D1509020

DATE DUE

MAY 2 1 1993			

THE ENVIRONMENTAL CLASSROOM

DONALD E. HAWKINS

*Research Professor,
Department of Health, Physical Education, and Recreation
The George Washington University*

DENNIS A. VINTON

*Consultant, Environmental Education Project
National Education Association*

With the assistance of Carol B. Epstein

PRENTICE-HALL, INC., ENGLEWOOD CLIFFS, NEW JERSEY

Library of Congress Cataloging in Publication Data

Hawkins, Donald E.
    The environmental classroom.

    Includes bibliographical references.
        1. Educational innovations—United States.
2. Human ecology—Study and teaching. I. Vinton,
Dennis A., joint author. II. Title.
LB1027.H384   301.31'07'1073   72-2495
ISBN 0-13-283135-X

© 1973 by Prentice-Hall, Inc.

10 9 8 7 6 5 4 3 2 1

Printed in the United States of America

Prentice-Hall International, Inc., London
Prentice-Hall of Australia, Pty. Ltd., Sydney
Prentice-Hall of Canada, Ltd., Toronto
Prentice-Hall India Private Limited, New Delhi
Prentice-Hall of Japan, Inc., Tokyo

Our ultimate concern is with the
human spirit and human minds and not schools.
In short we should concern ourselves with
human fulfillment. Schools are not ends
within themselves but rather vehicles
through which "the young and old unite
in the imaginative consideration of
learning."

The 1971 White House
Conference on Youth

contents

v

II

preface

We have become isolated and insulated from our environment, and our environment has suffered in the process. Our traditional system of education is ill-suited to reversing the trend; rather, it reinforces the process.

The extended family no longer exists. We live in nuclear families from which the old are excluded, and thereby lose perspective on a whole segment of our society. Often, our homes are only temporary settlements in a series of moves to material advancement, and we do not even know many of our neighbors. Housewives have become prisoners of their homes and small children. Employed persons travel to work in enclosed vehicles, oblivious of their surroundings, and engage in tasks that much of the time seem unconnected to any considerations of the larger environment. The necessities, amenities, and luxuries of our lives are neatly packaged in disposable containers that offer little hint of how the contents got there.

Young persons are alienated by an alienating society and an alienating educational system. School is a fortress against the very world about which young persons are supposed to be learning. Childhood has become a state of nonadmission to the world of work and decisions and responsibilities. Learning about work means going to a school of some kind—a vocational high school, a business school, a college or graduate school —but not practicing it until adulthood. Those who live in the suburbs are physically as well as psychologically detached from the adult world. Leisure for the young usually means either carefully planned, structured, prepackaged activities or aimless drifting for want of adequate facilities and the means to get to them.

Leisure time ought to be an ideal opportunity for contact with our environment. But far too many of us are unprepared to make productive use of it. Long weekends and retirement loom as threatening voids, during which we may become even more detached from the world around us. Weaned on the work ethic, schooled in the profit motive, graduated into the rat race, we find it difficult to view life as a total joyful experience. Living has become earning a living, and any other activity is seen as wasted time. Education truly ought to recreate and revitalize people, places, and things and, in so doing, improve man's environment.

It should come as no surprise that a society that lives this way has become increasingly careless about its environment.

To educate another generation in this manner is to risk the total destruction of the environment. To remove the young from the environment presupposes that they will care little about it when they are adults. They will care about it only if they know it intimately.

Young persons need to know where the material goods of our society come from and what happens during their transformation. They need to know how decisions are made, why they are made, and how policies can be changed. They need to be able to explore their environment without someone telling them what they are supposed to find. The environment is there to be discovered, and it is a far more exciting place in which to learn than any one school, a far more exciting teacher than any one person.

What we must do is move from traditional concepts of education to the concept of lifelong learning in the environmental classroom. Part I of this book describes the journey as a step-by-step process that allows thoughtful reconsideration of goals along the way. Throughout the book are numerous examples of programs already begun, ranging from those that take only the first uncertain steps to those well on the way to the environmental classroom. These programs have come to the authors' attention over the past few years. By now, some may be enjoying great success, while others may be of only marginal worth or no longer even in existence. It would be impossible to check on the progress of each; the purpose of including them is to show that what is desirable is also possible, that you *can* get there from here.

To be sure, there are many ways to get there, and undoubtedly many of the roads are still uncharted, unpaved, and even unimagined. Part II offers the ideas of some of the people who have thought about and worked on the problem of reconnecting human beings to their environment. The variety of probes, innovations, and alternative futures show that the problems lend themselves to uniquely creative solutions. They are presented with the hope that even more productive thinking will be stimulated by the contributions of the following:

Kaiser Aluminum & Chemical Company
Clifford Humphrey
Random House
Duane Robinson and Donald Clayton
The Conservation Educator
Catherine Watson
M. J. Ellis
Ladies Home Journal
Lynn and John Waugh
Educational Facilities Laboratories, Inc.
Roger Hudiburg
Earth Science Curriculum Project
Roland S. Barth
Elliot Richardson
Margaret Mead
Lyndon Baines Johnson
Robert E. Samples

William Van Til
George B. Leonard
Hugh Vallery
Rurik Ekstrom
Gordon A. Phillips
Roy L. Hyatt and Veronica S. Lish
Lloyd Fraser
Richard Saul Wurman
Herbert H. Swinburne
B. Ray Horn
Dick Palmer
Carroll G. Fader
Gary Nabham
Stuart A. Sandow
Louise Odiorne
Wayne O. Evans
Ivan Illich

Leslie Rich
Edward W. Weidner
Antioch College
Theodore Osmundson
Governor's Advisory Council
    on Community Schools, State
    Department of Education, Minnesota

Erika Pfeufer
Robert Theobald and J. M. Scott
Edward Stainbrook
Alfred A. Arth and Ronald N. Short

I

chapter one

two crises—one solution

The United States is a nation beset by crises. We have monetary crises, urban crises, youth crises, health care crises, racial crises, budgetary crises, and so on and on. Recently, the nation has focused particular attention on the environmental crisis and the educational crisis.

By definition, a crisis is a point in a series of events that determines the future course of related events for better or worse. Some are in fact only problems that bloom into crises in the fertile soil of political rhetoric. Perhaps our national ethic, which places such high value on the biggest, the most, and the best, causes us to ignore mere problems until they are termed crises. Certainly the environmental crisis is one that has been ignored until it is almost past the turning point. On the other hand, we have confronted problems in our educational system many times and considered them solved satisfactorily. Today the schools, as one of many national institutions, are in a state of crisis caused primarily by the impact of transitional social conditions. But whatever the difference in past perception, the nation is now taking a strongly critical look at the quality of both its environment and its schools.

In origins and causes, these two crises may be only tangentially related. In solution, however, the environmental crisis and the educational crisis may well become not-so-strange bedfellows. One of the roots of the educational crisis may lie in the idea that the educational establishment holds a monopoly on the learning process. Common sense tells us immediately that learning does not take place only in schools, protected in its virgin state by omniscient teachers, principals, and administrators. Human beings learn before, during, and after their formal school years. They learn wherever they are, for man is a curious animal who seeks out knowledge instinctively. Since learning takes place everywhere, the environment and the learning process are unalterably wedded to one another. The quality of the environment determines the learning opportunities available within the environment.

The present quality of the environment makes it inadequate in serving the total learning needs of the population. But that quality can be improved, once we become aware of the deficiencies. Awareness requires education; awareness of environmental deficiencies requires environmental education. Like all good marriages, this one calls for a give-and-take relationship: education can provide the impetus for improving the environment, and an improved environment can provide enhanced learning opportunities.

3

Environmental education is the bond between the environmental crisis and the educational crisis.

The solution of the two crises ought to provide a happily-ever-after situation. When the environment becomes highly conducive to learning, when it augments the quality of life, when it is totally accessible to all persons for satisfying and self-actualizing leisure and learning experiences throughout life, when education ceases to be a closed system, we shall have moved beyond the crises into the environmental classroom.

The Environmental Crisis

Man is doomed to relive the agonies of history only if he fails to learn from its lessons. Until now, man has remained oblivious to the lessons of his environmental history.

Ever since man first appeared on the earth, he has been polluting his environment. As soon as he acquired tools and discovered fire, he became more than just another element of the natural order. He began to change his environment, to control it, to dominate it—for better and for worse.

At first, the environment was vast and flexible enough to restore itself. Then man began to build civilizations. He forged cities from nature's bounty, and his population grew. Gradually, his impact upon the environment became so great that nature's restorative processes could not keep pace.

Civilizations rose to become the central powers of their time, then fell because man could not foresee that in his rush toward progress he would destroy the very support systems of the things he was creating. While the causes of the fall of any civilization are highly complex, it is safe to say in many cases that one factor was man's disregard for his environment. He cut away his forests to the point of no return, lost his farmlands to silted irrigation systems, polluted his water, dirtied his air with soot and smoke. In the biblical lands, in Greece and Rome, in Asia, Africa, and the Western Hemisphere, civilizations succumbed to an overused environment.

But man did not learn. There was always room to move from the rubble of one civilization to pristine lands on which to begin another. Europeans came to the shores of America in search of freedom and found a whole continent on which to exercise it. Inspired by Manifest Destiny, man settled the land from coast to coast and became convinced that the nation's resources were infinite. He took what he needed and passed the buck of conservation to future generations. He industrialized his society and created the highest standard of living the world has ever known—no mean accomplishment and assuredly one with significant social benefit.

In the Judeo-Christian culture, even God sanctioned such procedures. In *Genesis* 1 : 28 He told man, "Be fruitful and multiply, and replenish the earth, and subdue it; and have dominion over the fish of the sea, and over the fowl of the air, and over every living thing that creepeth upon the earth." One of today's popular conservationists notes: "The Judeo-Christian world heard every word except one. *Subdue it* came in loud and clear, and so did *multiply*. But practically nobody heard the word *replenish*." [1]

In the nineteenth and early twentieth century, a few voices pleaded the conservation cause—Thoreau, John Muir, Theodore Roosevelt. But conservation was regarded as mostly for the bird watchers, for short-sighted persons who could not see the bounty of the land, and for reactionaries who fought against progress. Growth in production, consumption, and population would keep the nation strong. The national ethic valued the biggest, the most, and the best.

Late in the eleventh hour of man's history—so late that many can already hear the bells of doom tolling—man has awakened to the fact that he and his technology have created an environment of decidedly mixed blessings. He has come to realize that the earth's resources of air, land, and water are finite and that man's manipulation of his resources is causing an environmental imbalance.

Our society has long extolled the positive blessings of technology. We enjoy longer lives, machines and gadgets that ease the burden of work, agricultural accomplishments that enable about eight percent of the population to produce more than enough food for the entire nation, communications that can boast of our prowess to all the world, transportation systems that deliver us even to the moon, unprecedented wealth and ease.

But now we have started to add up the debit side of the ledger. Each year we are discharging nearly 200 million tons of toxic particles into the air—almost a ton for every American—from 90 million motor vehicles, from factories, power plants, dumps, and incinerators. The estimated cost of the damage amounts to as much as $20 billion annually. The solid wastes of our production and consumption add up to 3.5 billion tons per year. We discard 8 million automobiles, 20 million tons of paper, 26 billion bottles, 48 billion cans each year. Dangerous chemicals poison our food; pesticides infiltrate every link in the food chain. Nearly half of the community water-supply systems surveyed by the Public Health Service in 1970 were contaminated enough to be potentially unsafe. Urban and industrial noise may be virtually deafening segments of the population. Occupational health hazards and accidents rise along with technological advancement. Radiation threatens us. Our population has risen from 4 million in 1790 to more than 200 million today, and it continues to rise and to concentrate itself in our megalopolises. The urban crunch—overpopulation, crowding, and other discomforting features—has produced an environment as alien to man as a cage is to a wild animal. Meanwhile, other species have been wiped out or are in critical danger of extinction; we watch with passive dismay as our wildlife vanishes. Overgrazed ranges are becoming deserts; overcut forests are leaving vast tracts of barren land susceptible to erosion; overpaved land is drastically altering water tables and climatic conditions. Take-it-while-you-can mining and agricultural methods have produced blighted and barren landscapes. In-

[1] Arthur Godfrey, "Confessions of a Polluter," *Reader's Digest*, 97 (September, 1970), 60–64.

creased life spans and increased leisure time have increased the desire for recreation, but uncrowded and unpolluted recreational areas are diminishing.[2]

We have begun to wonder whether the benefits of our lifestyle outweigh the banes. We are told that if we continue living as we do for the biggest, the most, and the best, our planet may be uninhabitable by the end of the century. The earth has been compared to a spaceship, a delicately balanced life-support system traveling in a universe otherwise hostile to life and in as great a danger of having its environmental balance wrecked as was Apollo 13 when an explosion ripped its side and imperiled the lives of its passengers. Today, there are neither undiscovered lands on which to begin anew nor places to which man can escape from his polluted environment—traces of pollution and DDT have been found in areas as remote from civilization as the Arctic Circle.

In his final address to the United Nations Economic and Social Council, the late Ambassador Adlai Stevenson described man's environmental condition:

> We travel together, passengers on a little spaceship, dependent on its vulnerable resources of air and soil; all committed for our safety to its security and peace; preserved from annihilation only by the care, the work, and I will say the love we give our fragile craft.[3]

Since late in the 1960s, when the environment became a popular topic of concern, the nation's air and water pollution have become worse. Our wildlife populations, generally more sensitive to polluted environments than man and therefore acting as an early warning signal, have continued to show losses. Our soil and mineral quality is down slightly. Our living space is deteriorating. Only the quality of our timberlands shows a gain during this period.[4]

The trends suggest that our life-giving spaceship will have difficulty supporting humanity—in numbers of about six to seven billion—by the end of the twentieth century. The quality and quantity of our food will be lower. Environmental diseases will afflict us. Living space and privacy will be at a premium.

The trends are, however, alterable. Those who point only to impending disaster have

[2] The statistics come primarily from the following:

James E. Allen, Jr., "Education for Survival," address before the 1970 Annual Meeting of the American Council of Learned Societies (Washington, D.C., January 23, 1970. Mimeo.)

Roger Revelle, "Population Growth and the Quality of the American Environment," *Background Book: 13th National Conference of the United States National Commission on UNESCO* (San Francisco: the Conference), November 1969.

U.S. Department of Health, Education, and Welfare, Environmental Health Service. *Environmental Health Problems* (Washington, D.C.: Government Printing Office, 1970), pp. 4–6.

U.S. Department of Health, Education, and Welfare, Public Health Service, *Community Water Supply Study: Analysis of National Survey Findings* (Washington, D.C.: the Department, July 1970).

[3] U.N. Economic and Social Council, *Official Records, 39th Session* (New York: the Council, 1965), p. 90.

[4] National Wildlife Federation, *National Environmental Quality (EQ) Index* (Washington, D.C.: the Federation, 1970).

been labeled "doomsday ecologists." For mankind is beginning to awaken and to learn from past errors in his use of the environment. Awareness, reason, and rational action offer a viable alternative to continued misuse of the environment.

We should remind the pessimists that the beginning of the cure is the pain created by the illness. Awareness of a problem is the first step toward its solution. Thus, the quality of life in the future becomes a matter of people and their sense of values.

It is absurd to suppose that if we all simply return to a nonindustrial, bucolic life, we shall no longer destroy our environment. Pollution occurs in rural as well as urban areas. The point is not to reject the benefits of our technology, but to learn to balance them with the preservation of our environment—to use them, in fact, to enhance rather than undermine the life-sustaining properties of our fragile planet. The nation's citizens must become aware of how man functions as the central figure in the environment and how man's activities affect the environment for good or ill. "We should strive," in the words of President Nixon, "for an environment that not only sustains life but enriches life, harmonizing the works of man and nature for the greater good of all." [5]

There is ample evidence that our scientific and technological communities have the knowledge and the resources to correct much of the damage from which our environment suffers. Nevertheless, it is also absurd to assume that since they know how to correct the damage, they will do so. In theory, scientists and technologists do not make public policy; aware citizens do, choosing priorities from the vast number of available options. The director of environmental affairs for a large power company summarized the problem of employing scientific initiative this way:

> We all agree the barn is on fire, perhaps it is burning down. Let's get the bucket brigade going. Attention has too long been diverted from the more fundamental questions: how to implement what we already know and how to choose rationally among technical alternatives and their alternative costs. The process of choosing does not involve science. It is political and social.[6]

Then surely the solution rests with the government, which must create a national policy on environment. But our government does not operate in a vacuum. It, too, depends upon aware citizens to indicate the direction of public policy. Until now, the people's mandate to the government has been that it create policies to enable our technology to grow and to continue to produce the biggest, the most, and the best. Environmental protection received little attention. The environment will be a matter of public policy only so long as aware citizens freely choose to make it so.

The solution to the environmental crisis thus rests neither with scientists nor with government officials but with a citizenry educated in environmental problem solving. An aware citizenry is crucial to making decisions on the balance to be maintained between technology and environmental preservation, on the priorities toward which our scientists should direct their energies, and on the policies our governments should

[5] Richard Nixon, "Presidential Message on Environmental Quality," *First Annual Report of the Council on Environmental Quality* (Washington, D.C.: Government Printing Office, 1970), p. xv.
[6] R. W. Comstock, "One Industrial Point of View," *Science Teacher*, 37 (September 1970), 23–27.

institute. The American people as a whole must become aware of how the forces in man's environment combine to create the precarious balance of life that sustains us; how the balance can be upset and in the process produce stresses of crowding, ugliness, disease, hunger, and discomforts that destroy the quality of life; how the structure of human organization must be changed in order to cope adequately with maintaining the quality of the world's environment. In the words of former Secretary of the Interior Udall,

> The movement to save our environment cannot depend on or be tied to an individual or a small number of individuals. It is a nation's commitment. . . . We will decide whether our water, air, soil, forest, wildlife, and public parkland resources will be adequate to meet the needs of the future. By our action, or inaction, we will determine whether our children will know the green and pleasant land which was our legacy.[7]

Along with an aware citizenry, we need a larger number of persons than ever before who are trained for and dedicated to the preservation of man's total environment. We need, first of all, persons informed enough about environmental problems that they can help us find out all we do not know about environmental relationships and sort out the facts from the emotional rhetoric. If certain species of wildlife are dying out, how will that affect the future quality of life? Are new and better species emerging? How much carbon monoxide can man expose himself to before undergoing biological harm? Has the oxygen level of the earth's atmosphere in fact declined? Are present levels of DDT really rotting our insides, or are we benefiting far more from having controlled malaria and improved our agricultural output through its use? Is Lake Erie really "dead," or is it a fact that its offshore water is still drinkable? To just how much environmental stress can man easily adapt? We know a great deal about the earth's ecology, but there remain many unanswered questions because we as a people simply have not learned enough about our environment.

Second, we need manpower skilled in identifying and combatting a wide range of environmental problems. We need large numbers of engineers, scientists, sanitarians, technologists, technicians, and technicians' aides who are educated to take a broad ecological view of the critical situations of man's environment. We need sociologists, doctors, educators, and politicians—in short, persons trained in a wide variety of disciplines—who can synthesize the many fields of human endeavor and concern into a universal, ecological focus.

The process has already begun. In the past few years, the awakening of concern for the quality of man's environment has caused the government of the United States to take the first steps toward creating a national policy on environmental protection. Its action is significant in light of the fact that our federal government is characteristically a slow-moving behemoth of a bureaucracy and poorly structured for a massive attack on a problem it once, in sheer innocence, helped to create.

[7] Stewart L. Udall, "Foreword," in *Focus on Environmental Education*, V. Eugene Vivian and Thomas J. Rillo (Glassboro: Curriculum Development Council for Southern New Jersey, 1970) p. iii.

A tentative first step toward population control was taken in 1969, when President Nixon sent to Congress the first message on population ever to come from the White House. In stressing the need for family-planning services and research and endorsing the proposal for a population commission, it opened the door to the adoption of a national policy on population. It was a "cautious, limited, but historically important, call for action." [8]

The most significant alteration in the federal government's approach to environmental protection came about with the signing of Public Law 91–190—the National Environmental Policy Act (also known as the Environmental Quality Act)—on January 1, 1970. The law set up a permanent three-member White House Council on Environmental Quality and established a policy of treating the root causes of environmental degradation rather than merely the symptoms.

Up to that time, governmental efforts toward environmental protection were fragmented among many departments, bureaus, and agencies. The earth's environment, however, is an exquisite entity; the deterioration of one aspect is likely to have profound effects on many others. Likewise, efforts to improve a single factor might actually be detrimental to other factors. Cleaning water and purifying air are at best only stop-gap measures that leave the origins of pollution undiagnosed. Piecemeal attacks permit the problem to rage on unchecked.

> A single source may pollute the air with smoke and chemicals, the land with solid wastes, and a river or lake with chemicals and other wastes. Control of air pollution may produce more solid wastes, which then pollute the land or water. Control of water-polluting effluent may convert it into solid wastes, which must be disposed of on land. . . . A far more effective approach to pollution control would:
> —Identify pollutants.
> —Trace them through the ecological chain, observing and recording changes in form as they occur.
> —Determine the total exposure of man and his environment.
> —Examine interactions among forms of pollution.
> —Identify where in the ecological chain interdiction would be most appropriate.[9]

Basing his request on this rationale, President Nixon called for the establishment, under the National Environmental Policy Act, of the Environmental Protection Agency (EPA), to pull together federal efforts on water quality, pesticides, air pollution, solid waste management, water hygiene, and radiation—efforts formerly scattered throughout the government. EPA is also concerned with training manpower to deal with the problems under its authority.

The National Environmental Policy Act is designed to be preventive rather than

[8] Population Reference Bureau, *Annual Report, 1969* (Washington, D.C.: the Bureau, 1969), p. 5.
[9] Richard Nixon, "President's Message to the Congress upon Transmitting Reorganization Plans To Establish the Environmental Protection Agency and the National Oceanic and Atmospheric Administration, July 9, 1970," *Hearings Before a Subcommittee of the Committee on Government Operations, House of Representatives, Ninety-First Congress, on Reorganization Plan No. 3 of 1970* (Washington, D.C.: Government Printing Office, 1970), p. 3.

curative. Its main purpose is to head off potential damage to the environment. Under its provisions, for example, each agency of the federal government has been directed to identify any of its proposals for legislation and other major actions that affect the environment, prepare statements describing the plans and programs with environmental impact, and clear such plans with the Council on Environmental Quality *before they are undertaken.*

In 1971 the Department of Justice took steps to coordinate federal litigation arising from environmental problems when it created the Consumer Affairs Section in the Antitrust Division and the Pollution Control Section in the Land and Natural Resources Division.

A second major piece of environmental legislation was Public Law 91–516—the Environmental Education Act—which was signed into law on October 30, 1970. The environment had by then taken on tremendous popular appeal as a political issue; the legislation passed the House by a vote of 289 to 28 and the Senate by a vote of 64 to 0. The Act is based on the concept that "we, as a society, can no longer afford the luxury of not knowing the environmental consequences of our decisions."

> The citizens of this country, both present and future, must understand the ecosystem and the interrelationships between its parts. Each phase of education, from preschool through adult and continuing education, must be reordered to permit the introduction of ecological understanding.[10]

Here, at last, was the recognition that citizen awareness and education is vital in the battle against environmental destruction. The Act established an Office of Environmental Education within the U.S. Office of Education, and authorized the Commissioner of Education "to establish education programs to encourage understanding of policies, and support of activities, designed to enhance environmental quality and maintain ecological balance." [11]

These much-needed laws are on the books, and their implications for the quality of human life in America cannot be underestimated. The problem is for the American people to voice their mandate strongly enough that Congress will appropriate the necessary implementing funds and that these laws will be enforced.

There can be no doubt that public attitudes toward environmental protection are changing. Recognizing that federal authority is limited to environmental damage that results from interstate commerce or that crosses state lines, many state legislatures have passed their own environmental quality and environmental education laws.

Like the cumulative effects of the damage man has done to the environment, awareness of the problem has crept up on us. People ignored the conservationists of the last century, but they paid attention when Rachel Carson wrote in 1962:

---

[10] U.S. Senate Committee on Labor and Public Welfare, *Report on the Environmental Quality Education Act* (Washington, D.C.: Government Printing Office, 1970), pp. 1–2.

[11] Public Law 91–516, 91st Congress, H.R. 18260, October 30, 1970.

It took hundreds of millions of years to produce the life that now inhabits the earth—eons of time in which that developing and evolving and diversifying life reached a state of adjustment and balance with its surroundings. . . . Given time—not in years but in millennia —life adjusts, and a balance has been reached. For time is the essential ingredient; but in the modern world there is no time.[12]

Within a year, bills banning pesticides had been introduced in forty state legislatures. People listen now to Barry Commoner, Paul Ehrlich, Rene Dubos, Ralph Nader, the Population Reference Bureau, the Environmental Defense Fund, and countless other Cassandras who are suddenly being heard. Disparate dissatisfied groups that protested against racial injustice, the war, the Establishment, and numerous other causes, found a point of coalescence in the environmental crisis. It appears that if you are bothered by any aspect of the quality of life, man's environment—central to the quality of life—can be your rallying point.

Suddenly the people are not so sure about the biggest, the most, and the best. It is popular to talk of small cars or no cars at all, of noise abatement, of zero population growth, of clothes that are less than whiter than white, of recycling the waste products of our "effluent society." In a 1970 Harris Poll, 66 percent of the respondents who were urban residents said they had considered moving out of the city because of environmental problems, 72 percent of all respondents felt we had developed our technology while neglecting human needs, barely half felt that the quality of most consumer goods is acceptable.[13]

Along with the change in attitudes has come a quest for the kind of action that will produce results. Carrying picket signs is likely to do little more than add to our mountains of litter, but citizens are seeking effective ways to make known their concern. Hundreds of conservation cases are pending before the courts. A group of students at Northwestern University have formed Northwestern Students for a Better Environment and, at the request of the city government, spent the summer of 1970 studying air pollution in Evanston and recommending corrective action. Citizens of Detroit reacted to the large number of gasoline stations in the city that failed and were abandoned by pressuring the city council to ban the construction of new stations. Radio station WINQ in Tampa, Florida, started a program called *Earth Patrol,* inviting listeners to call or write about suspected pollution violations, which are then reported to the State Control Board. A group of citizens calling themselves "For a Lesser Los Angeles" is attempting to stop the growth and sprawl of that metropolitan area. Students at Cornell College of Iowa have formed Students Organized for Survival (SOS) and, among other activities, produce an environmental periodical called *Eco-Log.* The American Association of University Women (AAUW) has published a booklet suggesting to housewives how they can help preserve the environment; the booklet has become AAUW's best seller. The League of Conserva-

[12] Rachel Carson, *Silent Spring* (Boston: Houghton Mifflin Company, 1962), p. 6.

[13] Louis Harris and Associates, *A Survey of Public Attitudes Toward Urban Problems and Toward the Impact of Scientific and Technological Developments,* Study No. 2044, conducted for the Public Broadcasting Environment Center, November 1970.

tion Voters, a national nonpartisan group organized before the 1970 elections, endorsed 22 candidates with good records on environmental issues, of whom 16 won the elections. In New York City, Citizens for Clean Air have studied air-pollution detection, now make sightings and report violations to inspectors. Bicycle Ecology, headquartered in Chicago, works for protected bicycle lanes on city streets and parking spaces in downtown areas.

One of the largest activities held to promote environmental awareness and action was Earth Day, April 22, 1970. The brainchild of Senator Gaylord Nelson, it was co-ordinated by Environmental Action, a group of young volunteers based in Washington, D.C. Earth Day was described as an environmental teach-in and was held primarily on college campuses throughout the nation, involving students and faculty as well as labor, conservation, and other citizens' organizations. Activities on each campus focused on local and national problems in ecology and attempted to make the country aware of the extent of the environmental crisis. Whether Earth Day succeeded, however, has yet to be determined.

Of all the segments of the nation, the one most on the defensive as a result of this new awareness is industry. But industry is not the only—or perhaps not even the major—culprit. Farmers and doctors and scientists and governments and consumers have all contributed to the environmental crisis. The problem was underscored at a recent environmental seminar:

> Industrial pollution is highly visible; industry is seen to be big, bureaucratic and greedy. So while it might be more objective to conclude that there are no devils in this story—or alternatively that just about everybody shares the blame—the chances are that industry is in for a large part of the pollution rap.[14]

Company executives are just as aware of the environmental crisis as other groups in the nation. *Fortune* magazine, in a survey in 1970 of 270 chief executives of some of the largest companies, found that 57 percent would like the federal government to increase regulation of environmental problems, 88 percent felt environmental protection is necessary even if it means inhibiting the introduction of new products, and 85 percent approved of such regulatory measures even if they resulted in reduced profits.[15]

Many industrial companies now employ a person to coordinate the environmental policies of the firm. New devices to control environmental damage are being created by America's industries, and the U.S. Patent Office has taken the unprecedented step of giving special priority to such inventions. The Coca-Cola company states that it is working to eliminate all forms of pollution in all phases of company activities, and it has acquired a company that develops water- and air-pollution prevention systems. The Humble Oil Company of Standard Oil (New Jersey) prides itself on the number of active oil fields in which it drills without destroying the wildlife of the area and the number of refineries it

---

[14] Thomas W. Wilson, Jr. of the International Institute for Environmental Affairs, *The Environment: Too Small a View,* An Occasional Paper (Aspen, Colo.: Aspen Institute for Humanistic Studies, 1970), p. 15.

[15] Robert S. Diamond, "What Business Thinks: The Fortune 500–Yankelovich Survey," *Fortune,* Vol. 81 (February, 1970), 118–19, 171–72.

operates with little or no environmental damage. On the other hand, the parent Standard Oil has a considerable interest in the completion of a pipeline for Alaskan oil—a project opposed by environmentalists as potentially dangerous to the ecology of the Arctic area. In March 1971, the New York Building Congress produced an advertising supplement that concluded with a caption: "The quality of life is not improved by preventing progress in the name of preservation." As the public's attitude toward environmental protection changes, business and industry are likely to respond to consumer demands—for this, in effect, is what they have always been doing.

But what are consumers going to demand? Will we pay the higher cost of oil refined without polluting by-products and of automobile engines designed for lower harmful emissions? Will we pay to have our labor-saving machines made more quiet? The fact of the matter is that we are paying dearly for not having considered our environment before it reached the crisis stage—but then, our wars and our domestic social problems prove that we begin to spend money on our problems only when they become, at least in name, crises. Will we accept less mobility in order to have fewer highways paving over our neighborhoods and recreation land? To what extent will we allow the use of pesticides to increase our food supply? How much of our water must be pure enough to drink, to swim in, to boat on? Which waterways should serve what purposes? Is irrigation more important than power, clean water better than paper production, a pristine forest more desirable than a public campsite, a park preferable to a housing development? At what point does family size cease to be a personal decision and become, instead, a social one? When does the biggest, the most, and the best—of anything—become a threat rather than a promise?

The answers to such questions do not come easily. They involve a view of man's environment that is not compartmentalized but is, rather, broad enough to consider the interrelationships of actions in many areas. In short, they involve the ability to perceive human ecology as a total fabric comprised of the many threads that make up the quality of life on our planet.

Few citizens today know enough about man's environment and how man's use and abuse can enhance or destroy it to make the kinds of decisions that direct government, business, industry, science, and the individual consumer to take the proper course of action. Given the obvious premise that we do not wish to abandon our technology, few persons are capable of sorting out the conflicting pressures and demands of growth versus protection to strike the balance that will maintain a comfortable, esthetic, and satisfying life for the earth's populations. Limiting growth may mean unemployment, loss of profits, fewer luxuries, less personal freedom to maintain the lifestyle to which we have become accustomed. At some point, it may also mean ceasing to upgrade the standard of living for the world's millions who have never experienced the benefits of affluence. We need to decide just how to harmonize our environment's economic potential, its recreational pleasures, its beauty, and its life-sustaining properties each with one another.

If we expect such decisions to be made by "outside" experts in government, we run the risk of submitting to dictatorship in an area where free choice is possible. We also run the risk that the experts on whom we rely have not been educated to take a total view—a systems view, if you will—of our environmental problems, so that they might perceive the wisdom of any given action in relation to its total effect. We should be allowed to establish our own priorities, difficult to determine though they may be.

> Today we are allowing priorities in use (and abuse) to be established by default, instead of assigning them with some rationale and purpose. The movers and effecters of these priority decisions are haphazard, dollar-directed, first-come-first-served, and utterly disconnected from any overall consideration of either life or the land, let alone the two interconnectedly. The total environment approach to planning would insist that all "side effects" be evaluated before any final decisions are made: no swamp would be filled, no new jetport sited, no nuclear power plant built, until the community as a whole had weighed the alternatives and determined that all possible actions had been taken to make the proposed development compatible with order and beauty.[16]

In order to make these choices, the community as a whole—all of the people—must be educated to acquire the values, knowledge, and skills needed to solve the problems of the environmental crisis.

The Educational Crisis

Like the environmental crisis, the educational crisis in our nation has been gathering momentum for some time, unnoticed by a relatively complacent populace whose values and priorities lay elsewhere. Not that education has not always been highly valued in this country. On the contrary, the American educational system has long been a source of pride to the people. But for the most part, we have assumed on little firsthand evidence that the schools were educating our children properly and effectively.

In the last few years, however, there has been a decided trend toward dissatisfaction and disillusionment. George Gallup recognized just such a trend in his "Second Annual Survey of the Public's Attitude Toward the Public Schools," published in the fall of 1970.[17] Most of the respondents to the poll expressed a wish for more objective measurements of school performance and for more information about the schools. A national test of achievement was favored by 75 percent, and 67 percent felt that teachers and administrators should be held accountable for what the schools are doing. Opposition to tenure for teachers was expressed by 53 percent, while 58 percent favored a system of merit pay for teachers—a little-used practice strongly opposed by both the National Education Association and the American Federation of Teachers.

The public schools have faced crises before, but each time they were considered

---

[16] Stewart L. Udall, "Introduction," in *It's Your World—The Grassroots Conservation Story*, U.S. Department of the Interior Conservation Yearbook No. 5 (Washington, D.C.: Government Printing Office, 1969), pp. 17–18.

[17] George Gallup, "Second Annual Survey of the Public's Attitude Toward the Public Schools," *Phi Delta Kappan*, 52 (October, 1970), 97–112.

successfully resolved. Just over a century ago, the call was for opening public education to all children instead of the small elite whom the schools originally served. The one-room schoolhouse was abandoned in favor of large schools that opened their doors to all and organized students on the basis of age and grade. Attendance laws made schooling mandatory, and the United States emerged with the first system of universal public education, which supposedly gave equal opportunity to all its children.

Around the turn of the century the great influx of immigrants created a demand for the schools to become a melting-pot operation. They molded a diversity of foreign cultures into an American work force capable of filling the needs of an industrializing society. Public high schools proliferated, and enrollment multiplied tenfold between 1880 and 1930.

With the Great Depression of the 1930s came a new educational crisis—the enforced prolongation of schooling for many more young people who found there was nothing else for them to do. No longer could the high school provide only a college-oriented curriculum, so the American school system created the comprehensive high school—a unique institution designed to serve all students, whether their interests were academic, vocational, or general.

In 1957, when Russia launched Sputnik, the American people suddenly came to the appalling realization that they might be only number two in the space race. Once again, the crisis was placed squarely on the shoulders of the school system, which bore the burden of not having produced enough technical experts to have gotten us there first. The crisis served to launch the curriculum reform movement, which had actually been in process since the early 1950s, into the forefront of priorities. New programs in mathematics, science, and, shortly after, in history, had the dual effect of changing classroom procedures to a more learner-centered focus but also of segregating subject matter into more discrete compartments than ever before.

When in the 1960s it became obvious that equality of educational opportunity was a figment of the imagination where the poor and minority groups were concerned, the educational system responded with Head Start, Upward Bound, Higher Horizons, and a host of other compensatory programs that were doomed to fail because, like early efforts at saving the environment, they treated symptoms rather than causes.

The peculiar trait of the American people has been to look to education to solve each new problem of society. Unfortunately, the procedure has usually been to gather a group of ardent supporters of a program to fill some new social need, and then add it to an already overburdened curriculum constructed according to no particular stabilizing educational philosophy or goal. Suddenly we are taking a whole new look at the entire system of education in the United States, and we are beginning to wonder if its very foundations do not need to be torn away and replaced with an entirely new structure.

What, in essence, do we do in our most traditional schools? We put our children into big boxes in which they pass through many little boxes at the dictates of the clock and gong, each box containing rows of desks at which the children sit and listen in docility as "education" is delivered from one omniscient being facing the group in opposition for a prescribed length of time. The curiosity of childhood, the give-and-take of true learning, the joys of discovery, the weighing of opinions and thoughts and values that may not represent the "right answer" and may even threaten the omniscience of the teacher are all quickly stifled and submerged under the efficiency of the system. One of the first lessons a pupil learns is how to operate in that system, how to reject his natural mode of learning by which he has acquired so much knowledge in his first five years, and take up instead the artificial style of the traditional classroom. We are beginning to wonder whether the whole system, instead of needing another program tacked on here or there, is not actually harmful in its very basic conceptions.

Alvin Toffler, in *Future Shock,* describes the system as possibly useful in another era but anachronistic in the modern world:

> The whole idea of assembling masses of students (raw material) to be processed by teachers (workers) in a centrally located school (factory) was a stroke of industrial genius. . . . The inner life of the school thus became an artificial mirror, a perfect introduction to industrial society. The most criticized features of education today—the regimentation, lack of individualization, the rigid systems of seating, grouping, grading and marking, the authoritarian rule of the teacher—are precisely those that made public education so effective an instrument of adaptation for its place and time.[18]

As the Grosses noted in their book *Radical School Reform,* it is no longer preposterous to call for a completely new system of education.[19] The critics are denouncing every aspect of the American educational process.

The most obvious harm is inflicted in the schools of our inner cities, and the books of personal experience with the inhumanity of such schools provide a painful indictment. James Herndon, author of *The Way It's Spozed To Be:*

> Sitting in a classroom or at home pretending to "study" a badly written text full of false information, adding up twenty sums when they're all the same and one would do, being bottled up for seven hours in a place where you decide nothing, having your success or failure depend, a hundred times a day, on the plan, invention and whim of someone else, being put in a position where most of your real desires are not only ignored but actively penalized, undertaking nothing for its own sake but only for that illusory carrot of the future—maybe you can do it, and maybe you can't, but either way, it's probably done you some harm.[20]

Jonathan Kozol, author of *Death at an Early Age:*

> On a series of other occasions, the situation is repeated. The children are offered something new and something lively. They respond to it energetically and they are attentive and their attention does not waver. For the first time in a long while perhaps there is actually some

[18] Alvin Toffler, *Future Shock* (New York: Random House, Inc., 1970), p. 355. Reprinted by permission of Random House, Inc.

[19] Beatrice and Ronald Gross, eds., *Radical School Reform* (New York: Simon and Schuster, Inc., 1969).

[20] James Herndon, *The Way It's Spozed To Be* (New York: Simon and Schuster, 1968). © 1968 by James Herndon. Reprinted by permission of Simon & Schuster, Inc.

real excitement and some growing and some thinking going on within that one small room. In each case, however, you are advised that you are making a mistake.[21]

Herbert Kohl, author of *36 Children*:

I frequently found that many of the children were deliberately choosing wrong answers because they had clever explanations for their choices. They had to be convinced that the people who created objective tests believed as an article of faith that all the questions they made up had one and only one correct answer. Over and over, it is striking how rigid teachers tend to be, and how difficult it is for children who haven't been clued in on this rigidity to figure out what the teacher expects in the way of suppression of original and clever responses. The children agreed to be dull for the sake of their future.[22]

While the educational crisis may be most blatant in the cities, it is not at all confined to the urban ghetto. One after the other, middle-class suburban schools—once presumed to be the benchmark of our educational system—are facing the problem of student unrest and dissatisfaction with the schooling process. Student rebellion in fact started with those considered to be the best products of the process—the college students. Searching for the causes of rebellion, the President's Commission on Campus Unrest described the process of higher education in terms that echo the denunciations of inner-city public schools. "The student's role in this process of education is largely passive: he sits and listens, he sits and reads, and sometimes he sits and writes. It is an uninspiring experience for many students." [23]

The suburban child may have an advantage over the ghetto child in the support he receives from his home environment, but he gets very little edge from his classroom experience. In a commentary on the decade of awakening to the educational crisis, James Cass pointed out that "the student rebellion . . . made clear that in large part the schools were failing the advantaged as well as the deprived.

The pervasive emphasis on conformity rather than creativity, on discipline rather than independence, on the defensive "put-down" rather than student support, on quiet orderliness rather than on the joy of discovery, on the neatness of administrative convenience rather than the often untidy environment of true learning—all highlighted the authoritarian rigidities of the system. Gradually, an increasing number of adults became aware that they were subjecting their children to a custodial environment that denied the very nature of childhood and youth—an environment to which they would not consciously submit themselves any more willingly than would their rebelling children.[24]

The key word of the student rebels is *relevance*. Early in their educational careers they perceive that they learn much from the real world outside of school, but that once

[21] Jonathan Kozol, *Death at an Early Age* (Boston: Houghton Mifflin, 1967).

[22] Herbert Kohl, "A Harlem Class Writes." *Radical School Reform*, p. 340.

[23] The President's Commission on Campus Unrest, *Report* (Washington, D.C.: Government Printing Office, 1970), p. 75.

[24] James Cass, "The Crisis of Confidence—And Beyond," *Saturday Review*, 53 (September 19, 1970), 61.

they enter the big box and start marching through all the little boxes they must suspend their knowledge of real life and their judgment of values and controversy so that they can parrot back the right answers and second-guess the teacher's motives. It is not that fundamental skills are necessarily irrelevant, but that students are not taught why and how they are relevant to their environment. As William Glasser says in *Schools Without Failure*, "schools usually *do not teach* a relevant curriculum; when they do, *they fail to teach the child how he can relate this learning to his life outside of the school.*" [25]

Students are force-fed an array of facts to memorize under the pressure of objective tests and possible failure, which can only be a vain attempt at education in an age when factual knowledge is proliferating at incredible rates. By the time a student leaves school, there is likely to be more knowledge available to learn than when he entered.

It must come as a terrible shock to most parents that the places to which they send their children each day—in part because they are required by law to do so and in part because these places represent to most adults the path to the good life in their children's futures—are actually destructive to their children. Here is truly a situation worthy of the label *crisis*. The sound of blind faith being shattered could be heard across the nation when Charles Silberman's study for the Carnegie Corporation was published:

> It is not possible to spend any prolonged period visiting public school classrooms without being appalled by the mutilation visible everywhere—mutilation of spontaneity, of joy in learning, of pleasure in creating, of sense of self. . . . Because adults take the schools so much for granted, they fail to appreciate what grim, joyless places most American schools are, how oppressive and petty are the rules by which they are governed, how intellectually sterile and esthetically barren the atmosphere, what an appalling lack of civility obtains on the part of teachers and principals, what contempt they unconsciously display for children as children.[26]

Silberman presents a multitude of examples of the rigidity, sterility, and constraint of the traditional public school classroom. Perhaps the most telling is the following:

> In lecturing the assembled students on the need for and virtue of absolute silence, an elementary school principal expostulates on the wonders of a school for the "deaf and dumb" he had recently visited. The silence was just wonderful, he tells the assembly; the children could get all their work done because of the total silence. The goal is explicit: to turn normal children into youngsters behaving as though they were missing two of their faculties.[27]

Those parents who have experienced the shock of finding out what really goes on in schools are probably a good deal less shocked by the fact that their children are rebelling. They see that their children are "turned off" by education; they know they are not turned off by everything. These same children are the ones who have given

---

[25] William Glasser, M.D., *Schools Without Failure* (New York: Harper & Row, Publishers, 1969), p. 50.

[26] Charles E. Silberman, *Crisis in the Classroom* (New York: Random House, Inc., 1970), p. 10. Reprinted by permission of Random House, Inc.

[27] *Ibid.*, p. 128.

evidence—sometimes of a kind that is truly frightening to the same "establishment" that lauds the schools—of deep concern over situations in the real world. They cry out against a meaningless war for which they are asked to give their lives, against injustice, against racial inequality, against the impending destruction of the world's environment, against slavish devotion to a lifestyle of materialism. The real world confronts them with problems begging for solutions; the false world of the school confronts them with a system to beat, a process to get through just for the sake of getting through it. It is no wonder that a student says,

> . . . The main thing is not to take it personal, to understand that it's just a system and it treats you the same way it treats everybody else, like an engine or a machine or something mechanical. Our names get fed into it—we get fed into it—when we're five years old, and if we catch on and watch our step, it spits us out when we're seventeen or eighteen, ready for college.[28]

Educators and education analysts who have recognized the existence of a crisis in education have tried to formulate new theories, goals, and methods for our public schools. The most radical have even suggested abolishing the schools entirely. One group, including Milton Friedman, Christopher Jencks, Theodore Sizer, and Kenneth Clark, have proposed a voucher plan, whereby all families—but especially the poor—would be able to choose from a number of educational options, public or private, and pay the institution of their choice with a credit voucher issued by the government. The effect of such competition could well be the destruction of the public school system.

But even current theories of education that seek some degree of reform *within* the present system of public schools lean heavily on ideas that do away with the factory-like atmosphere of schools, the suppression of creativity, and the notion of the teacher as the source of all knowledge and truth. They seek to make the learner central, to allow him to engage in exploratory activity that is to some extent of his own choosing, to change the role of the teacher to one of diagnosing the needs of the individual and facilitating the learning process. They usually stress the individuality of each child and the fact that different children learn from different methods and progress at different rates. They emphasize problem solving, experience-oriented education, learning how to learn for a lifetime rather than rote memorization for tomorrow's test. Many focus on independent study, and some conceive of a multidisciplinary approach to curriculum in response to the recognition that real life is not segmented into subject areas.

Recommendations for specific changes are practically as numerous as the critics of education. Charles Silberman sees an answer in the English open classroom. Dr. Glasser proposes schools without the kind of failure that leaves one convinced that any success is impossible, and schools that teach children to question without fear and make decisions on which they can follow through. Alvin Toffler calls for schools that enable children to adapt to future conditions that are inconceivable today: "[education's] prime objective must be to increase the individual's 'cope-ability'—the speed and economy

[28] Kathryn Johnston Noyes and Gordon L. McAndrew, "Is This What Schools Are For?" *Saturday Review*, 51 (December 21, 1968), 59.

by which he can adapt to continual change." [29] John Holt, long a gadfly to schools that operate under conditions of repression, advocates freedom:

> . . . a child who is learning naturally, following his curiosity where it leads him, adding to his mental model of reality whatever he needs and can find a place for, and rejecting without fear or guilt what he does not need, is growing—in knowledge, in the love of learning, and in the ability to learn.[30]

Edgar Friedenberg looks for the day "when you can't even tell education from living." And Arthur Foshay makes an urgent plea to reject schools that serve society's needs in favor of schools that work for the self-fulfillment of each individual:

> The school as an institution has to be devoted to human ends. It will no longer serve us well to consider the school as a form of business organization, with an input, a process, and an output. These are dehumanizing terms. A school is a place for people to grow into themselves, for a child to make himself into a man. Wherever this purpose is not central to the acts carried on in the school, the school is unworthy of continuation.[31]

Visibility and accountability to the community, freedom, relevance, equality of educational opportunities, new goals and purposes, commitment to education as part of life and as a lifelong process, learner-centered curriculums, a multidisciplinary problem-solving focus, value orientation, humane principles, individualization—these theories form the thrust of the movement to ameliorate the crisis in education. Awareness, value orientation, a multidisciplinary problem-solving focus, the ability to perceive the course of effective action—these qualities are deemed essential to a citizenry capable of ameliorating the crisis in the environment. The two crises have a common base from which to reach a solution—the environmental classroom.

In its final planning report, the Public Broadcasting Environment Center of the Corporation for Public Broadcasting noted a definite connection between the two crises:

> The rash of materials development and educational writing that has occurred during the past ten years is strong evidence of the discontent with existing educational practice. . . . Whether you read Holt, Bruner, Drucker or Silberman, you will find two major themes: the irrelevance of subject matter as now taught and organized, and the failure to truly individualize learning. . . . What is seriously wanting are materials that by their very arrangement invite teachers and students to explore their world, in and out of school, in a variety of ways. The current public concern with the quality of the environment offers an exciting intellectual scheme for organizing and promoting educational materials which provide the opportunities for exploring our individual and communal physical, social and psychological "environments." BUT the true legitimacy of the educational issues is that they are not unique

---

[29] Toffler, *Future Shock*, p. 357.

[30] John Holt, *How Children Fail* (New York: Dell, 1964), p. 220. Copyright © 1964 by Pitman Publishing Corporation. Reprinted by permission of Pitman Publishing Corporation.

[31] Arthur W. Foshay, *Curriculum for the 70's: An Agenda for Invention*, Schools for the 70's, Preliminary Series (Washington, D.C.: Center for the Study of Instruction, National Education Association, 1970), p. 22.

to the considerations of environmental quality. . . . For the moment, though, environment is the organizing theme, the organizing framework for transforming education from a reflection of society as it has been to a vision of what society can be.[32]

If we conceive of the environment as the total world in which man lives, and if we therefore conceive of all education as being environmental education (or else it is irrelevant), then the environmental classroom becomes not just another panacea applied to an unworkable and anachronistic curriculum structure, but a new conception of the purposes and methods of education. It deals with man's environment—past, present, future, natural, and man-made—as it relates to man today and in years to come. It uses man's environment, all of it. It opens the learning environment out of its succession of little boxes within big boxes and brings the learner to the real world and the real world to the learner.

Environmental Education—The Change Agent

Proposals to change the purposes and methods of American education to a more humanistic, learner-centered, problem-solving focus have been appearing in one form or another since the beginning of this century. They still do not have a very strong footing in our educational system. Many schools pay lip service to the ideals, include them in a statement of educational philosophy that rests untouched on the principal's or superintendent's bookshelf, and continue to operate as prisons of the bodies and minds of their students.

Single additions to the curriculum are the easiest changes to make, and so most schools—especially secondary schools—offer a veritable smorgasbord of different subjects for students to sample and find irrelevant to each other and to real life. Changes in total approach are far more difficult to institute. But there are many schools that pride themselves on the speed with which they adopt innovations, and they call in the community to view every new, experimental program in an atmosphere of a circus performance. Schools so encrusted with decaying tradition and aged methods that the slightest hint of change causes tremors of resistance and schools that hop blithely and blindly on each passing bandwagon are equally misguided—and probably do equal damage to their students.

Generally, the rate of acceptance of new educational ideas proposed at the research level has been 25 to 50 years. Two to three generations of students complete school before a "new" method is put into practice in a significant number of local school systems. Yet if we fear change and innovation in our schools, the products of

---

[32] Corporation for Public Broadcasting, *Final Report—Public Broadcasting Environment Center* (Washington, D.C.: Office of Education, U.S. Department of Health, Education, and Welfare, November 30, 1970), p. 586.

our schools cannot help but fear change and innovation in their lives. The entrenchment of the educational establishment militates against changes in the way things are done in our school systems, just as the structure of the federal bureaucracy impedes rapid action on problems requiring immediacy.

The U.S. Office of Education has called environmental education "education that cannot wait." Two or three generations from now, if the American public has not been educated to understand and solve environmental problems, the environment may well be hopeless. Certainly if the educational crisis drags on for that long, the situation in our schools—provided they are still standing—will be irrecoverable. The change that is brought about, however, must be intelligently and rationally conceived and must reach down to the very basic ideas of the structure and goals of education.

Environmental education can be the needed change agent. U.S. Commissioner of Education, Sidney P. Marland, describes environmental education as a "catalyst," a "triggering mechanism," deriving from its very nature as a pervasive concern and its emphasis on process over content.[33] Peggy L. Miller, writing in the *Journal of Outdoor Education,* points out that outdoor education (related to environmental education in purposes and goals) works as a change agent in schools by affecting people, process, and program, and providing new patterns of learning. "It leads one change in the curriculum to changes and innovations in other areas of the school program—its ramifications continually expand in ever widening circles of force for change."[34]

The manner in which environmental education can effect change in schools is significant, for it allows a school to begin the process of change and proceed at whatever pace is best in the light of its own circumstances, to retain from its present practices whatever it feels is worth keeping, and to review its progress as it goes along. It reduces the dangers of schools latching onto a new idea that is just another educational fad, but it also encourages the most tradition-bound school to move toward the kinds of sweeping changes demanded by the crises of our times.

Environmental education provides a change in focus for education. Its central concern is man, and it deals with man's environment in such a way that the learner perceives the interrelationships within the environment that he affects and that affect him. It is an integrated process involving experience, investigation, and problem solving in man's natural and man-made surroundings, using the total human, natural, and physical resources of the school and the community as an educational laboratory. While its ultimate goal is the survival of the human race, its immediate emphasis is on the individual learner, enabling him to develop self-reliance, self-direction, a feeling of self-worth, and improvement in the quality of life—his own and that of the larger society.

Environmental education includes conservation, outdoor, and natural resource education, as well as nature study, but it also includes everything else that relates to man and his environment. The breadth of the concept is indicated in the definition stated in the Senate report on the Environmental Education Act:

[33] Carlos Whiting, Office of Education, Dept. of HEW, "Environmental Education: Education That Cannot Wait," *American Education,* 7 (May 1971), 6–10.

[34] Peggy L. Miller, "Outdoor Education: Curriculum Change Agent," *Journal of Outdoor Education,* 4 (Fall 1969), 2–5.

Environmental education is an integrated process which deals with man's interrelationship with his natural and man-made surroundings, including the relation of population growth, pollution, resource allocation and depletion, conservation, technology, and urban and 'rural planning to the total human environment. Environmental education is a study of the factors influencing ecosystems, mental and physical health, living and working conditions, decaying cities, and population pressures. Environmental education is intended to promote among citizens the awareness and understanding of the environment, our relationship to it, and the concern and responsible action necessary to assure our survival and to improve the quality of life.[35]

One of the most important changes in focus is the shift from education as a teaching process (with the principal activity carried on by the teacher) to education as a learning process (with the principal activity carried on by the student). The requirements for educators involved in such a process are aptly summarized in the following quotation:

Teach your scholar to observe the phenomena of nature; you will soon rouse his curiosity, but if you would have it grow, do not be in too great a hurry to satisfy his curiosity. Put the problems before him and let him solve them himself. Let him know nothing because you have told him, but because he has learned it for himself. Let him not be taught science, let him discover it. If ever you substitute authority for reason he will cease to reason, he will be a mere plaything of other people's thoughts. . . . Undoubtedly the notions of things thus acquired for oneself are clearer and much more convincing than those acquired from the teaching of others; and not only is our reason not accustomed to a slavish submission to authority, but we develop greater ingenuity in discovering relations, connecting ideas and inventing apparatus, than when we merely accept what is given us and allow our minds to be enfeebled in indifference.[36]

A novel idea? The words were written by Rousseau in 1762! The validity of the idea in modern education is stressed by Commissioner Marland: "Inasmuch as we can avoid the use of the word 'teaching' and emphasize the concept 'learning,' we will convey the spirit and intent of our approach to environmental education."[37]

Environmental education, then, is the study of man and how he shapes his total natural and cultural surroundings for good or ill. Man—not his technology, not the physical or biological world as a separate entity, not the arts or professions operating in segregated spheres, but all of these as they affect the quality of human life—becomes the pivotal concern. Man cannot be separated from the earth's ecosystem, for he is the only conscious manipulator of the environment and his manipulation must be directed toward enhancing the environment.

[35] U.S. Senate Committee on Labor and Public Welfare, Report on the Environmental Quality Education Act, p. 3.

[36] Jean Jacques Rousseau, *Émile; or, Education*. Trans. Barbara Foxley. Everyman's Library Edition. (New York: E. P. Dutton & Co., Inc.), pp. 131, 139. Reprinted by permission of the publisher, E. P. Dutton, and J. M. Dent & Sons Ltd. (Quoted in *The Open Plan School*, Report of a National Seminar Cosponsored by Educational Facilities Laboratories and Institute for Development of Educational Activities, 1970, p. 5.)

[37] Whiting, "Environmental Education Cannot Wait."

Environmental education is not a separate subject. It is a multidisciplinary approach both to education and to the problems of the environment. All the subjects in a traditional curriculum pertain to the environment and deal with knowledge necessary for preserving the environment. But in their present form, the subjects fail to relate to one another. Just as piecemeal attacks on environmental problems are ineffective, so is piecemeal learning about the environment inadequate because it does not account for the interdependence of the pieces. Buckminster Fuller characterizes the universe as a synergetic system, the effect of the whole being greater than and unpredictable by the effects of its separate parts.[38] Learning must therefore be of wholes and not of parts, if we are to understand the totality of our environment.

> The most general of educations is usually made up of . . . specialized bits. It is no wonder that a housewife has difficulty seeing the connection between her laundry soap and the death of a lake. After all, soap is home economics, but detergents and phosphates are chemistry, the water system is health, the algae and bacteria are biology, and the lake is either geology or geography, she can't remember. To tell her that *she is the lake,* because of her effects on it and its effects on her, would be to present her with a riddle for which she is entirely unprepared.[39]

Subject areas must collaborate, integrate, and coordinate if education is to be relevant and the environment is to be saved.

Above all, environmental education is oriented toward development of values that are translated, ultimately, into action. Awareness, appreciation, and understanding of the environment are only first steps and do not necessarily lead to effective action. They are based on the factual information the students discover. Beyond this, each student must acquire an environmental ethic, a concern for and moral commitment to his responsibility to the environment. Further, he should have the motivation and the competence to make choices between what are often equally attractive alternatives and to act on his choices. His ethic must guide him both in living with the earth's resources and other species and in living with his fellow men in social, political, and economic relationships.

Environmental education should result in the knowledge, desire, and ability necessary to direct one's conduct toward improving the quality of life. It should enable the individual to perceive the problems that exist and to devise solutions to them. In order for students to develop an environmental ethic, their education must cease to laud the biggest, the most, and the best. Who cannot remember the pride with which American history books recounted the growth of the country's population, the industrialization of production, the submission of natural forces to science and technology? Man must now throw off his arrogance and perceive with humility his place in the earth's eco-

---

[38] R. Buckminster Fuller, *Operating Manual for Spaceship Earth* (New York: Pocket Books, Inc., 1969), pp. 65–66.

[39] Mark Terry, *Teaching for Survival* (New York: Ballantine Books, 1971), p. 83. © 1971 by Mark Terry. Reprinted by permission of Ballantine Books, Inc. All rights reserved.

system and his ability to manipulate his environment. His energies will have to shift from material growth to environmental protection. In short, his environmental ethic must provide him with a new reason for existence, or all his technology and power will not sustain his existence.

Although education about various aspects of the environment has been carried on through a number of recognized disciplines for a long time, the notion of environmental education as all learning, and of the environment as encompassing all of where man lives, how he lives, and why he lives, are fairly recent concepts. Before the advent of compulsory formal education, of course, almost all knowledge was obtained from the environment. Itinerant teachers roamed the countryside to provide instruction in the "three R's," but education beyond that came for most children through living and work- ing in the real world.

Formal programs in outdoor education for elementary school children originated at the Round Hill School in Massachusetts, which started the first school camp in America. The experiment ran from 1823 to 1843 and involved boys in camping, hiking, natural history, geological investigations, hunting, fishing, community living, and trips to places of interest. Frederick Gunn started the first camp for high school students in 1861 in Washington, Connecticut, providing a two-week experience in the summer as an aux- iliary to the regular curriculum. In 1919, Chicago became the first metropolitan area to open a school camp, and the movement spread rapidly thereafter.

Although the principal objective of outdoor education was to make learning more vivid through outdoor investigations and cooperative social experiences, the general public saw it as simply moving the class out of the classroom and providing recreational activities. It was regarded more as an extra frill than as an integral part of the cur- riculum.

By the turn of the century, most science curriculums included some kind of environ- mental studies. Conservation education gained established status with the formation of the U.S. Forest Service in the Department of Agriculture in 1905, and through such private groups as the National Audubon Society, the National Wildlife Federation, the Sierra Club, and the Appalachian Club.

Cutting across both outdoor and conservation education have been the interpretive naturalists, usually connected with the National Park Service of the U.S. Department of the Interior or with state park systems. These naturalists teach about the environment in a variety of natural settings and often act as resource personnel for school programs dealing with the natural environment.

A large number of associations have worked to promote outdoor and conserva- tion education in schools and communities, including the Conservation Education Asso- ciation, the American Nature Study Society, the Outdoor Education Association, the Association for Outdoor Education, the Association of Interpretive Naturalists, the Coun- cil on Outdoor Education and Camping (American Association for Health, Physical Edu- cation, and Recreation), the Natural Resources Institute, and the Pinchot Institute for Conservation Studies. But until the recent surge in awareness of the environment crisis, most of this type of education was concentrated in science curriculums, involved separate units on soil or water or wildlife or forests, stressed rural environments, and included a few days of classroom instruction and perhaps a trip to a zoo or museum or maybe a state park.

Today the focus is on man and his relationship to all the environment, with major emphasis on the problems of the city. The approach is multidisciplinary, and the demand is to integrate environmental learning into all learning, in all subjects, in all grades, all year long and beyond the formal school years to a lifelong concern. Environmental education should be viewed not as a new name that carries all its forerunners and their goals under one umbrella but as a transitional process that involves all of the environment and all of education in the transition to the environmental classroom.

Present-day programs in environmental education received great impetus from Title III of the Elementary and Secondary Education Act (ESEA) of 1965 which, by providing funds for creative educational projects, enabled more than 100 environmental education projects to get started. Among them are the Oceanographic Education Center at Falmouth, Massachusetts; Suffolk Environmental Biology Center at Port Jefferson, New York; the Conservation and Environmental Science Center at Browns Mills, New Jersey; the Napa Experimental Forest Education Center in California; and the Ecological Oriented Conservation Center in Missoula, Montana.[40]

Studies of current environmental education programs, however, reveal huge gaps between the theory of a total approach and actual practice. Before ESEA made available funds for experiments, the prevailing pattern of environmental education—when it was offered at all—was one week of conservation and natural science education through outdoor experiences in sixth grade.[41] The pattern has not changed significantly. Many courses dealing with aspects of the environment still fail to offer students any opportunities for direct experience with the environment. Lacking the training to introduce environmental studies in an integrated fashion, teachers have tended to tack them onto the curriculum haphazardly within existing segregated subject areas. A survey by the Council on Outdoor Education and Camping in 1968 revealed some attempts to move toward an ecological concept of the environment with the help of Title III funds, but it showed, nevertheless, a persistent emphasis on one-week programs for sixth graders.[42] A survey by the National Science Teachers Association in 1970 showed a marked trend toward using the real environment to teach about the environment, stressing problem identification and solution, and offering experiences in environmental learning at many grade levels, but the principal thrust of the programs, of course, was in areas of science only.[43]

In 1970, the Research Division of the National Education Association undertook a

[40] Roy C. White, "The State of the Art of Environmental Education," *Science Teacher,* 37 (November 1970), 38–40.

[41] Helen Heffernan, "They Grow Nine Feet High," *Journal of Outdoor Education,* 1 (Winter 1967), 3–5.

[42] Council on Outdoor Education and Camping, *Promising Developments in Outdoor Education* (Washington, D.C.: American Association for Health, Physical Education, and Recreation, March 1968). (Mimeo.)

[43] National Science Teachers Association, *Programs in Environmental Education* (Washington, D.C.: the Association, 1970).

major, nationwide survey of environmental education programs.[44] It polled 7,143 superintendents of school systems enrolling at least 1,000 students, which represented 90 percent of the nation's public school enrollment. Of these, 781 systems—barely 11 percent —were conducting a program in environmental education large enough to warrant the assignment of at least one half-time staff member. While more than half the programs were reported operating all year or throughout the school year, the median time spent on the programs was 10 days in class and 5 outside the classroom for elementary pupils, 12 days in class and 5 outside for junior high school students, and 20 days in class and 5 outside for senior high school students. The study showed that programs vary widely in content, goals, and scope. The courses operate under many different names. Only 14.4 percent listed the development of environmental awareness and ethics as the main intent, while the largest group—31.3 percent—described their aim as "education in and for the outdoors." Areas of study most often included are conservation, ecology, biology, insect study, geology, botany, general science, and weather. As would be expected, the largest school systems have the most comprehensive programs, but on the whole the sixth grade remains as the level at which the majority of school systems provide environmental education and science subjects remain as the major focus of the programs.

A 1971 special report on environmental education in schools, by the editors of *Education U.S.A.*,[45] revealed that most current programs fall short of the criteria expressed by authorities in the field. There are not enough programs to begin with, and those that exist generally are not multidisciplinary, year-round, or all-inclusive of grade levels. The report identifies New Jersey as a leader in environmental education and also describes worthwhile programs that are being carried on in Pennsylvania, South Carolina, Minnesota, California, and Washington.

The situation in our colleges and universities regarding environmental education is perhaps even more critical. Institutions of higher learning could be the ideal source of attack on environmental problems. They are also the training grounds for both the experts who deal with such problems and the teachers who staff environmental education programs in elementary and secondary schools. But entrenched procedures, territorial imperatives of subject fields, and vested interests make the necessary multidisciplinary approach practically impossible to achieve. Clay Schoenfeld underscored the problem a few years ago:

> If there is any agency capable of an objective role in determining the country's basic land and water problems, it is probably the university. Yet the ordinary posture of a university may not be optimum for the task. For the university has become composed of highly individualistic professors organized into departmental enclaves, marked increasingly by the break-up of knowledge into little pieces. . . .[46]

[44] National Education Association, Research Division, *Environmental Education in the Public Schools* (Washington, D.C.: the Association, 1970).

[45] The Editors of Education U.S.A., *Environment and the Schools* (Washington, D.C.: National School Public Relations Association, 1971).

[46] Clay Schoenfeld, "The Third American Revolution," *Everybody's Ecology* (Barns, New York, 1971).

Many colleges and universities offer courses in environmental studies, but most of these fall under the various science disciplines or else they are segregated into such other departments and schools as government, architecture, forestry, law, and medicine. Yet there have been a few noteworthy attempts at setting up a multidisciplinary approach to environmental education. Some have been sparked by Title I of the Higher Education Act, which has provided funds for environmental education and for use of resources in colleges and universities to help solve environmental problems.

In January 1970, Michigan State University established a Center for Environmental Quality as a coordinating center for contributions to environmental problems from numerous departments and disciplines within the university. Huxley College of Western Washington State College, at Bellingham, is seeking to allow students to spend their junior and senior years of college working on broad environmental problems. The hub of the college's activities is the Northwest Environmental Education Center, which contains numerous sites exemplifying the wide variety of environments to be found in the state of Washington. Hampshire College began in the fall of 1970 in Amherst, Massachusetts, based on the idea that the campus itself can be designed as an ecosystem in which students can become actively involved in environmental problems. In the fall of 1969 the University of Wisconsin-Green Bay (UWGB) opened its doors as an institution that deals with traditional disciplines in an untraditional way. The focus at UWGB is on man and his environment, and the entire program relates to the ecological crisis. According to the university chancellor,

> Whether it is teaching, research, or community outreach, the focus of the university remains consistently that of helping the student, professor, and community member to live in greater harmony with the environment and to do something constructive about the problems that beset it.[47]

Although the environmental education situation may appear dismal, there is good reason for optimism. Many of the programs now in existence were started quite recently, and all of those reported here were under way before the passage of the Environmental Education Act of 1970. They represent the awareness of the problem that is the first step toward solution. They may also be the change agents that will stimulate further changes in the whole process of education, until the day will come when learning is looked on as a part of living. Effective changes in the process of teaching and learning are not made overnight. The fact that the first steps toward change are being taken in schools all over the country is evidence that significant changes in education and in the way we relate to our environment are likely to follow.

The federal and state governments as well as national organizations are actively supporting the trend. In addition to the U.S. Office of Education, which administers grants under the Environmental Education Act, other federal agencies sponsor environmental education programs.

In February 1968, the National Park Service (NPS) of the U.S. Department of the

[47] Edward W. Weidner, "Ecology—Heart of Our University Program," *Today's Education*, 59 (December, 1970), 19–21.

Interior launched a program called National Environmental Education Development (NEED). An outgrowth of the NPS interpretive program, NEED is developing curriculum materials for students from kindergarten through high school. The materials relate to all subjects in the regular curriculum and focus on environmental awareness and understanding. They provide for experiences both in the classroom and in the real environment. In the elementary grades, the program stresses appreciation of the environment; the intermediate levels deal with the uses and abuses of our resources; and materials for senior high school students center on the development of an environmental ethic. The entire approach relates man to his environment in terms of the NEED watchword: "There is one web of life and you are part of it; the web is in trouble; you can do something about it."

The National Environmental Study Area (NESA) program is a related NPS program. The Park Service has identified sites on federal lands throughout the country that can be used as laboratories for direct experience with various kinds of environments. While the NEED materials are being prepared specifically for schools, the study areas are being developed for various groups and age levels who wish to use them.

In order to involve the educational community in evaluating the curriculum materials and disseminating information about environmental study areas, NPS called on the American Association for Health, Physical Education, and Recreation (AAHPER), a national affiliate of the National Education Association (NEA), to coordinate Project Man's Environment. In 1970, the Project produced a book and a filmstrip to help explain to teachers the new approach to environmental education. It also began to develop models for inservice programs to train teachers in environmental education. The following year, the Project was superseded by the NEA's Environmental Education Project, which reflects the increasing concern of this professional teachers' organization with environmental conditions and with the need for expanded and improved environmental education. Many other NEA affiliates have also been producing materials and holding conferences on environmental education.

The U.S. Forest Service also supports programs in environmental education. Forest Service specialists work directly with teachers in conducting workshops and producing materials for teachers to use in environmental education programs.

The Corporation for Public Broadcasting, a nonprofit organization funded by the federal government and private sources to promote the growth and development of the nation's noncommercial television and radio systems, set up the Public Broadcasting Environment Center in 1970. Its goals were to use the unique capabilities of the media—

To respond to the national mandate to raise the level of knowledge and understanding of the environmental status and to present viable alternatives;

To create an innovative system of environmental education to reach large and diversified audiences quickly at the primary, secondary, higher and continuing education levels;

To increase perception of the environment as a totality; to communicate an understanding and recognition of the parts, including man himself; and to stimulate the action necessary for man to move toward what he perceives to be a more desirable condition of life.[48]

[48] Corporation for Public Broadcasting, *Final Report* . . . , p. 3.

The National Recreation and Park Association is another large national association sponsoring several programs on outdoor and environmental education. There are actually hundreds more such national associations—among them the American Forestry Association, the National Audubon Society, the National Geographic Society, the Sierra Club, the National Wildlife Federation—that are putting increasing efforts into developing effective resources for environmental education.

Support by state governments for environmental education programs varies, of course, with the individual states. For example, New Jersey's leadership was established when it created the State Council for Environmental Education in 1967. The Council is funded through ESEA and administered by the Newark Board of Education. In 1970, the New Jersey legislature passed an Environmental Quality Education Act to provide for programs in each local school district, a network of facilities and centers, and a curriculum research and development center. California, Pennsylvania, Minnesota, Arkansas, Illinois, Kentucky, Maryland, and North Dakota now have statewide programs of environmental education, while the state of Washington is developing a model in its northwest region to be followed, eventually, by the entire state. On the other hand, the Michigan legislature killed a bill in April 1971 which would have made environmental education a part of the curriculum in all Michigan schools. While there are some promising environmental education programs in Michigan, they have developed without a statewide mandate.

At this point, what is needed most is a coalition of all the agencies, organizations, and interests that can make a contribution toward, as Professor Schoenfeld terms it, a national strategy for environmental education. It does not matter whether a program is called outdoor education, conservation education, resource use education, or environmental education. What does matter is that educators are working toward the common goals of environmental literacy. Whatever the education is called, it must be *effective* education—effective in reaching desired goals. John C. Hendee, a project director for the U.S. Forest Service, pointed out to a research symposium that environmental programs are guided now by a set of unproved assumptions, which need to be inventoried and tested.[49]

Higher education programs need to be made truly interdisciplinary. Elementary and secondary programs need to become broader in scope as well as in time, going beyond one week of outdoor experiences in the middle grades. Furthermore, resources outside the purview of formal education must become involved in the task of increasing environmental awareness and concern among citizens. These include the mass media, industry and commerce, trade and industrial associations, labor unions, and nonprofit organizations.

For it is not just the student who must be educated about the environment. We cannot wait for our student population to grow up to start saving our environment. From preschoolers to adults, each person must have the opportunity to learn about the system of which he is an inseparable part. The education, involvement, and support of

---

[49] John C. Hendee, "Challenging the Folklore of Environmental Education with Research," presented to the American Association for Health, Physical Education, and Recreation Symposium on Environmental Quality Education—Action and Research, April 4, 1970. (Mimeo.)

the whole community is necessary in order to improve the quality of the environment.

The common goals of environmental education programs should be to provide the learner with direct experiences in the real environment so that he may develop an awareness and appreciation of the factors and interrelationships operating in the environment, leading to an ecological understanding of man's oneness with his environment and how man both affects and is affected by it. Programs should encourage the learner to test the values of society as well as his own, so that he may ultimately select those values in which he believes and which are relevant to him in dealing with his environment. He must be free to investigate alternatives and choose among them. Based on his knowledge and beliefs, the learner should be guided to make rational decisions leading to constructive and effective action on environmental problems. Environmental education programs should seek to develop a commitment both toward the environment and toward learning that will last beyond the years of schooling and form a lifelong concern.

Central to all of these goals is the individual, who must discover his own role in his environment and develop concepts of his own self-worth. Through individualized learning activities the learner can become a self-directed person who can learn independently throughout his life and can use his knowledge to take successful action. The resulting personal enrichment of each learner will go a long way toward improving the quality of life for all learners as members of society. The rejection of the feeling of individual powerlessness that is so prevalent in an urbanized society is a prerequisite to the acceptance of personal responsibility for the environment by each member of society.

When directed toward such goals, environmental education can be seen as an evolutionary stage in the history of educational development. It is a synthesis of the most widely accepted modern learning theories. Just as environmental education has evolved from previous courses with narrower conceptions, so we might say that education in America has been evolving into the new theory of the environmental classroom —a concept that treats all the world and all of life as valid topics and sources of learning to enhance the development of the individual.

Current theories of education stress the individual and his needs, in an effort to move away from the rigidity and conformity that characterized traditional education. Abraham Maslow has proposed a hierarchy of the prepotent needs of each human being, which must be fulfilled at each successive level before the individual can pursue satisfaction at the next level. At level one are the basic physiological needs; level two includes the safety needs of justice, order, and security; at level three are the belongingness and love needs, the needs for friendship and for identity within a group; level four are the esteem needs, both of self and of others; and finally at level five is the need for self-actualization, the need "to become everything that one is capable of becoming." [50] The broad new theory of the environmental classroom addresses itself to the fulfillment of each of these levels of need.

Traditional education was based on the idea that students were to learn the body

[50] Abraham Maslow, *Motivation of Personality* (2nd ed.) (New York: Harper & Row, Publishers, 1970), pp. 80–92.

of knowledge that had developed up to their time. The fund of knowledge from man's history was sufficient for getting through life successfully in a relatively unchanging world. Today the very notion of attempting to learn all there is to know is absurd. What is more, the rapid changes that occur in modern life mean that we must unlearn and relearn periodically. Therefore, the process of learning is more important than the content of learning. Modern educational theories that identify relevant kinds of learning reject rote accumulation of facts in favor of discovery, analysis, synthesis, problem solving, and learning how to learn. Environmental education is consistent with these theories and is, by its very definition, relevant to all of life.

In fact, the broad view of environmental education epitomizes the kinds of changes that have gained wide support for dealing with the educational crisis. In 1970, H. Kenneth Gayer and Merrill Oltchick explained a "new system of education" devised for the Center for the Environment and Man in Hartford, Connecticut by Milton A. Young.[51] Among its principal characteristics were the following: (a) It emphasizes human values. Its major goals are establishing a positive self-concept and feeling of control over one's environment through active participation in decision making. (b) It emphasizes human interaction. Equipment and facilities are only tools for learning. (c) It responds to student needs and creates new learning environments and interests for the student. (d) It provides a range of direct, real, and relevant learning experiences. (e) It stresses individualized learning, using a variety of methods and permitting continuous progress by the individual. (f) It is responsive and accountable to the community. (g) Rather than fail students, the system adapts to the needs of each learner. (h) It uses resources for learning from the community, and the community is encouraged to use the facilities and resources of the system. (i) It operates all day, all year, and is open to all ages. (j) It emphasizes process rather than content. (k) It is flexible enough to change as needed. These characteristics of the (new system of education) are the essential characteristics of the environmental classroom at its best.

The kind of person we must fervently strive to produce through such an approach is one who is an environmental generalist, one who can take a broad view of problems and their solutions. To do this, we shall have to reverse the current trend of education and move from vertical specialization to horizontal generalization. It was a logical response to man's geometrically-increasing store of knowledge to train individuals to deal with ever-narrowing areas. The result, unfortunately, is that each specialist sees his own tree but not the forest, and the forest is now in imminent danger. Writing in *Today's Education*, J. Alan Wagar warned against the trend toward specialization:

> Our passion for specialization grew as times became increasingly complex and the way to success lay in doing one thing at a time. We purposely narrowed the view so that each specialist could delve deeply and solve problems of great difficulty in one small area of inquiry. But such specialization has more and more drawbacks. As John Muir pointed out long ago, you can't do just one thing at a time because there are always side effects.[52]

[51] H. Kenneth Gayer and Merrill Oltchick, *Toward a New System of Education* (Hartford, Conn.: Center for the Environment and Man, 1970), pp. 4–9.

[52] J. Alan Wagar, "The Challenge of Environmental Education," *Today's Education*, 59 (December 1970), 17.

We need experts, of course, but we need the kind of experts who are aware of the side effects of their actions.

Buckminster Fuller points out that man was never meant to be a specialist. While other species are designed for highly specialized tasks, man is adaptive in many directions: he can fly or swim and dive without the biological apparatus necessary in animals. "If the total scheme of nature required man to be a specialist she would have made him so by having him born with one eye and a microscope attached to it." What is more, over-specialization—achieved in many species through inbreeding—has been a major cause of extinction because it reduces adaptablity to new conditions.[53]

We have spent many years analyzing knowledge—breaking it down into small bits. We should now synthesize knowledge—put it all back together. If our environment is to be reborn, we shall need our own modern-day "Renaissance men."

To begin moving toward a system of education that can achieve these goals, we shall have to create the environmental classroom. It is a move that can start from even the most tradition-oriented base. It can proceed as rapidly or as slowly as a community desires, but it must get started immediately in order to reverse both the environmental and educational crises.

First, we should expand the learning environment. We should move out of the rigid boxes within boxes which, though they may have had some relevance to the factory-world in the early days of industrialization, have no relevance today to any environment but that of the school. The relevant environment for learning is the real environment.

In Bacon's *Essays,* there is a reference to an old myth in which Mohammed called a mountain to come to him. When it stood still, he merely said, "If the mountain won't come to Mohammed, Mohammed will go to the mountain." To expand the learning environment to its fullest extent, we shall have to move both ways: we must bring the learner to the environment, and we must bring the environment to the learner. In the former case, we can improve the design of facilities so that they are no longer a closed-in succession of boxes but an open structure that invites movement and freedom and use of all the resources within the facility. We can also move out of the school and allow the learner to deal with ever-widening environments—the school yard and grounds, the neighborhood, the entire community, the natural and cultural resources of the state, and ultimately what is popularly termed the "global village" or man's total environment. In the latter case, we can bring the environment to the learner in ever-larger shares—miniature environments and ecosystems in the classroom and in the area surrounding the school, simulated environments that produce all the sensations of their real counterparts, highly developed media providing the learner with vast and varied information sources, and ultimately the global village in which instant communication is possible between individuals or groups at any time and on any subject.

Second, we should restructure learning curriculums. We need to change the process in order to take an environmental view of the content. We shall have to move from a teacher-centered approach, from rote learning, from physical constraints, from a world in which knowledge is neatly divided into packages of subjects, from a single textbook

[53] Fuller, *op. cit.,* pp. 13, 35–37.

and a single test, from whole-class instruction, from education as an activity in preparation for a future event called adulthood—to a learner-centered method, to discovery and problem solving and decision making and value formation, to freedom to search for knowledge in the community of man, to a world where knowledge is interrelated and interdependent, to a variety of sources and ways of learning, to education that is a joyful and fulfilling part of one's entire life. We shall have to move, in short, toward making the whole world the environmental classroom.

chapter two

expanding the learning
environment i : mobility

Mohammed will have to go to the mountain. The learner will have to go to the environment.

As an environment, the typical classroom is like thousands of other classrooms. But it is not like a community, a city street, a garbage dump, a park, a forest, a river, a shopping center, an airport, an old mill, a battlefield, or any of the thousands of environments that comprise man's surroundings. There are many topics that are best explored in a classroom and many learning activities that are best carried on in such an environment. The classroom should continue to be the place for doing these things. But in a classroom you cannot see a tern flutter with the discomfort of oil-slicked feathers, smell the acrid stench of the open burning of solid wastes, taste a wild blueberry you have just plucked from behind a rock, hear the surf crash against a craggy coast, or feel the dew-soaked grass beneath your bare feet. Direct experiences with man's environment can only occur in man's many environments.

In testimony on the Environmental Education Act before the Senate Committee on Labor and Public Welfare, a representative from the Ford Foundation said,

> . . . the schools present a very special environment which is different from that of the community and quite separate from the life that surrounds them. This separation is pervasive throughout the school experience. . . . Children learn about the environment of their community from being in it, and from their experience in it. In schools, they learn about school environment and how to survive in that special setting.[1]

The indoor classroom can no longer be the only learning environment; in order for the learner to become capable of making rational decisions about many environments, learning has to take place in many environments.

If we are looking to achieve the kind of learning process that results in rational decision making, we should recognize that the typical classroom is not the sort of environment that lends itself to such a process. Stated succinctly, "education is a fluid process, and like all fluids, tends to take the shape of its container."[2] The shape of

---

[1] U.S. Senate Committee on Labor and Public Welfare, *Report on the Environmental Quality Education Act* (Washington, D.C.: Government Printing Office, 1970), p. 2.

[2] Education Facilities Laboratories, *Schoolhouse* (Newsletter), No. 1 (February 1971), p. 4.

the traditional classroom encourages a learning process that takes, to paraphrase Ole Sand, a two-by-four-by-six shape, confined between two covers of a textbook, four walls of a classroom, six periods of a school day.[3] Schools that resemble factories dictate a factory-like conception of education: raw materials in, standardized product out.

Nevertheless, there are many schools of the boxes-within-a-box design that are going to be used for many years to come. Although designers of schools are rapidly moving away from this kind of facility, which has been compared to an eggcrate, it will take even longer than two to three generations to replace all the existing eggcrates with facilities truly designed for human beings engaged in learning. Neither schools of traditional design nor, concomitantly, curriculums geared to separate subjects are appropriate to the concept of the environmental classroom. However, since environmental education is a change agent, it can start the process of change within even the

[3] Ole Sand, *On Staying Awake: Talks with Teachers.* Schools for the 70's, Preliminary Series (Washington, D.C.: Center for the Study of Instruction, National Education Association, 1970), p. 36.

most traditional facility and the most traditional classroom. It can help the educational process begin to move outward, expanding the horizons and experiences of learners in ever-widening circles, until we reach the goal of the environmental classroom.

Moving Toward the Environmental Classroom

The traditional classroom. Although the traditional classroom is not like any of the environments outside it, it is still an environment and exhibits many of the general characteristics inherent in any environment. Its physical features determine the kinds of functions that can be performed in it. Its inhabitants interrelate with and depend upon both one another and the physical environment. As such, it can be a logical first place to study environmental relationships. [Chapter 3 goes into further exploration of the classroom as an environment.]

The open school. However, the classroom itself is a confining place in terms of both space and time. It imposes physical restraints on the learner that work against joy and independence in learning. One method that seeks to encourage freedom of movement and self-motivated learning is the English open (or "free," "informal," or "integrated") school, which has caught the attention of many American educators in the last few years.

The most striking feature about the English open schools is that the children who attend them are no longer confined to a seat in a row in a classroom. As a matter of fact, there are no rows and few seats. The children are free to roam about their room to various areas containing an abundance of materials to explore, touch, and manipulate. They work at their own pace on projects that are largely of their own choosing and come to conclusions that have not been predetermined by a curriculum committee in another part of town. What is more, they may roam out of the classroom and into the corridors, which themselves become learning environments containing projects on display and additional learning centers.

All this is done not in a haphazard manner but under the firm and constant guidance of the teacher. Environmental education may be learner-centered, but the teacher plays a crucial—if untraditional—role. Learners cannot decide that a subject interests them if they have never heard about it. They cannot develop skills in a vacuum. Teachers must provide direction as well as an environment that expands the interests and skills of the learner.

Schools in England that use the open method range from the most modern in design to dreary, 100-year-old eggcrates. In each of them, whatever the architecture, the classroom doors are open and the students are free to encounter their learning environment and come to grips with it in the manner that suits them best.

American adaptations of the English method are being tried in various schools and school systems throughout the country—in New York City and neighboring West-chester County; in North Dakota, Vermont, Maine, Arizona, Texas, and Massachusetts; in Washington, D.C.; in Philadelphia. Some of these experiments are not specifically tied to the English prototype; they have evolved from a desire on the part of teachers and school administrators right here to develop a learning atmosphere in which children can be respected and can play an active role in their education.

One of the most noteworthy examples is the program at P.S. 84 on Manhattan's Upper West Side—a school of traditional design in a racially and economically mixed neighborhood. Getting such an experiment started in a school system marked by the obstacles it poses to even the most innocuous changes was the work of "a woman with a mission,"—Lillian Weber. "When I say that I came back [from England] determined to test the possibility," Mrs. Weber told interviewers, "it was not with ignorance of all the difficulty. It's that I decided that you have to *defy* all the difficulties and that then maybe you'd break through." [4] Others have had easier experiences in breaking down the classroom barriers—an enthusiastic young teacher experimented successfully with the open-school method for two years in a single class in a Bethesda, Maryland, elementary school, needing only the approval and support of a receptive and open-minded principal.

The movement toward breaking out of the classroom barrier, while emerging first in existing schools that were never designed for such a learning process, is stimulating new and creative thinking among school architects. The factories and eggcrates are beginning to disappear from the drawing boards and are being replaced by open, flexible, pleasing, and comfortable designs. At a school planning institute in 1969, a member of a group studying educational facilities in Toronto remarked:

> The school designer should assume that education in future schools will rest on the process of learning, rather than exclusively on that of teaching. There will be much less need of having students receiving instruction from a teacher in fixed, enclosed locations capable of seating 30 students.[5]

In a school design created by Bender Burrell Associates and exhibited by the Electric Heating Association,[6] the thirty-student classroom is given minimal space. The sixty-acre campus contains indoor and outdoor facilities for kindergarten through grade twelve, including a variety of playing fields, nature areas, gardens, and courts. The learning areas, designated by ability level rather than by age or grade, are designed to accommodate five kinds of learning arrangements—independent study, one-to-one

---

[4] Walter Schneir and Miriam Schneir, "The Joy of Learning—In the Open Corridor," *New York Times Magazine* (April 14, 1971), p. 92. © 1971 by the New York Times Company. Reprinted by permission.

[5] Hugh Vallery, "A Systems Approach to Educational Facilities in Metropolitan Toronto," *Planning Innovative Schools*, a Report of the Proceedings of the 19th Annual Summer School Planning Institute, sponsored by Stanford University School of Education School Planning Laboratory and Educational Facilities Laboratories, Inc. (New York: Educational Facilities Laboratories, 1969), p. 18.

[6] Electric Energy Association, *The Environment of Learning* (New York: the Association, 1969).

discussions, small-group activities, standard classes, and large-group activities. At the core is a resource center containing books and many types of technological learning media.

In traditional schools, the only space that is specifically designed for independent study is the library. But traditionally designed school libraries are not easily adaptable to housing modern technological learning resources. Since they are also quiet zones, they are inappropriate for working in small groups and engaging in discussion. The kind of independent study and small-group projects that arise naturally from the environmental classroom will require a variety of study environments such as envisioned in the Burrell model.

The trend today toward the open-plan school emphasizes access to information and different kinds of learning areas. The main spaces are usually large, multipurpose rooms accommodating three to five classes and teachers who proceed during the school day to group and regroup in clusters of various sizes, aided by movable partitions, areas designed for special learning activities, and a central resource center. Some of these schools look like contiguous hexagons, some are concentric circles, some are snail-like spirals, some are huge domes, some are merely rectangles or squares without the usual internal partitions, but whatever the shape, the idea is the same—

> . . . an educational process unbound by the barriers built into the conventional schoolhouse with its rows of standard classrooms. The major aim in these open-space schools is to provide an environment which encourages greater interaction between teacher and pupil, and between teacher and teacher. There are no partitions to fragment learning by dividing teachers, children, and subject matter into tight standardized compartments. And there are no halls to funnel children from compartment to compartment at the arbitrary dictate of a bell. Each child finds his own place, creates his own path.[7]

Schools like these have been constructed since the early 1960s in San Jose, Pacifica, and Cupertino, California; in Carson City and Saginaw, Michigan; in Beloit, Wisconsin; in Salt Lake City, St. Louis, and New York City; and in hundreds of other districts that have seen the need for form to follow function in facility design.

Ideally, the environmental classroom promotes the use of the school facility as a resource and study center for solving problems that are discovered not in the school environment but in the real environment. Some day the school will be a place to come back to, rather than a place to go out from—a place in which to analyze data collected at sites in man's world, to research information leading to solutions of problems, to think and to plan, to sharpen skills. When learners go to the real environment in order to study it, the school facility will become just one more part of the learning environment.

The school grounds. The real world begins right outside the school door. As the necessity for learning in the real world becomes clear to all educators, school sites will be planned to allow learners to experience a variety of environments close to their

---

[7] Educational Facilities Laboratories, *Profiles of Significant Schools: Schools Without Walls* (New York: Educational Facilities Laboratories, 1965), p. 3.

school buildings. They will no longer be stripped of their natural features and leveled before construction of a school begins. Rather, the unique educational features of the site will be preserved and developed to create an outdoor learning laboratory on the school grounds.

Yet even today, in the yard and grounds of just about any school—be it in city, suburb, or rural area—there are hundreds of environmental problems to be discovered and solved. All that is necessary is for the learners to walk outside with at least one teacher prepared to guide them in perceiving their environment. The area around the school is the most easily accessible environment beyond the classroom. Solving problems within it can provide the learner with the satisfaction of improving his immediate surroundings.

For example, seventh-grade students at Short Mountain Elementary School in Cannon County, Tennessee, collected four bushels of litter discarded by motorists along the highway frontage of their school. They separated, counted, and weighed the waste, then calculated the cost per mile to the government of cleaning the average monthly accumulation of litter along the roads.

Students pass through their school grounds every day, but most of them are unaware of the environmental problems that abound there because they have not been guided to be perceptive about their environment. They ignore or simply become accustomed to the litter, the ugliness, the pollution, the poor planning of their world, because they have not been trained to be keenly and critically observant of their surroundings.

A teacher in a Pennsylvania middle school conducted an interesting experiment in expanding perception. Each student took a lemon from a pile and was asked to describe it. There was a single restriction—that no two lemons could be described in the same terms—which forced each student to find something unique about his own lemon. The students described them, the lemons were put back into the pile, and each student was told to retrieve his own lemon. After participating in the exercise, the students actually were able to recognize their own lemons.

A schoolyard that initially exhibits features as ordinary as those of a lemon can also become a unique and varied environment to learners trained to use all their senses in perceiving their surroundings. A deep hole in the ground turns into a soil laboratory, from which texture, content, depth, and acidity can be determined. A hill of dirt only two feet high reveals erosion processes. Rocks and plants lend themselves to a variety of investigative activities. Trees, shrubs, plants, water areas (from streams to puddles), paving, and animal habitats disclose ecological principles. Even cracks in the sidewalk can be studied for plant and animal life, seasonal changes, effects on nearby areas, and patterns of development.

Two teachers involved in the Earth Science Curriculum Project funded by the National Science Foundation took a ninth-grade class outside of their inner-city school to observe and identify changes taking place on the building and surrounding grounds. After adjusting to the unusual and delightful experience of leaving the classroom in the middle of the day, the students eagerly went about noticing things they had never seen before—weeds, cracks, rust, different building materials, and so on. On their next foray onto the school grounds, they were each given a camera and asked to photograph evidence of changes. Being given responsibility for a valuable piece of equipment and achieving success with the technical aspects of it was an ego-building experience in itself for these youngsters. As to the results of the learning activity, one of the teachers reported: "From the pictures they took, from the reports and the discussion, it was . . . obvious that the students were becoming aware of the environment closest to them." She forecasts that "they should be better able to relate their own environment to environments elsewhere and understand environments wherever they exist." [8]

Given a reasonable amount of land and funds, a school can expand the learning potential of its outdoor site by developing a variety of environmental areas on it. A little more than 40 percent of the school systems identified by the NEA Research Division as conducting environmental education programs reported using sites within the immediate area of the school.[9] Since 1967, the Newark, Delaware, School District has been developing nature centers on the grounds of its schools. The grounds of the Millburn, New Jersey, schools are the focal point for elementary outdoor education programs. The Yarmouth, Maine, schools are creating a model outdoor site for environmental learning, improvement and conservation projects, and community recreational activities. And adjacent to the Shawnee Mission South High School in Shawnee Mission, Kansas, is a twenty-acre environmental science laboratory containing field, pond, stream, and woodland areas, staffed by six teachers, and used for small-group projects involving two to five days of on-site study.

School sites can be as simple as a small vegetable and/or flower garden planted by the students or as complex as a complete farming operation as well as varieties of plant and animal life, water areas, weather stations, nature trails, recreation areas and amphitheaters, and camping facilities.[10]

As site development for environmental education becomes more sophisticated, schools often move away from their immediate area to locate areas suitable for environmental projects. Sites owned and developed by the school or school system away from school grounds provide students with opportunities for extended field experiences. Resident facilities offer the additional social benefits of community living during the field experience and leadership training for older students.

Since 1938, schools in Ottawa County, Michigan, have leased land from the West

---

[8] Dorothy S. Curtis, "Designing Activities for Pupils in the Inner City," *Professional Growth for Teachers: Science, Junior High School Edition.* First Quarterly Issue, 1969–70. (New London, Conn.: Croft Educational Services, 1969).

Robert E. Samples, "Get Out . . . And Learn." *Environmental Studies Newsletter #1. Boulder, Colo.:* Earth Science Educational Program, undated.

[9] National Education Association, Research Division, *Environmental Education in the Public Schools* (Washington, D.C.: the Association, 1970), p. 40.

[10] Detailed specifications for school site development are contained in the following:

Peggy L. Miller, *School Gardens and Farms—Aspects of Outdoor Education* [Las Cruces, New Mexico State University Press (ERIC-CRESS)], December 1970.

Charles Trotter, *Use That Campus* (Norris, Tenn.: Division of Forestry, Fisheries, and Wildlife Development, TVA), undated.

U.S. Department of Agriculture, Soil Conservation Service, *The Community School Site: A Laboratory for Learning* (Berkeley, Calif.: the Service, March 1970).

Ottawa Soil Conservation District. With technical assistance from the District, students plant trees and care for them in a continuing conservation project. Teachers in Knox County, Missouri, felt that even a little puddle of water would help them teach biology. With the aid of Title III funds and technical assistance from various agencies, they constructed a nature pond at which classes study the biological, chemical, and physical features of an aquatic environment. Social studies, art, industrial arts, and history classes now also make use of the outdoor laboratory. Three Ohio school districts combined to create the Tri-District Outdoor Education Project, serving all 15,000 students in the districts with a variety of study sites. Elementary school children in Omak, Washington, enjoy the benefits of a school-owned forest camp, where they spend five days each year exploring the conservation needs of a particular area of interest. In Shelton, Washington, an elementary school owns a nearby fish hatchery, which is stocked by the State Department of Fisheries. Pupils visit their hatchery often to check on the progress of the fish and clean the hatching tanks. The Charlotte, North Carolina, schools have developed the Independence Outdoor Laboratory for field trips involving many curriculum areas and all grade levels. Elementary school children in Tyler, Texas, have opportunities for outdoor education at Camp Tyler and at school farms, both of which are owned and run by the school district. The Stepping Stone Environmental Education Center, in Sussex County, New Jersey, is sponsored by the Carteret School District but open to all districts in the state. It offers a multisensory and interdisciplinary program for either day or overnight field trips.

The variety of environmental education sites a school might operate appears to be limited only by the imagination of the school system and the interests of the learners—making the possibilities virtually endless. The important factor is that the learning that occurs at such sites be fully integrated into the school curriculum, so that the environment becomes something more than a place "out there" that is abandoned upon return to the classroom.

The neighborhood. Environmental learning need not and should not be restricted to areas owned and developed by school districts. The first environment beyond the home to which children are exposed is their own neighborhood, which offers a wealth of learning experiences within walking distance of the school. When used as a starting point for environmental awareness, the neighborhood—whether an urban slum or a glistening suburban development—provides a basis of comparison with other environments learners will explore.

Many teachers, however, hesitate to take a class on so simple an expedition as an exploration of their neighborhood. Once outside the security of their classroom, they are unsure of the reactions and interactions that a relatively unstructured learning experience will produce. While the typical thirty-seat classroom provides teachers with a familiar frame of reference, the many resources of the real environment are likely to give rise to unexpected responses.

One way to overcome the problem is to devise a loose structure for environmental experiences that involves preparation in the classroom for the kinds of situations the learners will encounter, free exploration by the learners during the field experience modified by teacher guidance toward a range of possible problem areas, and follow-up activity in class using a variety of learning resources provided by the school. This type of structure is known as the pre-site, on-site, post-site approach to environmental learning. In order for it to be effective, teachers should become familiar beforehand with the educational possibilities of the area the class will visit and understand some of the problems it illustrates in a variety of curriculum areas—social, scientific, esthetic, historic, mathematical, communicative, and so forth.

Focusing on the environment as a resource for discovering relationships and solving problems aids the teacher in recognizing the learning potential inherent in some of the most ordinary things to be found in a neighborhood: farms, fields, barns, wells, and fences; industrial sites, factories, and power plants; recreation and park areas; railroad tracks and terminals, tunnels, bridges, roads, culverts, airports, bus stations, canals, and waterfronts; parking lots, shopping centers, residential and commercial streets, broadcasting stations, telephone poles, and highways; water and sewage treatment plants, pipe mains, fire hydrants, reservoirs, fire and police stations, cemeteries, and vacant lots; municipal buildings and offices, subways, landmarks, street signs—virtually everything in a neighborhood offers possibilities for learning activities leading to a better understanding of the familiar environment close to home.

The community. From the use of the neighborhood for environmental learning, it requires only a small expansion of mobility to use the entire community as a learning environment. Furthermore, the community (read "town," "county," "city," "metropolitan area," or whatever is most descriptive in any given geographical location) can become more than a collection of places from which students learn. It can be a cooperative learning environment involving give and take between school and community and the active participation of many segments of the community.

It would be difficult to find a school curriculum that does not require students to study their city or town or county periodically throughout their school years. Yet such study is usually confined to the classroom, the textbook, and the teacher's authority, although it might include a "field trip" to a famous landmark, if there is one. It is platitudinous to assert that students really learn only what is interesting to them, but memorizing historical and descriptive facts about an area is not likely to be interesting to many students. If, however, students were encouraged to discover firsthand how some of the functions of their community really operate, why some things about their area are the way they are, and how some aspects of it could be improved, each student would probably find some topic relating to the community that would be especially relevant to him.

Instead of trying to teach about man's environment through the use of classroom materials alone, teachers and administrators should consider the total resources available in the community. They should enlist the cooperation of persons in business and industry, union leaders, government officials, and media personnel. At the same time, the school can perform a reciprocal function by sponsoring seminars, briefings, forums, exhibits, and information centers on environmental problems for the entire community.

The Milwaukee Public Schools, for example, use a variety of community resources for their environmental education program, including the zoo, a boat trip around the three rivers of the city, the Museum of Natural History, the planetarium, the Mitchell Conservatory (three large domes each of which contains plant life in a different climatic environment), an outdoor site, a resident camp, and a public forest. The Newark, Delaware School District makes use of a city park and local science museum as part of their Outdoor Laboratory program. The year-round day program in outdoor education for all grades in the Indianapolis Public Schools uses all city parks and scout camp areas; upper elementary grades have an additional six-week summer program at Eagle Creek-Geist Reservoir; and sixth graders participate in a resident program at Bradford Woods, Indiana University's outdoor education center. An experimental program entitled Environmental Problems for Individually Centered Studies (EPICS) in Tarrytown, New York, includes tours of local industry and seminars with local scientists and politicians. The Millburn, New Jersey Public Schools make use of Taylor Park, the delightful Turtle Back Zoo at South Mountain Reservation, and the Cora Hartshorn Arboretum. One cannot help but wonder whether such suburban communities as Millburn, West Orange, and Livingston ever break out of their insular boundaries and recognize the possibilities for relevant environmental learning in nearby Newark, New Jersey, as well.

An example of a cooperative community program is Project OUTREACH (Outdoor Unified Training for Recreation, Education, Appreciation, Conservation, and Health) in the Phoenix, Arizona, high schools. Personnel from cooperating agencies provide field activity programs at various county and city parks, and the project encourages the active participation of the community in conservation and outdoor learning experiences.

The Bellevue, Washington schools use their community for an integrated, multidisciplinary approach to environmental learning. While studying the physical and geographical features of their city, students also learn about its human resources, for the Bellevue schools find "teachers" in the thousands of persons who run the various enterprises, facilities, and resources of the community. The architecture, industrial parks, libraries, businesses, natural areas, and museums help comprise "the other classroom" for learning.

The South Kitsap School District in Port Orchard, Washington, operates a SKOOL (South Kitsap Outdoor Observation Laboratory), which includes a camp rented from a church and field trips to the Bremerton Watershed, the Minter Creek Salmon Hatchery, the Shellfish Laboratory at Purdy, the Webster Tree Nursery and Animal Problems Laboratory near Olympia, and Point Defiance Park in Tacoma. The Edmonds, Washington School District reaped great rewards from enlisting the aid of the PTA and the community in environmental education—they cooperated in developing the Marshall Outdoor Laboratory, a richly endowed nature trail for the use of 1,500 fifth graders.

On occasion, the initial impetus for an environmental education program will start in the community and move into the schools, rather than the other way around. TETE (Total Education in the Total Environment), for example, was conceived by ten science-oriented educators and community leaders in Wilton, Connecticut, in 1964. It is a total approach to ecological studies that uses the resources of public and private cultural and educational agencies in the community, because the originators of the idea realized that the breadth of the concept of ecology requires the involvement of many areas of community life in a program aimed at increasing ecological understanding. Title III provided funds for developing the approach, which is now also being used in an environmental education program for New York State at the Hudson River Museum. The Wave Hill Center for Environmental Studies in New York City is another community-based resource that has the potential to become a valuable aid to environmental learning for students in the city's schools. A third example is the Abraham Lincoln Memorial Garden and Nature Center in Lake Springfield, Illinois. The Center board decided that programs in outdoor and conservation education were the highest use consistent with the original purpose of the garden to which it could be put. It conducts courses in conservation and ecology for students and the community at large, has developed a curriculum guide, and holds inservice workshops for teachers.

Besides the educational advantages of using the community as a classroom, there is a distinct economic advantage as well. Facilities and environments in the community become subject to multiple use, thereby increasing their overall value to the community. The Southern River Swamp, a natural wilderness area in the Georgia Piedmont, is one such environment that lends itself to multiple uses. In addition to its natural functions as a conserve of water, plant life, and a variety of animals, it stands as a unique eco-system ready to be explored, within easy reach of a large metropolitan area (Atlanta) but unaffected by it. It is suitable for field trips, ecological research, and recreational use and is not likely to be damaged by such activities.[11]

The community, with all of its human, natural, cultural, and industrial resources that function to make it a community, is a real and relevant environment with real and relevant interrelationships and real and relevant problems to be analyzed and solved. It is a textbook on human and natural interactions and how they affect the quality of man's life, and it is far more revealing than any set of printed pages bound between two covers. Many a student has known instinctively at age four that to play on a seesaw, the heavier child must move toward the center, but at age fifteen he has had trouble understanding the concept of a fulcrum in the classroom. Such children find new pleasure in learning when they can grapple with real conditions in the community.

The community is especially appropriate for individual and small-group investigations. One student or a group of three or four, for instance, might be interested in finding out how and why their community is zoned the way it is into areas of residential sections, business establishments, industry, and so on. Did the area develop according to some master plan or did it, like Topsy, just grow? Their questions will be better answered by the county or municipal records and perhaps a local official who is concerned with zoning ordinances than by a textbook. This kind of information changes too rapidly to be kept up to date in printed classroom materials. After the students have completed their investigations, the entire class might benefit from a report, whereas other class members might have had little interest in doing the actual research in this particular field. The students might then be involved enough to attend a zoning reclassification hearing and offer their opinions as to why they support or oppose the zoning change.

11 Charles H. Wharton, *The Southern River Swamp—A Multiple-Use Environment* (Atlanta: Georgia State University Press, 1970).

Some schools around the country started taking a step toward using the community as a learning environment when the EFFE (Experiment in Free-Form Education) program, also known as the mini-course, began in 1968.[12] Walt Whitman High School in Bethesda, Maryland, and Wilson High School in Portland, Oregon, were among the first and most publicized schools to adopt the program, which has since spread even to the junior high and elementary school level. Typically, the school suspends classes either for a full week or two or for certain periods during a week, and students spend the time studying subjects that are not offered in the regular curriculum but which they are interested in pursuing. Courses include lectures, labs, or discussion groups conducted by experts from the community; work-experience assignments in local business and industry; community volunteer work; assisting teachers in elementary classes; field trips to governmental, historical, cultural, and scientific locations; and independent study contracts. Parents, community leaders, and businessmen have been willing and enthusiastic teachers, and many students have relished their first experience in curriculum planning and execution. A large number of the schools that have experimented with mini-courses are working to incorporate the program into the regular curriculum throughout the year.

A mini-course experiment at Hamilton-Wenham Regional High School in Hamilton, Massachusetts, resulted in better attendance than during the rest of the school year, although attendance was voluntary for the program. Students selected such topics as film-making, cooking, volunteer work at a school for retarded children, creative writing, mod music, and child care. One group planned and executed a mountain climbing expedition. Another studied marine ecology at nearby beaches and tidal marshes. One student commented, "Being *allowed* to learn, instead of being made to, changes everyone's attitude. This is how education should be structured." And the regular curriculum at the school is feeling the effects of the change agentry worked by the free-form courses:

> . . . sex education, using mini-course methods and materials, is now incorporated in the biology course. The Music Department now offers a full semester elective in music theory. The departments of history and English are busily studying the possibility of a changeover to a partially elective basis. By intention, the senior humanities elective is heterogeneously grouped as well as team-taught.[13]

In the spring of 1969, elementary pupils at Seth Lewelling School in Milwaukie, Oregon, planned their own courses for one period a day for a week. They invited guest lecturers on the topics they selected, scheduled field trips, and searched for source materials throughout the community. A local realtor guided a group studying interior design through homes in the area. Another group attended a rehearsal of the Portland

---

[12] Educational Research Service, American Association of School Administrators and NEA Research Division, *Experiment in Free-Form Education: Mini-Courses*, ERS Information Aid No. 6. (Washington, D.C.: American Association of School Administrators and National Education Association, October, 1970).

[13] Robert R. Hayward, "Maximum Results from Mini-Courses," *Today's Education*, 58 (September 1969), 55–57.

Junior Symphony. A high school junior demonstrated the equipment and technique of scuba diving. Still another group studied wilderness survival and built a lean-to shelter on the school playground.[14] Such experiments have proved to many schools that the community has virtually unlimited potential as an environmental classroom.

One of the most important results of studying the community is that students become aware of the forces that give their community its special character and possible solutions to situations they see as problems in their own environment. Through their observations of various environments, they perceive what is wrong with their own environment and what could be right about it. Through learning that focuses on the environment, they acquire understanding of man's technology and how it can be used to alter or modify the environment. When students have reached sufficient maturity to make rational decisions about their environment, they are able to select the kinds of alternatives that will improve rather than spoil their environment. Senator Gaylord Nelson told participants in a recent seminar on the schools and the environment:

> I think it is very important that the schools involve our young people in the practical aspects of their environment. The schools should encourage students to participate in projects right in their home communities—things like clearing up the local park or the streets. I also approve of inventories of environmental situations in their own communities. . . . An academic education in ecology is, of course, important. But I think you get much better understanding, better feeling, if the students are doing projects . . . or [dealing] with some aspect of the environment. . . .[15]

When education immediately becomes practical, it also becomes especially relevant to the learner.

Almost any existing course can be directed toward practical ends. Students at University High School at the University of Iowa were offered the P[3] course (Problems of Population and Pollution) in science during the 1969–70 school year. The class defined an ideal environment, and each student selected a problem area of the present environment that he felt prevents attainment of the goal. Their individual investigations sent students to listen to government officials, take opinion polls, test water samples, study problems of population control, and engage in numerous other explorations within the environment they sought to improve. They appeared before community groups to discuss the results of their investigations, their concerns, and their proposals for corrective action.

The Pollution Control Education Center of the Union Township, New Jersey, Public Schools is developing classroom lessons in air and water pollution control, solid waste and sewage disposal, noise pollution, and visual-esthetic pollution. It emphasizes making judgments about policies relating to environmental preservation and demonstrates successful solutions that have been implemented within the framework of governmental processes.

The concept of active participation in environmental planning is behind the ma-

14 Judith M. Brown and Don Emberlin, "Their Own Week," *Today's Education*, 59 (May 1970), 12.
15 I/D/E/A/, *The Schools and the Environment: A Report of a National Seminar* (Dayton, Ohio: Institute for Development of Educational Activities, 1970), p. 9.

terials being developed by GEE (the Group for Environmental Education), a coalition of educators and architects in Philadelphia. The idea is to provide opportunities for learners to become aware of their physical or man-made environment so that they can judge what they do and do not like, what is functional and attractive in city design, and what creative ideas for change can be devised. When students understand the processes of environmental planning, they become confident of their ability to contribute to the processes and effect changes in their environment.

A community that is both functional and pleasing to those who live and/or work in it should not just grow like Topsy. It ought to be planned—not by a few knowledgeable experts but by the entire knowledgeable community. So while the schools may be the logical central point of programs to educate the entire community about the environment, they ought not to have the entire responsibility.

Private organizations and businesses have considerable resources which could be directed toward educating and informing the community about the quality of the environment. Professional and labor associations can alert their membership to environmental problems and take positions on environmental issues. Business and industry can inform consumers about the proper use of products and educate the public on the kinds of alternatives about which decisions must be made in order to establish standards of environmental quality. Citizens organizations can stimulate action and exert pressure on government and industry to use appropriate measures to ensure environmental quality. Independent education organizations—such as private centers and institutes, foundations, and museums—can use their unique resources to promote and supplement environmental education programs in the community. The Youth Science Institute, a nonprofit organization in San José, California, offers several programs to school children in the community. During the summer, it sponsors Schamp (school-camp), which includes nine-day back-packing trips in the High Sierra preceded by three days of orientation at the Institute's Children's Natural History Museum. During the school year it runs a miniature version of Schamp on weekends and also supplements the school science program with loans of material and live animals, tours of the museum and nature walks, and special lessons.

When the entire community becomes an environmental classroom and all the citizens of the community are involved in environmental education, the result can be a dynamic social force motivated to take rational action to improve the quality of life. A number of schools have already moved toward this goal by going beyond the idea of the community as a place for isolated field trips and embracing the idea of the community as the place of learning. Educational activities are dispersed throughout the community, "teachers" include parents and local specialists as well as the school staff, and the school becomes a learning institution rather than a physical plant.

At the Murray Road Annex of Newton, Massachusetts High School, students use the school building for some courses while pursuing others where and when they find them. Local experts lead seminars evenings and weekends at whatever location is mutually convenient. At John F. Kennedy High School in Silver Spring, Maryland, courses may run for a whole semester or a few weeks and are marked by their interdisciplinary character: "The History of Ideas," "Law and Freedom," "Alternative Life Styles,"

"Geometry in Art." Students may also work during school hours for academic credit; some are interns in Congressional offices while others are aides at nearby schools and hospitals. At John Adams High School in Portland, Oregon, the students are divided into teams or "houses" with faculty leaders. Half the day is spent pursuing the regular curriculum, the other half working on a problem area such as pollution control or reducing racial tension at the urban school. Independent, self-directed study and optional grades or none at all are inherent in the structures of these schools and, unlike other schools that attempt the process, these schools truly make learning a part of living.

> Clearly, it is easier to assume the trappings of innovation than its substance. Thousands of high schools like to think that they are offering something called independent study; a handful really are. The rest are so heavily teacher-directed that the work deteriorates into little more than traditional homework or "projects" with a fancy new label. Indeed, it is not uncommon to hear a teacher announce, "Your independent study assignment for tomorrow is . . ." [16]

Going one step further is Philadelphia's Parkway School, the "School Without Walls"—it uses the city as a learning environment to the point where it does not have a separate facility for a school building. The rationale is that "school" is not a place, but a process.

The Parkway School began in February 1969 with an enrollment drawn by lottery from applications submitted from all eight Philadelphia school districts. Its name comes from the Benjamin Franklin Parkway, the downtown area where the city's institutions and museums—the school's "classrooms"—are located. The students are divided into groups with faculty leaders, and they learn basic skills in math and language arts as well as certain elective courses from the Parkway staff. In addition, they learn from some 200 participating institutions, generally in areas the students themselves have requested. They may, for example, choose to learn horticulture at the Pennsylvania Horticultural Society, broadcasting at WIP or KYW-TV or WHYY-TV, legal rights from an assistant district attorney, art at the Philadelphia Art Museum, advertising at an advertising agency, retail management from a local merchant, child development at a number of day-care centers and nursery schools, home economics or electricity at the Philadelphia Gas Works, or any number of courses at nearby colleges and universities. Students are also encouraged to conduct courses in areas of their own interest and to work at the Parkway institutions as an extra activity. At the Parkway School, learning really does take place in the environmental classroom.

None of these schools—Murray Road, Kennedy, Adams, or Parkway—is without its critics in the community, who feel that a great deal is lost in the rejection of structure and that students waste a lot of time finding their own structure in learning. Certainly some individuals gain more from this type of learning than do others, which indicates perhaps that there ought to be a variety of learning approaches available in any school system to match the variety of learning styles that exist in the community.

[16] Arlene Silberman, "Bold New Directions for U.S. High Schools," *Reader's Digest*, Vol. 97 (August 1970), 90–91.

It is not necessary to abandon the idea of the school building in all—or even in most—cases. But if we are going to move into the environmental classroom and if the school is going to become an institution of learning rather than a place for learning, then the school facility ought to function as such. The school itself ought to become a multiple-use resource serving the educational, recreational, and social needs of the entire community, and the school as an institution ought to be the coordinating center for a variety of community endeavors. This is the essential concept underlying a movement that has been growing in force for about two decades—the community school.

Originating in Flint, Michigan, and stimulated by the support of the Mott Foundation, the community school is grounded in the following philosophy, adopted by the National Community School Education Association (NCSEA) in 1968:

> Community School Education is a comprehensive and dynamic approach to public education. It is a philosophy that pervades all segments of educational programming and directs the thrust of each of them toward the needs of the community. The community school serves as a catalytic agent by providing leadership to mobilize community resources to solve identified community problems. This marshaling of all forces in the community helps to bring about change as the school extends itself to all people.
>
> Community School Education either affects all children, youth, and adults directly or it helps to create an atmosphere and environment in which all men find security and self-confidence, thus enabling them to grow and mature in a community which sees its schools as an integral part of community life.[17]

The community school offers its services all day, all year, to citizens of all ages in the community. It uses all the combined resources of the school and the community to provide regular, formal education for school-age children; retraining for the unemployed; recreational, social, educational, vocational, and avocational opportunities for all; a forum for community problems; facilities for health services; and a focal point for community planning and community projects. Community education stands for social improvement, a life-relevant curriculum, and total absorption of the school into the community's lifeblood. The community has always owned its schools; the community school, in effect, returns the schools to those who own them.

Early experiments with community schools drew largely on existing school programs of adult education, opening the schools for adult classes and recreation during late afternoon and evening hours. From seven schools in 1959, the NCSEA documented 275 community schools in 1968 and 620 in 1972. Along with the increase in number has come a concomitant enlargement in scope—from high school completion, basic education, enrichment, and recreation to programs and projects on poverty, pollution, criminal rehabilitation, health, overpopulation, personal anonymity, and man's relationships with his fellow man.[18] At community schools, services to all members of the community are

---

[17] Quoted in *Community Education Journal*, 1 (February 1971), 18.

[18] Phillip A. Clark, "If Two and Two and Fifty Make a Million," *Community Education Journal*, 1 (February 1971), 9.

no longer an afterthought but are available twelve to sixteen hours a day, at least six days a week, fifty-two weeks a year.

Institutions of higher learning, too, are realizing the need to raze their proverbial ivory towers and become an integral part of the community, providing services for all community members and using their resources to help solve problems within the community. The president of Cornell University defines the role of the university in modern society in these terms:

> Our society . . . recently has become concerned with a whole range of problems that either did not concern it before, or may not even have existed. This change demands that the universities reconsider their own educational priorities and curriculum offerings. If the universities fail to be relevant to the times, they will invite a lack of confidence from the very society they seek to serve. If they fail to heed the persistent cry of this generation of students for tangible steps toward a better world, the resulting disaffection of this generation could well make the America of the future into an underdeveloped nation.[19]

A program to serve the community with the resources of the university was developed recently by the Cornell Law School. Entitled "Basic Legal Concepts and Processes for the Secondary School Curriculum Project," it was undertaken by the Law School in cooperation with the Ithaca School District and the New York State Education Department. Law students assist social studies teachers in presenting the legal topics to junior and senior high school classes, then report observations and suggestions for revision to the committee preparing the curriculum materials. The object is to provide young people with an opportunity to learn about an area that concerns them in their day-to-day living but which has generally been neglected by the schools.

The skills and resources of the university can and should be directed toward solving a whole array of problems relating to the quality of the environment. Through its research facilities, it can help discover ways of improving environmental quality. Through its educational facilities it can help train more and better professionals to deal with environmental problems. By enlarging its adult education and extension programs, it can inform the general public about issues concerning man's many kinds of environments.

The university has always been a place where professionals have been trained in their skills and then have gone into the community to practice them. But the problems of modern society will not be solved by professionals trained in ever-narrowing specialties. As Robert Theobald has warned,

> . . . if universities and colleges are to survive, they must move in one of two directions—or indeed in both simultaneously. Either they must become the "communications and information center" of the community in which they are located, or they must become the center of knowledge about a specific problem/possibility of state, national, or international interest. The universities which continue to turn out graduates equipped only with theoretical knowl-

---

[19] Dale R. Corson, "Cornell Appraises Its Goals," *Cornell Alumni News*, 73 (April 1971), 53.

edge of disciplines are fated to die. . . . The university should be involved in the community so that it becomes possible to eliminate the concept that one is either being educated or one is living. It seems clear that one of the necessary changes for the next generation is that we cease to see life as being for earning and begin to see life as being for learning.[20]

There is a real need to address the education of all kinds of professionals and experts in all fields to the broad problems of society. An essential component of the task is an interdisciplinary thrust toward moving higher learning into society and bringing society into the institutions of higher learning. This was the concept inherent in the formation of the University of Wisconsin at Green Bay (UWGB). Community advisory committees provide counsel for the university, and the students join the community in mutual learning experiences off the campus. Separate courses are pursued toward the end of solving environmental problems that require the knowledge gleaned from many courses. Similarly, the Center for Environmental Quality at Michigan State University provides for university-wide participation in the development of programs and policies on environmental problems and in assisting faculty members, students, and citizens to become better informed about environmental issues.

At Wayne State University, recognition of the fact that environmental problems include urban environmental problems as well as pollution of natural areas, led to the formation of the Council on Urban Affairs early in 1970. It is designed to enlist the cooperation of students and faculty from many disciplines in research, community activities, and courses aimed at improving the urban environment.

The College of Idaho, at Caldwell, has been developing the Snake River Regional Environmental Studies Program, using the region as a laboratory for the study of environmental problems and involving the community—represented by industry, labor, agriculture, and government—in projects on environmental planning and problem solving. In this case, the "community" is actually a group of at least six states in the region, all of whom contribute to and benefit by the activities of the program.

One of the most interesting proposals to bring the college into the community and vice versa has been made by the Union for Experimenting Colleges and Universities, a consortium of eighteen institutions joined together to foster research and experimentation in higher education. It is an alternative plan for undergraduate study leading to a degree, called the "University Without Walls." Like the Parkway Program at the secondary level, it abandons the idea that learning occurs only in a particular place. It provides for students from sixteen to sixty to learn at one or more colleges; at work; in their homes; through internships, independent study, and field trips; in travel and service abroad; and within areas of special social problems. It enlarges the faculty to include knowledgeable people outside the academic world and makes flexible the time in which a degree can be obtained. Its object is not to produce "finished" graduates but lifelong learners. The plan began with a small pilot program in February 1971. The hope is that the University Without Walls will offer a real alternative to areas of higher education needing reform rather than fit new pieces into an old framework.

[20] Robert Theobald, *An Alternative Future for America II* (Chicago: Swallow Press, 1970), pp. 81, 176.

Community colleges, too—as their name implies—are ideal resources for community education on environmental problems. Interdisciplinary courses on such problems, open to all citizens, are one means by which they can serve the community. Community service programs, such as forums and debates on the issues, are another. The location of community colleges within large population centers makes them logical clearinghouses of information on environmental topics. The rationale behind the community college has always included community involvement, and involvement in improving the quality of the community environment ought to be a commitment of high priority.

The nationwide environmental teach-in, Earth Day 1970, brought students and faculty together with community leaders at many universities for the first time. If it succeeded at all, it will have provided the impetus for institutions of higher learning to make a regular procedure of using the environmental classroom that is their community for mutual programs in learning and problem solving.

The state. It is evident that there is no exact definition or limit to "the community." Modern means of transportation enable students to learn about man's environment over considerable distances. Certainly the nature of environmental problems—which quickly spread over international boundaries—demands that students have the opportunity to trace environmental patterns through different kinds of environments and to compare environments that are different from their immediate surroundings.

Every state has, within its borders, examples of different types of environments—urban, suburban, rural; natural, physical, cultural. The state, therefore, is an environmental classroom that offers numerous possibilities for students to acquire a broad view of the concept of man's environment.

A teacher in Washington State, for example, guided her students around the school grounds to collect data about a deciduous forest. Later, the class took a two-hour bus trip to a state forest, where they could compare findings on a coniferous forest. The students learned history, geology, health, science, language arts, and outdoor skills in the many educational situations the trip presented, and they also had a chance to observe in detail an environment unlike any near their home.[21]

The publicly owned land of a state is an ideal classroom for environmental learning. Parks, forests, reservoirs—all kinds of areas that lie untouched during school hours are waiting to be discovered and explored. A single teacher or an interested adult group can locate such areas and use them for environmental study. In many cases, an interpretive naturalist is available to assist the teacher and the group in their explorations. If an area has educational possibilities; is accessible; is reasonably free of physical hazards; has adequate eating, drinking, restroom, and parking facilities; and can withstand a learning activity without significant damage, it is suitable. Cities, small towns, rural areas, deserts, forests, lakes, rivers and estuaries, mountains, and seashores abound with potential learning experiences.

The federal government has, in recent years, increased its program of making

[21] Karol Nevers, "The Million-Acre Classroom of Mother Earth," *Washington Education*, 81 (March 1970), 33–34.

federal lands available as educational sites. In 1963, President Kennedy assigned to the Tennessee Valley Authority (TVA) the task of developing Land Between the Lakes—a 170,000-acre strip of forestland in western Kentucky and Tennessee—as a national demonstration in outdoor and conservation education. The entire peninsula has become an outdoor classroom in ecology, with particular focus on learning activities at the Conservation Education Center. One of the Center's major facilities is the Youth Station, which cooperates with schools in providing outdoor and conservation education programs for students. This resident facility officially opened in April 1966 to serve a wide region, and it has since served thousands of college, elementary, and secondary school students from Tennessee, Kentucky, Indiana, Illinois, Texas, and Michigan, and teachers from these states as well as Georgia, Alabama, and Missouri.

The U.S. Department of the Interior considers all of its land as dedicated to ecological awareness and education. In particular, lands managed by the National Park Service are being selected on the basis of educational potential as part of the previously-mentioned National Environmental Study Area (NESA) program. A network of NESA's has now been developed, each with interpreters and printed materials to assist classes using the sites for environmental learning. The sites are intended to serve as models to help teachers identify similar areas outside parklands that can be used in the same way as environmental study areas.[22]

Each state has its own special environmental problems, which ought to be the first its students attack. Connecticut, for example, is particularly concerned with the marine environment. The Thomas School in Rowayton, a private girls school located on Long Island Sound, has long used nearby marshes for biology field study. Recently, the students formed PYE (Protect Your Environment), to focus their learning on action to save the marine environment. They were instrumental in convincing the state legislature to pass a bill declaring a moratorium on the use of tidal areas until a survey determines what areas should be retained for the public domain and what areas can be given over to private use.[23] A sailing school in Rowayton has organized an oceanography institute complete with a floating laboratory. Many of the youngsters of the area have rejected summer camp in favor of the institute's five-day-a-week program in July and August, during which the young people from elementary school through college study and try to solve problems in marine ecology. In New Hampshire, a nonprofit organization called New Hampshire—Tomorrow has been formed to coordinate teams of citizens studying legislation to protect the beauty of the state, plans for economic growth that will not damage the environment, recreational systems that open the state's bounty to all of its citizens, and programs to increase citizen awareness of environmental problems.

School systems and state departments of education have begun to recognize the educational potential of the various environments to be found in an entire state, and many have moved toward establishing a system of environmental learning sites throughout the state. The NEA Research Division described the typical school system with an

---

environmental education program as using two sites of approximately twenty acres in the immediate school environs, one day-use site of about seventy-seven acres within twelve miles of the school district, and one resident site of approximately two-hundred acres about fifty miles from the district. About seventy-five percent of the school systems own the sites, but many use sites free of charge. Sites with resident facilities are the ones most often leased, usually from the YMCA, the Boy Scouts, the state government, or private camps. A little more than a third of the school systems are within fifty miles of a National Park Service area.[24]

The resident facility allows students to encounter an environment that may be very different from his home area for an extended period of time and for an intensive learning experience. Beyond that, there are the social gains which accrue from living together with classmates and—in joint programs—from living and working with students from other areas. Often the students are called upon to participate in planning and executing the program and some of the logistics of the group's stay at the site, which encourages the development of leadership skills. Of environmental education programs in school systems, sixty-three percent make use of a resident facility.[25]

Northern Illinois University runs the Lorado Taft Field Campus at DeKalb, staffed and directed by professionals from the University. It serves school and college classes, community organizations, and other interested groups in the area. The Nolde State Park Environmental Education Center near Lancaster, Pennsylvania, provides many natural and man-made features suitable for environmental study. Schools in the New York Metropolitan Area make use of the Fresh Air Fund's Hidden Valley Camp near Fishkill, New York. During the summer, it is a camp for underprivileged children, but during the academic year the Fund and the schools cooperate in providing a staff to guide environmental studies at its winterized facilities.

The Superintendent of Public Instruction of the State of Washington leases the Cispus Environmental Education Center in the Gifford Pinchot National Forest from the U.S. Forest Service. Resource personnel from a number of state and federal agencies assist students in exploring rivers, ponds, forests, and soil. Cispus also contains education buildings, dormitories, an infirmary, and a gymnasium, making it a unique combination of facilities and outdoor study areas.

Several schools in the North Franklin, Washington School District make week-long trips to Camp Wooten, a facility operated through its Association by those who use it. The Stockton, California Unified School District sponsors a one-week residential program at the San Joaquin County Outdoor Education School, concentrating on such activities as conservation education, ecology, marine tidepool studies, earth science, safety, and survival studies. The Jefferson County (Colorado) Outdoor Education School accommodates sixth-grade pupils for one-week resident programs emphasizing ecological relationships. Frederick County, Maryland students make use of an outdoor school on NPS land, a church camp, private areas, a state park, and the city reservoir. The Battle

---

[24] National Education Association, Research Division, *Environmental Education in the Public Schools,* pp. 39, 43.
[25] *Ibid.,* p. 49.

Creek, Michigan Public Schools run a resident Outdoor Center, which has a staff of five certified teachers and a director, cooks, custodians, teacher aides, counselors, and farm workers and a physical plant that includes a lodge, the director's residence, winterized dormitories, summer cabins, classroom laboratories, historical buildings, and a farm. The Kansas City Parks and Recreation Department sponsors a Natural Science Resident Camp during the summer, providing three ten-day camp sessions stressing ecological investigations along with a regular camp program. Four districts in the state of Washington expand their learning environment even a little more, with a "Flying Classroom." Used by children from kindergarten through grade twelve, the program allows younger pupils to view their environment from the air, while older students plan itineraries for flying and resolve time and distance problems with charts, plotters, and computers. Using an airplane to study the environment seems rather appropriate to children of the space age.

Unfortunately, most of the environmental education sites, resident and day-use, are overused because there are not enough good ones. Many sites lack necessary safety and health facilities. In 1970, a conservation and outdoor education advisory committee submitted a proposal for a statewide environmental education program for Oregon. Among its recommendations for a network of educational facilities it included state facilities—an environmental center for research and development of programs, a teacher training center, resident outdoor sites, mobile touring classes, summer schools, conference centers, and day-use centers; local centers in urban and rural areas; use of existing agency facilities—Boy Scouts, church, YMCA; mini-centers at private camps, logging camps, etc.; and local study areas. A state that developed such a network of facilities would go far toward making the state an environmental classroom.

The global village.   State boundaries limit the environmental classroom only because of political or practical considerations. Actually, the environmental classroom is nothing less than the entire world and beyond into the universe, for these are the boundaries of all that comprises man's environment.

Regional environmental education facilities such as the Snake River Regional Environmental Studies Program and Land Between the Lakes attest to the fact that environmental problems do not respect political boundaries. Man's environment is an intricate ecosystem involving interdependencies that are worldwide in scope. "His environment is his world, though he does not consciously take part in all the activities in his ecosystem." [26]

We have seen photographs of the earth from the moon, and it no longer appears as a series of political entities marked off in Rand-McNally colors. The fragile qualities of our "spaceship" seem painfully evident when the earth is set against the dark background of vast and empty space. Yet even from a terrestrial vantage point we can perceive the global nature of our most pressing crises: "Race problems, poverty, pollution, danger of nuclear war, the population explosion, and epidemics such as the Hong

[26] Frank Fraser Darling and Raymond F. Dasmann, "The Ecosystem View of Human Society," *Impact of Science on Society*, 19 (April–June 1969), 113.

Kong flu, while not necessarily manifest in the same way in each country, are world problems that can best be dealt with as such." [27]

Even the practical considerations that once limited our attention to our own neighborhoods are quickly disappearing. Modern transportation and communication methods are rapidly shrinking our earth into what Marshall McLuhan aptly termed "the global village." Viewed from this standpoint, the isolated classroom seems an inappropriate learning environment indeed. There is more and more to learn outside of it and less and less within it. When the potential of the whole world to become the environmental classroom is realized, then all education, in a sense, becomes environmental education and all the world becomes an educational resource.

Students now travel outside their home states to participate in educational activities. Even fifty years ago, such programs would have been impossible. And our mobility is likely to increase in speed and decrease in cost and discomfort. Computerized highway travel, pneumatic tube trains, and considerably more efficient air transport may be realities in only ten to fifteen years, so that by the end of the century "the youth of today, following our example, will travel fifty or a hundred times more mileage per year than did their fathers." [28] Since we are rapidly approaching the possibilities of global learning, it is not too early to begin conceiving of the world as the environmental classroom.

The Urban Environment as a Unique Educational Problem Setting

Until fairly recently, the urban environment was excluded from environmental education. When outdoor programs were offered at all to city children, teachers generally headed for city parks to conduct a nature study class. The city as an environment was hardly ever given any consideration. Yet the city is the area most profoundly affected by the environmental crisis.

Ever since man began to develop civilizations, he has been drawn to the city. After the industrial revolution began only a little more than a century ago, the gradual influx toward urban areas became a stampede. Settlements on the most desirable pieces of land with the best transportation access attracted large populations. Industrial manufacturing proliferated. Prepackaged goods became available at city stores. More people lived in less area. All of the human activities of the city created unprecedented wealth—and unprecedented waste.

Industries poured their wastes into the waterways. Housewives threw away the containers and packages that held their store-bought goods. The biological wastes of

[27] James M. Becker and Lee F. Anderson, "Riders on the Earth Together," *American Education*, Vol. 5 (May 1969), 2–4.

[28] Gabriel Bouladon, "Transport," *Social Speculations: Visions for Our Time*, ed. by Richard Kosterlanetz (New York: William Morrow and Co., 1971), p. 142.

large populations moved through sewers into rivers. As automobile transportation became more efficient, some city dwellers moved to outlying areas in search of green trees and fresh air, then fouled the air with automobile exhausts during their trips to and from the city for employment, shopping, and cultural and social activities.

> Now the suburban areas are becoming sicker with many of the same problems that plagued the city. In some areas of the country there is limited direction in which to run from the rivers man has converted to sewers, the land he has saturated with material waste, the air he has polluted with smoke as well as poisonous gases from the automobile.[29]

Air and water pollution, solid wastes, and less available space for comfortable living are more extensive problems in cities than in areas with low-density population. Today's cities also produce stresses of noise, crowding, inconvenience, and disunion from natural environments that combine in a unique threat to personal mental and physical health. The inner-city poor bear the greatest brunt of the effects of the urban environmental crisis, for they are more crowded and their dwelling units are less sound.

Yet urban areas continue to attract people and to grow. Three compelling facts about the trend emerged from a recent United Nations symposium on urbanization:

> (1) urban population will increase five-fold over the next generation; but (2) urban facilities are already overloaded and the environment dangerously polluted; therefore (3) each increment of urban growth will lead to a further deterioration of the environment.[30]

What is more, urban residents, comprising as they do more than seventy percent of our nation's population, control the fate of the total environment through their decisions and votes on environmental policy.

Just as the urban resident feels the environmental crisis most acutely, he is also hardest hit by the educational crisis. Granted that there are difficulties in schools everywhere and that young people from all kinds of environments are turned off by force-fed schooling, yet the inner-city child is most afflicted by an educational system that is irrelevant and unresponsive to him. Middle-class education, governed by middle-class school boards, determined by middle-class curriculum committees, and taught by middle-class teachers who make the self-fulfilling prophesy that those children "can't learn" drives thousands of the city's poor to drop out of school imprisonment and then flounder under the middle-class demand for a diploma.

They drop out into the inner-city environment that screams with problems, yet their education has never consisted of tackling the solutions. Their surroundings are the most egregious examples of squalor and ugliness, yet they are largely unaware of how bad things are and how good things could be. A truly relevant education for the urban dweller would deal consciously with his environment, how to survive in it, and how to

---

[29] Thomas J. Rillo, "Toward an Urban Ecological Structure," *Journal of Environmental Education,* 2 (Spring 1971), 40–43.

[30] United Nations, *Symposium on the Impact of Urbanization on Man's Environment: Statement and Conclusions* (Washington, D.C.: United Auto Workers, 1970), p. 5.

improve it. Instead, the inner-city dropout learns "survival" on the street corners and often succumbs to the overwhelming pressures of environmental forces.

Even the more fortunate city children grow up with little awareness of their environment. Urban environments are constricted; they offer little room for imaginative play and almost no contact with nature. They are often confusing, dysfunctional, and even dangerous. Although the city is notable for the diversity of cultures, values, lifestyles, and services it shelters, these are to a great extent segregated from one another so that children have few opportunities to experience the different environments within their city. The children move from their homes to their egg-crate schools and back and fail to observe the nuances of even the small environment in between. Instead of learning to perceive with all their senses, they learn to blot out unpleasant sights, sounds, smells.

Environmental education for the urban child—and most of our children now grow up in metropolitan areas—would enable him to perceive his environment, appreciate both its good and its bad aspects, and participate in improving it. It would take him out of what are usually gloomy school buildings and provide an environment for learning different from the one in which he has too often faced only failure. It would allow him to investigate real things instead of artificial ones and to develop all of his senses. Children of poverty, more than children of affluent backgrounds, tend to be what the Gesell Institute of Child Development terms "reality bound." They learn better dealing with the concrete rather than with the abstract. Environmental education could be a means of providing success-oriented learning experiences for such children.

Environmental education for the urban child would provide experiences in many kinds of environments, so that he could know of worlds beyond the tenement, the subway, and the street corner. Best of all, he might build a positive self-concept from success at solving problems in his own environment, which could encourage him to participate in ameliorating the problems of the larger urban environment.

All of our urban areas are tied in the same Gordian knots. Most of them grew with little planning at the whim of separate developers who were unaware of John Muir's warning that you can never do just one thing. Then city governments tried to patch together services and transportation systems to meet the needs of haphazard developments, the end result being only confusion and inefficiency. As one architect has puzzled over the problem—

> One might imagine that poor planning, jammed highways, overcrowding, dirt, noise, and ugliness could only serve as a warning to newer cities that the same mistakes would not be made again. Unfortunately, this is not the case. There is a strange similarity in cities, and all in one way or another seem to share the same problems.[31]

An essential beginning to finding solutions to urban environmental problems—as to all environmental problems—is to take a total, or systems, approach. Just as cleaning up only a water area can result in increased air and land pollution, so can piecemeal solutions prove detrimental to the city as, for example, when a slum is replaced by beautiful

[31] Elliot L. Whitaker, "The Architectural Point of View," *Science Teacher*, 37 (September, 1970), 28.

and expensive living units and the poor are left to crowd themselves further into the remaining low-income housing.

The city is actually an ecosystem, a community of physical and biological entities interacting with each other and with the total environment. Education that deals with the urban environment should help learners conceive of the city as such a totality. The city, moreover, does not end at a specific boundary, but influences environments far beyond itself. Urban environmental education thus includes investigation of all types of environments. In addition to the study of the effects of the city on the natural environment, urban environmental education must deal with public health, transportation, architecture and landscaping, and zoning and planning.

The most traditional forms of environmental education—nature study and conservation—are easily adaptable to urban surroundings and points of reference familiar to the city dweller. At least one educator has suggested that examples of urban rather than rural phenomena can clarify conservation principles for the learner in the city: "A watershed consists of areas having a common drainage outlet, such as land comprising a river valley" can be changed to "A watershed consists of areas having a common drainage outlet, such as a roof and eaves trough [the outlet for which is] the drain spout"; "diversification of risk is an economic principle of importance in conservation; it may be illustrated by avoiding large plantations of a single species and single age" or "by avoiding planting only one species, such as elm, in our attempts to beautify city streets." [32]

The National Audubon Society has prepared curriculum materials for elementary school pupils that relate ecological principles to the urban environment. Entitled *A Place To Live*, the workbook and teacher's manual deal with such fundamental concepts as the nature of plant and animal life, the community as a composite environment, and change and adaptation. Suggested learning activities include walks around the school and neighborhood to discover the variety of building materials in a city; food chains as familiar to an urbanite as garbage-rat-cat; changes that occur in the city environment; changes the city works on the natural environment; and such environmental problems as air and water pollution, noise pollution, litter, population, and solid wastes.[33]

Even in the earliest grades, children can become aware of the kind of total planning necessary to make the urban environment pleasant and functional by observing the area between home and school. A survey of protection and maintenance services (police, refuse, road construction, street cleaning, firemen) and of conditions requiring such services (speeding cars, full garbage cans, holes in the streets, litter, fires) illustrates the amount and kinds of such services a local government needs to provide. The distance to school, traffic along the way, and safety of pedestrian routes indicate the need to plan for schools in safe areas in the center of a neighborhood and to construct arterial routes along the periphery. The location of parks, residential areas, and commercial areas points to the zoning plan of the community.[34] Such observations and the conclusions

[32] Paul A. Yambert, "Let's Urbanize Conservation," *Journal of Outdoor Education,* 3 (Spring 1969), 16–19.

[33] National Audubon Society, *A Place To Live* (New York: the Society, 1970).

[34] Alfred A. Arth and Ronald N. Short, "City Planning in the Elementary School," *NJEA Review,* 45 (December 1969), 42–43.

drawn from them help young children become keenly aware of their surroundings and lay the foundation for building an environmental ethic.

The Parkway School is the prime example of environmental education in the city. The city itself is the learning environment, and subjects pursued are not merely academic but also intensely practical and indicative of what the city has to offer. The city as an environment is capable of being a vivid learning laboratory.

Traditionally, education designed by and for the white middle class has taken little notice of the rich and diverse cultural offerings of the city. Puerto Ricans, Mexicans, and blacks are termed "culturally deprived," when in fact they inherit strong cultural traditions that are merely different from white, European-based cultures. Since late in the 1960s, with the help of federal support for urban arts programs, community arts centers have been springing up in cities all over the country. Through these programs, young people in the cities participate in such activities as street theater, film-making, improvisational theater, dance troupes, and rock bands.

> Drawing on Negro, African, or Spanish-American history, poetry, dance, and drama, store-front academies like Studio Watts in Los Angeles, the New Thing Art and Architecture Center in Washington, D.C., and Harlem School of the Arts in New York City give the minority child a sense of historical pride, a knowledge of the roots of his own culture, something with which he can readily identify and on which he can build confidence in his own worth and ability.[35]

These young people are using a resource of the city to learn about their cultural heritage and at the same time contributing to the cultural offerings of the city through their participation.

Some of the arts programs have resulted in even more direct influence on the urban environment. Students near San Francisco used a videotape recorder to film an area they wanted developed into a neighborhood park, then made presentations of their proposal to the community and the city council. Their drive was successful in gaining support for construction of the park. Students in New York City used tape recordings to study the sound environment between 85th and 86th streets and create awareness of the need for noise abatement in the city environment. These projects go beyond identifying learning resources that exist in the city by using some of the unique characteristics of the city to create learning environments that have never existed before.

The architects who helped form GEE! in Philadelphia would go even further and make the city itself one big classroom that continually educates the public about its functions, design, and activities. While the urban arts programs have taken a step toward making the diverse cultures of the city observable, there are other aspects of city life that remain hidden from public view. Richard Saul Wurman, a partner in the Philadelphia architecture firm of Murphy, Levy, Wurman and vice-president of GEE!, points out that more than half the city belongs to the public—streets, sidewalks, parks, recreation facilities, hydrants, highways, parkways, utility and transportation systems, public buildings. He designed an exhibit, which opened in June 1971 at the Philadelphia

[35] Don D. Bushnell, "Black Arts for Black Youth," *Saturday Review,* 53 (July 18, 1970), 43. Copyright 1970, Saturday Review, Inc.

Museum of Art, called City/2 ("city over two")—showing the educational potential of the publicly-owned half of the city. If the ground floor of buildings (public and commercial) contained exhibits on the activities carried on within the building, the pedestrian would find a walk in the city both an interesting and an educational experience. If traffic and directional signs were more clear, if subway systems were easier to comprehend, if route maps were made uniform from city to city—the traveler in the city would be able to get around with less difficulty.[36] Two city planning professors at the Massachusetts Institute of Technology have expressed similar ideas:

> An urban region is an immense storehouse of information. Its stimuli, diverse ways of life, events, and facilities are a prime occasion for learning. Developmental policy should aim at making this information accessible. One straightforward way is to provide a free public transportation system, bringing all parts of a metropolitan region within some reasonable time distance. . . . A more limited policy would subsidize educational trips where the destination was a school, museum, or other specifically educational locale. It might even be possible to subsidize "first-time" trips by distributing free tickets to random destinations.
>
> The transportation system should be easy to use, as well as cheap and ubiquitous. It should be designed to be completely legible—the system of routes and transfers easy to follow and the destinations clear. Symbolic maps should be displayed, and direction-giving devices installed at all critical points. . . . There should also be a network of paths along which young children can move safely by means under their control: by foot, bicycle, cart, pony, or otherwise. Even the prosaic walk to school might be an educational device.
>
> All vehicles and routes should give a clear view of the region being traversed—its most important activities and particularly of its changes. The environment itself might be designed to be "transparent," wherever possible without intruding on individual privacy. The form of structures and of land, as well as signs and electronic devices, can communicate the activity and function of a place, express its history or ecology, reveal the flow and presence of people, or signal the social and environmental changes that are occurring. In an industrial area, factories would be encouraged to let their machines be seen in action, to label raw materials and their origin, to distinguish the different kinds of operatives and explain what they do, to exhibit finished products, to make their transportation containers transparent. Thus the city, like a good museum, would be designed to increase the physical and perceptual accessibility of its contents.[37]

Wurman takes Parkway School students on walking tours of the city, pointing out how the city could be a more functional environment. He poses such questions as, "Wouldn't a three-foot wall make more sense than a curb? Wouldn't it, in addition to doing what a curb does, keep cars from parking illegally, prevent jaywalking, and eliminate rainy-day splashing?" Students ponder the absence of a clock in the bus station, empty lobbies and sterile facades to look in at public courts, lack of arcades to

36 Richard Saul Wurman, "Making the City Observable," *Design Quarterly 80* (Minneapolis: Walker Art Center, and the MIT Press, Cambridge, Mass., 1971). Copyright 1971, Walker Art Center.

37 Stephen Carr and Kevin Lynch, "Where Learning Happens," *Elementary Education Today: Its Impact on Children.* Ed. by Robert D. Strom and Mary Elizabeth Bell (Washington, D.C.: American Association of Elementary-Kindergarten-Nursery Education, 1971), pp. 44–45.

protect shoppers from bad weather, anonymity of companies behind plate-glass windows.[38] The materials being created by Wurman and GEE! president Alan Levy are an attempt to help all school children become aware of the man-made environment, how to judge environmental criteria, how to improve the man-made environment. In the form of workbooks, these materials challenge students to manipulate miniature environments in order to discover just what goes into the making of an urban environment that would be truly functional, observable, and pleasing.

It is encouraging to note that the design of urban facilities has begun to move toward functional form in recent years. Of particular significance to environmental education are trends in the design of schools, recreation facilities, and environmental study areas.

Urban schools take longer in being replaced than suburban or rural schools, primarily because of scarcity of land area on which to build new ones. All school systems have faced increased construction and credit costs in the past few years as well. One solution has been a concept known variously as joint occupancy, mixed use, or multiple use of land and buildings. One of the principal advantages of the plan is that when the joint use is both public and private, it does not require removing school land from the tax rolls.

> The concept includes combining schools with housing, commercial space (retail or office), community services and facilities, other civic agencies such as health units and municipal offices, recreation facilities, parking garages, and so on. Various combinations of these create environments that are in effect small cities or towns that could almost act as independent communities but which are still linked to their surrounding cities.[39]

Friends Select School, a private institution in Philadelphia, leased one of its three downtown acres for commercial development and built a new facility on the remaining two. The new building contains more than twice the indoor space of the old and compensates for the loss of an acre with an outdoor recreation area on the roof, covered with artificial turf. Income from the commercial acre is more than enough to amortize the principle and interest costs incurred in constructing the new facility.

New York City, badly pressed for school space, has a number of joint-occupancy schools and more in the planning stage. An addition to P.S. 99 will house a gym, an auditorium, a cafeteria, and community space, with 224 upper-income apartment units above it to pay the full share of taxes. P.S. 126 in the Bronx combines an elementary school with 400 middle-income housing units. Residents are provided with recreational space on the school roof. P.S. 169 is a school for emotionally disturbed children. The city leased the air rights over the school for upper-income apartments, the income from which will pay for the school.

The Dade County, Florida, School District needed a new school in a densely popu-

[38] Beth Gillin, "A Critic's Tour of the Public Environment," *Today Magazine, the Philadelphia Inquirer* (June 13, 1971), pp. 30–31.

[39] Evans Clinchy, *Joint Occupancy: Profiles of Significant Schools* (New York: Educational Facilities Laboratories, 1970), p. 3.

lated area of Miami, where the land would have cost $2 million and its purchase would have displaced as many as 150 families. Instead, the district chose to use land under an expressway which is elevated 80 feet above ground level. The land is leased from the State Road Department without charge, and the 900-student school will have all normal facilities, including a playground, for an estimated cost of $1.5 million.

Even the open-plan school has begun to invade the city, although it is still a rarity and city schools that wish to use open-plan methods still rely more on converting traditional buildings by opening doors and allowing freedom of movement. Steuart Hill School is in an integrated neighborhood in Baltimore—a fully carpeted, air-conditioned, nongraded, team-teaching school that has no fence around its playground but invites the community to use it at any time. Steuart Hill has an open-plan design, with large multipurpose spaces and no corridors. The principal, Doris Hammond, explains:

> Our goal was to get away from the institutionalized jail-like atmosphere of most inner-city schools. We have no bells ringing. We have a relaxed atmosphere. Inner-city children are probably better able to use an open-plan school than suburban children. So much attention has been given to the weaknesses of these children, but not enough to their strengths. One strength that you find is that they are self-propelled. Many of them assume a lot of responsibility for their own living. Consequently, they can do the same for their own learning, if we give them a chance.[40]

New York City's P.S. 211 is also an open-plan school, but it is not a new building. The school is housed in a converted factory loft, which has been carpeted and furnished with tables and chairs, bookshelves, cabinets, and chalkboards. There are six large areas, small-group and office spaces, a library, an auditorium and lunchroom, and a gymnasium. The open spaces have encouraged a free, self-directed, individualized learning program.

One of the most unusual city schools is a 2,350-ton, three-masted Norwegian barque containing an experiment called the Oceanics. The ship has space for ninety boys, thirty teachers, and a captain and crew. It was launched as a school in New York City by a couple, Charles and Stephanie Gallagher, who were looking for a solution to educating hard-to-teach boys. The boys learn regular subjects from the teachers as the ship sails through its itinerary, but they are also exposed to the real-life and environmental situations of living and working on an actual sea-going facility.

Facilities designed specifically for environmental learning are also rare in urban areas, partly because of lack of space and partly because the city has long been considered not to be part of "the environment." Yet every city contains such resources as parks, zoos, and water areas at which students can explore the natural environment. And urban schools can be constructed so as to provide outdoor study areas on the school grounds. Even wilderness areas within an hour or two from the city could be leased or purchased by a school district, and private or organizational camps usually abound within a 150-mile radius of a city. In a feasibility study of outdoor education

---

[40] Educational Facilities Laboratories, "Open-Plan School for the Inner City," *Schoolhouse* (Newsletter), No. 2 (May 1971), p. 3.

for New York City, Eugene Ezersky recommends the following complex of facilities for a program for urban children: resident facilities; laboratory facilities for the study and accommodation of living specimens; outdoor stations at school-owned sites, including those for photography, animal- and bird-watching, astronomy, art, water ecology, soil-erosion study, geology, plant life, and compass use; portable field kits; an outdoor meeting site for large groups; campsites; individual consultation sites; nature trails; and recreation facilities.[41]

Leisure and recreation facilities pose an especially critical problem in urban areas, yet making use of leisure time may be one of the most significant activities of tomorrow's adult. When leisure is viewed as all time that is not spent providing for basic needs, it is evident that in the future there may be little distinction between work and leisure. Machines will take over most of the dullest tasks, and it is likely that most persons will be provided with the resources to fill their basic needs with little effort. Work will either be subordinate to leisure or absorbed by leisure in man's quest for self-actualization and social approval. Leisure will increasingly be considered a central focus of life.

Leisure is at once free, discretionary, or unobligated time; a particular set of activities; and a set of attitudes or state of mind.[42] Schools will have to take an increasing role in opening the learner's horizons to understand what leisure is all about. Implicit in the concept of the environmental classroom is the goal of understanding and using environmental resources for leisure activities as well as developing a commitment to environmental preservation that may well become a leisure (nonwork) activity for many persons in the near future.

Play—an essential component of leisure activity—is also an important determinant of the quality of life. Play and play opportunities in urban areas are especially important when space is limited, when the natural environment is choked, and when the street world is the basic territory for living. Meaningful play environments in city areas are a means toward counterbalancing the destructive, unwholesome aspects of the environment. Because the child has little control over the forces influencing him, it is necessary to provide an environment through which he can work out his problems, develop skills to cope with life, and gain a better understanding of himself and others.

Play environments should be geared to the developmental needs of children. Play cannot be separated from other basic life needs and processes. The city interferes with the spontaneity of play; play environments encourage spontaneity. The traditional playground, however, provides an extremely limited choice for those who use it. The equipment is generally one-dimensional, fixed to a certain spot, and designed to eliminate experimentation and often even the rudiments of fun. There is little or no landscaping to bring into a sterile environment some of the vitality of life. Physical facilities are constructed to support highly organized, constrained, discrete activities. The design is based not upon scientific rationale or a well-conceived set of behavioral-change objectives, but

[41] Eugene M. Ezersky, City to Country: Outdoor Education for New York City (New York: Educational Facilities Laboratories, 1969), pp. 57–58.

[42] Rolf Meyersohn, "Some Problems in Recreation Research Planning," Conceptual Approaches to Research—Recreation for Older Americans (Washington, D.C.: National Recreation and Park Association, 1969), pp. 5–14.

upon the concept of play as defined by the institutional buyer or manufacturer of equipment. The typical playground is insulated against change. It is unimaginative, unresponsive to the needs of children, and unrelated to a total view of man and his relationship to the environment.

In an attempt to improve leisure facilities in urban areas, there is now a growing trend toward multiple use of open space, physical facilities, and natural resources for educational and leisure programs. Memphis transports twelve portable swimming pools to the grounds of its inner-city schools so that the children can learn to swim. Cleveland conducts a similar program using twenty-two portable pools serving 10,000 inner-city children. All physical education facilities built by the Pittsburgh Board of Public Education will now be used by the community as well for recreational purposes. Chicago is moving toward the construction of field houses for gyms, located so that a number of schools can use the same facility during weekdays and the whole community can enjoy recreational activities at other times. Many cities are turning to rooftops, "vest-pocket" parks, and vacant lots for additional play space.[43]

Day-care facilities for urban children are becoming similarly innovative. In Washington, D.C., the roof above the conference room for the Secretary of Health, Education, and Welfare (HEW) has been turned into a playground covered with artificial turf and equipped with swings, climbing apparatus, and tricycles for the children of HEW employees. A sunken plaza outside the building shared by the U.S. Office of Education and the National Aeronautics and Space Administration will soon become an outdoor play area containing a geodesic dome, a bridge, ramps, a sliding hill, and a "crow's nest." [44]

Such facilities are termed playscapes—open ecological systems supporting an infinite variety of play activities. They include as many elements of the natural landscape as possible and simulate those not available but considered essential to the play experience. Geared to the individual and social needs of children, these systems provide almost unlimited opportunities for self-starting exploratory play, for the development of motor skills, for challenge and variety in expressive behavior, and for enhancing a child's understanding of himself and his relationship to the environment of people and things. The Infant Learning Landscape, to be installed at the Durham Child Development Center in Philadelphia, has been designed to provide elements of environmental learning for infants up to eighteen months of age. It contains appropriately scaled examples of nature (river, plain, tree, mountain, cave) and man-made environments (house, wall, road, tower, bridge) linked by ramps and other devices for movement and exploration to form an example of the real-world relationships of such objects.

> It provides the opportunity for an endless spatial odyssey, crawling or toddling through a rich variety of clearly differentiated forms. Individual toy play, exercise, the observation of other infants and socialization of all sorts are also facilitated.[45]

[43] American Association for Health, Physical Education, and Recreation, *The Trouble with Cities: Meeting the Urban Challenge* (Washington, D.C.: the Association, 1970).

[44] John Methews, "A Day Care Center in the Sky," Washington Star (Tuesday, July 6, 1971), p. B1.

[45] Chuck Burnette, "The Beginning of Observation in the City," in Wurman, "Making the City Observable," p. 73.

Playscapes can help increase the environmental perception of the child. The city itself can be a means toward increasing the environmental perception of all its citizens by increasing the "environmental mobility" of the urban dweller. In most cities, it is impossible for persons to travel from the inner-city environment to other environments without the use of motor vehicles. Thus, young persons and persons without access to automobiles are "bound into" the city environment. Simply because such a consideration was never included in city planning, streets with minimal traffic lead only to other similar streets; busy streets and intersections consistently come between the urban dweller and the nonurban environment; paths along water routes are blocked in many places by bridges and highway structures, industry, utilities, or railroads; bicycle paths and trails in city parklands generally come to a dead end within the city—and often require some intricate maneuvering to get to them from city residential areas.

One solution to the problem is to establish nature centers in the city as a community resource for urban environmental education. The urban nature center allows city residents who have little access to natural areas to enjoy one in the city and learn ecology from it. Joseph Shomon defines such a center as "an area of undeveloped land (at least fifty acres) within a city or town or near it with the facilities and services planned to conduct community outdoor programs in natural sciences, nature appreciation, and conservation education." [46] The National Audubon Society operates four such centers, at Greenwood and Sharon, Connecticut; El Monte, California; and Dayton, Ohio. There are also the Kalamazoo Nature Center, the Carver Park Nature Center outside of Minneapolis, and the Rock Creek Park Nature Center in Washington, D.C., as well as others in Stamford, Connecticut; Peoria, Illinois; and Cincinnati, Ohio, to name just a few examples.

Unfortunately, it is difficult to find fifty acres of undeveloped land near enough to any city today to be really convenient to its residents. Still, there are natural or park areas within most cities, if programs can be developed to encourage the young people of the inner city to use them. The National Park Service inaugurated such a program in 1967 in Washington, D.C. called "Summer in the Parks" and developed with the aid of the District of Columbia government, the program calls for bus excursions to take children to different parks in the District, Maryland, and Virginia each day of the week; a wide variety of portable equipment available to neighborhoods wishing to present entertainment and cultural programs in community parks; and imaginative uses of inner-city parks, such as cultural events and exhibitions by the Smithsonian Institution.

NPS has also begun to use Theodore Roosevelt Island, in the Potomac River, as a National Environmental Study Area, where it has been conducting workshops for teachers since March 1970. Getting the children to the island, however, poses the same transportation problems—the Washington, D.C. School Board has been reluctant to provide busing facilities. Yet NPS interpreters have found that when inner-city children do get there, they learn more and appreciate the area more than suburban students do, because the urban youngsters are more confined to an unpleasant environment in their everyday lives. NPS has identified seven other sites in the Washington metropolitan area as NESAs.

---

[46] Joseph J. Shomon, "Nature Centers—One Approach to Urban Environmental Education," *Journal of Environmental Education*, 1 (Winter 1969), 57.

The National Park Service has also experimented with hosteling excursions to nearby NPS facilities as part of its Environmental Interpretive Program for inner-city youth. In the belief that such bicycle trips would provide an additional dimension of environmental learning, the Potomac Area Council of American Youth Hostels (AYH) coordinated a pilot program for Washington, D.C., children in May and June 1969. Although the experiment was generally successful, AYH recommended the development of better cycling trails that would extend from the heart of cities to NPS facilities. Because travelling "under one's own steam" allows for close observation of the environment, learning through discovery, and, above all, a sense of personal enrichment, AYH also recommended expansion of the program to other cities near NPS sites.[47]

Access to people, places, and things is a major concern in today's urban centers. The lack of open space and natural areas in the inner city is further aggravated by inadequate transportation systems. What is really needed is an urban trail system, using open-space corridors, parks, sidewalks, utility rights-of-way, easements, stream valleys and their flood plains, waterfront jettees and breakwaters, canals, and so on. A system of designated trails would link home, school, recreational sites, natural areas, and the cultural resources of the community. It would expand the environmental mobility of the urban dweller by opening new opportunities for environmental learning, social integration, and outdoor recreation.

Federal support for the development of urban trails is available through the National Trails System Program, the Land and Water Conservation Fund Program, Open Space Land Grants, and the Urban Beautification Program, but to date these programs have emphasized limited natural trail approaches rather than a broad set of educational, recreational, and health specifications. In March 1970, the Open Lands Project and the Council of Governments of Cook County, Illinois, held a conference, entitled "Trails in an Urban Setting," to discuss the broad development of scenic and recreational trails in the Chicago metropolitan area. Under the federal support programs, such trails could be used for hiking, horseback riding, bicycling, trail biking, and snowmobiling. The year-round educational potential of the trails is extensive, encompassing nature study, weather observations, map construction, first aid courses, a wide variety of art techniques, camping, planting, astronomy, and many other fields. The extensive trail, in short, would link the urban resident with recreational land and provide a pathway out of the constricted city and into new worlds to explore.

Once the mobility of the urbanite is thus increased, the "city" as an environmental classroom actually becomes an entire region, embracing home, neighborhood, city, urban fringe, suburbs, and rural areas. The urban dweller would have at his disposal the resources of any of these elements for learning and could use whichever ones were most appropriate for his learning or recreational needs at any given time.

At the hub of such a learning environment would be the community school, which can serve an additional and vital role for today's urban citizens by providing a "sense

---

[47] American Youth Hostels, Potomac Area Council, *The Impact of the National Park Service Environmental Interpretive Program on the Inner-City Youth Through Hosteling* (Washington, D.C.: National Park Service, 1969). (Mimeo.)

of community," a feeling of identification with a particular geographic area and social group. A handful of demonstration community schools on American Indian reservations are already proving that they can help dignify and preserve tribal culture, draw the community together for purposeful endeavor, enlist the talents of the community in planning for the use of the facility, and improve health and nutrition in the community. In the same way, the community school can serve to improve conditions in urban neighborhoods now marked by blight, decay, and fragmentation.

More properly, the urban community school would actually be a community resources center, in which a variety of essential urban services share a facility complex and function as a neighborhood city hall. It would serve as a center for education, recreation, public health, and welfare, and it might also house a branch of the public library, art gallery, or museum. It might be used for voting, obtaining licenses and permits, listing and paying taxes, paying fines for minor infractions of the law, and other public purposes. It could contain small businesses, a theater doubling as a commercial stage and a hall for public forums, a restaurant, and other similar public and private establishments that might be appropriate.

The newly-opened Human Resources Center in Pontiac, Michigan, is an example of such a facility. Originally planned as an elementary school for 1,800 pupils, its location in the downtown area near the city hall, school department, and fire and police headquarters stimulated a broader concept for the complex. Although the U.S. Department of Housing and Urban Development (HUD) had never before released funds for facilities associated with schools, the planners convinced the agency to finance parts designed specifically for community use and to provide partial support for areas shared between school and community. The school consists of three wings, housing upper-elementary, lower-elementary, and kindergarten classes and sharing centralized recreation space, a cafeteria, and an auditorium. HUD helped finance the kindergarten, a preschool, and the gymnasium, as well as a theater, vocational education area, home economics rooms, meeting rooms, and adult education spaces. Portions of the complex house such civic and social agencies as county health and mental health groups, the Urban League, the Office of Economic Opportunity, the local community college, and community recreational and social organizations.

Plans to replace the 120-year-old Quincy School in Boston—which had the dubious distinction of being the first graded school in America—led to a seventeen-story structure which includes the school, community health and welfare services, stores, parking, housing, and a 25,000-square-foot playground on the roof. The housing is designated for the personnel of the nearby Tufts-New England Medical Center. The Drake-South Commons School in Chicago was planned as part of a housing project by developers who sought to promote the stability of the project by including the school, a church, and a community activities center. All three share facilities in a single community building, which also contains parking space, meeting halls, and offices. Creating such facilities for joint community/school use throughout the school day and for total use after school and on weekends makes possible substantial cost reduction as well as the increased accessibility of public services.

The urban community school would also be the coordinating center for the educational and recreational use of resources throughout the region. The most exciting possibility for environmental design is to develop environmental resources for educational use: zoological park and aquarium areas, historical sites, museums, libraries, limited-space urban recreation areas, parks, outstanding natural areas, key ecological areas, water and waterfront resources, wetlands, public buildings and grounds, open space, farms, camps, playgrounds, and related areas. When an urban region is thus developed and the urban citizen is enabled to move freely to educational and recreational resources— via low-cost transportation and an urban trail system—the city's potential as an environmental classroom is expanded in multiple ways.

The state of New Jersey is in the process of such development. At once the most highly urbanized, most densely populated, and most industrial state, New Jersey may be viewed as a prime example of one large urban region containing cities, urban fringes, suburbs, and rural areas, none of which is more than three hour's travel by automobile from any other. In 1970, the State Council for Environmental Education prepared a master plan for environmental education throughout the state which, in part, would link the educational agencies and resources of the state in order that they be of benefit to all of its citizens.[48]

New Jersey's network of environmental education facilities includes, at present, (a) the Conservation and Environmental Science Center at Brown's Mills, a consortium of more than sixty school districts, which produces curriculum guides, operates teacher-training courses, and maintains a one-day field-study program all year and a limited resident program during the school year; (b) the Deserted Village in Union County, which has a day-use program in such areas as ornithology, living-off-the-land, ecology, and field math for school districts in the county; (c) Stepping Stone Environmental Education Center in Branchville; and (d) the Spermaceti Cove Science Interpretive Center at Sandy Hook State Park, which offers a shore and marine environmental program to all Middletown Township students and to students of Brookdale Community College. Individual school districts, in addition, operate such programs as (a) Action Bound School-Within-a-School in Trenton, which offers gifted but underachieving male high school students opportunities to develop self-reliance through hiking, cliff-climbing, and survival training; (b) A Classroom of Today's World in Madison Township, which uses a variety of educational environments for a program that reaches all grades, including mobile units to take students and teachers to environmental study areas throughout the township, a mobile arts center that comes to the schools, school planetariums, and an environmental study center; and (c) the Learning Camp of Kearny, which provides a three-day outdoor living experience for sixth graders each fall and spring. County parks and museums, such as those in Monmouth, Bergen, Somerset, and Morris Counties, have also developed day programs in conservation and natural history studies. This type of network, providing different kinds of facilities for school children and adults, ought to be created in every urban region.

As the trend toward urbanization continues, the development of urban regions

---

[48] State Council for Environmental Education, *Master Plan for Environmental Education: A Proposal for New Jersey* (Mountain Lakes: the Council, 1970). (Mimeo.)

should be based on achieving a high-quality environment—one that is favorable to the greatest number of living beings, conducive to their health and well being, and responsive to a broad range of needs including solitude, sociality, education, and recreation. As participants in the U.N. seminar on urbanization concluded,

> It is no longer necessary that the urban environment have degrading effects upon its occupants and on the natural features of the territory it occupies. . . . Governments must now think in terms of rational planning of the urban environment and assign a higher priority to human environmental needs. This involves, first, the planning of urban activities in locational patterns which offer the maximum of human convenience, comfort, pleasure, and peace of mind; with minimum congestion, health hazards and other disturbing influences. Second it involves increased expenditures for the essentials of such an environment: housing, water supply, sewage disposal systems and other community services and facilities; more open space and recreational opportunities. . . . In the natural area within which urban development takes place and which it influences, the rational management of the resource base is needed. . . . Although human intervention results in constant change to the total natural environment, this disturbance must be minimized, and where necessary must be repaired to maintain the natural balance that existed before intervention took place.[49]

One of the most significant opportunities for rational planning of urban centers is appearing in the rise of "new towns" and, more particularly, of "new towns in town." Much attention has been given to the development of Reston in Virginia, Columbia in Maryland, Fort Lincoln in Washington, D.C., the new cities under construction on the west coast of Florida, and the planned development of a new town on Staten Island, New York. Natural settlement has ceased to be the method by which residence is established, and it is likely that a systems approach toward creating entire new towns will be the developmental trend of the future. The neighborhood multipurpose center, with provision for both commercial and institutional facilities within the same complex, can become the background for the downtown of the "new town in town." From there, the entire region can be planned as a high quality, observable environment in which citizens can live and learn in the environmental classroom.

[49] United Nations, *Symposium* . . . , p. 11.

chapter three

expanding the learning
environment ii : communications

The mountain can go to Mohammed. It is possible to bring the environment to the learner.

Actual physical travel is only one kind of environmental mobility. It is the traditional kind, involving movement of the person from one environment to another. But no matter how advanced our transportation technology becomes, physical travel will always take time, require the resolution of complex logistical problems, be hazardous to some extent, and in the case of student travel, involve legal and scheduling considerations that become prohibitive when more than a relatively short distance is to be covered.

The other kind of environmental mobility is achieved through communications. The person remains in one place, while the environment "travels" to him. Time, logistics, hazards, and legal considerations are all reduced when communications is the vehicle of mobility. Modern technology already makes possible a high degree of environmental mobility through communications. Projections of further advances in communications technology indicate that in the future more and more environments that are more nearly real will be able to "go" to learners, eliminating the necessity to undergo the inconveniences of physical travel in order to study any aspect of man's environment. A long-term projection made in 1966 by the Stanford Research Institute forecast that in the United States the communications industry will overtake the transportation industry in dollar volume by 1977, reaching around $60 billion per year. The trend will be for more persons to choose the electronic experience over the "real" experience—bringing the environment to the learner rather than the learner to the environment.[1]

For most people, however, it is easier to conceive of the changes being wrought by transportation technology than of those made possible by communications technology. This phenomenon is simply another illustration of the fact that we grasp the concrete more readily than the abstract. Being transported from place to place—even at supersonic speeds and through the once forbidding territory of outer space—is more concrete than communicating with a place that is beyond one's physical reach. It is likely that when Neil Armstrong took the giant leap for mankind by setting foot on the moon, the majority of people witnessing the event were less astounded by the actual physical pres-

[1] Don Fabun, ed., *The Dynamics of Change* (Oakland, California: Kaiser Aluminum & Chemical Corporation, 1967).

ence of a man on the moon than by the fact that they could watch the event live and in color in their own homes.

The principles of physical travel, for one thing, are more readily demonstrable than the principles of communications. One can observe the operation of a steam engine, a diesel engine, an internal combustion engine, or a jet propulsion engine. But one cannot see an air wave, a laser, or even a communications satellite in operation. While most of us have seen the inside of our home telephone receiver, it seems to be a mass of multi-colored wires that bear little relation to the nearly instantaneous movement of our voices over thousands of miles.

Yet advances in transportation technology have been relatively recent compared to those in communications technology, which has been developing for centuries. Not until James Watt patented his steam engine in 1789 did man have the potential to travel faster than the fastest animal he could harness or the fastest wind he could catch in his sails. At that, it took the better part of a century to improve on the natural transportation methods that had been used for thousands of years, for the first steam engines puffed along at only four or five miles per hour. The internal combustion engine became a practicality late in the nineteenth century, and only early in the twentieth century were the principles of air flight adapted to man's transportation needs. Indeed, a significant number of people lived through the period from the Wright Brothers' experiment at Kitty Hawk in 1903 to man's moon landing in 1969.

On the other hand, man's first giant leap in communications appeared with the formation of a written language thousands of years ago, and the second—toward mass communication—came with the invention of movable type by Johann Gutenberg in the 1430s. In 1844, Samuel F. B. Morse sent his famous message, "What hath God wrought," over the world's first telegraph circuit between Washington and Baltimore, and mankind could do by communication what he cannot even today do by transportation—travel instantly over many miles. In 1875, Alexander Graham Bell proved that man's own voice could do the same, and today his image, his ideas, in fact his very environment can be transported in split seconds anywhere on earth and even beyond.

In terms of potential for learning, then, communications deserves more acceptance than transportation, for it can do far more to enable the learner to experience the environmental classroom. Starting with the communicating environment of the classroom itself, the learner can expand his environmental perception through miniature ecosystems and mobile units that bring real environments, through simulated environments that reproduce some or all of the sensations of their real-life counterparts, through media that transport information both on a mass scale and in response to individual needs and, finally, through the realization of the global village concept, at which point the learner may be at home or at school or at any facility containing the technological means to obtain any kind of information instantly from anywhere.

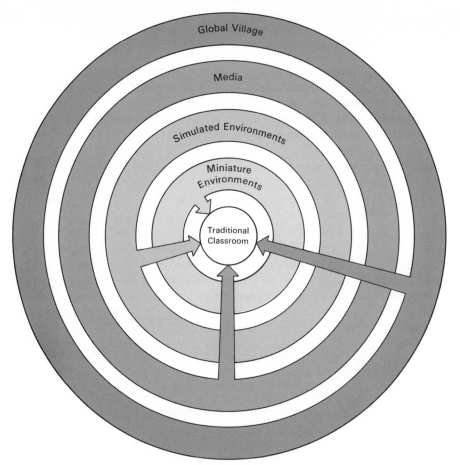

The Traditional Classroom as an Environment

The traditional classroom—occupied by most children for six hours a day, five days a week, approximately 180 days a year, for most of their developmental years—is an important environment in the lives of our children. However good, bad, functional, unpleasant, restrictive, challenging, or innocuous it may be, that classroom *is* the environment of children for a significant part of their lives. As is any environment, the environment of the classroom is fraught with lessons in the relationships of living beings to the environment, the effect of the environment on the nature of activities carried on within it, and most other kinds of environmental interaction that exist in the real world.

Used consciously as an illustrative environment, the classroom and the school can offer a starting point for environmental learning. These areas are both easily accessible and familiar to all students. A kind of subconscious environmental education, however, has always been going on in the classroom. Teachers have always been communicating in subtle ways to students about man's environment. The kind of instruction that lauds the biggest, the most, and the best has transmitted a persistent message about the nature of man's role in his environment. Mark Terry recalls that one of his first environmental lessons in school was that paper is in infinite supply, and the stocks of newsprint always available in an elementary classroom are proof that paper need not be conserved. He lists some other environmental lessons taught early in the school years:

- Any amount of garbage is all right, just don't litter.
- Population growth is good, bigger families are more fun and more people mean more friends.
- The Asians won't starve, as long as I eat everything on my plate and we harvest the sea.
- Water won't be polluted, as long as we pay "them" to build sewers.
- Man has always had problems, and he'll always be able to solve them through science and industry.
- Wildlife is a precious, but unnecessary, resource.
- Hydroelectric dams bring nothing but good: power, irrigation, recreation.
- Standard of living is based on annual income and purchasing power.
- Driving to school is approved if I am licensed, permitted by my parents, and safe.
- The history of man is the history of his growing mastery over nature.[2]

We have all learned such lessons, and they are evidence of the fact that environmental education goes on all the time in all subjects and at all grade levels. These are indeed interdisciplinary bits of learning, fully integrated into the ongoing curriculum.

In sharp contrast is the teacher who requests that the back of the paper be used for the next assignment or for jotting down notes, who keeps a store of bits of string and material and perhaps even melon seeds to be used at the creative whim of the children to make collages and other art objects, who discovers that frozen food trays are convenient receptacles for paper clips or melon seeds or crayons, who plants seeds in empty milk containers for science experiments, and who in a thousand ways each day in the classroom illustrates that valuing the biggest, the most, and the best can have tragic consequences for the human environment. Such a teacher reverses the subliminal communication of attitudes that are environmentally destructive and does more for the cause of environmental preservation than a specific course in environmental education that may fail to relate environmental principles to the routine of everyday living.

Just as the classroom teacher cannot help but be a communicator of environmental attitudes, so is the classroom, as an environment, a communicator of evironmental relationships. That the form and shape of the classroom determine the form and shape of the activities within it is demonstrated by the freer and more mobile approach to learning

2 Mark Terry, *Teaching for Survival* (New York: Ballantine Books, Inc., 1971), pp. 4, 7–8. Copyright © 1971 by Mark Terry. Reprinted by permission of Ballantine Books, Inc.

encouraged by classrooms without doors or fixed walls. While function ought to determine form in facility design, form has traditionally dictated function in American schools. A conscious effort to open the classroom doors and create learning centers in a variety of spaces, however, modifies the form of the traditional classroom and stimulates new kinds of functions. An easy object lesson on the impact of environmental form can be undertaken by rearranging the classroom furniture and observing how various arrangements aid or inhibit such basic classroom processes as communication, independent study, or small-group projects. What happens, for example, when the chairs are all grouped in a circle? In separate clusters? In a circle with everyone's back to the center? In a random pattern?

The items within a classroom communicate something about environmental concepts as well. Desks, chalkboards, paper, books, writing implements, light and heat resources, and similar objects can be analyzed as to their function, their efficiency in implementing certain activities, their natural origin, the changes they have undergone before taking their present form, and the changes they will undergo before becoming useless in performing their present functions. The classroom population relates in specific ways to the objects in the environment. The environment must meet certain basic needs, such as light, air, protection from natural elements. What other basic needs must it meet, and which human needs do not have to be met in a classroom?

Since a classroom is part of the man-made environment, it also illustrates how man builds structures in his environment to suit himself. Measuring the environment and translating the measurements into human terms enable children to grasp this idea. A door, for example, may be wide enough for two children to pass through, a window only enough height from the floor to be at eye level, a desk high enough for a seated child to rest his arms comfortably, and so on.

One of the most striking examples of the impact of environmental form on the environment's inhabitants is the fact that in open classrooms modeled on the British prototype, there are no desks or chairs assigned to specific individuals. (There are, of course, places where each child can store his belongings and his own learning materials and projects.) "Children who have a need to relate to a particular space," explains a teacher who uses open-plan methods, "are usually quick to find a spot in the room that they consider their own territory. Children who do not feel such a need move from learning center to learning center without claiming a special area as their own."

The school itself is also an environment. In fact, it operates more or less as an ecosystem during the hours when its population is present. The arrangement of its rooms, halls, and stairways illustrates systems of movement. It meets certain basic needs through its light, heating, and water systems and through its eating facilities. It meets other needs pertinent to the function it houses through areas devoted to learning materials and resources, storage, administration, and different types of learning activities. Its design and construction illustrate land-use concepts and building materials. Students who first inventory the environmental elements of the school and then analyze and evaluate them as to whether the school as an environment facilitates learning and its related functions in the best possible way will discover basic principles of environmental awareness and judgment. These principles will hold up in transference to other, less familiar environments that the learners will explore.

Real Environments in and Around the School

The school's own environmental elements constantly communicate about the environment to the school's population. When additional aspects of the environment are brought to the school, the possibilities for richer and more varied environmental communication are enhanced. Any classroom can become a more vivid learning environment when different kinds of environments are brought in for study, observance, and cultivation.

Plants, for example, are an element of the environment easily brought to the classroom and cultivated there. They have often been used by teachers both as an esthetic improvement to the otherwise institutional environment of the classroom and as illustrations of certain elementary scientific principles. When plants are grown in the classroom, the learners have an opportunity to observe day-by-day changes, growth patterns, and reactions to specific situations over extended time periods, which they would not have in the course of a day trip or even a week's experience at a natural botanical habitat.

Too often, however, the plants are simply "there," and only casual mention is made of the fact that plants need water, soil, and sunlight. Environmental perception does not develop without guidance. Teachers need to direct learners' activities toward an understanding that good soil contains food for the plant in the form of minerals, that water carries the food to the leaves, and that sunshine converts the food to growth energy. By using cuttings, carrot tops, potatoes, bulbs, and seeds; by carrying out such experiments as providing varying degrees of sunlight for a number of plants of the same kind, using different types of soil, varying the amounts of water, and planting in containers of different sizes; and by keeping records of planting conditions and growth patterns, learners can be guided not only to draw conclusions about the effects of the environment on the plant but also to understand the essential procedures in a valid scientific test.[3]

More sophisticated environmental observations are possible when the classroom contains complete ecosystems of plants or small animals in combination with plants. An ecosystem is an enclosed environment containing all the elements necessary to support the life within it. It reveals the basic elements and processes of nature that are vital to all ecosystems—the necessity of proper temperature and humidity, the importance of proper light for plant growth and stimulation of animal behavior, the requirement of food

[3] Environmental Science Center, *Plants in the Classroom* (Golden Valley, Minn.: the Center, undated).

and the operation of food chains. It communicates to the observant student the behavior of plants and animals under natural conditions and the effects of man-made changes in the combination of air, water, and land on the processes of nature's self-correcting mechanisms to restore balance to the environment.

The aquarium is perhaps the best-known kind of ecosystem, containing varieties of aquatic animals and the plant life essential to their life-support systems. Lacking the sunlight and warmth of a natural outdoor setting, indoor aquariums require lamps and simple sewage-treatment systems in the form of pumps and filters. Terrariums, on the other hand, contain land plants and animals and usually duplicate the natural environment by providing at least two climates, one a cool and dry atmosphere and one an enclosed area that can be kept warmer and more humid by the use of a lamp that causes water in a dish to evaporate into the surrounding air. Totally enclosed terrariums can maintain the warmth and humidity suitable for tropical or warm-climate reptile life. These enclosed worlds of aquatic or terrestrial life can be left for weeks to care for themselves with only the addition of one outside element, light, to provide the energy source needed to perpetuate life.

Enclosures for such ecosystems may range from specially designed commercial containers to cake covers and other kitchen equipment used with imagination. They may also be constructed from easily obtained materials according to specifications that meet the life requirements of particular kinds and combinations of plants and animals. Some of the more easily maintained species include turtles, bluegills, crayfish, anoles (the American "chameleon"), iguanas, lizards, snakes, small ferns, partridge berries, lichens, mosses, and a wide variety of insects. The Bureau of Outdoor Recreation of the U.S. Department of the Interior provides instructions for building and maintaining minia-ture ecosystems and praises their educational value in the following statement:

> The educational applications of these tools are broad and flexible. They can serve the goals of early school years for initial exposure to appreciation of the natural world. Equally well, they can provide a means for advanced instruction in the processes of plant and wildlife behavior, or the problems of pollution. They offer opportunities for first-hand experience with a wide range of environments—deserts, marshlands, forests, prairies, and ponds. The students' experience can be a daily event, carried on over long periods of time during which growth and change may be studied.[4]

Larger animals that thrive in cages or similar enclosures—gerbils, guinea pigs, rabbits, white mice, and some birds—may also be brought to the classroom. Students might note how environments built for such animals differ from human environments. However, these larger animals require constant care, feeding, and cleaning, and pro-vision must be made for their maintenance over weekends, holidays, and vacations. Nevertheless, they are effective communicators of the requirements of living creatures and the need for continued attention in order to sustain the higher forms of life in our environment.

---

[4] Bureau of Outdoor Recreation, U.S. Department of the Interior, *Miniature Environments: An Environmental Guidebook* (Washington, D.C.: Government Printing Office, undated).

The area around the school should likewise be developed for environmental learning. Environmental elements requiring more space than is available in a classroom can be brought to the school grounds to help form an environmental study area. Even urban schools might consider the possibilities of a rooftop development for gardens, weather equipment, air pollution detection equipment, and sound pollution devices; a courtyard development using a partial enclosure; tree planting, shrubbery, student sculpture, glacial boulders, and changes in texture and colors of surfacing material—both to improve the esthetics of the site and to provide sources for environmental study.[5] Gardens —from the simplest window box to the most elaborate development—can be used to illustrate nationality, when plants from a variety of geographic regions are grown; to teach about food crops (edible "weeds" will grow in even the poorest soil); to aid in pollution detection, when such pollution sentinels as petunias or gladiolas are included; to provide a natural outpost in an urban area, when a thicket is allowed to grow wild in a small corner; or to provide a practical application for mathematics learning, when symmetry, rates of growth, ratios, and other similar phenomena are measured. Students might write about the garden or study the economic, social, and political factors involved in planning and maintaining a garden. One small activity offers potential for interdisciplinary education, recreation, human relations improvement, conservation, and pollution control.

One of the outstanding examples of benefits accruing by chain reaction from a school garden can be found in a low-income neighborhood of Washington, D.C. There, in 1969, the Madison Elementary School developed a garden on a 1,500-square-foot plot of rocky ground, an abandoned lot adjacent to the school playground, with the assistance of the National Park Service (NPS). The students and members of the surrounding community call it Our Block of Earth, but NPS considers it the first urban National Environmental Study Area (NESA) and has supplemented the school's environmental study program with curriculum materials, camping sessions at nearby NPS facilities, and field trips to other NESAs around Washington, D.C. Our Block of Earth has been divided into forest, grassland, desert, and cropland, each containing varieties of plantlife representative of that kind of environment. The cropland has yielded corn, beans, tomatoes, collards, squash, and radishes for use by neighborhood families. Students patrol the area to avert vandalism and to alert the sanitation department when refuse pickups are needed. There has been virtually no vandalism of the garden, largely because of community cooperation and enthusiasm—which has spread to private planting and beautification projects by nearby residents. Members of the community have formed "Block Clubs" to remove litter in the neighborhood, protect and maintain the NESA, and organize gardening projects for their own homes. Cooperation in maintaining the garden and initiating related cleanup programs has also been extended by the police department, the rodent control unit, the department of highways and traffic, the Humane Society, and the Society for a More Beautiful National Capital.

Across the nation in Los Angeles, the Monlux Science and Conservation Center for

---

[5] Educational Facilities Laboratories, in cooperation with Project Man's Environment, *Places for Environmental Education* (New York: Educational Facilities Laboratories, 1971).

the Los Angeles Unified School Districts has developed a similar program. On 1,200 square feet of land, the Center created an environmental study area called Conservation in Miniature. Part of the area is devoted to models of principles of scientific farm conservation, such as contour farming, terracing, windbreaks, waterways, and conservation grazing. The area also contains a miniature replica of the Los Angeles basin flood-prevention project. Equipped to involve children on an investigational or experiencing level, the facility is staffed by trained volunteers. The Center's teacher resource building contains instructional materials and produces resource kits to aid teachers and students. The Center has "brought" a living example of conservation to city-dwelling children.

Examples of aquatic life may also be brought to small outdoor areas near urban schools. A concrete or stone pool, at least one and a half feet deep and with recirculating water, can maintain fish, turtles, and water vegetation during months of temperate climate with little care other than food. Tadpoles, crayfish, and turtles help keep the water clean, and once the pond gets started bluegills and sunfish can thrive and spawn in such an environment.[6]

When elements of the natural environment are thus brought to the school—even to a school in the deepest recesses of the inner city—the school becomes a communicator of the fascinating store of information in the natural environment. But the natural environment is only a part of man's total environment. The man-made environment, too, can come to the learner.

One way to bring the man-made environment to the school is to bring in persons who deal with some aspect of that environment to explain their specialty area to the learners. The idea that professional teachers are unlimited sources of wisdom on unlimited numbers of subjects and that only teachers can teach is gradually succumbing to the more realistic idea that the community contains persons who are both highly knowledgeable about specialized areas of interest to learners, as well as effective and enthusiastic teachers. Talks, demonstrations, and film or slide lectures by selected adults in the community on travel, jobs, hobbies, pets, and the like offer students multiple sources of information and understanding about their world. A municipal councilman is immersed in the daily problems of local government; an architect is constantly searching for new ways of designing the structures that house human activities; a traveler to some distant land has a fresh and vivid impression of the sights, sounds, and culture of the place; a public health worker has a personal reaction to the effects of drug abuse or venereal disease; a policeman has intimate knowledge of methods of crime prevention. If such persons—and a host of others—are able to communicate their experiences effectively, they can "bring" a part of man's environment to the classroom, whereas a single teacher would find it physically impossible to have more than secondhand knowledge of more than a few of these aspects of man's environment.

Another way to bring communication about man's environment to the classroom is through the various disciplines of the arts. In whatever form it may take, art is essentially a medium of communication about some facet of the human condition or the human

<hr />

[6] U.S. Department of the Interior, *Nature Downtown* (Washington, D.C.: Government Printing Office, 1970).

environment. The artist works through his medium to communicate not only factual information ("cognitive domain") about the environment he perceives but also his emotional reaction to it ("affective domain"). In traditionally conceived curriculums, however, the arts have been considered expendable "frills," compared to the necessary disciplines of language arts, mathematics, science, and the social studies. Young people with special artistic talent have often been the only ones offered in-depth instruction in any artistic medium. Yet if environmental perception is to be a goal of learning, there is no more effective way of sharpening the perception of all the senses than through the arts. Art is, first of all, perception, and secondly, it is the process of communicating what is perceived through manipulation of artistic media—painting, sculpture, dance, drama, music, and the like.

Today, the emerging trend in school curriculums is to place increasing emphasis on the arts as a part of the general education of all students. In a recently revised curriculum handbook for school administrators, the authors of the chapter on art education make the following observation:

> One of the most encouraging signs to art teachers has been the implications of the vocabulary in education in recent years, exemplified by such phrases as "quality of life." . . . The phrase implies the developing of greater emphasis on appreciation of that quality through values that are nurtured by art education. Perception, sensitivity, critical awareness, and creative problem solving—all items high on the priority list of the art educator—are beginning to receive an increasing emphasis as we begin to strive for true quality and appreciation of life in an increasingly complex environment.[7]

By developing perception, sensitivity, critical awareness, and creative problem solving through the arts, the learner as artist is able to confront some of the problems presented by the esthetic conditions of the environment.

> These problems and their implications for the visual dimensions of both the man-made and the natural environment are becoming content areas for art education programs. In one sense, the total environment becomes the learning environment for the visual arts, for it is from perception of our surroundings that creative expression receives it impetus.[8]

And the first place in which to exercise esthetic problem solving might well be in the school itself.

> The predominant look of schools today is a very austere environment for learning. Many art education programs have taken on the task of redesigning the school environment as part of their study of the environment. Such projects as painting the halls with supergraphics and filling spaces in the lunch rooms and in the classrooms with images start to give the school a feeling that it has some personality. . . . Even administrators are coming to realize that

[7] Stanley Madeja and John Mahlmann, "Art Education," *Curriculum Handbook for School Administrators*, rev. ed. (Washington, D.C.: American Association of School Administrators, in press).
[8] *Ibid.*

the environment has a significant effect on how the child learns, and if the student can have a part in altering and changing the learning environment the learning process will be enhanced.[9]

The Aesthetic Education Program of the Office of Education's Central Midwestern Regional Laboratory (CEMREL) is based on the premise that the sensibilities and capacity for judgment and effective action can be trained within the school. Through the arts, the program aims to guide students to make informed esthetic judgments so they can appreciate and interpret esthetic qualities in their lives, make intelligent decisions about such practical things as material possessions, and participate actively in shaping the cultural life of the nation.

Environmental perception is only one aspect of learning improved through the arts. In searching for a more humanistic approach to learning, we are also seeking ways for students to develop greater self-understanding and appreciation of their individual worth—a necessary first step toward understanding the total environment and appreciating the worth and dignity of all humanity within it. Such understanding and appreciation are a concomitant outcome of learning in the arts. At the 1970 White House Conference on Children, the forum on creativity and the learning process reported that:

> . . . [the arts] can make a crucial contribution to academic performance as well. The child often "finds" himself through immersion in the arts. . . . Those who frame curricula must recognize the immeasurable contribution the arts make toward the fulfillment and enrichment of the human spirit.[10]

At the Escarosa Humanities Center in Pensacola, Florida, the value of the arts in fostering personal and cultural understanding has been proved by the new outlook on learning of the 3,000 elementary and secondary students who have participated in the experiment. Through exposure to artistic creations in both the visual and performing arts, as well as through experience in creating their own artistic productions, these "culturally deprived" youngsters have discovered that learning is a delightful endeavor, that all academic disciplines are related and many emerge in new perspectives through the arts, and that products of their own creative attempts are worthwhile. At the Minnesota Museum of Art, a group of volunteer citizens guide children through a range of exhibits featuring a variety of kinds of artistic expression—Chinese shadow figures, satirical drawings, hand-crafted lace, ceramics, and sculpture, to name only a few examples. The students respond by creating their own versions of art objects and artistic performances back in their classrooms. Similar experiments in many school districts provide evidence that the sense of accomplishment and pride resulting from such activities in artistic problem solving encourages young people to become confident problem solvers in many other areas, as well.

[9] *Ibid.*

[10] White House Conference on Children, "Creativity and the Learning Process," Report of Forum 6, *Report to the President, White House Conference on Children* (Washington, D.C.: the Conference, 1970), pp. 96–97.

Still another way of bringing the environment to the learner is to do so in literal terms—to transport environments by means of mobile units. A mobile unit might contain live animals and plants and travel from school to school or to other public locations to present its program. An interpreter traveling with the unit guides learners in observing the environmental information illustrated by the unit and, perhaps, arouses their curiosity to the point of stimulating trips to actual environmental sites. In Kansas City, Missouri, the Lakeside Nature Center sends the "Good Friend Nature Wagon" to schools. It uses native live animals in discussions and demonstrations of adaptation, community, survival, and family life and development.

A mobile unit set up as a well-equipped environmental education facility can be a catalyst for involving people with the natural environment, for creating awareness of the interaction between people and the biophysical resources of environments, and for expanding the use of such environmental areas as public parks. It may be a portable storage box, a small trailer, a step van, or a large moving van. Along with samples of environmental objects, it should contain equipment designed to increase environmental perception—study kits, such as water-testing kits and weather kits; human sensory extensions, such as temperature guages and hand lenses; and reinforcement literature, such as field manuals and publications on pollution. Learners might be guided to explore temperature changes or map the differences between open-space and closed-space environments or focus on noise pollution by wearing blindfolds.

Crucial to the maximum effectiveness of such a unit is the environmental guide who travels with the unit. His principal goal is to encourage discovery, inquiry, and the enjoyment of the sensations of man's biophysical surroundings by creating perceptual awareness of the environment as well as an attitude that will evoke additional sensitivity and inquiry beyond the moment. He should pose problem questions about environmental issues, guide learners' investigations, provide multisensory experiences, and stimulate active involvement by participants in problem-solving and decision-making situations.[11]

Another type of mobile unit—one designed to educate educators—was created by the Soil Conservation Service and has traveled to many locations in the northeastern states. Its exhibit is modeled after an actual outdoor classroom in Freehold, New Jersey, and it is meant to show teachers and administrators how outdoor classrooms for schools can be developed and used. This "outdoor classroom on wheels" contains various plantings illustrating different kinds of environments, along with its major attraction—six mallard ducklings in a tiny pond.

Mobile units may be used for recreation as well as for education, an idea that started taking practical shape at Southern Illinois University (SIU) in 1962 and has since been duplicated in many communities. SIU's recreation and outdoor education department began with a Nature-Outdoor Education Wagon, the sides of which open out to reveal equipment for outdoor living and a library of nature-study reference materials. A few years later, they developed the Show Wagon, which opens out into a

---

11 B. Ray Horn, "Creating Environmental Awareness: The Development of a Mobile Environmental Education Program," *Trends*, 8:2 (April 1971). Published by the National Recreation and Park Association, the National Conference on State Parks and the National Park Service, U.S. Department of the Interior.

stage and has held such events as rock-and-roll concerts, dance acts, vocal acts, baton twirling, comedy skits, contests, and award presentations. In 1966, they completed the Puppet–Marionette Wagon and followed with the Teen Dance Party Wagon. A Craft Shop Wagon rolls through nearby towns with a program of craft instruction and a display. William Ridinger, the department head, calls the whole concept Portomobile Recreation, and he has on the drawing boards plans for a mobile zoo, science wagon, infant playground, swimming pool, tiered band wagon, and movie theater. Small towns that find expensive park hardware beyond their budgets and urban areas pressed for open recreation land have been the major beneficiaries, but there are added bonuses to the community members who cooperate to plan the functions for the wagons and to the students of recreation and outdoor education at SIU who gain practical experience to balance classroom theory.

Simulated Environments

Apparently, anything in the environment that is small enough to be carried in a highway vehicle can be brought to the learner, as some ingenious designers have been proving for some years. But there remain many environments that are not transportable, and learners should be able to experience these, too, without the hardships of physical travel.

Simulation can provide the answer. An ordinary photograph, of course, is a kind of simulation, as is the "manufactured" humid environment of a terrarium. One kind of simulation that has been gaining popularity for classroom use is the game. Educational games simulate conditions or situations that require certain kinds of problem solving on the part of the player. They enable the student to apply abstract principles to concrete problems. An educational game focuses on a very limited aspect of the real world, defined by the problem area and by the rules of play. Two or more independent decision makers must work within the rules to solve the problems the game presents and thereby achieve their objectives. If a player makes the wrong decision, he probably learns the consequences of his error. But the stakes that exist in real-world problem solving are not present in games, and a bruised ego is about all the player suffers.

Games can simulate the situations in occupational selection or the intricacies of decision making in industry or government. There are games that require selection among the social or technological alternatives of the future, games in which learners design communities, and games in which international considerations are necessary. Games involving environmental choices illustrate the interaction within the environmental web and the fact that it is impossible to do just one thing. Games dealing with population, for example, show how the choices of one generation as to family size affect the environment for many generations thereafter.

Such limited simulations have great value for learners in the environmental classroom. Sometimes, however, we may wish to produce the opposite effect—to enlarge rather than limit the environment. If we rely on more complex technology, we can create simulations that are all but the real thing in every sensation produced by the environment.

A firm in Ohio has developed The Tree House Learning Environment, a modular system of space-arrangers, rear-projection screens, seating blocks, and graphics designed to furnish a school or learning center with a versatile environment. The space-arrangers are steel-and-canvas partitions that shape spaces to accommodate the size and function of a learning activity. The rear-projection screens receive single or multiple images from hidden projectors. The portable seating blocks are of colorful corrugated cardboard, designed for both storage and seating. But the graphics begin to create a visual environment that stimulates awareness by enlarging small elements of the world and reducing big ones. They are a series of black-and-white panels, either photographic or graphic art representations of some environmental element, each thirty inches wide by fifty-six inches tall. A huge photograph of a spider web takes three panels which, when hung together, give the observer an impression of what the spider might be seeing from within the web. A three-panel optical illusion created by undulating lines shows how certain patterns affect the eyes. Other panels show the planets looming out from the darkness of space. Even so simple a visual addition to a learning center as these wall hangings can create a number of vivid environmental sensations.

A multimedia dome, constructed in the McDonald Elementary School in Warminster, Pennsylvania, with the aid of Title III funds, recreates the sights and sounds and smells of environments ranging from a forest to a tenement, from a farm to outer space, from the familiar to the previously unimagined. The circular room is forty feet in diameter and topped by a dome rising thirty feet above the carpeted floor. It is equipped with projectors, tape recorders, aerosol spray cans, temperature controls, a planetarium projector that retracts into the floor, twenty-three speakers, and twelve projection ports. Called the Special Experiences Room, it holds about thirty children at a time comfortably seated on the floor, who are exposed to and completely surrounded by a simulated total physical atmosphere. Although it cost nearly $300,000, the Special Experiences Room was intended to serve as a model, and one school district near Erie, Pennsylvania, has converted a classroom into a small version of the dome at a cost of $8,000.

Mobile units carrying such environmental simulations from place to place could further reduce expenses by serving a number of school districts. As it is, mobile units already carry other types of simulations. The Cooperative Science Education Center (CSEC) uses a simulation of a county environment—actually a three-dimensional map on a large board, indicating the physical features of the area—to aid in discussions of environmental problems. CSEC calls these discussions Enviro County, and they enable schools and organizations to deal with economic, social, and environmental issues by using the simulations to visualize problems and possible solutions. Originally, the program could be held only at the Center, but since the construction of new portable models—some of them illustrating new environmental problems—groups are able to schedule the sessions at their own sites.

In the foreseeable future, simulated experiences may well replace real ones outside of school, as well. Alvin Toffler predicts the creation of "experiental enclaves" that

will reproduce all the realities of such past environments as ancient Rome or Eliza-
bethan England and enable participants, in effect, to live for a brief time in other times
and other places.[12] There already exist artistic environments that use sight, sound, smell,
and touch to envelop the participant in whatever total sensory impression the artist
wishes to create. A 1969 issue of *The Futurist* predicted that future tourism may consist
of a replication of the physical environment of another country, projected into the home
or created at a nearby touring center, spiced by adding full two-way video communication with the country being "visited." [13]

Processes for creating complete and very realistic simulations are already a reality,
as evidenced by the Special Experiences Room. But this is a highly individual application,
requiring a great deal of manipulation of numerous sensory elements right at the time
the participants are going through the experience. Mass production and projection of
simulations, however, may become a reality within a decade or so. Consider the following scenario, devised by Boyd Evison of the National Park Service as a proposal for
bringing the experiences of the National Parks within the reach of every person in the
United States:

> June 23, 1989. A balmy morning, . . . as you glide on a conveyor walk toward the com-
> munity center. Ahead of you, and to the right of the walk, a building complex that is like
> a giant cluster of crystals rests lightly amid grass and trees at the base of a slender, soaring
> skyscraper. As you step off the conveyor and walk along a shaded path toward them, a
> sense of delicious anticipation rises in you. Almost a week has passed since your last national
> park experience in three dimensions.
>
> Inside, you no longer see walls—only curtains of light and darkness. Projecting from some
> of them are vivid, moving, three-dimensional images. For a moment, you seem to be walking
> in the cathedral quiet of a grove of coast redwoods; the image fades, and you are passing
> between the sheer walls of the gorge of Rio Grande National River. Your heart leaps as you
> catch a glimpse of a mountain lion, sprawled like a hearthside tabby on a ledge just above
> the level of your shoulders. Behind you, a small boy in a family group claps his hands in
> glee at the sight of the big cat; but there is not the twitch of an ear or blink of an eye in
> response from the lion. Almost 2,000 miles separate child and lion, and the sights, sounds,
> and aroma-activators are flowing only *from* the park. The fist-sized sensor unit, gliding on a
> gyroscopic mount down the Rio Grande, does virtually nothing to disturb the wildlife along
> the way. You are not watching a film; the lion breathes at the moment you watch his chest
> rise and fall.
>
> Spotting a vacant alcove, you step in, pick up a headset, and fit it to your ears. The touch
> of a button brings a fresh carbolon mesh into place on a recliner frame. Lying back in the
> mesh, you quickly become totally absorbed in the scenes around and above you. Two
> hundred million people could be sharing these scenes with you—many of them on home
> sets, in two dimensions—but not one person intrudes on the scenes or your reverie. By a
> phenomenal extension of your senses, you are experiencing all but the tactile sensations of

---

[12] Alvin Toffler, *Future Shock* (New York: Random House, Inc., 1970), p. 228.

[13] John LaHult, "Cheap Communications," *The Futurist*, 3, 3 (June 1969). (Published by the
World Future Society, P.O. Box 19285, 20th St. Station, Washington, D.C. 20036.)

immersion in your choice of park environments, precisely as they exist at the moment of your pleasure, while the resources you're enjoying remain undisturbed.

At your hand, a dial glows softly in the dusky light of your alcove. You spin the dial to the Yellowstone symbol, then switch to the area scan control. Interpreters at a control board in Yellowstone, monitoring the views picked up by dozens of sensor units, have picked the best of them for the ten relay screens to which you have access. From the three-dimensional images that flash around you as you turn the dial, you opt to linger on the view of a sage-brush-covered slope. You are facing downslope, looking toward the Gardner River and the precipitous slopes of Mt. Everts beyond. The tangy-sweet scent of an aspen grove drifts to you from your left, mingling with the sharp, spicy aroma of sagebrush. From behind the shoulder of the ridge that slopes off to your right, a female pronghorn trots nervously into view. The sensor picks up the movement and zooms in for a closer view as she turns and stops, looking intently at something that is still blocked from your sight.

Now you see it, though—two coyotes saunter into view, and behind them, two more. . . . You are not in the mood to look at a natural act of wildlife population control. [You select another sensor], and in an instant you are at Ozark Rivers, drifting on clear, greenish water beneath arching elms and maples. Ahead of you, the rumble of a rapids rises; from the bluff on your right, the liquid song of a Carolina wren rolls out to you.

As the sensor carries you to the lip of the rapids, you see the dark shadow of a bass dart away to a submerged tangle of roots and brush near the bank. The sight of the fish, followed by the mild exhilaration of a run through the rapids, gives you such a lift that you decide to try the real thing. You push the reservation button; a pleasant voice says "Yes?" and you ask for the first open date for a two-day float for two adults and a child. A date is spoken; you accept it, give your identification number, and pluck your reservation card from the console beside your recliner. The date is more than three months off, but you know that you and your family will have an uncrowded river to enjoy firsthand. It would be worth a far longer wait.

Once more you turn the dial, halting it this time at Acadia's symbol. The fresh-clam taste of ocean air mingles with the scent of spruce forest, as a sensor puts you at the edge of a tidal pool. Now it slips into the crystalline water, and you are gliding past long blades of kelp. Flower-like sea anemones wave lavender-pink tentacles from the rocky bottom, but the sensor sweeps up to the pool's silvery ceiling, to pick up a close look at the barnacles clinging to a rocky wall, just under the water's surface. Through the recorder's eye, you see a barnacle's feet emerge from its miniature volcano of a shell and begin to kick plankton into its hungry depths. You press the interpretation button, and a voice rich in down-east inflections comes to you, describing the special set of conditions essential to barnacle success.

A tour through Independence Hall and another through Mesa Verde's Cliff Palace round out your hour in—or with—the parks.[14]

This rather incredible scene was originally predicted possible for the NPS centennial year, 2016. In fact, it is technologically possible right now and could perhaps be made a practical reality by—to choose a year that connotes very different images of the future—1984.

[14] Boyd Evison, "Parkscapes '89," adapted from a communications research program proposal, January 1969. (Mimeo.)

The technological basis for the creation of such possibilities is the laser, and the process is known as holography. The laser, whose name is acronymically derived from light amplification by *s*timulated emission of *r*adiation, is an instrument that produces an enormously intense, pencil-sized, and sharply directed beam of light over long distances. The laser beam consists of light waves all of the same frequency and all in phase. When such a beam, rather than a camera, is used to take a picture, a high-resolution photographic plate is exposed to a subject illuminated by the laser. The distance from each point of the subject to the plate is represented by a specific number of wavelengths, and the plate thereby records not only light and dark (or color) in two dimensions but also information about depth. The developed plate shows only a meaningless pattern that looks something like a fingerprint, but when viewed properly it produces a hologram (whole picture)—a high-quality, three-dimensional image, with complete representations of all objects on all depth planes.

Evison's futuristic park simulation relies primarily on holography, which would be used to reproduce the visual experiences of the park in three-dimensional, color images. Holography also has tremendous potential to revolutionize communications media. Its potential is so great that the inventor of the hologram, Dennis Gabor, was awarded the 1971 Nobel Prize for Science for his work. With or without the marvels of holography, the communications media stand to enlarge the environmental classroom beyond the wildest science-fiction predictions of only a few years ago.

Media

Media—under the broad umbrella of instructional technology—have been part of the learning scene for a long time. Although great claims have been made for them, on the one hand, and great disappointment expressed about them, on the other, instructional media are actually nothing more than the name implies. They are merely a reflection of the fact that schools today exist in a society that has produced electronic and technological media. Instructional media are not teachers; they are only communicators of information. Neither are they a teaching method; a teacher can use any method of instruction ever devised with the aid of media. The wide range of instructional media only makes it possible to dispense information and facilitate learning in a variety of ways instead of just through lectures and books.

It is a paradox that the schools, so often excruciatingly slow to change in response to changes in society, quickly embraced the products of educational technology in the 1960s, only to suffer bitter disillusionment when the machines and media did not live up to their heralded promises. The results are understandable, however, when we realize that the technology was introduced without the essential accompanying changes in philosophy of education, without a critical overhaul of the basic purposes of schools. Thus, the forum on educational technology at the 1970 White House Conference on Children was compelled to conclude:

Most American schools are still organized around the notion that all children can (and should) learn the same things, in the same way, at the same time. Standardized schoolrooms, standardized instruction, and standardized texts are reflections of the technology of mass production that took hold in American society during the years when public education was coming of age. . . . In our attempts to make the system more "efficient," enormously proficient technological means are being applied to an anachronistic end: we continue to inundate our schools with hardware and software aimed at mass instruction of children. But such technological products have only served to intensify the destructive dehumanization that already characterizes the American school system.[15]

The technological implements were introduced because it was said that they would teach better. Teach what . . . better than what? Little research had been done on the effectiveness of these implements in reaching specific goals. The situation is now changing. Robert W. Locke, executive vice-president of McGraw-Hill Book Company, indicates that the direction of change is toward research on the ability of media to implement the objectives of individualized learning:

We are finally, slowly, painfully beginning to find better ways of measuring educational results, not just in terms of achievement in broad areas as measured by standardized tests and compared with group norms, but in terms of learning outcomes compared with objectives stated in behavioral terms. . . . The most encouraging sign is that educational research is finally beginning to lead instead of follow educational experimentation. . . . It remained for a handful of men trained in educational psychology and research to point out that preoccupation with the tools of instruction was putting the cart before the horse; that instead of concentrating so single-mindedly on *products* for sale to schools, we should instead concern ourselves with the *processes* by which skills and knowledge are acquired.[16]

Communications technology, far from encouraging the continuation of standardization in education, could actually be the very thing that allows individualization. Toffler points out that as technology becomes more advanced, it becomes easier to produce a diversity of items that, under simpler technology, appeared as mass-produced, assembly-line products. Customization of the production process is the hallmark of advanced technology.

Computers, for example, . . . make it easier for the school to cope with independent study, with a wider range of course offerings and more varied extracurricular activities. More important, computer-assisted education, programmed instruction and other such techniques, despite popular misconceptions, radically enhance the possibility of diversity in the classroom. They permit each student to advance at his own purely personal pace. They permit him to follow a custom-cut path toward knowledge, rather than a rigid syllabus as in the traditional era classroom.[17]

[15] White House Conference on Children, "Environmental Technology: Constructive or Destructive?" Report of Forum 9, *Report to the President: White House Conference on Children* (Washington, D.C.: the Conference, 1970), pp. 145–56.

[16] Robert W. Locke, "Has the Education Industry Lost Its Nerve?" *Saturday Review*, 54 (January 16, 1971), 44. Copyright 1971, Saturday Review, Inc.

[17] Toffler, *Future Shock*, p. 243.

Technological media provide multiple ways of learning. They accommodate the child who learns best from the printed word, the child who learns best from visual sources, the child who learns best from auditory cues, and the child who learns best from some combination of sight and sound, words and pictures, or anything else the media can communicate. They will not teach by themselves, though. They require teachers who believe deeply in the individual worth of each child and the value of individual learning styles and who are able to facilitate the learning of each child by matching the child to the learning materials—hardware and software—that are available. The process of education and of using educational technology then becomes a process of meeting individual needs, and the technological tools of education can help bring to the learner the world that is the environmental classroom.

The types of technological equipment available today to facilitate instruction are many and varied. Each has the potential to communicate about certain aspects of man's environment in certain ways. Educators need to understand the capabilities of each in order to select those most suited to particular kinds of subject matter and particular learning styles.[18]

One of the oldest audio devices used in classrooms is the phonograph, which can bring to the learner accurate reproductions of music and drama, as well as the spoken word. The tape recorder offers the additional advantage of enabling students and teachers to record live performances and lectures, other recordings, and their own voices. There are also special kinds of tape recorders designed to facilitate language learning or to be used as dictating machines.

A research project begun in 1970 by the University of Idaho's College of Education, Communication Skills Through Authorship (CSTA), is attempting to find out whether recording original material can enhance the reading ability of first- and second-grade pupils. The children compose orally and record their compositions on casette recorders located in private booths in their classroom. They are taught to operate the simple machines themselves and are free to record at any time except during large-group instruction. A typist transcribes each child's stories and places them in the child's own folder. Although a young child's speaking vocabulary always surpasses his reading vocabulary, most children have been able to read their own dictations by the end of the first year. Second graders tested at the end of a year with CSTA showed a significantly higher gain in paragraph comprehension than did a control group.[19]

There are also wireless audio systems, which transmit sound by radio waves and require a loop antenna. Language laboratories, wired or wireless, exemplify a complex application of audio technology. They generally consist of several learning stations connected to an instructor's console, enabling the student to hear the program source and, in some cases, respond or record his voice.

Telephone teaching systems permit instructors to reach larger numbers of students

[18] For a detailed description of technological devices for school use, see Educational Facilities Laboratories, *Instructional Hardware/A Guide to Architectural Requirements* (New York: Educational Facilities Laboratories, 1970).

[19] Lewis Smith, et al., "Communication Skills Through Self-Recording," *Today's Education*, 60 (January 1971), 18–20.

than possible otherwise, transmitting material live over long distances. One type transmits the lecturer's voice and also the illustrative material he writes with an electronic stylus on a special transmitter. Instructors are also able to reach home-bound students by such means.

Dial access information retrieval systems let a student sitting at a single console receive information from many different audio and/or visual sources, including some that may be many miles away—in a large, central library, for example. As these systems are improved, students working at their own pace and in their own manner will have virtually unlimited access to information.

Visual devices start with the simple and well-known slide, filmstrip, and motion picture projectors, which are found in almost every school. Newer devices include the overhead projector, which allows the teacher to face the class and project clear images in normal room light, and the opaque projector, which projects book pages and other opaque material directly onto a screen without the need for intermediate photography. The film loop is a means of packaging a short lesson or an explanation of a single concept into a film cartridge that can be projected by a student or teacher and be run again immediately without rewinding. Microform systems—microfiche, microcard, and microfilm—enable an instructional materials center to store vast quantities of information in relatively little space and still have it readily available for student access.

Teaching machines, and the entire field of programed learning, appeared on the instructional scene backed by more research than perhaps any other technological device. Their use—and misuse—has been the subject of great debate, nevertheless. On the one hand, the teaching profession voiced concern over the possibility that the machines were being introduced to take over teachers' jobs. But on the other hand, far too many teachers have sat every child in front of a console to work through the same program at the same time in the same way. Teaching machines and programed learning were actually devised to present routine instruction—for example, basic reading or math skills—and thereby free teachers to give individual attention to single students or small groups and to prescribe personalized courses of learning to meet individual needs. The instruction is programed to allow the student to make responses and, if he is correct, to proceed to more advanced exercises at whatever pace he can handle. Some of the more complex programs contain a number of branches, from which the computer selects either remedial drill or more advanced presentations, depending on the student's responses. The more apt students may then pass over certain phases and proceed more quickly to material suited to their higher ability levels.

A very basic element of the potential success of programed learning is that there be effective programs—or software—available. Some of the initial software developed for instructional computers was put together so hastily in response to demand that it was never worthy of the concept of programed instruction. A second element is that programed learning needs to be used by teachers in a truly individualized manner. Teaching machines should only be used with learners who learn well from an impartial and unemotional "instructor" (and for some children, these characteristics of the computer are its biggest asset). Programs should never be so standardized that every child works through the same material in the same way. Theoretically, the computer provides enough free time for the teacher to investigate a variety of learning sources suitable for the variety of learning styles found in any class.

The system known as computer-assisted instruction (CAI) consists of a sequence of learning activities comprising a complete curriculum. The computer dispenses information, asks questions of the student, then either goes ahead or repeats and explains previous material. Since CAI involves a more complex program, it comes closer to individualization than do simple programs dealing primarily with rote learning. Systems that actually respond to student inquiries and carry on discussions with the student are being developed by corporations formed through mergers of textbook and electronics firms. Some companies are also set up to operate and manage the programs within schools. The first computerized elementary school classroom in the country was opened in 1966 in Palo Alto, California, by the Institute for Mathematical Studies in the Social Sciences at Stanford University. Stanford's computer network now supplies instructional material to a number of schools around the country. Other computer centers operate at Florida State University, Pennsylvania State University, the University of Illinois, the University of Michigan, and the University of California at Irvine.

Television is another technological device that has proved its value as an instructional aid but has nonetheless been a disappointment in practice. Again, the fault lies more in the programs broadcast and the way teachers use instructional television than in the medium itself—for the medium is not the message; it is only the carrier of the message, and the message must be presented well in order to be effective. The most successful uses of television in schools are as an auxiliary to the teacher in presenting some types of material (e.g., complicated demonstrations that are difficult to duplicate in a single classroom), as a mass medium to bring the teaching of unusually high-qualified instructors to many learners; and as an extension medium to bring additional or enrichment instruction to a class. Television is least effective when the classroom teacher has no advance preparation in the content of the program and when there is no discussion period before and after the program to enable learners to clarify the material in a give-and-take situation. As the Educational Facilities Laboratories points out—

> The reasons television has not had wider acceptance are essentially the same reasons that have held back the full development of all electronic teaching systems, namely:
> - economic constraints on school districts;
> - lack of indisputable research as backup for validity of the system as a teaching tool;
> - resistance to innovation on the part of faculty; inexperience and lethargy on the part of school administrators;
> - failure on the part of industry to cater specifically to the education market as a separate field;
> - mediocre programs;
> - lack of adequate professional help in assisting school administrators to design and set up electronic teaching systems.[20]

[20] Educational Facilities Laboratories, *Instructional Hardware/A Guide to Architectural Requirements*, p. 48.

Along with the transmission and distribution systems currently available—VHF, UHF, closed-circuit, and cable—there are likely to be great expansions in the potential use of instructional television if certain predictions become reality. One is a device that would allow students in a school to interact with a live instructor in a television studio, asking questions through a two-way communication setup. Another possibility is a device that will record programs from television to be played back on the receiver at a convenient time. Still another is the use of the laser to open up the now limited number of broadcast channels.

There is one certainty—education technology will continue to advance and to produce more sophisticated kinds of equipment as instructional aids. If the technological media are used in conjunction with teaching methods directed toward helping each student realize his full potential and become a rational member of the world's environment, then they can be the indispensable tools for bringing the environment to the learner and creating the environmental classroom in the school.

One of the more intriguing implications of the concept of an environmental classroom created by communications is that it will be able to exist anywhere and not just in a building called a school. Just as physical mobility takes learners away from the school and into the real environment more and more, so may communications "mobility" obviate the need for a school by bringing the environmental classroom to the learner wherever he may be. Thus the forum on the future of learning at the 1970 White House Conference on Children hypothesized:

> It is possible that advanced technology will return the family to the center of the stage as the basic learning unit. Each home could become a school, in effect, via an electronic console connected to a central computer system in a learning hub, a videotape and microfilm library regulated by a computer, and a national educational television network.[21]

Communications media offer a tremendous potential for bringing the environment not just to the classroom but to persons everywhere, in all of life.

Certainly much of the credit for the emerging awareness of environmental problems ought to go to the mass media. Newspapers, magazines, books, radio, motion pictures, and television have reached millions of persons with environmental messages, helping to place environmental preservation and improvement among the top national—even international—concerns. Given the necessity for educating two generations about man's environment, these media are the most effective means of reaching and teaching the out-of-school population.

The need to strengthen environmental communications prompted the formation of the Center for Environmental Communications and Education (CECES) at the University of Wisconsin at Madison. Working internally with the journalism, education, and ecology faculties and externally with mass communications media, resource manage-

---

[21] White House Conference on Children, "The Future of Learning," Report of Forum 5, *Report to the President: The White House Conference on Children* (Washington, D.C.: the Conference, 1970), p. 79.

ment agencies, scientific groups, conservation organizations, schools, and other organizations concerned with environmental quality, CECES describes its mission as helping to train more and better environmental communicators, helping to discover new and better ways of building public understanding and support for environmental preservation, and assisting the various groups in developing broad ecological awareness and action. By training media personnel, school teachers, and adult educators, CECES is, in effect, sponsoring a new profession—that of the environmental communicator.

The effectiveness of the mass media, and especially of television, in reaching large numbers of persons was the force behind the creation of the Public Broadcasting Environment Center (PBEC) to apply the unique capabilities of public broadcasting to the broad challenge of environmental education (see Chapter 1). From its initial study, completed in November 1970, PBEC concluded that "there is a need for an effective communications system to stimulate broad public awareness of the environment, opportunities for its improvement, and dangers with respect to its deterioration and to develop environmental education programs to give that awareness focus, to encourage widespread responsible action, and to reach national and local audiences." [22] The study found that seventy-five percent of the fifty-eight million television households are reached by public television, representing as a conservative estimate some eighty-six million potential viewers. Furthermore, the public television market is growing and gaining increasing numbers of viewers from population segments heretofore unreached.[23] Since public television already functions as a communications, information, and educational medium, it seemed logical to develop within its purview a center that would administrate, evaluate, and coordinate an environmental education program to be taken to a broad national constituency through local stations. It would create educational programs both for schools and for the general public

> by using the power of public broadcasting to make available to the general public and to education institutions in particular a comprehensive educational program. Such a program could be a tool for educational institutions to influence the collective outlook of all people, with special emphasis on children, on their lifestyles, their surroundings, their responsibilities, their hopes and their possibilities as mankind, in and of environmental/ecological networks of mutual dependency.[24]

Used in this way, public broadcasting would have the potential to create community forums on environmental issues. It could become a two-way communication medium, through the use of group discussion, telephone tie-ins, panels, town meetings, and the like, which would enable local citizens to respond directly to program content. It could engender a whole new concept of community education and involvement. Some local stations have already experimented with this type of programming; PBEC would add a

[22] Corporation for Public Broadcasting, *Public Broadcasting Environment Center*, Final Report (Washington, D.C.: U.S. Department of Health, Education, and Welfare, Office of Education, November 30, 1970), p. 5.

[23] *Ibid.*, pp. 63–64.

[24] *Ibid.*, pp. 107–108.

central focus to such efforts by coordinating local projects, identifying national trends, and evaluating results on a nationwide scale.

For far too long, television's potential to inform and involve has been eclipsed by the bulk of mediocre and even harmful programs. In the early 1960s, Senator Thomas J. Dodd's Subcommittee to Investigate Juvenile Delinquency concluded that programs of crime and violence stimulate aggressive reactions in normal children. But through the decade such programs continued to proliferate. In 1969, the National Commission on the Causes and Prevention of Violence concluded that television programs desensitize children to violence by giving them the impression that it is an everyday fact of life. Senator John O. Pastore's Subcommittee on Communications came to similar conclusions. Even programs not steeped in violence can be harmful. The White House Conference forum on child development and mass media noted that television programming in general

> tends to perpetuate a certain narrow and distorted version of human behavior. This version is based on a theoretical group of idealized human beings who appear to be able to cope easily with the hazards of human existence and even to transcend common difficulties. When this group of idealized human beings is accepted as standard, the myth of ideal human behavior is then perceived as normality. The corollary myth is that each member of society has an ideal to attain; failure to reach it implies abnormality and causes various degrees of uncertainty, fear, frustration, and feelings of inadequacy.[25]

By bringing distorted views of the environment, by encouraging aggression, by diminishing feelings of self-worth, television contributes to the degradation of the environment. But television has amply proved its ability to produce positive results. Documented evidence has come from tests on viewers of *Sesame Street,* a children's program that set out to prove that television can teach the preschool child, regardless of his background, and that children are sophisticated viewers who can be attentive longer and learn more at an earlier age than was previously supposed. Evaluation by the Educational Testing Service showed that *Sesame Street* effectively taught all groups who watched, that children who watched most gained most, and that disadvantaged children who watched regularly gained more than middle class children who watched infrequently.[26]

Television can enrich the lives of children and adults. It can educate, excite, and enlighten. It can foster environmental awareness and encourage active participation in confronting the issues of the times. Public television has taken the lead, and where it has achieved success, commercial television has followed. After *Sesame Street* proved itself, all the major commercial networks formed children's programming departments to upgrade their offerings in this area. After public television brought high-quality dramatic series to this country from the BBC, commercial networks began airing similar series. If

[25] White House Conference on Children, "Child Development and the Mass Media," Report of Forum 20, *Report to the President: White House Conference on Children* (Washington, D.C.: the Conference, 1970), p. 326.

[26] Samuel Ball and Gerry Ann Bogatz, *A Summary of the Major Findings in "The First Year of Sesame Street: An Evaluation"* (Princeton, N.J.: Educational Testing Service, October 1970).

public television takes the lead in forming a massive educational program on the environment, it could well precipitate a tremendous expansion of the environmental classroom.

Future developments in communications technology will likewise increase the capabilities of media to bring the environment to all individuals. Although most kinds of predictions are based largely on educated guesses, predictions about technological advances are based on groundwork already laid and the direction and scope of present efforts. Such predictions are therefore relatively accurate, and the margin of error exists not in the answer to *whether* but in the answer to *when*.

The home television set, for example, may soon expand its communication "mobility" through videotape recorders which allow the viewer to record a program and play it back on his set at a convenient time. The logical outgrowth of this convenience will be cassettes or cartridges of programs available for purchase, similar to today's records and audio tapes, enabling the viewer to see programs that may not have enough mass appeal for regular network broadcasts. Cable television, which uses wires rather than the already overloaded airwaves, can also expand viewing potential by sending out programs of limited appeal on otherwise empty channels. Laser holography may add three-dimensional pictures to television's capabilities. Enlarge the screen to allow pictures to come through in life size, add stereophonic sound, and almost complete realism comes to the home viewer. Then bounce the signal off an orbiting communications satellite, and you have instant, live, color, realistic broadcasting between any two points on the globe.

The versatility of the television receiver may also allow a viewer to select the kind of picture he wants. Watching a football game, for example, he may be able to press a button and receive his picture from the camera angle he specifies. Or he might wish to see detailed segments of a work of art. Or he may be able to request amplification of a story on a news broadcast, pressing a button to receive a fuller account tailored to his special interests. Furthermore, the viewer may also be able to receive selected high-resolution print-outs of television pictures, which in turn suggests an electronic newspaper —broadcasting the newspaper page by page, while the viewer selects print-outs of those pages he wishes to retain for deeper perusal.

Picturephone and Touch-Tone telephones form the basis for some equally remarkable predictions about telephone communication. As the Picturephone is perfected, it will allow business meetings to be held among persons many miles apart. They will be able to see not only each other but visual material pertinent to the conference as well. A related application would be to hold small classes over a Picturephone system. Any material presented in a classroom that requires only sight and sound for full understanding could be presented in this manner with equal effectiveness. Touch-Tone dialing already provides the advantage of speed in placing a call. In the future, with the use of portable telephones, it will enable the user to lock his front door or turn off his oven while away from home, dictate to an office machine, pay bills through a bank computer, and purchase goods—all by pushing coded sets of numbers on the Touch-Tone panel.

When a Touch-Tone telephone is linked to a computer, which then transmits information on the Picturephone screen, the whole process of information retrieval takes on almost unbelievable dimensions. Microform—or high-reduction photography—has already eased the burden of storing the huge amounts of information published annually.

Advances in this field are still forthcoming: supermicrofiche has recently been perfected, enabling the information of six books to be stored on one three-by-five card. It is the computer, however, that is necessary to retrieve the information in a minimum of time. The near future will see computers that can carry on a dialogue with a person looking for information, research the sources of the information, translate it if necessary, then display the information (either in full or in abstract form) on a screen or print it out or even transmit it to a home information center—all within split seconds. The information will be stored in data banks linked by data grids, so that virtually any information would be obtainable by a call to a single source.

The Global Village

These very real possibilities of communications technology lend strong credence to the global village concept. Consider the following scenario, constructed by Hal Hellman:

After dinner, Andrew Mann settled down into his favorite armchair and touched the "Program" button on the control box. The lovely fishing scene his wife had chosen that morning to decorate the picture wall faded and a complete listing of the evening's programs flashed on. Seeing that there was nothing of interest at the moment, he decided to watch a video tape of that old master, Arturo Toscanini, conducting Beethoven's Ninth Symphony. . . . Andrew set the electronic echo characteristics for "Music" and settled back to enjoy the performance.

Just then his son Jimmy came in and said, "Aw, Dad, I wanted to watch the Smithsons."

"First of all," Andrew said sternly, "you can watch them on one of the small sets upstairs. But more important, it seems to me you have homework to do. I'll tape the program for you and you can watch it later. Will you need the computer hookup for your homework?"

"No, not tonight," Jimmy said sadly as he went up to his room.

Again Andrew settled back; but a moment later the buzzer on the InstaMail printer indicated an incoming message. As he pushed the "Stop" button on the control box he thought irritably, "Will these interruptions ever stop?"

But his mood changed as he tore the sheet off the printer. [It was a letter to his daughter announcing her acceptance to the University of Tokyo to study Japanese and requesting a call for confirmation.]

Andrew walked quickly into the kitchen to tell his wife the good news. "Fran, Janis' application has been accepted."

"That's nice. She said to call her right away if the message came in."

"Where is she?"

"At the basketball game in the high school."

Andrew went back to the communications center in the living room and touched the "Call" button. A moment later a voice, just audible over the sounds of the crowd, answered, "This is Janis."

"Janis. Dad. We just heard from Tokyo. You've been accepted."

"Oh, that's marvelous. Thanks."

"How's the game going?"

"It's awful. We're losing, 52–42."

"Too bad. See you when you get home."

Andrew then turned his symphony back to the beginning and settled down with a sigh into his favorite armchair.

The next evening the family assembled at the communications console. Janis sat at the picturephone and placed the call to Mr. Sushiu. . . . Then she pressed the CompuTrans button and said "English/Japanese."

The signal light flashed on, indicating the computer had heard, and immediately there appeared on the screen, "CompuTrans English/Japanese Computer Translation Program. Extra cost: seventy-five cents for each five minutes or fraction thereof. Please speak as distinctly as possible."

Andrew also pushed the "Printed Record" button. "This way you won't have to take any notes. And," he added, "you'll have a record of the conversation in both languages to study if you wish."

Mr. Sushiu came on and began speaking in Japanese. A moment later the English translation began to appear under his image, like English subtitles on a foreign film.

After all arrangements were made, and good-byes were said, the image faded. Janis, of course, was bubbling with excitement. Mrs. Mann, though smiling bravely, was obviously wondering how wise it was to send a fifteen-year-old girl off to Japan by herself.

Andrew looked at his wife for a moment, then said, "You know, I've been thinking; why don't we fly over a few weeks early and see a little of the country first? I've got some vacation time coming to me."

Mrs. Mann nodded, "That would be lovely."

"Me too?" piped Jimmy.

"Of course," said Andrew. "Incidentally, does anyone happen to have a road map of the country?"

All shook their heads.

"Well, no problem." He tapped out the number for Information Central and asked for a road map of Japan. Thirty seconds later it began to appear on the printer, in color.

They spent a good part of that evening and the next morning planning out their route, making travel reservations, and so on.

By afternoon of the second day, Jimmy began to get restless. "Dad, you promised to take me fishing today, and it's getting late."

"Right you are, Jimmy; I guess we can finish this tonight."

Mrs. Mann said, "Before you go, Andrew, there's something I want to ask you. Bergdorf Goodman in New York is showing its new spring line; I've seen two things I like very much and I can't decide between them."

She walked over to the communication console and spoke a series of numbers. Two dresses, a red and a blue, appeared. "Which of these do you prefer?" she asked.

"I'm not sure. Let's see how they look on you."

Mrs. Mann stepped into the image of one and then the other.

"I like the blue," said Andrew. "Let's go, Jimmy."

A few weeks later the big day had arrived. As the Manns were driving toward the Long Distance Terminal, Mrs. Mann wondered aloud, "Did we remember to lock the front door?"

Andrew tapped out the proper combination on the car telephone pad and listened for a moment.

Hearing a low-toned buzz, he answered confidently, "Yes, we did." [27]

When this projection becomes reality, the individual will in effect have the world at his fingertips. Man's environment and virtually all that it comprises will come to the individual at his call.

The most obvious implication of this prediction is that the whole world will be a school, and the school building as such will no longer be the essential learning facility. Although some place for congregating students will be necessary, a place for interaction and group activity where learners can experience the self-development that can come only from real human contact, learning will be able to take place anywhere.

> Whether at home or elsewhere, each student, of whatever age, will have at the touch of a button access to a comprehensive "learning package," including printed lessons, experiments to be performed, recorded information, videotaped lectures, and films. . . . Learning need not take place in a box, from nine to three each day, five days a week, 180 days per year. . . . The biggest block to the kind of learning future we are endeavoring to describe is not its availability. It is our individual difficulty in seeking to shake ourselves loose from the vice-like [sic] grip of our present stereotyped thinking. Let us begin simply, with the young man who wrote, "All the world is a school and you don't need permission slips to get out into the halls and everybody should exchange classrooms and, Hey! what about the lawns . . . ?" [28]

The implication expands to include many other human activities in addition to learning. Cities—the focal point of the world's environmental crisis—grew because people needed to be close to the centers of commerce, manufacture, culture, and all the other aspects of economic and social life that human beings could most efficiently provide only where persons congregated in large numbers. The automobile, enabling persons to come and go at will, produced a situation where workers could move out from cities to a limited extent and commute to their places of work. But still, the great proportion of mankind lives in urban-suburban clusters that are eroding the life-sustaining elements of the earth. Isaac Asimov writes of three revolutions in communication—speech, writing, printing—and then asserts that the fourth—instantaneous global communication through technology—could produce a vital solution to the environmental crisis:

[27] Hal Hellman, *Communications in the World of the Future* (New York: M. Evans and Co., 1969), pp. 3–6.
[28] White House Conference on Children, "The Future of Learning," pp. 79, 83–84.

With every man possessing his own television outlet, men can both hear and see each other at global distances. . . . No one would need to be at any particular spot to control affairs, and businessmen need not congregate in offices. Nor, with the advance of automation, need workingmen congregate in factories. Men can locate themselves at will and shift that location only when they wish to travel for fun. Which means that cities will spread out and disappear. They won't even have to exist for cultural reasons in a day when a play acted anywhere can be reproduced electronically at any point on Earth—and a symphony, and an important news event, and any book in a library. . . . The benefits will be enormous. The greatest problems of the third revolution arise, after all, from the fact of overconcentration, which many times multiplies the impact of overpopulation. It is the great cities that are the chief source of pollution and the chief deprivers of dignity. Let the same billions be spread out, and the condition will already be not so acute.[29]

Robert Theobald makes a similar prediction, based on the premise that communication may be the only answer to a livable planet:

Those who believe in continued progress argue that we must make room for the development of huge, homogeneous megalopoli whose presumed physical ugliness can only be matched by their hideous suggested names: Boswash, Chidet, etc. Those who disagree argue that we must anticipate large numbers of unique small communities linked by communication rather than transportation. Those who perceive life as a "spiral staircase" state that it is only if the total society learns to organize itself around communication rather than transportation that survival in small communities will be possible.[30]

The day must come when mankind will use the earth's resources more evenly, when humans will stop crowding together, when people will communicate—rather than commute—to work.

Once again, advanced technology will serve to individualize. Communications will become more "mass," in that it will reach more people. With the expansion of voice and picture channels, any person will be able to speak with any other person anywhere in the world. The individual will be able to direct computers to prepare printed and visual material custom-tailored to his interests. Teachers will direct computers to prepare learning packages suited to each individual.

The Earth for the first time will be knit together on a personal and not a governmental level. There will be the kind of immediacy possible over all the world as had hitherto existed only at the level of the village. In fact, we will have what has been called the global village. . . . There are no boundaries in a global village. All problems will become so intimate as to become one's own. No problem can arise at one point without affecting all points immediately and emotionally, and world government will become a fact even if no one, due to past prejudices, particularly wants it, and perhaps even if no one is particularly aware that it is taking place.[31]

[29] Isaac Asimov, "The Fourth Revolution," *Saturday Review,* 3 (October 24, 1970), 17–20. Copyright 1970 by Saturday Review, Inc.

[30] Robert Theobald, *An Alternative Future for America II* (Chicago: Swallow Press, 1970), p. 65. © 1968, 1970. Reprinted by permission of The Swallow Press, Inc., Chicago.

[31] Asimov, "The Fourth Revolution."

The inevitability of the global village is the most compelling reason for starting to move education into the environmental classroom right now. The young people of today who are getting their education in boxes within boxes are going to be living in the global village of tomorrow. They must be able to cope with change and with differences and to select on a rational basis from available choices—choices that do not even exist today. They must learn how to process information so that they will be able to deal with the enormous amounts of it that will be so readily available to them.

In a study contracted by the U.S. Office of Education, Becker and Anderson concluded that children need this kind of learning as well as learning based on the following consideration:

> If it is true that the world is becoming more and more a single unit, then it is equally true that a person will fill many roles, some related to local institutions, some to nations, and some to mankind in general. The issue is not loyalty to one or another but recognition of the various roles, some of which transcend national boundaries. . . . What is needed seems to be greater recognition that one can be loyal to many different groups at the same time.[32]

The less communication is available, the more people are isolated in their communities and their nations. Fragmentation is the result in lifestyles, ideas, customs, and culture. When everyone is linked by a communications network, the lifestyles and ideas and customs and cultures will clash with one another—unless some effort is made toward understanding and cooperation. When the technology of communications breaks down all the remaining physical barriers separate peoples have always hidden behind, there will have to be a way of breaking down psychological barriers as well so that true communication can take place.

Becker and Anderson cite a number of efforts at structuring learning from a global village approach. One is *Man: A Course of Study,* developed by Jerome Bruner and his associates at the Education Development Center in Massachusetts. A social studies course for elementary pupils, drawn largely from anthropology, it asks such questions as: "What is man? What makes him human? How is he distinguished from other forms of life? from other animals?"

The kind of learning that takes place in the environmental classroom relates man to all of his environment. It breaks down artificial barriers that separate men into enclaves, in response to the fact that man's environment and its problems no longer respect artificial barriers. It transports the learner to all of man's environment and brings all of man's environment to the learner. It sees all the world as a school, all of life as a learning process, and all the environment as part of the environmental classroom.

[32] James M. Becker and Lee F. Anderson, "Riders on the Earth Together," *American Education,* 5 (May 1969), 2–5.

chapter four

designing interactive man/ environment learning

We confront two crises—environmental and educational. Although man's technology has brought him from the horse and buggy to the space vehicle within the span of this century, his environmental habits and his educational theories and methods still stumble along at the pace of the buggy.

We search for solutions. Improving the environment and improving education lead us toward similar goals—improving the quality of life. During the past forty years, environmental and social deterioration have gone hand in hand in America. Whether a causal relation actually exists, the compelling fact remains that environmental systems impose limits on the prospects for quality lives of whole populations.

The need for the development of an interactive man/environment learning system has never been more pressing than it is today. To conceive of man's environment in its broadest sense (and in its dictionary definition) as "the aggregate of surrounding things, conditions, or influences, especially as affecting the existence or development of someone or something" and to conceive of education as being relevant only when it deals with man's environment in a useful and positive way leads to the conclusion that environmental education can be the answer to improving the quality of life. So conceived, environmental education becomes a change agent, a catalyst to bring about a complete restructuring and reform of the educational system that exists today.

Piecemeal approaches to environmental problems do not work. Patching up one element of an integrated system leads only to further breakdown in the other elements. Piecemeal approaches to educational reform do not work. Adding new courses and renaming old ones produce an overstuffed curriculum containing more of the same approaches that caused the critical conditions in the first place. Spending more money on the same old approaches only produces more costly failures.

There are encouraging examples of truly innovative approaches to restructuring education to deal with the problems of contemporary society, but there are too few of them. The growing number of schools dedicated to the use of nonformal, out-of-class experiences as the core of the learning process indicates that educators are beginning to recognize the potential of these heretofore ignored sources of learning. They seek, in these preliminary attempts, to produce alternatives that capitalize on all experiences relevant to the learner's world. The World of Inquiry School in Rochester, New York; the

Urban School in San Francisco and Project Gold Mind in Woodland, California; Metro in Chicago; and the Parkway School in Philadelphia are schools that use the entire community as a legitimate learning resource. They attempt to narrow the disparity learners perceive between school and the real world. Perhaps the greatest contribution these pioneer efforts are making is in showing that revolutionary approaches to education are, in fact, not beyond the realm of possibility.

When questioned individually, most educators will state a sincere desire to break out of the box of tradition. Many inspired and capable teachers will also provide examples from a repertoire of horror stories illustrating frustration of and outright opposition to efforts to bring about significant change. For the most part, "change" occurs haphazardly and in limited areas. The curriculum reform movement that bloomed and burgeoned so healthily in the 1960s concentrated on improving science and mathematics and social studies but not on improving education.

Today, when a school board reviews its budgetary priorities, it continues to ask, "Do we want to improve students' reading abilities? Do we want more intensive mathematics education? Do we want broader science offerings?" Parent associations, teacher organizations, and community groups respond to the board, "Our children do not get enough physical education. We need smaller classes. There is not enough emphasis on spelling. The amount of money spent on language equipment is the lowest of all school systems in the area." Hardly anyone starts at the beginning by inquiring, "What is the purpose of education, what kinds of human beings should education produce, and what do we need to do in order to accomplish the task?"

The separate disciplines that contribute to the curriculum constitute the educational *program*. The philosophy of the educational system must be defined in terms of *goals*. It makes no sense to pick apart the program without reference to goals. Re-examination of goals may prompt one to say, "We want persons to be lifelong learners. Since it is impossible to learn on one's own without sophisticated reading abilities, we should strengthen the reading program." The manner in which reading would be strengthened would also have to relate to goals, which would be the basis for identifying content, methods, and proposed outcomes of the reading program. Re-examination of goals might also prompt one to say, "We want learners to be able to cope with real problems in the real world, so we ought to begin to emphasize experience-oriented, multidisciplinary, problem-solving approaches to learning rather than stress the subjects as separate entities."

This kind of educational program planning, relating as it does to broad purposes rather than to narrow curriculums, is likely to lead to the institutional reform that must undergird any efforts at meaningful change in education. Neither teachers nor administrators nor school boards nor students nor interested community members can effect the change alone—but all must contribute to it, whether actively or merely by opening their minds and saying, "It's worth a try." Just as a living organism requires a harmonious environment in order to survive, so does the broad concept of environmental education require an institutional structure supportive of its unique requirements and its impetus toward change. Mario Fantini states that "institutional reform is the key to improved education for all. Relevance will be achieved when the reformed institution actually serves the needs of its clients." [1]

The need for institutional reform in education has been documented in Chapter 1. Why has the reform been so long in getting under way? Partly because reform proposals are often rejected out of hand with the idea that such things simply cannot be done. We cling desperately to horse-and-buggy myths about education at the same time that we are trying to educate young people for the global village. Some of these myths were identified by the forum on myths of education of the 1970 White House Conference on Children:

1. *Children have to go to school to learn.* Our worshipful attitude toward formal schooling reveals a resistance to exploring alternatives which maximize learning outside the classroom.

2. *Teachers know and children don't.* The educational consequence of this myth is teacher-oriented rather than student-oriented schools.

3. *Schools prepare children for the future.* Our children are sent forth with little preparation for improving the skills they do possess; they are even less able to modify their previous learning to accommodate the difficult but inevitable changes of a society in technological, social, and spiritual explosion. We must educate for adaptability in an ambiguous future, rather than merely train the memory to recall past "certainties."

4. *Schools teach the truth.* The sins are primarily those of omission rather than commission, and the perpetration of misleading partial truths. We do not honor the intelligence of children when we insist upon focusing children's attention almost exclusively on those external, predetermined, and easily manageable bits of information which teachers and school administrators find convenient to evaluate.

5. *All children should be treated alike.* Human differences are viewed as obstructions to efficient classroom operation to be administratively eliminated. Children should not be considered raw material to be "improved" by teachers into a socially viable finished product.

6. *Competition in class is good and grading is good.* Competition for grades has become a zero-sum game in which the possibility of winners requires the existence of losers.

7. *Schools can only be changed slowly.* In addition to providing a perspective for accurate evaluation of both the innovations and the old system, radical change may enable an idea to be tested where the present educational structure foredooms single reforms.

8. *You shouldn't experiment with children's schooling.* The risks of maintaining the status quo are now as great, or greater, than the risks of exploring educational alternatives.

9. *You can't change education because "they" won't let you.* As Walt Kelly's Pogo said so well, "We have met the enemy and they is us."

10. *You can't change education without more money.* Clearly, changes in the educational structure which do not require additional resources are more favorably received and are more likely to be continued. The easiest way to avoid major recurrent costs is through the reallocation of resources.

---

[1] Mario D. Fantini, *The Reform of Urban Schools*, Schools for the 70's, Preliminary Series (Washington, D.C.: National Education Association, Center for the Study of Instruction, 1970), p. 40.

11. *Local school boards control education.* Studies both in* large cities and the suburbs indicate that school board members have neither the information nor the facility, much less the authority, to control policy. Policy decision rests largely with school professionals.[2]

Reform of educational structure is not only possible, it is imperative. The irresistible force of an alarmingly complex, deteriorating, yet dynamic environment is about to meet the immovable object of educational perversity, and as the song goes, something's gotta give. The result could be chaos and destruction or it could be a powerful thrust in positive directions, depending on how we react and how well prepared we are to turn crises into constructive catalysts.

To paraphrase the old definition of outdoor education, environmental education may be viewed most simply as education in and for the environment. *For* implies that all education is directed toward improving the quality of life—that is, enabling the individual to strive to become all that he can be and developing a commitment in every learner to enhancing all of man's environment for all mankind. *In* implies that education takes place in the environmental classroom, that the learner uses all educational resources in and out of the school facility as learning experiences. Based on goals oriented to the future rather than the past and developed according to these goals in such a way that the learning environment is designed to encourage the attainment of the goals, the learning environment becomes all the environment, and the kind of learning that takes place makes free and integrated use of the environment. What actually takes place in the environmental classroom might most appropriately be termed *environmental learning.*

Environmental education viewed in this way is not just another curricular innovation but a whole new philosophy for educational change. It carries with it directions for educational reform that are entirely consistent with the best we know about educational theory, environmental design, and operational strategy.

Principles of Educational Theory

Fantini states that reform must take place in governance, shifting educational decision making from bureaucracies to parents, teachers, community residents, and students; in substance, emphasizing individual and group problems in a humanistically oriented curriculum; and in personnel, involving a broader base of talent for facilitating learning than the conventionally prepared career educator. The public then becomes a partner with the professionals in policy decisions, parent organizations participate as active agents in substantive educational matters, authority becomes decentralized and flexible, educational objectives are derived from a humanistic orientation, curriculum relevance is determined by the needs of the learner, professional proficiency becomes a function of

[2] Adapted from the White House Conference on Children, "Confronting the Myths of Education," Report of Forum 8, *Report to the President. White House Conference on Children.* (Washington, D.C.: the Conference, 1970), pp. 123–32.

effective performance with learners, the institution becomes accountable to the learner and to the community (failure is failure of the system rather than of the learner), and the basic learning unit ceases to be the classroom but becomes instead the entire community and its resources.[3]

Oran Smith points to similar directions in comparing a laboratory model with traditional schools: the learner becomes involved in all decision-making processes relating to education, the traditional learner and teacher roles dissolve and are replaced by functions of interaction suited to particular learning situations, learners identify problems and resources with the aid (but not control) of teachers, learners identify problem-solving techniques and standards for solutions, learners work with both the abstract and the concrete, the individual seeks to know himself rather than compete against external measurements, and learning becomes a self-directed process of increasing understanding and participation through self-motivation.[4]

William B. Stapp, professor of resource planning and conservation at the University of Michigan, reviewed the literature on learning theories to select those that apply to environmental education. He selected the following principles as most relevant to environmental education concepts:

- Behaviors that are reinforced are most likely to recur. It is important that desired behaviors be reinforced by the home, school, church, youth organizations, etc.

- The most effective effort is put forth by youth when they try tasks that fall in the "range of challenge"—not too easy and not too hard—where success seems likely but not certain.

- Youth are more likely to throw themselves wholeheartedly into any project if they themselves have a meaningful role in the selection and planning of the enterprise.

- Reaction to excessive direction by the teacher is likely to be apathetic conformity, defiance, or escape from the whole affair.

- What is learned is most likely to be available for use if it is learned in a situation much like that in which it is to be used and immediately preceding the time when it is needed. Learning in youth, then forgetting, and then relearning when need arises is not an efficient procedure.

- The learning process in school ought to involve dynamic methods of inquiry.

- Research shows little correlation between cognitive achievement and concern and values. Able students who achieve well in traditional "content-centered courses" do not necessarily demonstrate commitment to positive social goals.

- Learning takes place through the active behavior of the student. It is what he does that he learns, not what the teacher does. The essential means of an education are the experiences provided, not the things to which the student is merely exposed.

- One of the keys to motivation is a sense of excitement about discovering for oneself, as opposed to having a generalization presented by a teacher and requiring a student to prove it.

[3] Fantini, *The Reform of Urban Schools*, pp. 39–40.
[4] Oran Smith, "Comparison of Two Educational Frameworks." (Informal unpublished paper.)

- Attitudes may not be formed through a rational process by which facts are gathered and a reasonable conclusion drawn, but rather through repeated exposure to ideas.

- Helping citizens to acquire technical knowledge alone regarding an environmental problem may not increase their concern for the problem.

- Citizens are more likely to become involved in environmental issues if they are aware of how they can have some effect upon decision making.[5]

Stapp concludes that environmental learning occurs best in a curriculum structure based on problem identification and solution, drawn around "encounters" (experiences) that focus the attention of the learner on the environment and link all relevant economic, social, technological, and political information.

Environmental education demands restructuring of both the learning environment and the curriculum. To do one and not the other would eventually involve fitting a square peg into a round hole. Put another way, the learning environment represents the playing field; curriculum is the game plan to be implemented upon it. It makes no sense to attempt basketball on a football field. If we expand the learning environment as discussed in Chapters 2 and 3, we shall have to devise curriculums suitable to the new learning environment. A number of curriculum projects geared to environmental education have also been discussed here. Most focus on narrow areas, and only a few consider "environment" as more than the natural environment. As far as they go, however, those that are better are those that break away from traditional discipline-oriented approaches and adhere to the principles and concepts underlying the broad idea of the environmental classroom.

A number of such principles and concepts have been posited throughout this book. Environmental education is seen as a whole new approach to learning—not a renaming of old conservations or outdoor programs, not a narrow focus on pollution or natural resources depletion, but a broad idea that includes all of man's environment and that insists that all relevant learning deals in some way with man's environment. It demands that learners have access to all of man's environment, both by going to it and by bringing it to the learning facility. The learning facility itself encourages freedom, movement, access to information, a variety of learning activities, and a variety of kinds of human interaction. Its form is a direct result of its function. It is a place in which to analyze, to synthesize, and to share real experiences. It is available to the entire community all day, all week, and all year and functions as the central locus of essential community activities. Where traditional education suffers from resource myopia, environmental learning opens out to gather in all resources that facilitate learning.

Environmental learning is an experience-oriented, investigative, problem-solving concept that seeks and nurtures diversity in learners. It deals with development of sensory perception, with problem identification, with attitudes and feelings and commitments,

5 William B. Stapp, "Environmental Education—Opportunities, Encounters and Experiences with Natural, Physical, and Social Environments," from a paper presented at the National Consultation on Environmental Education Areas and Faculties, Belmont Center, Maryland, June 1970.

with self-awareness and growth toward self-potential. It fosters joy and involvement in learning. It rejects a Skinner-box concept of controlled environment and embraces, instead, the idea that learners will strive for self-actualization if given the opportunity and the trust. It sees the teacher as anyone who facilitates learning and the learner as central to the process. It seeks to develop individuals with the self-confidence to identify and solve problems on their own and the larger societal environment through an open-ended, multidisciplinary, concept-based orientation. It results in generalized knowledge accompanied by those specialized skills that enable a human being to be a productive and happy member of society. It seeks lifelong learners who can process, not parrot, information and use it to improve the quality of life.

Principles of Environmental Design

Principles derived from the best elements of current educational theory provide a logical baseline for a restructured learning environment. They indicate directions for changing primarily the program—or curriculum—aspect of the educational system. They point to new methods of instruction developed with an eye toward enhancing the potential of the individual. They lead away from the educational box, the prison surrogate, the fact-trough, the passivity inducer and toward a humanistic environment in which humane means are employed to reach humane ends.

But the instructional environment will not easily be changed unless the physical environment of learning is changed at the same time. Guidelines directing the course of this second dimension of educational reform toward a truly interactive man/environment learning system can be derived from the best and most appropriate elements of current theories of environmental design.

The environmental design field today encompasses a broad range of professions, including architecture, city planning, research psychology, and engineering, as well as many more that relate—if only tangentially—to improving man's surroundings. Current recognition of the importance of the field has led to increasing research and experimentation to determine optimal environmental designs for a variety of purposes. The resulting body of literature has become a prime source of environmental design theories from which we can select those that relate to the learning environment.

In general, the literature reveals that environmental design lends itself to evaluation in terms of its compatibility with human goals, that conclusions drawn about the relation of design to goals can be stated as principles, that design objectives are an integral aspect of culture, that changes in environmental design require acceptance by large numbers of persons in a given culture, and that to gain such acceptance design objectives must involve individuals through the promise of achievement of personal goals. Environmental education thus cannot wait for the changes in environmental design that are essential to its success. It must begin before the changes occur to create awareness and acceptance of the necessary changes at the same time that it points to the urgent need for such changes.

The present emphasis on quality of life and hence on quality of environment presents a great challenge to those who are to design the prototypes for the man/environment learning systems of the future, for they must derive models that educational institutions will use for a long time to come. These models may be constructed from a new vision, or they may be pieced together from the relics of past systems. The chief danger lies in constructing them on less than a total cultural systems concept and with little or no relation to real alternative futures in the American social system. It is crucial that they be designed on the basis of existing needs and emerging future needs, with the flexibility to adapt to unknown but possible future conditions.

Man's behavior is a product of man and environment interacting. Man and environment interacting constitute the human ecosystem. The nature of the interaction often depends as much on the nature of the environment as it does upon the personality background of the individual. If man is dissatisfied with any aspect of the ecosystem, he must have a means of evaluating that aspect so that he can correct it. When persons interact with environments they make evaluations, consciously or subconsciously, in terms of degree of familiarity, behavior linkages, adequacy of space, amenability of the environment to their control, and so on. One of the major criticisms leveled against the school is that place and activity have become so specialized as to separate related activities from one another in an artificial way. An optimal environment, on the other hand, would promote the kind of behavior that identifies a high quality of living. It would contribute to the satisfaction of all the basic needs described by Maslow, as well as to the fulfillment of the need at the pinnacle of his hierarchy—the need for self-actualization. What designers need is a conscious and all-inclusive statement of such principles as they relate to design decisions.

A comprehensive study of the literature of environmental design, covering the many fields concerned in some way with problems of the human ecosystem, was completed by Matrix Research for the Office of Naval Research in 1970.[6] The purpose of the study was to generate guidelines for designing a total living environment for personnel on a naval base. The researchers surveyed the total literature of environmental design, identified more than 1,000 bibliographic items, reviewed approximately 800, and eventually abstracted 300 as those most closely concerned with man/environment interaction. The aggregation of data about design from so many different fields is the unique contribution of the study. As such, it lends itself as an important reference tool for identifying basic principles of environmental design as they apply to just about any aspect of human activity. In this case, it enables identification of those principles applicable to design of the learning environment.

Definitions of man/environment interaction, as it applies to learning, appear on the following chart adapted from the Matrix study:

[6] Robert D. Campbell, Lawrence Schlesinger, and Betty Jane Schuchman, *Planning the Man/Environment Interaction,* final report for the Office of Naval Research, Contract No. N00014–69–C–0290, April 30, 1970.

definitions of man, environment, and interaction

man

The individual man surrounded by and interacting with his four environments is recognized as having a potentially great range of characteristics. Depending on his genetic and cultural background, his potential corresponding to various environmental stimuli is extremely varied, and thus the range of possible learning environments is almost unlimited.

Man's interactions with environment depend on his world-view and self-view, respectively—that is, his concept of what environment really is and what his role is with respect to environment. Basically, it is in terms of these concepts—which he shares with some group of "others"—that he not only perceives his ambience but of whether it will induce or support changes in behavior which are consonant with world- and self-views.

environment

Distinguishing four environments may appear to be somewhat arbitrary and a little artificial. However, the basis for distinguishing them is that each represents an aspect of the ambience which man perceives and responds to somewhat differently. One result is a compartmentation of knowledge about each of the environments by *discipline*, a compartmentation which is necessary if each is to be understood as an entity but which must somehow be shown to be structurally associated with the larger package if all compartments are to be understood as parts of a whole.

Natural environment. The natural environment consists of the physical earth and all of the forms of life it supports—except man. We refer to the natural environment in its present state, as modified by man. The land, water, atmosphere, and biota on earth's surface are constantly undergoing change, even without man. But the changes introduced by man are immediate and far reaching. Nevertheless, it is the present ambience—however exhausted, depleted, polluted, or enriched—with which present man interacts.

Human environment. The human environment consists of people— not in terms of their beliefs or learned behavioral systems, but in sheer

interaction

The four environments influence man's behavior—in the broadest possible sense of the term "behavior"—and man's behavior changes or creates the environments. In other words, there is a mutual interaction of forces, some of which are largely controlled by man and some of which are completely outside the control of man. In the sense that the changes which man is capable of making are made in the direction of increasing his control over the system, the system is man-dominated; and that is basically man's perspective.

The interactions we are concerned with, therefore, are those which either cause or reflect various kinds of learning behavior. Of course, in a system such as this everything *relates* to everything else, but not always directly. We believe that the gross relationships are graphically expressed by the arrows joining man and the various environments, each arrow representing a different direction of action–reaction and therefore a different relationship.

Briefly the categories of interactions are the following:

(1) Interactions between man and the natural environment, man and the artifact environment, and the natural and artifact environments:

demographic terms: numbers, sex, age, distribution, density per unit area of earth, rate of increase, etc. In effect, the human environment can be thought of as too many people in the ambience of a mentally disturbed person, the right density-mix of people in a neighborhood to provide optimum social contacts for all members of a given family, or as the basic ingredient of both social interaction and privacy.

Intervening artifact environment. The artifact environment consists of all the physical things man has added to the natural environment. Analogous terms are "structures," "built," "carpentered." This includes everything from bandaids to bathrooms to jet aircraft to universities to megalopolises. The rationale is that all products created by man were created for some man-purpose, and as such they become a part of his environment. The purpose behind much of the artifact environment we assume to be man's perceived need to modify what nature has supplied him, and behind *all* of it is a perceived need of man.

Intervening social environment. The social environment consists of all rules of human behavior, implicit and explicit. This includes all rule structures, such as institutions, legal codes, organizations, etc. We assume that most of these rules were created for the purpose of regulating man's interactions with all of his other environments, but in particular it is the perceived equivalence, or lack of it, of the social environments of two individual men which permits or denies the communication processes which in turn determine the limits of interpersonal interaction.

(2) Interactions between man and the human environment, man and the social environment, and between the human and social environments:

(3) Interactions mediated by man, between the artifact and social environments, and between the natural and human environments:

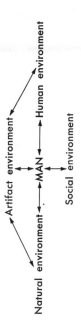

The Matrix study found that architects of suburban houses, for example, do not attempt to create functional living environments that support the normal activities of a family; rather, they attempt to create eye-catching structures that suggest an image of status and success—and that sell. The same holds true for schools. They are not designed for optimizing learning but to fit the public stereotype of educational places and spaces.

Designing the learning environment as an open system has many ramifications. The open school environment produces decisive influences on human behavior through such architectural elements as carpeting, modular construction, movable furniture, and other flexible features allowing freedom of movement to interactive as well as solitary activities.

Clearly defined educational goals free the architect from the myriad of structural and mechanical problems long enough for him to concentrate on improving learning design. Furthermore, the overriding concept of this book—that learning takes place everywhere—demands accessibility to places and spaces in the home, neighborhood, city, and global village—the totality of the biophysical and man-made environment, which constitutes the environmental classroom.

The Matrix researchers developed a model for extracting environmental design principles and guidelines from the literature. They found that reports of investigations of some aspect of the man/environment relationship tended to have the following common features:

1. They specify the nature of the environment (school, hospital, isolation, etc.) and the nature of man (aged, ill, students, etc.);

2. They make explicit statements about the interaction (how students choose seats in libraries, which seating locations in the classroom seem to be associated with greatest student participation, etc.);

3. They tend to draw some conclusions about the nature of the interaction as it relates to the environment, and this can be interpreted in most instances as an evaluation of the *quality* of the interaction as it relates to environmental design (arrange seating so that all students participate equally: in design terms, that is the *problem* for which a design *solution* is sought);

4. There are many bases for evaluating the interaction, and these are stated either explicitly or implicitly as design objectives (increase student participation in learning activities) which contribute to more abstract goals (improve the learning environment for all students);

5. Very often suggestions are made for changing the environmental design to improve the quality of the interaction.[7]

From each study reviewed, the Matrix researchers extracted each of the above points, as illustrated in the following example of a study reported in *Progressive Architecture* (August 1966): ——▶

To use this model to analyze data for the purpose of improving the learning environment, however, we need to emphasize the goals. After viewing the environment, the

[7] Matrix Research, Design of an Interactive Man/Environment, pp. 112–13.

model #1

man	environment	interaction	task or job performance activity (activities)	guidelines or suggestions to meet objectives	objectives	goals
Architectural students.	Classroom building, office space.	Architectural students work at private office space in classroom building.	Components necessary for good working conditions are private work areas, storage space, lighting, and areas for display and teaching.	Movable walls to use for private partitions. Lamps on overhead tracks. Display space on walls of unit. Storage space within each unit.	To provide for privacy and flexibility within a given space.	To facilitate learning and teaching.

humans within it, the interaction between the two, and the activities taking place, then, we should establish broad goals and specific objectives that *lead to* the guidelines for change. In other words, guidelines should evolve from goals, rather than the converse. Adapted to the learning environment, the model thus shifts its order to the following. So reordered, the model allows us to understand the learning goals and objectives that support human growth and development, the link between human activity and achievement of learning goals and objectives, and the link between activity and environmental design. We can then evaluate activities in terms of learning goals and objectives, the extent to which they contribute to those goals, and the effect of the environment on the quality of the activities.

The following table presents, in the form of the adapted model, the data from those studies abstracted by the Matrix researchers that are most relevant to the learning environment.

This model, based on a small sample of available studies, shows that data from research on many types of learning environments and learning situations can be used to formulate design concepts and principles. It also shows that studies of environments not immediately related to schools as such produce data that relate to the learning environment, especially if the learning environment is perceived as the environmental classroom, the total environment. It could be a useful format for all designers of future learning environments, enabling them to gather relevant data and analyze it according to the general goals and specific objectives their designs must achieve. The format helps clarify the goals and objectives, permits establishment of priorities, and provides a basis for evaluation of environmental design.

The goals, objectives, and priorities can help keep the design process going in the right direction, for they offer guidelines as to the kinds of environments most conducive to certain activities. Evaluation determines whether the environment actually does promote the desired activity; for example, whether a particular design encourages the kind of interpersonal relationships that facilitate learning.

The simplicity of the overall model ought to allow designers to communicate with educators, parents, students, and the interested community about possible future designs. Certainly, everyone who will be involved with the final design product (the learning environment) ought to be involved in stating principles for the design—and in the environmental classroom, that means literally *everyone*. Unless the concept of a plan is widely accepted among those who are to use it, it simply is not implemented.

The Matrix study, as well as discussions of the learning environment throughout this book, reveal some general concepts related to design of the learning environment, from which goals and objectives and the guidelines that enable us to reach them can be drawn. Among the most important principles are the following: ———▶

The learner spends most of his time in a man-made environment, which is built to fulfill man's needs but which ultimately determines the quality and content of human activity. In a rapidly changing society, human needs may change rapidly. Adaptation to an impoverished or deteriorated environment may have short range advantages, but long-range effects may be deleterious. Humans learn best in an environment that challenges their abilities but allows for more success than failure. When an environment

model #2

man	environment	interaction	task or job performance activity (activities)	goals	objectives	guidelines or suggestions to meet objectives
Architectural students.	Classroom building, office space.	Architectural students work at private office space in classroom building.	Components necessary for good working conditions are private work areas, storage space, lighting, and areas for display and teaching.	To facilitate learning and teaching.	To provide for privacy and flexibility within a given space.	Movable walls to use for private partitions. Lamps on overhead tracks. Display space on walls of unit. Storage space within each unit.

man	environment	interaction	task or job performance activity (activities)	goals	objectives	guidelines or suggestions to meet objectives
Not identified other than people.	Not identified other than environment.	Man living in his environment.	As man interacts with his environment: he has needs; he searches for new and relevant information in environment; he retrieves information from his memory and uses it to select possible action; he executes the action which is appropriate; he assesses results to guide future actions.	An environment which will support "planful" behavior and facilitate man's search for meaning. (Increase the quality of life)	To provide choice. To show possibilities and opportunities; To increase aspiration level; To raise curiosity; To promote exploratory behavior.	Increase exposure of people to variety of settings and interactions. Decrease ambiguity so that elements of environment are easier to recognize. Provide alternative routes same area or point.
					To provide information for mental representation of city form.	Simplify structure of city areas and increase information aids (maps, information boards, etc.). Enhance unique qualities of environmental settings.
					To promote identification and foster attachments to a setting. To increase individual meaning of environmental value. To accommodate several activities without conflict.	Single family house with yard. Build town center as a general purpose environment.

Stephen Carr, "The City of the Mind," from *Environments for Man: The Next Fifty Years*, ed. William R. Ewald, AIP (Bloomington and London, Indiana University Press, 1966), pp. 197–231.

man	environment	interaction	task or job performance activity (activities)	goals	objectives	guidelines or suggestions to meet objectives
Not identified.	City	City as environment.	Physical deficiencies of city: Perceptual stress—symbolic and sensory.	Perceptual enrichment of the city.	Aesthetic balance.	View the city as landscape: Dramatize the characteristics of the city and reduce noxious stimulation.
			Lack of visible identity of city centers.		Identity of city centers.	Sharpen the diversity by emphasizing the unique quality of each center.
			Illegibility—parts of the city cannot be read as system of signs.		To convey information about the city.	System of paths organized to provide a visual source of information.
			Rigidity—the city is not responsive to human efforts.		To encourage more active participation in the use of space.	Provide open spaces.

Kevin Lynch, "The City as Environment," from *Cities*, a Scientific American Book (New York: Alfred Knopf, 1965), pp. 192–201.

man	environment	interaction	task or job performance activity (activities)	goals	objectives	guidelines or suggestions to meet objectives
College students.	Study facilities.	College students utilizing various study facilities.	An effective study environment was discovered to be a result of administrative rules and educational procedures; single aspects of the study environment had no impact on where the students studied.	To enhance learning.	To provide optimal study facilities to meet students' needs for quiet, privacy. A place to study alone, a place to study with date or small group, etc.	Students, faculty and administration should examine the existing rules and regulations on (their) campus and make recommendations for revision or changes when appropriate.

Robert Sommer, "The Ecology of Study Areas," Man-Environment Systems, July, 1969.

man	environment	interaction	task or job performance activity (activities)	goals	objectives	guidelines or suggestions to meet objectives
Students, Faculty, Staff.	School building; identified as the School of Art and Architecture at Yale.	As people use a building, activity patterns develop and can be observed.	The physical design of a space can provide a principal means of communication and control; examples: A coffee lounge was set up; after it was in use a while it was used by participants who no longer attended special "coffee hours" which had been established to bring together members of different departments. Exhibition hall was not used for informal social interaction; it became an important place for students to find out what was going on when it was used for all-school assemblies and when bulletin boards, tables, and chairs were installed. Space may seem unimportant —entry hall used by all students and for this reason was used to display personal and community notices. Space is used in a way not intended by the designer—students must travel through a faculty office to get to a corner classroom; communications were enhanced by this activity pattern.	Utilize space to accommodate necessary activities (to enhance learning).	To change or increase the scope of activities within a given space to accommodate changing needs and provide variety.	To bring about changes. 1. develop new activities or relocate activities; 2. by relocateable furniture, walls, or by use of short term and reusable materials, 3. modify the physical design by adding or eliminating stairs, elevator stops, halls, doors, etc.

Donald Watson, *Modeling the Activity System*, prepared for First Annual Conference EDRA, North Carolina State University, 1969.

man	environment	interaction	task or job performance activity (activities)	goals	objectives	guidelines or suggestions to meet objectives
Dental students.	Dental school.	Dental students interacting with faculty and other students at the dental school.	Students feel that learning is enhanced by interaction with faculty and other dental students.	To promote learning opportunities and professional attitudes.	To increase the possibilities for contact and interaction.	Design features most likely to facilitate this interaction: hallways either wide enough or with irregular bays for conversation groups, faculty offices near other areas of interest such as clinics, laboratory, and cafeteria.
Dental students and instructors.	Dental school clinic.	Dental students interacting with instructors in the clinic.	Instructors feel they are isolated from other groups in the school; long hours curtail any further involvement with students; students express dissatisfaction with student-faculty relationships.	To promote learning opportunities and professional attitudes.	To increase the possibilities for contact and interaction.	Design implications to solve these problems: locate basic sciences and operative clinic in proximity to one other, routes within school and to parking lot, etc., planned to maximize the number of contacts between students and faculty, eliminate student cubicle and instructor's office and provide eye contact, make work visible to others, and supervision easier.

Richard Myrick, *Planning Study: Behavioral Factors in Dental School Design*, Investigation supported by Public Health Service Grant DH-00042-01A1, Division of Dental Public Health and Resources.

man	environment	interaction	task or job performance activity (activities)	goals	objectives	guidelines or suggestions to meet objectives
College students.	Study facilities.	Students use various study facilities in preparation of college work.	Students preferred studying in small places. Students liked to study in small groups (or alone). Students disliked large library reading room.	More effective and efficient use of study facilities to enhance learning.	Privacy. Comfort. To meet individual needs of students.	Large study halls should be broken with facilities (walls, small study rooms for groups) which will both decrease noise and provide study opportunities. Rooms which can accommodate from 20 to 40 students should be planned to take care of only 15 to 20% of that number. There needs to be a variety of study spaces. (See two suggestions above.)

S. M. Stoke, R. F. Grose, et al., *Student Reactions to Study Facilities—With Implications for Architects and College Administrators,* a report to the Presidents of Amherst College, Mount Holyoke College, Smith College, and the University of Massachusetts. Committee for New College, Amherst, 1960.

man	environment	interaction	task or job performance activity (activities)	goals	objectives	guidelines or suggestions to meet objectives
College students.	Residence halls.	Students living in residence halls on the college campus.	Market research by architect of university residence halls indicated that:	Enhance learning by improving college environment.		
			Students had no strong preferences for low wide buildings over high rise buildings (residence halls).			Adequately research the other criteria which will enter into decision on building type.
			Twenty to thirty percent of a student's time was spent studying in his own room.		Comfort and convenience of student.	Provide desk, bookshelves, and study lamps in student rooms.
			Noise from typewriters was a serious problem.		To provide space for special activity and remove conflict of that activity with other activities in hall.	Include special typing room in residence hall design—sound absorbent table, walls, etc.
			Men and women students wanted different types of social and recreational spaces.		To meet students' needs and desires.	Ascertain specifically what these social and recreational spaces will be for each group and include in hall design.
					To meet need for flexibility in hall assignments.	Facilities should be of a convertible and movable nature.

Lawrence Wheeler, Behavioral Research for Architectural Planning and Design (Terre Haute, Indiana: Ewing Miller Associates, 1967).

man	environment	interaction	task or job performance activity (activities)	goals	objectives	guidelines or suggestions to meet objectives
Students, Secondary School	Library	Students using school library.	Secondary school students act in several ways to use information in the school library: take book home for study, sit down and read book there, use reference collection, take notes, go into small discussion group, ask questions of the librarian or teachers, use machines—typewriters, calculating machines, phonograph, take book to classroom or laboratory, stretch out in lounge chair or couch and read as he would at home.	To foster learning.	To provide study facilities which will be used by a variety of students for the numerous activities of a library.	Different types of study carrels for independent study: rooms for small groups, 2'x3' space for each reader at table, tables limited to 9' in length, table heights varied and intermingled, table tops with good writing surface, 5' space between tables, reading chair to use at table, occasional chair for short periods of reading, lounge chair for longer periods of reading.

Ralph E. Ellsworth and Hobart D. Wagener, The School Library, Facilities for Independent Study in the Secondary School (New York: Educational Facilities Laboratory, 1963).

man	environment	interaction	task or job performance activity (activities)	goals	objectives	guidelines or suggestions to meet objectives
School children.	Educational environment- school.	School children involved in the learning-teaching process at school.	Learning is faster in an environment with more perspectives and in an environment to which a learner can bring his own perspectives.	To enhance learning.	Facilitate learning a skill.	In teaching a child to read, other communication skills (speaking, writing, listening) are an aid. (Specific example Moore gave of children 5 years old who edit, write, type and stencil their own newspaper.)
			An environment is more conducive to learning if autotelic principle is followed—is easier to learn more difficult things if you are in environment where you can try things out, make a fool of yourself, guess, etc. . . . without serious consequences.		Safety—both psychological and physical.	Since the 5 year old children used typewriter, a special plastic shield was designed to protect the fingers from automatic return.
			A learning task is more productive if it has properties which allow the learner to make deductions after his initial exposure to it.		To offer a simpler and more productive method.	Provide a private space where children can go when they want to be alone. Use the Pitman system of 40 phonemes instead of standard alphabet.
			An environment is more conducive to learning if it responds to the learner's activities and permits the learner to make interconnected discoveries through exploration.		Permit discovery through exploration.	A talking typewriter was devised with cues and signals built into keyboard to help the child make discoveries about how to use the typewriter.

Omar K. Moore and Alan Ross Anderson, *Some Principles for the Design of Clarifying Educational Environments* (Pittsburgh: University of Pittsburgh, Learning R & D Center, Reprint No. 32).

man	environment	interaction	task or job performance activity (activities)	goals	objectives	guidelines or suggestions to meet objectives
College students.	Library study hall.	College students using library study hall.	Students engage in various behaviors relating to space in library study hall: Students maintained distance between themselves and strangers by sitting alone at table or sitting as far apart as possible. (Seat least likely to be chosen was adjacent to person seated.)	To enhance learning.	To allow more students to study in comfort.	Plan library or study hall with study tables which allow adequate room between each occupant.
			Students who arrived in pairs sat adjacent to one another.		To artificially assist in defining space.	Use markers on table to designate an area for one person.
			Conversing pairs were likely to sit side by side and to be of the same sex.		To help break space of room.	Plan room to accommodate less persons than it takes to fill it.
			In rooms with smaller tables with one person seated at them—newcomers chose a table where there was a member of the same sex.			Plan numerous individual and group study spaces.
			Physical objects such as coats, handbags, books, and personal belongings are used by the students to mark their personal space at a table.			

Robert Sommer, "Sociofugal Space," American Journal of Sociology, Vol. 72, 6 (1967), 654–60.

man	environment	interaction	task or job performance activity (activities)	goals	objectives	guidelines or suggestions to meet objectives

High school students.	Large and small high schools.	The activities of students in a large high school and a small high school.	Barker's study of the high schools in Kansas showed: The behavior settings within the schools were more similar than the number of students.
			
			Students from the small schools participated in greater proportion in festivals, dramatic, journalistic, and student government competitions.
			
			Students in the smaller schools reported more attraction, obligation, and external pressure to take part in activities. They also report more satisfaction related to:
			  development of competence the challenge offered
			  being engaged in important activities
			  being identified with their school
			  learning about the school's affairs and persons.
				To enhance learning.	To foster sense of involvement independence achievement exploration.	By providing a smaller setting we increase the individual's chances for participation and responsibility.

R. G. Barker and P. V. Gump, "Big School, Small School," *Social Psychology*, Vol. 1 (1964).

man	environment	interaction	task or job performance activity (activities)	goals	objectives	guidelines or suggestions to meet objectives
High school students.	Large and small high schools.	Students may have different experiences and different opportunities for responsibility in a small school than in a large school.	Occupants of an under-manned setting are more likely to be performers in the activity; occupants of an overmanned setting are more likely to be non-performers. Student's level of responsibility for group tasks was related to their having satisfactory experiences. The level of responsibility was important to the relationship of school size to student's experience in school activities. Experiences students have may depend on the kind of behavior setting.	To increase learning opportunities.	Participation, responsibility in group tasks.	In larger high schools (over-manned population) offer a variety and number of activity groups to meet interests and needs of the students; build in facility to change activities to satisfy changing needs and interests.

Allan H. Wicker, "Undermanning, Performances, and Students' Subjective Experiences in Behavior Settings on Large and Small High Schools," *Journal of Personality and Social Psychology*, Vol. 10, No. 4 (1968), 255–61.

man	environment	interaction	task or job performance activity (activities)	goals	objectives	guidelines or suggestions to meet objectives
People	Noise within buildings: hospitals offices schools homes	People engaged in various aspects of living, exposed to noise nuisance.	In addition to simple annoyance and dissatisfaction with noise nuisance, the quality of sleep, work, and learning, is also adversely affected by noise level.	Increased comfort and well-being.	Decrease annoyance and possible ill effects on health from noise pollution.	Consideration of the variations in individual noise tolerance when establisihng noise control limits.
	Road traffic noise					Approach all the noise pollution difficulties with an awareness of their magnitude.
	Aircraft noise					Further research into control of noise.
	Railroad noise					Attention to the problem by city planners.

J. Langdon, "Noise in and around Buildings," paper, Royal Society of Health, November 14, 1968, Research Project No. EP 5/66.

man	environment	interaction	task or job performance activity (activities)	goals	objectives	guidelines or suggestions to meet objectives
Students Teachers Administrators Parents	Nongraded elementary school.	Students, teachers, administrators, and parents using elementary school constructed for non-graded teaching.	The school environment (walls, furniture, materials) should contribute to the many activities (reading, talking, listening, meeting, observing, sitting, moving, writing, etc.) which equal the process of (enlightenment and understanding) education.	Promote the excitement of learning.	Economy and acoustics.	Floors covered with carpets.
				Support the best verbal communication.	Make a natural backrest for seating.	Carpets curve up wall in some areas.
					To define (activity) areas.	Carpet pattern; weave or textile to designate specific areas.
					Ease of maintenance.	Heavy, waterproof carpet material used in entrance ways.

man	environment	interaction	task or job performance activity (activities)	goals	objectives (continued)	guidelines or suggestions to meet objectives (continued)
					To foster self identity. To provide objective presentation of scenes (variety, widen vista).	Walls should contain: mirrors large photos of geographic areas not usually seen by children.
					To define (activity) areas To create private space.	Ceilings Should vary in height and lighting. Use awning or arbour.
					To provide space and facilities for many uses.	A Solarium as a multi-purpose room.
						Pogo tables (which adjust in height and can be arranged in various groupings).
					To encourage imagination—to increase safety of playground.	Use earth excavated from school to build fantasy components into playground—"magic mountain", etc.
					Provide easy, colorful graphic symbols for identification of sites.	Mark areas in building with "glyphs" established by the U.N. as international marks.
					To allow control of inter-personal community privacy.	Areas for teachers and for administration arranged to follow principles of Action Office.

Research and Design Institute, *Motivating Space: A Report on Elementary School Landscape*, REDE Experience and Proposals, Vol. I, H 014 EC.

man	environment	interaction	task or job performance activity (activities)	goals	objectives	guidelines or suggestions to meet objectives
Not identified other than man.	The environment which is perceived by man.	Man perceives the environment in terms of stimulus which may vary in complexity, novelty, and elements of incongruity and surprise.	Optimal level of stimulation varies for individuals. Individual level varies by cumulative experience. Optimum level of stimulation is not one to which individual is accustomed but one which deviates slightly (in negative or positive manner).	Perceptual growth (learning) thru broadened experiential background.	Encourage exploration, examination and understanding.	Present stimuli of varying degrees of complexity.
			Individual has a level of complexity of stimulus which is optimal—the intermediate between the most simple and most complex. (In experiment, subjects asked to see a complex picture again but preferred one of intermediate complexity.)		Provide elements of interest to preclude boredom and lethargy.	Present large number of stimuli.
			An element which is incongruous will not be overlooked by the individual whether he likes it or not.		Capitalize on shock value of unusual.	Present stimuli which are inconsistent and not in harmony with other.
			A novel stimulus (which differs from those in past) will also attract attention of individual whether he likes it or not.			Present stimuli which are surprising in context.

Jochim F. Wohlwill, "Man as Seeker and Neutralizer of Stimulation," paper presented at Institute of Environmental Quality Management, University of Connecticut, Storrs, Connecticut, December 12–13, 1968.

man	environment	interaction	task or job performance activity (activities)	goals	objectives	guidelines or suggestions to meet objectives
Residents of a new town.	Basingstoke, England.	Social issues arise in planning a new town for residents.	Physical design does not overcome social and economic differences in a community; however, social and physical planning can contribute to social goals.	To promote social interaction.	To provide rooms for meetings and for clubs.	A town hall social center.
				Inhibit development of class animosities.	To provide a place where residents can easily congregate until they have an opportunity to develop their own local meeting places.	In neighborhoods, provide limited meeting places.
					To reduce the possibility of labeling a section of homes as "inferior" or "superior."	Sharp boundary lines should not be drawn between homes of different social classes; there should be people from each class who use the facilities of the neighborhood such as shops and schools.

Maurice R. Broady, "The Social Aspects of Town Development," from *Taming Megalopolis*, Vol. II, ed. H. Wentworth (New York: Frederick Praeger, 1967).

becomes over- or under-stimulating, the individual will try to change it back to an acceptable level. People tend to prefer familiar environments; when confronted with a new environment, they will try to maintain habitual patterns. A changed environment, however, eventually leads to change in human behavior. Any environment is adaptable to changing functions: the effective variables within it change as human activity changes.

A satisfactory environment allows stress-free activity, provides easy links between related activities, and provides appropriate spaces for interactive and solitary activity. The greater the opportunities for human interaction, the more attractive is the environment. Social interaction increases when there are limited numbers of points where people converge. The design of the environment affects the user's perception of his role in the activities carried on within it. His satisfaction depends on the degree of influence he feels over the environment. Smaller environments permit greater individual participation and involvement.

The quality of learning and living is enhanced when the environment is perceptually enriched. The learning-living environment should provide choice, exhibit possibilities and opportunities, increase aspiration levels, arouse curiosity, and promote exploratory behavior. It is most conducive to learning when it enables the learner to experiment with ideas and things without serious consequences.

These environmental design principles, along with principles derived from educational theory, begin to point compellingly to the kind of learning environment essential in American society. But there is yet a third source of principles that can guide us toward the necessary reform of American education.

Principles of Operational Strategy

The learning theorist and the design theorist may well produce some provocative hypotheses while completely disregarding the practicalities of implementation. The implementers who fail to consider such realities as public enthusiasm, administrative intransigence, teacher competence and commitment, student involvement, political pressures, budgetary limitations, existing power structures, and the like, do so at tremendous risk. Those who will actually perform the restructuring of American education must select guidelines from the best we know about operational strategy—the third dimension of educational reform—in order to devise an organized method for systematically and effectively coping with problems encountered along the way.

Environmental education that leads to environmental learning in the environmental classroom moves far beyond the realm of traditional notions of environmental education, exemplified by outdoor education, conservation education, nature study, and other such limited approaches. Consequently, the number of variables with which the implementer must contend are greatly compounded, and no single approach to implementation will be effective in all situations and circumstances. Nevertheless, it bears repeating that this broad concept of environmental education permits a step-by-step process of change; starting from even the most traditional educational structure, a small but deliberate movement toward environmental learning provides direction for the logical next step, and the next, and so on. This process should not be confused with patchwork reform, for it does require an overall change in philosophy and goals and a commitment to the ultimate restructuring of the entire framework of the educational system.

The operational strategy that has come into the most widespread use in the past decade and has been employed to reorganize and evaluate virtually every kind of institution in American society is the systems approach. It has been used extensively to solve complex management problems. It is the only rational approach to solving environmental problems, because it requires all the variables within the total system—resources, alternatives, inputs, and so on—to be considered as they affect one another before a total plan is decided upon. Obviously, some systems applications involve highly sophisticated and complex technical processes and require intricate computers and highly trained technicians.

A systems approach to planning and implementing educational reform need not be an undertaking of these proportions. It need only be a means of looking at institutional objectives in such a way that management of complex problems becomes realistic and achievable. It should involve the identification of all the tasks required to achieve the goals in a practical and effective manner. It should be viewed as a means of organizing and managing the many variables that affect the implementation of the environmental classroom. The environmental classroom is the system—albeit an open-ended and not easily defined system—and the systems approach is the means for integrating the various parts that comprise the system.

The basic characteristics of a system, as identified in a study of organization and management in the social welfare field, include the following:

A system

- is composed of interrelated and interacting parts or components in such a way that a change in one affects all other parts and the whole.
- is dynamic and changing rather than static.
- is purposeful.
- has boundaries that can be identified for purposes of analysis, so that the system can be differentiated from its environment.
- is characterized by three attributes which determine performance: purpose, parameters, and processes or procedures; so that performance operationalizes and modifies procedures; procedures operationalize and modify parameters; and the parameters operationalize and modify purpose. Thus, the process is circular, and the nature of the process is more important in determining systems performance than are the categories of input.
- is characterized by a sensing apparatus, a feedback of information into a control center, and an adjustment of systems behavior.[8]

The environmental classroom does not have identifiable boundaries by which it can be differentiated from its environment—it *is* the environment. Like the environment, it is a

8 Jean Szaloczi Fine, " A Systems Approach to Management Utilization," *National Study of Social Welfare and Rehabilitation Workers, Work and Organization Contexts,* Working Papers, No. 1. (Washington, D.C.: U.S. Dept. of Health, Education, and Welfare, Social Rehabilitation Service, 1971), p. 22.

synergetic system, the parts of which together produce greater effects than can be predicted from the effects produced by each in isolation. Thus, a systems approach is useful only if it is adapted to the unique characteristics of the environmental classroom.

Among the many approaches to systems analysis in current use, the Planning, Programming, Budgeting System (PPBS) is perhaps the best known. It is a cost-analysis system, in which allocations of money are made not to large line items, as administrative costs or building maintenance, but to each activity carried on in the institution on the basis of its unique costs as well as its share of the total overhead, including supervision, operations, administration, supplies, debt service, and the like. Evaluation can then be carried on in terms of the share of the total budget consumed by a given program and its resultant output (which should justify its share of available funds).

Two other schemes—Phased Project Planning (PPP) and Program Evaluation Review Techniques (PERT)—rely on flow charts to project the sequence and time span of events in a program. The first is useful when many persons are involved in a single project, for its chart shows the time at which each person is to complete a phase of the project as well as the relation between one person's contribution and the activities of others. PERT uses a flow chart on which expected achievements are scaled against a time line projected into the future.

An adaptation of systems analysis to educational situations is provided by Stufflebeam's Context, Input, Process, Product (CIPP) Evaluation Model,[9] in which these four strategies are employed in a continuous and circular relationship. The context evaluation identifies broad goals on the basis of needs, implementation, and expected results. Input evaluation catalogues all the resources available, all possible solutions, and alternative procedural designs. The process evaluation involves a detailed plan for using all inputs for each strategy, in an attempt to anticipate any barriers to the smooth flow of the program. The product evaluation assesses results in terms of behavioral changes.

Each of these "alphabet soup" strategies is simply another way of perceiving the total system. Whichever viewpoint one takes, the necessary steps include recognizing and defining the problem, suggesting alternative strategies for solution, collecting relevant data, analyzing and evaluating the alternative solutions, and reaching a decision. In educational terms, the process implies identifying the needs of learners, determining how to meet them, considering alternative solutions, involving the learner in selecting strategies, planning and implementing the selected strategies, evaluating, and revising when necessary.

The New Jersey State Council for Environmental Education adapted the systems approach to construct a model for self-evaluation of environmental education programs. It divided the system into four categories of variables—planning and design, content, operation, and productivity. The categories included the following elements of the system:

A. Planning and Design
   1. Origination of the Idea
   2. Pre-planning

---

[9] Daniel L. Stufflebeam, "The Use and Abuse of Evaluation in Title III," (Address delivered to the National Seminar on Innovation, July 1967.)

    3. Identification of Needs
    4. Philosophy
    5. Community Involvement
    6. Outside Involvement
    7. Resource Identification
    8. Design Production
    9. Financing
    10. Priorities

B. Content
    1. Goals and Objectives
    2. Curriculum
    3. Faculty and Staff Activities
    4. Student Involvement
    5. In-Service Preparation
    6. Resource Utilization
    7. Material and Equipment Utilization

C. Operation
    1. Organizational Pattern
    2. Personnel
    3. Facilities
    4. Materials and Equipment
    5. Budget
    6. Student Participation
    7. Scheduling
    8. Dissemination
    9. Record Maintenance

D. Productivity
    1. Fiscal Policies
    2. Personnel Evaluation
    3. (a) Personnel Growth and Attitudes Project Personnel
       (b) Personnel Growth and Attitudes Local Education Agency Personnel
       (c) Project Personnel Growth—Skills
       (d) Local Education Agency Personnel Growth—Skills
       (e) Success in Role—Project Personnel
       (f) Success in Role—Local Education Agency Personnel
    4. (a) Student Changes in Attitudes
       (b) Student Changes in Knowledge
    5. Project Effectiveness
    6. Effect in School District
    7. Project and Community Long-Term Effects [10]

Obviously, there is no one system and no one model ideal for the environmental classroom. The choice must certainly depend on situations in individual school systems and individual communities. It will also depend on the nature of the needs, goals, and

[10] New Jersey State Council for Environmental Education, *Evaluation for Environmental Education: A Systems Analysis Approach for Self-Evaluation* (Mountain Lake: the Council, 1969), p. v.

objectives as they are eventually determined in a given situation. One possibility of adapting systems theories to the environmental classroom is presented here as an example. It would analyze the environmental classroom in terms of its philosophy and goals, strategic processes, program options, program needs, and resources required for program support. The first phase would involve determining from such an analysis what planning data are necessary, what decisions on alternative options must be made, and what implementing mechanisms will be used. The second phase would be application of the plan to the process of implementing the environmental classroom system.

The model might consist of the following major components:

functionaries	*processes*	*outputs*
Students	Identification of needs and goals	Curriculum
Teachers	Research and Development	Activities
Administrators	Program Coordination	Areas and Facilities
Consultants	Teacher Training	Teacher Guides
Community Support Groups	Administration	Resource Materials
Resource Personnel	Program Evaluation	

The model offers a framework for identifying the appropriate roles of each of the system components and their relation to other components, defining the relationship of components to each other in the total program, determining specific needs of program elements in terms of functionaries and processes, inventorying resources to be used in meeting program needs, developing a step-by-step or phased plan and determining available coordinating mechanisms, integrating financial planning with program planning, and suggesting guides for evaluation.

The simplicity of this model is indicative of the adaptability of the systems approach as an operational strategy. Whatever model is used, it is probably best to start with a simple framework that identifies variables, relationships, and options. Because the system to which the strategy is being applied is so vast, simplicity keeps the process open-ended and flexible and allows changes to be made as new elements are identified, without destroying the basic structure of the plan.

Guidelines for the Environmental Classroom

The principles and concepts derived from these three sources—educational theory, environmental design, and operational strategy—produce a set of guidelines for restructuring the learning environment into an interactive man/environment learning system, the environmental classroom.

The guidelines direct that the learning environment be designed to accommodate persons at all stages of life, for learning should be a lifelong activity. Furthermore, if learning is perceived as both a formal and a nonformal process, persons other than those who are specifically students should be able to carry on learning activities of many kinds within the learning environment.

The learning environment should provide access to relevant information—that is, information about all of man's environment—both by enabling the learner to have direct experience *out* in the environment and by bringing *in* as much of the environment as possible in real, simulated, or informational form. Both transportation and communications mobility render man's environment unlimited by variables of distance and time. The trails outward and the retrieval inward must be designed to provide an easy flow in and out for learning experiences, as well as spaces suited to solitary and interactive learning activities. The areas outside the learning facility should be perceptually enriched in order that they can contribute to learning experiences. The areas within should have the technological capacity to obtain man's storehouse of knowledge. Simulations should allow the learner to experience elements of the real world and make decisions without social consequences.

The accessibility of the learning environment to the user also implies that if the users comprise the total community, then the total community should be involved with and have a voice in the planning, design, and use of the learning environment. The city should become observable to its inhabitants, and towns should be designed with central meeting places where the community can come together. It further implies that if the learning environment is to undergo such radical change (from school building to total environment), there will have to be an educating process to secure the acceptance of educators, students, and the public at large.

The learning environment needs to be open, flexible, and conducive to diverse learning styles and rates. It should encourage individuality and cease to stress uniformity and conformity. It must be receptive and adaptable to new ideas and new needs by incorporating a large number of effective variables that can change as human activities change without imposing stress on the new activities.

The learning environment should facilitate the acquisition of broad concepts rather than narrow facts, of knowledge of how to obtain and process information rather than how to memorize available information. It should encourage imaginative and creative activity. Its major activities should be experience-oriented, problem-solving investigations rather than dull, repetitive exercises.

The learning environment should encourage the development of skills that enable human beings to be productive and happy members of society, to find pleasure in both work and leisure, to exert a measure of control over their environment. It should offer a full range of such skills so that as an individual's needs change, at various stages of life, he will be able to meet those needs through the offerings and facilities of the learning environment.

The learning environment should be staffed by learning facilitators (professional and nonprofessional) who value individual worth and nurture individual self-acceptance and self-confidence. The design of the learning environment should be based on learning goals, so that change will proceed in the desired direction; it should focus on the centrality of the learner and should promote a humanistic philosophy of learning. The classroom should be an example of how man's technology harmonizes with the natural world, both in the resources it contains and in the kinds of human relations it encourages. It should be alive with the joy of learning, not deadened by teacher- and administrator-satisfying routine. The learner should be actively involved in the total process of learning, and the process should be learner-oriented rather than institutionally created. The learner should be able to influence his goals and activities as a first step in learning to cope with and modify all his environments. His basic needs should be met so that he is able to strive to be all that he can be. The learning environment should be designed to meet learners' needs, not to conform to stereotypes of educational facilities. The level of challenge for each learner should be within "the range of challenge"; that is, the learning environment should provide enough stimulation and incentives to make the learner reach for his goals but not so much that his goals are beyond his reach. The learning environment should provide not only for teacher-to-learner interaction but for learner-to-teacher and learner-to-learner interaction as well, to capitalize on the many kinds of relationships that enhance learning.

The learning environment should be designed for total resource use. All resources in the environment should be viewed as learning resources and should be built into the learning environment. The central learning facility should contain as many learning resources and materials as possible, and it should be augmented by a network of study areas in the wide variety of environments accessible by transportation. Learning facilities should be designed to take advantage of the compounded effects of multiple use, joint occupancy, and maximum trade-off. The unique problems of the urban setting must be turned to unique advantages for learning through redesign and redevelopment of cities to render their facilities, cultures, and spaces observable and educational. Learners should be exposed to a variety of settings, should be able to take a variety of routes to the same point (literally and figuratively), and should be able to recognize easily the elements comprising a given environment.

The learning environment should unify or transcend the separate disciplines and focus on sensory stimulations and development. All kinds of environmental communications—not just the visual ones—should be perceptible to the learner. The learning environment should encourage esthetic creation, appreciation, and judgment by exposing learners to and involving them in all forms of artistic expression. It should emphasize affective as well as cognitive learning. Learning should include multidisciplinary problem-solving activities—for real-life problems rarely fall within the confines of a single discipline—to enable individuals to deal with the world as a system, not as an array of separate and unrelated subjects. Learners should be encouraged to use their specialized skills from a generalized orientation.

The implementation of such a learning environment should be based on a systems approach that remains flexible but takes into account the essential variables of the system in order to enable implementers to cope with problems effectively and evaluate results constructively.

The country we and our ancestors have forged, based on the biggest, the most, and the best, has produced a standard of living for most of its citizens unsurpassed anywhere else in the world. But the environment we have created at the same time diminishes the quality of our lives. The air we breathe, the food we eat, and the water we drink are less than ideal. All of our affluence has not yet been able to stem the noise, the over-crowding, the deterioration, the health hazards built into our surroundings. Our educational system fails to equip most of us to cope with the problems and the stress we perceive now, let alone with the urgencies we foresee arising in the near future. If the creation of the environmental classroom seems a mammoth task, requiring totally new concepts of institutions that are now immovably encrusted in the American system, we must nevertheless face the fact that such institutions evolved for other times and other purposes. Either we recognize the priorities of today and tomorrow and take the first big steps to redesign those institutions, or we shall confront and pass on to future generations an increasingly degraded quality of life—until, eventually, we shall reach the limit of the adaptability of the human organism.

There is already a movement under way to effect change through learning, an experiment that now accepts many of the concepts and principles posited here and could, if modified to embrace them all, provide for future educational reform in the direction of the environmental classroom. The community school movement is an emerging force to help solve human problems. It challenges the educational system to assume leadership for bringing into concert all of the learning forces and factors in the community. Its full power to bring about social change depends on the extent to which the community beyond the educational establishment endorses the idea and becomes involved in advancing the movement.

Central to the community school idea is the multipurpose educational facility serving all members of the community at all times. Concomitantly, the public school becomes the school of the public, with the community taking an active part in the planning, implementation, and programs of the educational system. The central facility will be even more essential to meet the technological needs of the future. The global village of future communications is almost a certainty. But equipping each home with information-retrieval facilities shades somewhat into the twilight zone of prophesy. Cost will be the most severely limiting factor. If we look to communications to spur a return to the community as a way of life, reversing the trend toward congregating in large urban centers, the multipurpose community school would be the ideal locus for the technological equipment necessary to link each community with the information and communication grid that will form the global village.

Evidence from experiments in community education indicates that it is helping to solve some major social problems. Some of the communities report improved human relations, decrease in juvenile delinquency, and reduced recidivism of former convicts. Elderly persons are again contributing to society, the literacy level of adults has risen, and the voting turnout has improved. In the formal school program, academic achievement has increased and the dropout rate is lower.

To the community school concept of the central facility bringing in all the resources of the community add a modification of the Parkway School concept, which sends the learner out to all the educational facilities of the community, and we begin to come close to total resource use. It follows logically that the environment to which the learner goes would need to be made accessible, safe, obervable, clean, and pleasing, thereby improving the quality of living and learning.

The community school movement also supports a humanistic, learner-centered, multi-disciplinary approach to education. It would have to be strengthened to embrace full thrust of the learner's drive toward self-actualization, but it goes a long way toward providing an environment conducive to allowing the learner to be all he can become.

One of the most noteworthy observations of the leaders of the 1971 White House Conference on Youth was that the young delegates were not seeking to abandon "the system" but rather to have a greater voice in it. As students, they asked to be thought of as participants in, not merely recipients of, the educational process. In the report of the task force on education, they made the following recommendations:

> Students need to be allowed to learn outside the formal classroom and to receive academic credit for these experiences. . . . Educational systems must perceive and build their curriculum on the basis that the total community is the context in which education occurs. . . . A concerted effort should be made to enable man to develop a real and basic understanding of how he exists within his environment, and to become aware of the tremendous impact he has upon his world. . . . The limited use of [school] facilities must be expanded. The community school concept must be seriously considered by all state and local school boards. . . . We recommend the establishment of a new type of community learning center, a center that would marshal the services and make available the cultural . . . , educational, and business and industry resources of the total community.[11]

In order to move the community school idea closer to full implementation and closer to the environmental classroom, the groups and organizations within the community must join hands with the educational system to support such change. When the community and the school act as partners for learning, the consumer has the widest possible array of learning resources from public, private, commercial, and voluntary sectors. Such cooperation and collaboration should lead to a resource brokerage, matching users with resources (including information resources involving media).

Approached systematically, the first step in the process should be an analysis of learning resources provided by public, quasi-public, and private sectors in the community, conducted in a phased process with natural review stages for spot checks. The investigation phase would identify resources, locations, barriers, activities, management, facilities and features, and equipment and supplies. The evaluation phase would analyze resources in terms of adequacy of facilities, sufficiency of activities, and efficiency of management, as well as the work and cost necessary to integrate such resources into the learning system. The recommendation phase would suggest the most effective ways of improving and using the available resources.

American education is handicapped by a severely limited perspective that sees only a formal process undergone by students at specific times in a specific facility. There is

---

[11] White House Conference on Youth, *Report of the White House Conference on Youth* (Washington, D.C.: Government Printing Office, 1971), pp. 87, 90–92.

greater acceptance today of leisure as an opportunity for learning and a growing trend toward viewing education as an ongoing process encompassing both formal and non-formal activities. Learning is properly viewed as the entire life process, without distinction among work, education, and leisure. The school building shifts from being the only center of education to a point of reference in a continual educational process. Learning extends well beyond the formal walls of the school facility to the family, to the community and its geographic environment, to the total world—the environmental classroom.

Work, as a matter of modern fact, is being challenged by leisure as the central focus of life. We have more money to invest in leisure and recreational pursuits, more nonwork hours to fill in more ways, increased mobility, and a greater desire for exotic and diverse experiences. Recreation and culture pursued through the arts, media, sports, crafts, and the like can form a valuable base for stimulating many forms of learning.

But first, learning must be perceived by all persons as a joyful activity, a relevant pursuit, a process that can and should go on everywhere in man's environment leading to the betterment of man's environment. It should offer its own justification for inclusion in man's leisure time; learning and living should become a single, total process.

Unfortunately, our living environments fail to provide adequate educational and leisure opportunities for children, youth, adults, and special populations. The special physical patterns of cities and the unique behavior patterns of their inhabitants have not been successfully matched and blended by those who shape the design and destiny of a larger portion of American demography and geography. In most instances, urban planning has not been based on a systematic plan for open-space use, population flux, zoning, and provision of total resources for leisure and learning. Changes in population composition render original master plans obsolete in a short time. Many facilities and opportunities for leisure and learning and for full use of environment are inaccessible because of inadequate and expensive transportation systems, lack of awareness, limited mobility, and lack of interest. Existing facilities and opportunities are often inappropriate for the potential users.

Our environment is deteriorating; our educational system is collapsing. Yet our schools continue to try to shelter us from the environment and to force us through an irrelevant mill until we emerge unable to cope with the real problems of the real world. They can no longer continue to be fixed-time, fixed-place institutions serving administrative domains and conveniences. They must become all-time, all-place coordinators serving all citizens and directed toward improving the quality of life of each individual and the entire community. The rallying cry of current social reform movements—"Now!"—is in no case so crucial as here, directing us all to take the first step toward enhancing living and learning through the environmental classroom.

There is no one route to the environmental classroom. The pathways to learning are many, and the pathways to environmental learning are multiplied even further.

Think . . . dream . . . suppose . . . conjecture. Why does learning happen? How does it happen? When does it happen? Why, how, and where *should* it happen?

What is today like? What will tomorrow be like? What do we need to learn in order to face today and tomorrow, to build better worlds for ourselves and all mankind? What is different from yesterday? What changes ought to be made? What from yesterday is good enough, relevant enough, valid enough to keep?

The following items—probes, innovations, alternative futures—were selected to provoke thoughts, dreams, suppositions, and conjectures that may lead to the environmental classroom.

PROBES

view of the world and man

driftwood from the conceptual beach

how a man of that age might describe his view of the world

I

THE AGE OF
PRIMITIVE
REALISM
From ? B.C.
to 650 B.C.

"We are two, the world and me. The world is just as I sense it (see it, touch it, taste it, smell it, hear it). The world is like me. In me there is a spirit; in the world as a whole, and in each part of the world that I deal with, there are spirits who rule. I have come to terms with these spirits. I do so by rituals, by magic. *The superior man is the magician or witch doctor who knows the spirits and how to deal with them.*" (In many parts of the

II

THE AGE OF
REASON
From 650 B.C.
to 350 B.C.

FROM THALES THROUGH ARISTOTLE "We are now three: the world, I, facing the world, and I, observing myself looking at the world. To put order into the world, I classify things, qualities and actions in the world and in me. I take this classification into account when I want to guide my behavior. My ideal is to be as 'objective' as possible. My thinking must be orderly, as the world is orderly. My brain mirrors the world; to each thought corresponds a fact; to each word corresponds a thing, a person,

III

THE AGE OF
SCIENCE
From 1500 A.D.
to 1900 A.D.

FROM COPERNICUS TO PLANCK "I do not confer with the spirits as did the primitive. Nor do I deceive myself as did the Metaphysician (II) who mistook his own voice for that of Nature. I ask Nature definite questions and Nature gives me clear-cut answers. I translate these answers into mathematical formulas that project my conclusions into the unknown, where I discover other facts that Nature has kept hidden since the beginning. *The superior man is the experimenter-mathematician, the man who expresses relations in formulas that reveal how the properties and the actions*

IV

THE AGE OF
RELATIVISM
From 1900 A.D.
through
1966 A.D.

FROM ROENTGEN THROUGH RUSSELL "I find that the further I ask questions, the less and less the world seems like a giant machine. I have trouble even asking the 'right' questions and the answers frequently baffle me. Even when I ask the 'right' questions and get the 'right' answers, I find that the answers are in terms of my frame of reference to the world I have *myself* created through centuries of observations. The structure of my world is built of *my own* postulates, which must be re-examined relentlessly. They

V

THE AGE OF
UNITY
From 1966 A.D.
to ? A.D.

FROM PEIRCE THROUGH EINSTEIN AND REISER TO? "Having discovered that I cannot separate what I observe from my own act of observation, I begin to study my own way of observing. When I do this, I find that my observation does not consist solely of what goes on in my brain, but that my total organism, with all of its history, is also engaged.
"I discover that my most clever formulations take their origin and their significance from an immediacy of felt contact, of fusion and oneness with what is going on, beyond the dimensional limits of symbols, and without the distinction between the self-and the non-self. Out of this knowledge comes an awareness of my inter-relatedness with everything, from blind cosmic energy to fellow human beings; the old, verbal distinctions between art and science and religion disappear—becoming an overall oneness of experience." (This concept, which after 2,000 years offers the promise that

world today, in all cultures and societies, there are still people who believe that there are "spirits" whose help can be invoked, or whose wrath avoided, through incantation of magic words and the performance of rituals.)

"The world is what I feel it to be."

an action or a quality. If my thinking goes from one thought to another according to logic, it directs me through the world from one fact to the next. *Within my brain there is a miniature of the universe.*" (Even after 2,000 years, there are still many people who think this way today. They are the 'practical' people; they accumulate 'facts' and pin labels on them, and base their conduct—and their appraisal of others—on 'facts' and labels.)

"The world is what I say it is."

of men and things follow measurable sequences." (The man of affairs today; the one who runs business and industry, serves in high governmental posts; writes and edits our journals and newspapers, is the product of colleges and universities whose curriculum is largely based on the experimenter-mathematician concept; he speaks in charts and graphs and figures, and bases his conduct upon them and his appraisal of others on the extent that they do so.)

"The world is an immense machine and I can discover how it works."

appear to be relative to my own spacetime relationship but the cosmos, and with every unique event that I single out for study. What the primitivists thought of as spirits in nature, and the philosophers considered the 'facts' of nature, and the rationalists considered the 'laws' of nature, I find now to be but gross irregularities in the world as I see it through my inadequate senses and instruments. The only 'laws of nature' I can discover are statistical averages that provide rough indications of probabilities."

"The world consists of probabilities that I create by my way of looking at them."

the powerful ethical systems of Christ, Buddha and Mohammed may fuse with the relativistic world of Einstein, the cyclic, recreative universe of Hoyle, the "participative iconology" of McLuhan and Ellul, is a still, small voice in our world of today. It can be heard in the enclaves of a handful of universities; in the words of a bearded poet somewhere east of midnight; and in the voiceless contemplation of a Zen disciple besides the dripping water and stone pools somewhere west of a Shoji screen. But it *can* be heard.)

"My world has a structure that no formulation can encompass; I conceive of the world as my own total experience with it, and I play with my own symbolic constructs in a spirit of easy detachment."

clifford humphrey

constructing new life styles from an ecological perspective

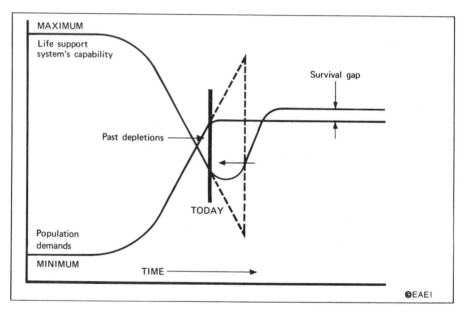

Environmental education has not yet come to grips with the massive task implicit within the ecological perspective. This perspective calls for a period of more intensive change and adaptation than either the agricultural or industrial revolutions. Studying natural communities, the biogeochemical cycles and pollution is not the study of ecology. While these topics are concerned with our relationships to the environment, they have little meaning until the implications for our behavior and aspirations are developed.

Ecology in its broadest sense means household knowledge. The ecological perspective then means interpreting our behavior as contributing to or overseeing household function. The other word in our language that begins with "eco" (from the Greek *oikos;* which means household) is economics, meaning household management. We have de-

Clifford Humphrey is director of Ecology Action Educational Institute and co-founder of Epicenter.

Reprinted by permission of Ecology Action Educational Institute.

veloped economic practices without adequate knowledge of what we are managing, or of management goals that would complement rather than threaten household function.

Economic thinking has come to focus on monetary growth, which has pushed all other factors to the periphery of our management decisions. Many are blaming technology and science for today's environmental problems and alienation; but science would not have been "misapplied" if our economic institutions were knowledgeable and holistic. To promote the general welfare, economics (household management) must derive from ecology. Such a major reorganization of our affairs will require an unprecedented period of rapid cultural transformation. This requires a general consensus as to the nature of our present situation and a willingness to recognize our dependence on a life support system that is finite.

Some groups still perceive environmental concern as a means to an end, such as overthrowing or scoring revenge on all or part of the "establishment." Others simply see it as a movement to force a long overdue cleanup of smoke, smells, and spills. Such positions are not only naive, but are making an adequately clear understanding of the ecological perspective difficult to grasp. The advocate system of settling a dispute in court or justifying a revolt in the streets is an archaic mechanism in the face of the task before us. Everyone is adversely affected and threatened by the inequities generated by a culture that does not understand what it is dependent upon. Only by massive education and through defining new values by which to make decisions and transform our institutions may we assure ourselves of a future.

The above figure is a *conceptual tool* to help us in realigning our decision making mechanisms. It is a survival crisis graph, illustrating our present tenuous situation and how this situation can be relieved. The lower curve represents population draw, that is *the number of people times their withdrawals from and depletions of the life-support system.* As this draw has increased, the health of the life-support system has proportionately decreased. The upper descending curve represents such things as topsoil erosion and mineral depletion, ecosystem simplification, mining of ground water, watershed destruction, fisheries depletion, disruption of incoming solar energy and retardation of escaping heat or infra-red radiation. Social factors would also be included such as suicide and homicide rates, drug and medicine dependence, mental illness, decreased life expectancy, etc.

The crossing over of these curves prior to 1971 indicates that we have been mining our life-support system. While a farmer may be increasing his annual yield, such gains are not only temporary, if quantity and quality of the soil is diminished in the process, but they create a most dangerous illusion. The subtle threat to us is that these two factors, population draw and life-support system capability, may become so out of balance that there would not be sufficient resources to re-establish a sustained yield situation. It is as if a financier needed more funds than his interest provided and began dipping into his capital. How long could he do so and still have a chance of rebuilding back to his original capital?

This task has two basic parts: first, trying to precipitate a minimum impact on our total environment in our daily affairs, as they are now constituted. Second, transforming the man-made environment, both social and physical, into a shape and structure that will best facilitate a future for everyone. These tasks may appear to be contradictory in terms of energy and resource utilization, but both are moving in the same direction.

The environmental movement thus far has concentrated on the importance of changing personal life styles. Project *Epicenter* seeks to expand the movement to include a wide range of community groups, and to work toward the transformation of American government by focusing on local issues and local government units. If you would like information on how to work for a better, more stable environment where you live, write to *Epicenter* at *Clear Creek.*

From *Birds* by Robert J. Lifton. Copyright © 1969 by Robert J. Lifton. Reprinted by permission of Random House, Inc., Robert J. Lifton and the International Famous Agency.

PROBES

learning to change

john a. gustafson

education's third dimension

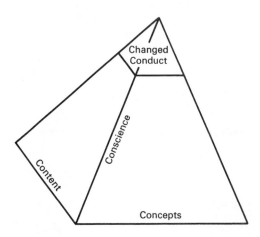

Education is a three-dimensional thing. The most obvious dimension is content—the simple transfer of information, either from person to person directly or through various media. Most of the time we attempt to go to a second dimension—the concept. We recognize that knowing many facts is pointless unless these facts are integrated into meaningful generalizations. What we generally fail to realize is that education has failed if it does not result in changed behavior—and changing behavior comes only through a third dimension—conscience. Rational, productive behavior is the result of the practical application of a body of ethical principles—principles which a person lives by even if he cannot state them or is unaware that he has them. As James stated so long ago, in his New Testament epistle: "Show me that what you believe is real though not accompanied by deeds, and by my deeds I will show you what I believe." The effectiveness of our educational program is demonstrated by the things people do—by the way they live.

John A. Gustafson, "Education's Third Dimension," in *The Conservation Educator*, 3, No. 2 (November/December, 1970). Reprinted by permission.

PROBES

the joy and fun of learning

catherine watson

learning and liking it

Lincoln school in Staples, Minn., an imposing brick edifice built in 1907, looks at first meeting as tradition-bound as it is old. But inside, warm and bright and busy, it is what its administrators call "a school for kids." It is home for a grade school without grades, where at any given time 150 youngsters may be doing 150 different things, and where the three R's are relevance, readiness, and responsibility.

Teachers don't take roll, for example. Pupils check themselves in every morning by turning over their name tags on a panel by the door. There are no letter grades and consequently no need to compete for them; tests are given only to determine a pupil's weaknesses so they can be strengthened. Grade barriers between classes, which traditionally kept youngsters of the same age together regardless of their individual differences, have all but been abandoned for that purpose.

Lincoln is not the kind of school one expects to find in a small northern Minnesota town. But then Staples, like its model school, is exceptional.

About 10 years ago, Staples was one more little town on the railroad, slowly dying as rail employment diminished and as surrounding farming began to be less profitable. The 1960 census showed Staples to be in the poorest economic area of the State. Today, however, the community appears to be in the midst of a mild boom, and the schools and their officials have had an important hand in the change of fortune.

In 1960, Staples bid for—and got—an area vocational-technical school, part of a network of such schools across the State funded largely by Federal and State monies. As part of their classwork, its students built a municipal airport, reclaimed a weedy lake as a recreation area, and started an experimental farm. Ten new industries moved into Staples and citizen morale began to rise.

By the mid-1960's, when several school administrators were talking seriously about starting an experimental elementary school in Staples, the climate in the town was such that the idea could take root and grow.

"The model school began with our dissatisfaction with what we were doing," says Duane R. Lund, Staples superintendent. "We were looking for a vehicle to shake up our

Catherine Watson, "Learning and Liking It," in *American Education*, Vol. 6 (May, 1970), pp. 18–22.

methods, and we felt that nongradedness (on an age basis) was the best way to individualize instruction."

When the model school opened in 1967 it offered Staples youngsters individualized instruction, starting right out in kindergarten. "If a child is ready to learn to read when he comes to school, we teach him reading," explains Donald D. Droubie, a former teacher with a master's degree in curriculum who now directs the Staples model school project. "We take them where they are, not where they should be."

But individualized instruction is not the only reason that this school in the middle of Minnesota's rural north calls itself a school for kids. "A lot of schools have individualized education, but they haven't personalized it in the sense that youngsters are taught according to their personal needs and interests," says Droubie. "You can test a child to find out what he knows and doesn't know in academic areas, and assign him work on that basis. But how meaningful will that work be for him if you ignore his learning style and the kind of learning experiences he'd really enjoy?"

At Lincoln, each child's personal dignity, his work, and his preferences are respected. If a youngster learns some skills better with a tape recorder than a book, then he uses the tape recorder. If he learns more slowly than some of his classmates, his efforts are nonetheless treated with respect. Sometimes children are grouped solely on the basis of interest, rather than achievement, aptitude, or age. Each child spends part of several afternoons each week on special activities such as baking, photography, knitting, carpentry, guitar, sewing, French, or baton-twirling—things that he and his classmates do mostly because they want to. . . .

The pupils also have some say in choosing their activities in subjects like reading and math, although the degree of structure in each child's program depends upon his maturity. Lincoln faculty are convinced that children learn best if they have some responsibility for their own education. "They must be made partners in education," says Droubie. "Children have the right to be wrong, and the only way to raise responsible youngsters is to give them responsibility and permit them to make their own mistakes."

Which explains why the school lunch fund was $28 short the first month—just after pupils were put in charge of selling their own lunch tickets last fall. But they have been operating in the black ever since.

Teachers provide several avenues for learning and students are allowed to choose how they want to learn. A supreme effort is made, reads a Lincoln staff report, to get every child to work at his potential without frustration.

"One of the teacher's biggest jobs," says Droubie, "is to motivate pupils, to make them curious about learning by creating an atmosphere that makes the child, at every step, want to try something different."

Teachers do this partly by keeping up warm relationships with the students that make the youngsters feel personally involved in education. A 10-foot papier maché dragon that stands in the school is a monument to an early effort to pull faculty and pupils together.

"The kids liked the song, 'Puff, the Magic Dragon,' so we decided to build a dragon," Don Droubie says. "Everyone—all the kids and all the teachers—had a part in it. Everyone made some contribution."

Lincoln's teachers also expend plenty of mental energy thinking up new ways to make learning exciting and interesting for their pupils. One of their ideas is a 50 feet by six feet polyethelene tube with see-through walls. Children can walk through it, with psychedelic lights flashing through the walls during their stroll. Or they can just sit down in it and read for a while. "It's an exciting place for a kid to be," says Droubie. "There's really no sophisticated educational goal behind it. The idea is just to turn kids on."

Recently teachers came up with another idea for motivating their pupils; they call it multimedia. It's a kind of sensory bombardment designed to trigger individual learning that looks more like a psychedelic light show than anything else. Pupils pack together in the center of a horseshoe-shaped screen made of white sheets while movies, filmstrips, and slides are projected simultaneously around them. Teachers produce the multimedia shows, spending as much as 15 hours on a 45-minute session, planning things so that room decorations and all the various media contribute to certain objectives.

During a recent show on Alaska, for example, youngsters cringed and squealed as pictures of rangy king crabs, moose, and blubbery whales flashed around them. "Some youngsters learn a lot from these sessions, others little, but everybody learns something," says Droubie. The educational value, he points out, is that some of the youngsters will usually be interested enough to learn more, and all materials used in the presentation are available for further study.

Lincoln school itself has been designed to make children involved and interested in learning. That first year, when the Staples school system was given a $100,000 Federal grant for the project, the district had a dilapidated hulk of a building that had stood boarded up for a year—ever since the completion of the town's other elementary school.

The project staff moved in the summer before the school was to open and renovated the antiquated building to suit their own specifications. They had the high ceilings lowered about four feet, had the big old-fashioned windows boxed in, the walls paneled, and most of the floor space carpeted. The result is a cheerful, modern building, with two enormous classrooms on the second floor and one on the first. Left-over first floor space was turned into a comfortable room for kindergartners, and the first floor hallway became all-purpose space, put to good use by youngsters who want a quiet place of their own to work.

Classroom areas are broken up by a rearrangeable assortment of odd-shaped tables, portable carrels, folding screens, bookcases, and such items as the top half of a young oak tree, complete with its drying leaves, for the science area. The layout of the rooms—especially on the second floor where older youngsters spend most of their time—changes almost daily. The furniture, much of it designed by teachers, is moved around to create a constantly interesting, unschoollike environment, full of nooks, study alcoves, and mini-rooms for small groups.

The second floor hallway is now a 2,000-volume library which Droubie calls an "advertisement for learning." It exposes youngsters to books every time they walk from one study area to another. Other study materials are also laid out where children can come and select what they want. "And it looks neat, not sloppy," Droubie emphasizes.

"It teaches the youngsters that they must handle materials with care and respect for others."

Even the names of classes have been changed to make them sound a little more intriguing. English, reading, writing, and so forth have become "communications," math is "calculations," and science is "investigations."

"Grade"—whether applied to achievement or age—is another word that seldom appears in the Lincoln staff's vocabulary. The ages of pupils at the school cover a range that in a traditional setting would be kindergarten through fifth grade. Pupils are referred to as members of levels, which correspond to the traditional grades for their ages.

The distinction between grades and levels is more than one of words, however. The levels are not thought of as barriers which children cannot cross for instructional purposes. They're simply a "convenience, a starting point," says Droubie. "Youngsters are free to move across these boundaries as the need arises."

The levels have been kept, according to Droubie, because sometimes Lincoln teachers do like to present materials to youngsters of a certain age and because instruction in some subjects—physical education, for example—has not been individualized. Droubie himself prefers to call Lincoln a fluid rather than a nongraded school.

Students are not assigned to one teacher or one classroom, and they may be placed in whatever grouping arrangements suit the day's activities. Teachers work in teams or as individuals, and Lincoln's atmosphere encourages them to try out new ideas spontaneously.

Each student has his own folder that tells him when and how much to study each subject he's taking. Made out to fit his specific needs, it tells him exactly which tasks and assignments he has in each area. It includes both structured and nonstructured time.

Intermediate students (fourth and fifth levels) keep their folders in a bank of file cabinets on the school's second floor. A nearby file bank holds study materials, booklets, puzzles, tests, and worksheets under titles like Phonics, Math 4, Vowel Sheets, Using Dictionary. It is up to the student to get the required materials and to complete his assignment.

When he has done that, and testing shows he has learned the skill or concept he needed, he moves on—always at his own speed, whether that is faster or slower than others his age, whether or not his skills in other areas are keeping pace.

"We never push youngsters or put pressure on them," says Droubie, and that's part of the reason that Lincoln doesn't give marks in the usual sense or send a child home with a report card that spells out his success or failure.

Instead, teachers tell parents about their children's progress through a minimum of three conferences a year and a home visit. They hold as many conferences each year as are necessary. Also, they sometimes send a child home with a tape recording of the teacher's comments. Other ways of reporting are by a weekly newsletter and parent teas every other week. "We want to get across to parents that there's more to learning than just the academic areas. Enthusiasm, happiness, responsibility—these are worthy and important goals, too," Droubie explains.

The several thousand visitors who come to Lincoln annually to watch what's going on are living evidence of the interest the experimental school has stirred in Minnesota and elsewhere. "It has had a profound effect on our other schools," says superintendent Lund, pointing to the fact that Staples' other elementary school has borrowed team teaching and the use of multimedia from Lincoln.

The community seems sold, too. Ninety of the pupils were volunteered by their parents for the experimental program; the other 60 youngsters were enrolled when their rural districts consolidated with Staples. Since the school opened, only four parents have withdrawn their children.

After its initial $100,000 grant under title III of the Elementary and Secondary Education Act, Lincoln received a second-year grant of $70,000 and a third-year grant—for the present school year—of $35,000. Gradually most of Lincoln's costs have been absorbed by the Staples district. When the third grant expires, the school will be on its own. To continue, it must be supported by local funds. No one, however, seems worried about any lack of community support.

To win over skeptics, school officials have simply let the school speak for itself. Droubie recalls one father who came for a visit: "He said, 'This shouldn't work. It isn't how I went to school. I know it shouldn't work but it does. For the first time, my boy is having success.' "

"The best public relations agents we've got here are the kids," says Droubie. "If Johnny goes home and can read—and read well—that does it."

m. j. ellis

the rational design of playgrounds

Children achieve about half their adult intelligence by the age of four, and during their early years they are most plastic and susceptible to their environment. They become less so with time. This early plasticity is a two-edged sword since while a youngster is highly responsive to the challenge of an appropriate environment, he is also highly susceptible

M. J. Ellis is currently Assistant Professor in Recreation and Park Administration, Motor Performance and Play Research Laboratory Director in the Children's Research Center of the University of Illinois. He is interested in the motives for and the bioenergetics of play.

M. J. Ellis, "The Rational Design of Playgrounds," in *Educational Product Report* (Educational Products Information Exchange Institute), 3, Nos. 8 & 9 (May/June, 1970). Reprinted by permission.

to the deprivations of an impoverished one. The early experiences of our young are crucial. They are not something to while away the time as they grow.

Duplication Produces Monotony

Playgrounds can be a significant part of the environment and their design should not be taken lightly. But, playgrounds in general are duplicated from site to site in a monotony of stereotyped apparatus. They are essentially static, tubular, safe, predictable, and are often pathetic imitations designed to catch an adult's eye. Some newer playgrounds are guilty of similar errors, as they approximate a contemporary art show. They all too frequently are not designed with some child-oriented rationale in mind. Planners buy the equipment presented by the industry because they presume that it was designed by an expert and/or because they can build a play area by merely placing orders. Few people have the time or energy or talent to design and construct original playthings from first principles, so most play areas are designed by leafing through catalogs. . . .

Theorists have attempted to understand and explain play by following the lead of others concerned with describing behavior in general. This has proved difficult since the general theories usually assumed some obvious motive for the behavior. Yet enigmatically, the behavior called play has been categorized as being without use to the animal; it was something that did not aid in survival by producing food, shelter, or progeny.

Old Theories Still Used

At present, much of the knowledge and practice of those concerned with the informal activities of children are based on a variety of these older theories of play. . . . The expenditure of large and ill-directed energies in freer situations, where big muscle activity is encouraged, smacks of the old surplus-energy theory of play and seems to explain the sudden explosion of a group of youngsters into a playground or gymnasium after being cooped in a classroom. The purging of undesirable behavior via its redirection to a condoned activity harks back to a cathartic theory of play that still appears useful to practitioners. It is assumed that opportunities to hit, strike, throw, or roll that are inappropriate to one setting can be controlled by providing opportunities for that activity elsewhere. In another old theory, compensatory activities have long been considered to account for the free activity choices of adults and children. Here the child is seen to select play activities that complement his habitual activities, thus leading to a balanced activity regimen and, therefore, development. Juxtaposed to this is the theory of response generalization, claiming that people recreate by using activities that they habitually indulge in and in which they are presumably competent. This theory argues strongly for the teaching of appropriate recreational activities so that the children can carry with them from school skills to use during their free time.

All the above theories are in part weak since they can be dismantled by an aggressive critic, but they are useful to modern practitioners. It seems good sense to allow them to stand for the time being as partial explanations of some of the behavior we are likely to see in our children until the modern theories of play and recreation that are just emerging are tested.

A modern theory that considers play as information gathering derives from observations that an animal continues to emit behavior even though apparently its every need has been met. Some animals just cannot be still; they constantly interact with the environment. Monkeys manipulate; rats sniff, exercise, and explore; and children constantly disturb their surroundings. On the other hand, another class of animals seems content, once their needs are met, to curl up and relax, to idle till it is time to catch the next meal. Why? . . .

Generalists and Specialists

The two classes of animals can best be labelled the "generalists" and the "specialists." Specialists are animals that are very well adapted to a particular environment doing the few things necessary for their survival extremely well. When not performing their limited number of responses they relax, uniquely adapted to the *status quo*. They are exemplified by snakes, frogs, etc. Generalists are quite different. They are not adapted exclusively to any particular niche but are capable of adapting to a variety of environments. They are opportunists living by their wits. They maintain a large variety of responses and are forever testing and probing the environment, playing with it, even when not hungry. By this process they keep abreast of change and the more up-to-date ones tend to survive. The generalists' curiosity, their tendency to explore, manipulate, and control the environment is characteristic of rats, bears, and primates. Man is the prime example.

Generalists have an abhorrence of sameness; in our terms they become bored. They need constant opportunities to deal with the environment. If they are deprived of opportunities to do this then they create them. Men cannot tolerate the absence of stimulation and may be considered to play when they maintain their interactions with the environment after insuring their immediate survival. Play can be seen, then, as a type of knowledge-seeking behavior. It prevents boredom and generates a base of information about the environment from which to operate.

Animals are changed by their experience and become more complex as they get to know things. Things that become completely known cease to be interesting. Only things that are somewhat new, or to some extent uncertain, are interesting. Thus, with increasing experience an organism's interactions with its natural environment gradually increase in complexity. Presumably there are limits to this, either set by the complexity of the environment or by the animal's ability to deal with complexity. A dumb generalist in a rich environment is limited by its own capacity to get to know the environment, whereas a sharp generalist in a limited environment soon knows it well and begins to suffer, from stimulus deprivation.

Play seems to be knowledge-seeking behavior that leads to an increasing complexity of the players and their play. Further, the evidence suggests that appropriate opportunities to deal with unknown elements in the environment are crucial to the development of our children. If you accept the above, then shed a tear with me for the opportunities we have lost to enrich our children's lives. . . .

An Enriched Environment

Researchers with rats on the West Coast have determined that rats reared under enriched conditions did better at a variety of learning tasks than those reared as usual in little cages. These workers put a great variety of play apparatus in the cages at first—the kitchen-sink approach—but since then have been whittling down the apparatus to find exactly what experiences are necessary to allow a rat to get smart. With our children we are in most cases, still in the pre-kitchen-sink stage. . . .

It seems reasonable, however, to bring some order to the process of designing these environments. There seem to be two major changes of outcomes from play activity. It is desirable that our youngsters develop the capacity to make novel or creative responses to situations. These by definition are hard to foresee and plan for, often coming by surprise. At this time in our planning we must allow plenty of opportunity for this potential expression.

Taking the opposite tack, we know that our children need to master certain knowledge—of numbers, for example—and that others are desirable; say, gravity or conservation of momentum. Rarely do we invade an informal environment with our contingencies rigged so that children will be led into making responses that will tend to increase their grasp of what we want them to know. Thus, it becomes legitimate to ask what a child will learn as a result of playing with such an item. Playgrounds should be designed unashamedly to produce learning. That process is only just beginning in the area of playground design.

This is not so in the realm of small playthings, which have had a long history of being considered "didactic material.". . .

Children Will Play With Anything

Luckily for our planners and manufacturers children will play with a cardboard box, a scrap of wood, and playgrounds. Their propensity to play, explained by one or more of the theories that seem to hold water, ensures this. Yet a hard-nosed look at usage patterns of our conventional playgrounds show that they do not sustain the attention of their clients. For example, a recent study in a variety of different locations in Philadelphia showed that children visited only once per day and then for only fifteen minutes. Children in the most depressed environment with presumably least opportunities for play and perhaps greatest need showed the same pattern. Further, the study showed that on the average the play apparatus was vacant at least 88 percent of the peak time. So it is my conclusion that playground activity features very low on the behavioral popularity poll. . . . It is feasible to compare the behavior in many traditional playgrounds to those aimless stereotyped mechanical responses of our furry relatives caged in stimulational vacua.

The golden rules for selection need to be based on a theory, and frankly, the one outlined in brief above is the theory of play that recommends itself by seeming to explain best much to be happening during play. To use it then leads to the following:

1. Children play for the stimulation they receive, not just to burn up energy.

2. Children need to indulge in activities that become increasingly complex with time.

3. Children by playing learn about their physical surroundings and about their own roles in a social group.

The essential ingredients for a playground are that it should elicit new responses from the child as he plays and that these responses increase in complexity as play proceeds. The plaything should avoid as far as possible pre-empting the actions of the child. To erect an *ersatz*-rocket indicates an intent for the children to play as astronauts. The actual behavior in the rocket will show that they might sustain the expected behavior for a limited time, but go on to using the assemblage of parts as just that—a matrix of sub-units to be played in and on.

For new responses to be elicited, the objects in the play environment must be manipulatable by the child. Currently much apparatus merely allows the child to manipulate himself by swinging or whirling. This is important, but goes only half way. The items that sustain attention and generate the greatest number of responses are those that are manipulatable. The items manipulated should by their interactions demonstrate relationships that exist in the physical world, and some should require social organization among the players. Finally, in Utopia, the playground would change regularly, say once a month, so that the children it serves are regularly challenged to explore and exploit a new environment.

Most of the concepts contained above are exhibited by adventure playgrounds, those delightful areas filled with bricks, lumber, dirt, scrap metal. Here the children can dig, build, change their environment, and undertake cooperative projects that can last a whole summer. If we can add to those kinds of playgrounds the new devices as they are developed that seek for specific goals by leading the child to learn by his own actions, then we have achieved the pinnacle of our current state-of-the-art.

With the above in mind the following questions might be asked about items being considered for inclusion in a play area.

Which manipulates the child in the greater variety of ways?

Which allows the child to manipulate it in the greater variety?

Which pre-empts the behavior of the child least?

Which allows for cooperation between children?

Which seems to be capable of teaching most, and which seems likely to teach what you want the children to learn?

Moving to a higher order of question:

Which combination of items maximizes the variability of behavior exhibited?

Which set or combination will allow different ages (on site or in the school or park district) to rearrange the setting to extend the possibilities for play either by the introduction of change or by increasing its complexity through a season?

. . . Just as every architect should be made to use the building he designs, so should the playground planner use (vicariously) the play area. If the behavior it forces on the child is stereotyped or dependent entirely on the presence of others and generates short attention spans, then the chances are that the play area is not doing its job. If, on the other hand, there is a rich variability of responses either in isolation from, in parallel with, or in association with other children, if attention spans are of varied length, and if adults are not required to maintain the play, then what has probably been created is a learning environment. . . .

come out & play

Come out and play!   In parks and playgrounds, on beaches and patios, . . . an old spirit revived [during the summer of 1971]. Come out and play! It's a spirit rooted in our national tradition, as old as Tom Sawyer and Huck Finn. It's a rallying call to all sorts of childhood games—from stickball to tag to jacks to marbles to hide-and-seek—all the games that are unstructured, free. On July 5, [1971] Come Out and Play Day [was] celebrat[ed] in many cities including New York City, [which staged] a giant Play Day in Central Park. As Mrs. Richard M. Nixon [said] in a special message (see it in its entirety on page 8), "To all the young people and their parents, a happy celebration on Come Out and Play Day, July 5, in all the parks, playgrounds and backyards throughout the land. The President joins me in sending our warmest wishes that they will enjoy our land and its pleasures in happy, carefree games and recreation, all of which are so much a part of our American Heritage."

Little League?   Some kids make the League teams, and some kids love them. But many experts think a diamond is a boy's best friend when he and a few buddies decide on the spur of the moment to play and choose up for teams hand-over-hand on a bat handle. Some kids watch TV, and the only muscles they use are the ones in their wrists as they—finally—switch it off. But an organization called the Outdoor Game Council of the U.S.A. headed by dedicated business executive Julian Burg, has for [six] years been serving as ombudsman for free play for American youngsters. Says Mr. Burg: "The playing of games is a child's natural way of maturing; making decisions on his own without the interference of adults is his way to independence. Indeed, in playing the natural games of childhood, he is learning to play the game of life."

How to have a come out and play day in your family or community.   Organize it through your recreational department or your family recreational leaders (Mother and Dad?). Consider the possibilities of all the available games. A partial list: punchball, dodge ball, handball, volleyball, marbles, balloon-blowing contests, hide-and-seek, hopscotch, jump rope, leap frog, Follow the Leader, jacks, nature hunt, etc. Says Mr. Burg, "Urge children to bring their own equipment, from roller skates to boxing gloves, quoits, bikes, trikes, Frisbees. And don't forget the opportunity for spontaneous play in such things as old tires and tubes, empty cartons, cheese boxes, and so on. For safety's sake, avoid knives, bows and arrows, hard baseballs, trampolines, and firecrackers. And don't forget such mass ice-breakers as a group tug-of-war, or a downhill rolling contest. Above all, the fun's the thing."

The professionals' views.   Among the government officials who [gave] Come Out and Play Day their blessing [was] Dr. Edward Zigler, former head of the Psychology Section of the Yale University Child Study Center and now Director of the Office of Child Development and Chief of the Children's Bureau of the United States Department of Health, Education and Welfare. Writes Dr. Zigler: "Remember how much fun it was to roam through the woods as a child . . . to play Follow the Leader on a summer's evening . . . to dig canals in the sand and trap the ocean's cool water . . . to ride a bike out to a place under a tree and spend an hour or two lying in the grass, staring up at the leaves, thinking deep thoughts."

"When we recall our childhood, chances are we remember most happily the joys and adventures of these hours of free, relaxed outdoor play.

"Unfortunately, too many children lack just this kind of healthy outdoor play today. I have in mind the child who sits in a semidarkened room, staring at a television screen. The inner-city child who tosses a basketball in a barren, fenced-in playground. The suburban child who hangs around the nearby shopping center, wondering where to go, what to do. These children have never had the opportunity to discover the world around them through play.

"We who are professionals in the field of child development know how important play can be in shaping the total child—in creating the awareness, the perceptions, the attitudes that make each child an individual. I believe that we should concentrate more on the total child today. In our country during the past few years, there has been far too much emphasis on the intellectual achievement of children. Child experts have said: give your youngster a superior mind, teach him to read at age three, raise his IQ. Parents have been urged to try new educational techniques and to buy special records and toys—in order to produce better, brighter children.

"But we need to pay attention to the social and emotional needs of our children—

not just to their intellectual development. After all, the proper goal of education is not to produce a generation of geniuses. Rather, our task is to provide children with an opportunity to develop their individual interests and abilities, so that they can become socially competent adults who can contribute a variety of skills to our society and who can, in the process, achieve satisfaction and self-fulfillment.

"To help our children grow in this way, we need organized school activities, of course. But we need more than that.

"As often as possible, we need to free children from school, from home, from parents giving orders. We need to let them play, wander, discover, take risks, make things—and make their own decisions. We need to let our children *enjoy* their childhood.

"Many parents have the idea that a child learns only in school. But I am convinced that children do a great part of their learning on their own, and that it's important for parents to know when to be at their side and when to simply leave them alone.

Play Is Valuable

"At the Office of Child Development, we are pleased to support this nationwide "Come Out and Play Day." We believe that free, healthy, unregimented play is a wonderful idea for youngsters not only on this special day but throughout the year. We like to see children encouraged to go outdoors, where they can discover the world—and themselves."

"Play is valuable," adds Catharine V. Richards, Chief of the Youth Activities Division of the Office of Child Development, Department of Health, Education and Welfare. "Many of our nation's children are being deprived of the opportunity to play. Play is not a waste of a child's time, but a valuable way for a child to learn through experience. It is a major factor in the development of a child's concept of self and in his learning about his roles in society.

"Too often in congested cities, there are no safe, accessible areas in which a child can enjoy adventurous activity. But if we are to help each child realize his full potential, we must encourage creative and inventive play and provide the necessary resources at the national and local level.

"In this busy, crowded world, we must see that children have the opportunity to play, the play areas and equipment they need, and the encouragement of caring adults—so that they can learn and grow through the many activities of play."

Come out and play. Such simple words, yet so nearly lost in a world that encourages children to monitor TV instead of stars, Scrabble indoors instead of scramble outdoors, and be structured and strictured at play by adults and adult rules all the livelong day. Why shouldn't an adult tell a child how to play? Bruno Bettelheim, renowned child psychologist, answers the question meaningfully: "Free-play games are so spontaneous that their value is immediately lost if somebody tells the child how to play them. It is absolutely essential to the game that the rules are self-chosen and self-imposed. What must never change is that the rules are self-set and that a child is convinced that obeying them will achieve magical results.

"These games are experiments in self-mastery and prove to the child that he is capable of commanding his own activity. He learns that even if he can't control the outside world, at least he can control his own actions. Through his own efforts the activity helps to bring meaning into an otherwise chaotic world. This is why the rules need to be self-imposed. Otherwise the child would merely be doing what others tell him and no experiment in self-regulation would be taking place. There is popularity and value in games in which the rules or obstacles are self-imposed. . . . The self-imposed rule or obstacle leads to the development of self-respect and self-mastery.

"The child must first learn to give orders to himself and to obey them, before he can learn to accept rules set by others.

"Adults often expect the results of play activity to be obvious and tangible. But the value of play resides in the act, not in the outcome.

"Through play, children can develop inner strengths and self-mastery, which will enable them to grow into socially confident and mature adults who can easily accept the rules of the group while maintaining their individuality."

Dr. Arthur Weider, Senior Supervising Psychologist, Roosevelt Hospital, New York City, concurs, adding, "Psychiatry, social work and related mental health fields are effective and I do not doubt their validity in toto, but what I do doubt is the rationale of spending millions on therapy and practically nothing, by comparison, on prevention—especially in terms of thirty-six million American children between the ages of five and twelve.

"The Outdoor Game Council's total environmental approach to the child can create a positive development of healthy emergent attitudes and ego within the mind of every pre-teen child in America, regardless of his status or need. So, though I continue in psychology as a practitioner, I also pour my energies into this preventive program for all children while continuing to therapeutize the 'daily few' where it was almost too late.

"The action of free play is the developing playground for maturity for the individual child. The child focusing in real terms upon real children playing real games is left with a residue of anticipation that can provide him with all-important healthier alternatives replete with ego fulfillment and enhancement of his own self-image among his own peer group. Whether he wins the game is irrelevant. Within the *gestalt* of 'free-play' is the mind-filling experience of the world of childhood. Most important, in free play lies the essential opportunity for the successful resolution of childhood conflicts now and adulthood conflicts a brief ten years later."

Message To Parents

Does all this mean "keep off" for parents? On the contrary, parental participation is a childhood-enricher devoutly to be desired—but participation, not patronage; spontaneity, not planning. The message is loud and clear: let's love and play with our children, but let us not overprotect them during their childhood so that we deprive them of their essential peer contact.

And let's not fret if they appear to be enjoying themselves aimlessly, so long as they're enjoying themselves. Or if they're unconcerned about being track stars if they'd rather track stars. Or worry, if they don't, about winning. Or shove them into structured recreational groups if they'd rather play in their own backyards with a pal or two or with *us*. Yes, let's set this day aside and get our towns to turn out for it—games for the kids to play *by themselves*, or games for the kids *and* their folks if the kids want it that way. Let's make Come Out and Play Day a rallying call for joyous play that encourages individual growth, physical and emotional; self-reliance; and pride in personal achievement—qualities essential for success and happiness when the child becomes an adult.

lynn and john waugh

albuquerque's free-wheeling library

Above the door inside the storefront library at the corner of Lead and Broadway avenues in Albuquerque a sign reads: NO SILENCE. It just may be the most ardently obeyed sign in all of librarydom.

In a corner of one room a "Peter and the Wolf" film flickers merrily, its soundtrack scratchy from much use. An audience of children, most of them Spanish-speaking, sits entranced with Prokofiev's music as Peter and Ivan capture the wolf. In another room a television set blares above the cadence of youngsters counting to ten in a "Sesame Street" exercise.

Even the adults comply with this library's weird code of ethics. They move freely among the stacks, looking through books or chatting easily with one another or with the librarians. This is a library that has never known a whisper.

In a rear office cluttered with open boxes, piles of books, and laminating and poster-making machines, the crew that makes this library function bustles at a hundred tasks and demonstrates its allegiance to the "no silence" rule. Next to the poster-making machine behind a desk that blends perfectly into the clutter sits Richard Levine, chief

Lynn and John Waugh, "Albuquerque's Free-Wheeling Library," in *American Education*, Vol. 7 (August/September, 1971), 33–35. Reprinted by permission.

librarian of the Albuquerque Model Cities Library and a man at ease with chaos that would frazzle an ordinary member of his calling.

Levine presides over one of the most unusual education experiments in the country. And beyond its novelty, this remarkable enterprise appears to be achieving such success in reaching minorities and the poor as to attract national attention. Already several Model Cities programs in other States have sent representatives to catch the action in Levine's establishment, which looks more like a used book store than a library. This summer a group of Model City librarians and chicano aides attending a two-week institute sponsored by the U.S. Office of Education will make a comprehensive analysis of the library and the depth and extent of its impact on the community.

The Albuquerque Model Cities Library was conceived in the wide-ranging, impatient mind of Donald A. Riechmann, director of the Albuquerque Public Library. "For a long time," Riechmann says, "I grieved about our almost total failure to serve the Spanish-speaking, and the blacks, Indians, and low-income anglos in this city. We only reach 25 to 35 percent of the people in Albuquerque anyhow, and very few of them are Indians, chicanos, blacks, or poor whites."

The day he first heard of the Model Cities concept, Riechmann began to plot a library that might fit into such a program—if one was ever assigned to Albuquerque. When Albuquerque subsequently appeared on the list of selected cities, Riechmann had a library plan all ready to go.

The strip of inner city ultimately designated as the Model Cities area is 81 percent Mexican-American, 12 percent black, two percent Indian, and five percent anglo. Riechmann persuaded officials of the program to allocate $150,000 for the rental of an old printing shop on Lead Avenue in the heart of this depressed area. There he and the three librarians temporarily assigned to help start the library sat down and tried to figure out what kinds of books might appeal to such a clientele, most of whom rated the attractions of a library as minimal.

Riechmann's initial impulse was to follow the standard procedure of first evaluating the need and then trying to fill it. But that would require time; moreover, Riechmann and the other librarians felt a bit shaky about their ability to determine what the need might really be. So they decided to move ahead backwards, first filling the need, or at least the library, and then evaluating the results later.

With the help of four trainees from the community, they started ordering at random from any publishing house offering books even remotely dealing with things they thought, felt, or hoped, would appeal to people in the Model Cities area. The assortment of publications that soon began to arrive covered just about every conceivable taste and ranged from comic books and militant newspapers to ethnic classics and best sellers. The library quickly built the best collection of recent literature about blacks, chicanos, and Indians in all of New Mexico.

Then Riechmann made the new venture virtually autonomous. It didn't have to operate under downtown library or branch rules. Its central policy dismissed tradition and the restraints that frequently proliferate in its folds. Today, operating with an open-door friendliness that sweeps through the neighborhood like a fresh breeze, the new library, now rounding into its second year, is attracting 4,200 people a month.

The key characteristic is informality. Silence is strictly not maintained. There are no card catalogs—just go to the shelf and find it, friend, and if you can't let us know. The books are only roughly sorted according to subject matter under a system that would probably decimate Dewey. Because fines for overdue books are unthinkable, the library may well have as many volumes it can't locate as volumes it has tabs on.

Points of Returns

"The point is," says Levine, who took charge of the library shortly after it was launched, "those books, wherever they are, are out in the community and, we hope, helping somebody. And that, after all, is what this library is all about. Of course, we encourage the return of library property. That, too, is what a library is all about. Friendly post cards help us do a fairly good job of it, and as we learn library skills, so do our users."

The decor of the Model Cities library breathes vivacity. Reproductions of paintings by old Dutch masters hang side by side with "Viva Zapata" posters. The walls are lined with drawings by children who have come in, pulled their chairs up to the art table and turned loose their imaginations. Original poems, stores, and nonsense lines composed by young patrons hang above the desks and around the rooms.

After only a year, the 3,000 square feet of the library's original quarters proved inadequate, so last March a children's branch was opened on Broadway several blocks from the main building. But children don't limit themselves to their designated branch; they flock to both places. Youngsters who either had never been in a library before or who were cowed by the experience and never went back feel right at home. They browse through some 15,000 books in Spanish and English, pore over magazines, and never hesitate to ask help of the staff or just talk.

The allure for adults is no less powerful, according to Lionel and Mary Curtis, who as chronic library-goers qualify as expert witnesses. "The first place we make a bee-line for in any town we move to," Mary Curtis says, "is the library. Here in Albuquerque we go to three of them—the city's, the one at the University of New Mexico, and this one. And this is our favorite."

The Model Cities library operates on what the staff regards as a rather slender shoestring. After its initial $150,000 budget to get stocked and started, last year's appropriation dropped to $102,000. Levine feels that another $28,000 or so is needed to put the operation at an optimum level, with $20,000 of that going for new acquisitions, $10,000 for workshops, and the remainder for salaries.

Locating appropriate new materials remains a somewhat baffling exercise, though Levine is gradually learning which publishing houses specialize in Indian, chicano, and black-oriented books, and he has come to rely heavily on the trainees to share in the picking and deciding. Levine says, "They know better than anybody else what the people here want to read."

The fundamental reason for the library's success is the trainees, who know the families and where everything in the community is. They have carried the word to the community: "Here is your library and we are pleased to help you use it."

Family Affair

The library has come to place particular emphasis on motion pictures and especially those dealing with black and brown history and culture. By now its collection includes more than 100 films for adults and children in both Spanish and English. One of the library trainees, a secretary, clerk-typists—any handy adult or Levine himself—will run off a film for as few as two children, a number the library considers to be a legitimate movie audience. During the school year the entire Albuquerque school system draws on the Model Cities library film collection. Levine says that at least 40 percent of the films in the library are always in circulation in the winter.

In setting up the Albuquerque experiment in library science Riechmann sought to design an operation likely to have a special appeal to people living in a minority neighborhood. He has since reached the conclusion that the free-wheeling storefront library and its children's branch have much to teach the Albuquerque library system as a whole.

"The Model Cities experiment," he says, "could greatly affect our total approach to library management. It is already changing some of our attitudes. We librarians have too long discouraged the use of our libraries by the way we operate. Already we have had people stop in at the Model Cities libraries and then come to us and ask, 'Why don't you have something like that in our community?'

"Already it has forced us to look at all the rules and regulations that we thought were necessary to run a library but that just aren't proving necessary—or even desirable—down on Lead and Broadway. This thing has loosened up our thinking."

Then, similing he adds, "Just as I hoped it would."

PROBES

openness

a whole new way of life

"The largest group of people incarcerated in this country today consists of youngsters between the ages of 6 and 16," commented an educational psychologist. "These children must be freed from their feelings of restriction and confinement, or educators are going to be faced with increased disruption of their schools through student demonstrations and other forms of protest. Teachers and administrators must open up the students' school lives to the wonderful world of knowledge and the possibilities this knowledge presents. This cannot be done behind the classroom door."

The Open Plan School: Report of a National Seminar. Co-sponsored by the Educational Facilities Laboratories, Inc. Copyright 1970 by the Institute for Development of Educational Studies. Reprinted by permission.

Poster by Robert E. Samples. Reprinted by permission.

roger hudiburg

some frank comments from a teacher on openness

Openness scares the hell out of me—it also makes me feel good! It scares me because of:

SAFETY—A kid fell off the mountain once on a field trip, a light bulb blew up in a girl's face, hot paraffin spilled in a guy's lap.

DOUBT—Am I really on the right track?

NOISE—Constant, the sound of busy students.

LONELINESS—This occurs in a school where my openness is an island.

MESS, CONFUSION, IMPACT—Inevitable and ubiquitous, answering questions, rapping, always on call, a constant barrage of demanding, inquisitive students, broken glass, mud on the floor, spills, no time for meditation or reading, no respite from pressure. I yell a lot!

It makes me feel good because of:

DECREASED FEARS—I am less afraid of extrinsic intervention, the administration, bureaucracy, myself, the kids.

INCREASED TRUST—Much less soul-searching when I am asked for permission to do this or that; I try to consider things as legitimate as long as nobody gets hurt.

DECREASED DISCIPLINE PROBLEMS—Nuff said!

SHARED LEARNING THROUGH INQUIRY AND DISCOVERY—Excited girl peering through microscope at snow crystals: "Wow, look at this, Teach!"; Boy experimenting with electro-magnetism inadvertently produces copper carbonate: "What's this weird blue stuff? Where'd it come from?"—he follows this for weeks, happy and excited; Others surprised when they put alcohol and salt in snow and frost forms on outside of container: someone says "ice cream"—they learn much more than this, for they fool around for days; in fact they turn the whole class on to their "freezer."

Students do learn in an open environment. They learn about the excitement and importance of discovery, about their capabilities, their limits, self-discipline, and responsibility. They also learn facts. How many? Who knows? I just know that they learn some facts. They know this, too. I don't think I ever *really* knew this before, and I don't think that they did either. It makes me feel good to *really* know something and to know down deep that we are learning.

Openness promotes happiness and joy, it has good karma, it's groovy, Aquarian, cosmic. Somethin' else—it's like Zen; stop it to describe it and you've lost it. You've got to experience it, live it, do it!

One more thing. I have been frank as promised in the title. If you don't believe, then that's your problem. I have shared this with you because you're part of me and vice versa. But, you've got to learn to swim by yourself and only when you're ready. No coercion, no justification. O.K.

roland s. barth

so you want to change to an open classroom

Another educational wave is breaking on American shores. Whether termed "integrated day," "Leicestershire Plan," "informal classroom," or "open education," it promises new and radical methods of teaching, learning, and organizing the schools.[1] Many American educators who do not shy from promises of new solutions to old problems are preparing to ride the crest of the wave. In New York State, for instance, the commissioner of education, the chancellor of New York City schools, and the president of the state branch of the American Federation of Teachers have all expressed their intent to make the state's classrooms open classrooms. Schools of education in such varied places as North Dakota, Connecticut, Massachusetts, New York, and Ohio are tooling up to prepare the masses of teachers for these masses of anticipated open classrooms.

Some educators are disposed to search for the new, the different, the flashy, the radical, or the revolutionary. Once an idea or a practice, such as "team teaching," "nongrading," and (more recently) "differentiated staffing" and "performance contracting," has been so labeled by the Establishment, many teachers and administrators are

[1] For a fuller description of this movement, see Roland S. Barth and Charles H. Rathbone, annotated bibliographies: "The Open School: A Way of Thinking About Children, Learning and Knowledge," *The Center Forum*, Vol. 3, No. 7, July, 1969, a publication of the Center for Urban Education, New York City; and "A Bibliography of Open Education, Early Childhood Education Study," jointly published by the Advisory for Open Education and the Education Development Center, Newton, Mass., 1971.

Ronald S. Barth, "So You Want to Change to an Open Classroom," *Phi Delta Kappan* (October, 1971), 97–99. Reprinted by permission.

quick to adopt it. More precisely, these educators are quick to assimilate new ideas into their cognitive and operational framework. But in so doing they often distort the original conception without recognizing either the distortion or the assumptions violated by the distortion. This seems to happen partly because the educator has taken on the verbal, superficial abstraction of a new idea without going through a concomitant personal reorientation of attitude and behavior. Vocabulary and rhetoric are easily changed; basic beliefs and institutions all too often remain little affected. If open education is to have a fundamental and positive effect on American education, and if changes are to be consciously made, rhetoric and good intentions will not suffice.

There is no doubt that a climate potentially hospitable to fresh alternatives to our floundering educational system exists in this country. It is even possible that, in this brief moment in time, open education may have the opportunity to prove itself. However, a crash program is dangerous. Implementing foreign ideas and practices is a precarious business, and I fear the present opportunity will be abused or misused. Indeed, many attempts to implement open classrooms in America have already been buried with the epitaphs "sloppy permissivism," "neoprogressive," "Communist," "anarchical," or "laissez-faire." An even more discouraging although not surprising consequence has been to push educational practice further away from open education than was the case prior to the attempt at implementation.

Most educators who say they want open education are ready to change *appearances.* They install printing presses, tables in place of desks, classes in corridors, nature study. They adopt the *vocabulary:* "integrated day," "interest areas," "free choice," and "student initiated learning." However, few have understanding of, let alone commitment to, the philosophical, personal, and professional roots from which these practices and phrases have sprung, and upon which they depend so completely for their success. It is my belief that changing appearances to more closely resemble some British classrooms without understanding and accepting the rationale underlying these changes will lead inevitably to failure and conflict among children, teachers, administrators, and parents. American education can withstand no more failure, even in the name of reform or revolution.

I would like to suggest that before you jump on the open classroom surfboard, a precarious vehicle appropriate neither for all people nor for all situations, you pause long enough to consider the following statements and to examine your own reactions to them. Your reactions may reveal salient attitudes about children, learning, and knowledge. I have found that successful open educators in both England and America tend to take similar positions on these statements. Where do you stand?

Assumptions About Learning and Knowledge [2]

INSTRUCTIONS: Make a mark somewhere along each line which best represents your own feelings about each statement.

Example: School serves the wishes and needs of adults better than it does the wishes and needs of children.

strongly   agree   no strong   disagree   strongly
agree   feeling   disagree

I. ASSUMPTIONS ABOUT CHILDREN'S LEARNING

Motivation

Assumption 1: Children are innately curious and will explore their environment without adult intervention.

strongly   agree   no strong   disagree   strongly
agree   feeling   disagree

Assumption 2: Exploratory behavior is self-perpetuating.

strongly   agree   no strong   disagree   strongly
agree   feeling   disagree

Conditions for Learning

Assumption 3: The child will display natural exploratory behavior if he is not threatened.

strongly   agree   no strong   disagree   strongly
agree   feeling   disagree

Assumption 4: Confidence in self is highly related to capacity for learning and for making important choices affecting one's learning.

strongly   agree   no strong   disagree   strongly
agree   feeling   disagree

Assumption 5: Active exploration in a rich environment, offering a wide array of manipulative materials, will facilitate children's learning.

strongly   agree   no strong   disagree   strongly
agree   feeling   disagree

Assumption 6: Play is not distinguished from work as the predominant mode of learning in early childhood.

strongly   agree   no strong   disagree   strongly
agree   feeling   disagree

Assumption 7: Children have both the competence and the right to make significant decisions concerning their own learning.

strongly   agree   no strong   disagree   strongly
agree   feeling   disagree

Assumption 8: Children will be likely to learn if they are given considerable choice in the selection of the materials they wish to work with and in the choice of questions they wish to pursue with respect to those materials.

strongly   agree   no strong   disagree   strongly
agree   feeling   disagree

Assumption 9: Given the opportunity, children will choose to engage in activities which will be of high interest to them.

strongly   agree   no strong   disagree   strongly
agree   feeling   disagree

Assumption 10: If a child is fully involved in and is having fun with an activity, learning is taking place.

[2] From Roland S. Barth, "*Open Education*," unpublished doctoral dissertation, Harvard Graduate School of Education, 1970.

Assumptions About Learning
and Knowledge—Continued

strongly agree	agree	no strong feeling	disagree	strongly disagree

Social Learning

Assumption 11: When two or more children are interested in exploring the same problem or the same materials, they will often choose to collaborate in some way.

strongly agree	agree	no strong feeling	disagree	strongly disagree

Assumption 12: When a child learns something which is important to him, he will wish to share it with others.

strongly agree	agree	no strong feeling	disagree	strongly disagree

Intellectual Development

Assumption 13: Concept formation proceeds very slowly.

strongly agree	agree	no strong feeling	disagree	strongly disagree

Assumption 14: Children learn and develop intellectually not only at their own rate but in their own style.

strongly agree	agree	no strong feeling	disagree	strongly disagree

Assumption 15: Children pass through similar stages of intellectual development, each in his own way and at his own rate and in his own time.

strongly agree	agree	no strong feeling	disagree	strongly disagree

Assumption 16: Intellectual growth and development take place through a sequence of concrete experiences followed by abstractions.

strongly agree	agree	no strong feeling	disagree	strongly disagree

Assumption 17: Verbal abstractions should follow direct experience with objects and ideas, not precede them or substitute for them.

strongly agree	agree	no strong feeling	disagree	strongly disagree

Evaluation

Assumption 18: The preferred source of verification for a child's solution to a problem comes through the materials he is working with.

strongly agree	agree	no strong feeling	disagree	strongly disagree

Assumption 19: Errors are necessarily a part of the learning process; they are to be expected, and even desired, for they contain information essential for further learning.

strongly agree	agree	no strong feeling	disagree	strongly disagree

Assumption 20: Those qualities of a person's learning which can be carefully measured are not necessarily the most important.

strongly agree	agree	no strong feeling	disagree	strongly disagree

Assumption 21: Objective measures of performance may have a negative effect upon learning.

strongly agree	agree	no strong feeling	disagree	strongly disagree

Assumption 22: Learning is best assessed intuitively, by direct observation.

---

strongly agree no strong disagree strongly
agree feeling disagree

Assumption 23: The best way of evaluating the effect of the school experience on the child is to observe him over a long period of time.

---

strongly agree no strong disagree strongly
agree feeling disagree

Assumption 24: The best measure of a child's work is his work.

---

strongly agree no strong disagree strongly
agree feeling disagree

II. ASSUMPTIONS ABOUT KNOWLEDGE

Assumption 25: The quality of being is more important than the quality of knowing; knowledge is a means of education, not its end. The final test of an education is what a man *is*, not what he *knows*.

---

strongly agree no strong disagree strongly
agree feeling disagree

Assumption 26: Knowledge is a function of one's personal integration of experience and therefore does not fall into neatly separate categories or "disciplines."

---

strongly agree no strong disagree strongly
agree feeling disagree

Assumption 27: The structure of knowledge is personal and idiosyncratic; it is a function of the synthesis of each individual's experience with the world.

---

strongly agree no strong disagree strongly
agree feeling disagree

Assumption 28: Little or no knowledge exists which it is essential for everyone to acquire.

---

strongly agree no strong disagree strongly
agree feeling disagree

Assumption 29: It is possible, even likely, that an individual may learn and possess knowledge of a phenomenon and yet be unable to display it publicly. Knowledge resides with the knower, not in its public expression.

---

strongly agree no strong disagree strongly
agree feeling disagree

Most open educators, British and American, "strongly agree" with most of these statements.[3] I think it is possible to learn a great deal both about open education and about oneself by taking a position with respect to these different statements. While it would be folly to argue that strong agreement assures success in developing an open classroom, or, on the other hand, that strong disagreement predicts failure, the assumptions are, I believe, closely related to open education practices. Consequently, I feel that for those sympathetic to the assumptions, success at a difficult job will be more likely. For the educator to attempt to adopt practices which depend for their success upon general adherence to these beliefs without actually adhering to them is, at the very least, dangerous.

---

[3] Since these assumptions were assembled, I have "tested" them with several British primary teachers, headmasters, and inspectors and with an equal number of American proponents of open education. To date, although many qualifications in language have been suggested, there has not been a case where an individual has said of one of the assumptions, "No, that is contrary to what I believe about children, learning, or knowledge."

At the same time, we must be careful not to assume that an "official" British or U.S. government-inspected type of open classroom or set of beliefs exists which is the standard for all others. Indeed, what is exciting about British open classrooms is the *diversity* in thinking and behavior for children and adults—from person to person, class to class, and school to school. The important point here is that the likelihood of successfully developing an open classroom increases as those concerned agree with the basic assumptions underlying open education practices. It is impossible to "role play" such a fundamentally distinct teaching responsibility.

For some people, then, drawing attention to these assumptions may terminate interest in open education. All to the good; a well-organized, consistent, teacher-directed classroom probably has a far less harmful influence upon children than a well-intentioned but sloppy, permissive, and chaotic attempt at an open classroom in which teacher and child must live with contradiction and conflict. For other people, awareness of these assumptions may stimulate confidence and competence in their attempts to change what happens to children in school.

In the final analysis, the success of a widespread movement toward open education in this country rests not upon agreement with any philosophical position but with satisfactory answers to several important questions: For what kinds of people—teachers, administrators, parents, children—is the open classroom appropriate and valuable? What happens to children in open classrooms? Can teachers be *trained* for open classrooms? How can the resistance from children, teachers, administrators, and parents—inevitable among those not committed to open education's assumptions and practices—be surmounted? And finally, should participation in an open classroom be *required* of teachers, children, parents, and administrators?

elliot l. richardson

each livingroom a schoolroom

Should not educators try harder to increase the number of homes that encourage learning as the next big effort to help break the cycle of poverty through educational means?

Is it not in the educator's self interest to minimize, if possible, the number of educationally deprived children of 1978 and 1980? Can educators, perhaps working in close concert with other specialists in the community, help turn an educationally deprived home into one that encourages and supports learning achievement? And into one that will add to rather than detract from the future quality of life in the community? I am sure this wonderful transformation happens spontaneously in thousands of homes each year. Can we find out how to make it happen deliberately so the children of a new newly enlightened home can, in their turn, provide the magic catalytic effect to other disadvantaged children when they go to school each day?

Research on the effectiveness of "Sesame Street"—a program which the Office of Education had a major role in creating and supporting—points to the potential. Children who watched most and learned most tended to have mothers who watched the show with them and who often talked with them about it. Perhaps our slogan for the 1970's should be: Each livingroom a schoolroom.

Elliot L. Richardson is Secretary of Health, Education, and Welfare.

Elliot L. Richardson, *Perhaps our Slogan for the 1970's Should Be: Each Livingroom a Schoolroom.*
American Education, Volume 7, Number 1, page 11. Reprinted by permission.

schools involve the people who own them: a summary of community education

A COMMUNITY SCHOOL:

Extends its services around the clock and throughout the year.

Includes all people of all ages within the community as members of its student body.

Is for the whole family. It builds individual and family strength.

Uses all the resources of the school and community.

Sets the environment for the community to get to know itself and its difficulties.

Provides programs and counseling which can make a big impact on unemployment.

Furnishes supervised recreational, educational, social, vocational, and avocational opportunities.

Provides a forum for the discussion of social problems.

Furnishes facilities for health services.

Serves as a catalyst for family, neighborhood and community economic planning.

Provides initial leadership in planning and carrying out constructive community projects.

Promotes democratic thinking and action.

Constructs its curriculum and activities creatively and is less reliant upon traditional education patterns.

Is genuinely life-centered as a social institution.

Develops a sense of unity and solidarity in its neighborhood. Oneness of purpose overcomes community problems.

Initiates programs of usefulness for persons of all backgrounds, classes, and creeds.

The community is the classroom.

The facilitators of community education are community school coordinators and directors.

margaret mead

urban quality
community services and culture

The ideal community is one that can take responsibility for the well being of all its members from conception until death. One of the basic problems of environmental planning is the discrimination between the community services which should be provided, locally, within walking distance of children and the elderly, and which should be part of large regional organizational structures. We are moving towards an examination of this question, and a recognition that it may be much better to leave people within a home neighborhood most of the time, and bring the specialized services to them, physician, teacher, vocational consultant, etc., that we can better afford the traveling time of specialist consultants than the wear and tear on mothers and children and the aged of bringing them to central spots. At the same time greater demands for specialization will mean ever high levels of service, and these in turn will require funding on a metropolitan or possibly regional basis.

But the adequate use of the facilities which we already know how to design but do not use—electronic retrieval and information delivery services—should make it possible to combine the nearby, neighborhood-centered, person-oriented community center, with the widest possible scale of expertise, as the clinic nurse can tune in on a city wide system of information, or the social service worker place her client within a past and future network of vocational and advisory services.

The nature of expertise will change; instead of half a dozen highly specialized workers operating locally, one person with a clientele small enough so that he or she can know them all, can still draw on resources far greater than any local team of specialists can do today.

UNESCO Conference Summary. Man and His Environment: A View Toward Survival. Conference held in San Francisco. Reprinted by permission.

lyndon baines johnson

from an address on schools

Tomorrow's school will be a school without walls—a school built of doors which open to the entire community.

Tomorrow's school will reach out to the places that enrich the human spirit—to the museums, the theaters, the art galleries, to the parks and rivers and mountains.

It will ally itself with the city, its busy streets and factories, its assembly lines and laboratories—so that the world of work does not seem an alien place for the student.

Tomorrow's school will be the center of community life, for grown-ups as well as children—"a shopping center of human services." It might have a community health clinic or a public library, a theater and recreation facilities.

It will provide formal education for all citizens—and it will not close its doors any more at three o'clock. It will employ its buildings round the clock and its teachers round the year.

Lyndon Baines Johnson, *From an address delivered at the annual convention of the American Association of School Administrators, February 16, 1966.* Reprinted by permission.

INNOVATIONS

curriculum

robert e. samples

toward the intrinsic: a plea for the next step in curriculum

Modern education is orchestrated coercion. The professionalism of educators is generally measured by the efficiency with which they coerce. Times change, however, and the coercive criteria also change. Gone are the "traditional" days when substantive content provided the standards for educational evaluation. We are now crushed by a wave of behavioral research, and the dominance of content has waned in the name of progress. Currently the students are being tossed and tumbled about in the result of that research, the work of behavioral scientists who are infatuated with definable, measureable objectives.

The Measurement Syndrome

The prevailing claim holds that measurement (the virtuous necessity of research) is required in all legitimate education. This measurement syndrome can be related directly to the educational research practices currently in vogue. . . .

Looking at the past 10 years of curriculum revision, we find that the educational community is still bobbing in the ripples created when the great rock was dropped in its still waters at Woods Hole in 1958. With Jerome Bruner as their spokesman, the Woods Hole conferees gave a pushoff to science and mathematics revision that has kept it in motion ever since. The list of people who have contributed is impressive. But even more impressive is the list of professions that have become involved. Psychologists, teachers, medical doctors, social workers, priests, oceanographers, aeronautical engineers, philosophers, and nurses have all entered the fray. Everybody seemed to think something should be done.

Now, slightly more than 10 years later, there exists a feeling of unrest among many of us who have been involved in the enterprise. Though we have created books, films, records, lab equipment, courses of study, and a snarled new statement of old philosophies, we feel as yet unfulfilled. Several points of view have emerged, and two of them

Robert E. Samples, "Toward the Intrinsic: A Plea for the Next Step in Curriculum," *The American Biology Teacher*, March, 1970, pp. 143–48. Reprinted by permission.

have created a disparity between ends and means. It appears some feel we have created a finished model, while others are convinced we have just discovered the raw materials that must undergo yet another phase of evolution.

The S-R Creed

At about the turn of the century the brightest circle of light was created by those who were applying the stimulus-response (S-R) theories originally elaborated by E. H. Thorndyke. They held that when an organism is somehow stimulated it will respond. This led to what psychologist Dorothy Sherman once called "the rats, cats, and graduate student" era of psychological research. Using laboratory animals of the kinds mentioned by Sherman, researchers bent on internally consistent results limited themselves to studying a variety of simple stimuli that produced reasonably simple responses.

In a sense the research could have been ignored, had it not so profoundly colored the educational practices that followed. Curriculum writers were confused as to which kinds of stimuli should be selected to produce the appropriate responses. Many didn't care; they wrote curricula based on any vested interest that was popular with them, and they invoked the S-R technique to prove that their curricula were really working. S-R became primarily a tool of evaluation rather than of teaching. However, teachers still used it as if they were teaching with it.

They would "teach" the curriculum and then test the students by stimulating them (with questions) until they responded (with answers). Though this technique was at least as old as Socrates, it at least had the sanction of then-current research. S-R as described in psychological research was being applied to teaching as an evaluation technique that plagues us to this day.

No distinction was being drawn between teaching and learning. . . .

Enter the Cognitive

As if this weren't enough, another source of structure in educational practice lurked in the underbrush of the times: industry. The growing industrial institution bred its own mystique. The cult of productive efficiency provided another quality to be reckoned with. Some educators were quick to recognize that the mechanistic learning theories were compatible with the mechanistic systems approaches so favored by "forward-looking" industries. With the wedding of systems approaches and mechanistic psychologies becoming more and more imminent, there dawned an era of cognitive dominance.

The work of the cognitive psychologists really began to surge forward about 15 years ago. Piaget, Bruner, Inhelder, and others began to argue more than convincingly against the still-extant elaborations of S-R. Though cognitive theory differed remarkably from S-R, there remained a structure that was behavioristic in quality. True, the criteria for cognitive performance were far more complex, but there still existed an immutable link: stimulus → response. S-R behaviorism had metamorphosed into a more beautiful and legitimate form of its earlier self. Distressed by the accomplishments of Russian technology, the American educational community was jolted into cooperation at all levels. With workers armed with cognitive research and federal money, education began to experience a vigorous period of reform. The pebble had hit the pond.

And Now—Two Camps

Here we stand more than a decade later and what do we see? A camp of educators who consider the cognitive behavioral research results to be inviolate and a camp that views them with suspicion.

The behaviorist camp says education is extrinsically purposive. There is a reason for educating. The professor of education (the spokesman of society) is ordained to determine the curriculum and train teachers to manage students. Teachers, in turn, train the students so they will demonstrate (when evaluated) that they have assimilated the curriculum by displaying certain identifiable behaviors.

The suspicious camp feels that education should be intrinsically purposive. They feel that children should explore and discover their own capacities—indeed, should learn that they *have* the inclination to explore and discover. The professor of education has a very different role from that of the teachers. He must sensitize the teachers to the needs of the students in such a fashion that the teachers allow the students to create the curriculum. In this model, evaluation is primarily intrinsic rather than extrinsic. . . .

Someone Else's Bag

Today the problem we face is much simpler than the decisions we must make in the attempts toward its solution. Education will remain orchestrated coercion for many years to come. The problem as I see it is that we must decide upon *the nature of the coercion.* Shall we continue training children to jump through the extrinsic hoops of our behavioral objectives, or can we afford the sacrifice we must make and exert our energies to nurture environments in which school children can create their own behavioral objectives?

Traditional curricula provided environments in which children were coerced by someone else's selection of content. Modern curricula provide environments in which children are coerced by someone else's selection of behaviors. In both of these environments children learn. The sponsors of each can argue that they learn different things; I would argue that they learn the same thing. They learn how to be coerced by somebody else. *It is always someone else's game!*

Though "cognitive" and "affective" are terms invented a long time ago, the last 10 years of heavily funded curriculum revision have been heavily invested in the cognitive. With behavior being couched in locutions like "inquiry," "investigative," and "laboratory approach," it was assumed that the affective was being served; that is, through involvement with someone else's content in someone else's way the students' feelings of self-worth were supposed to be nurtured. I feel this assumption must be challenged.

To phrase it in the popular idiom, we do not necessarily get a thrill out of being in someone else's bag. Currently, I see curriculum revision as still being someone else's bag. True, it's a different bag now, but it still belongs to someone other than the student.

It is no secret to teachers working with students in ghetto situations that the my bag-your bag syndrome is being severely challenged. Black students seem the most eloquent in their statements discrediting the bag that society has put them in. Today's environment of electronic media completely tears away the shroud of ignorance that once protected the city-trapped Negro from an awareness of the middle-class norms of American society. He suddenly became capable of a total awareness of the organized intimidation that had been focused on black Americans. In the face of the new freedom wrought by communication, the black parents and students have rightly begun to question the schools.

It is absolutely clear that the schools, in an effort to cling to the past, have sustained social and academic traditions that were exposed as faulty long ago. Suburban middle-class students have never been threatened enough by deprivation to do anything but accept their lot in public-school environments. After all, they were, by the rules of society, expected to go on to higher education. College is the incubator of middle-class society.

Black students in an environment of deprivation can look to entrance into the middle class only through conformity-buttressed access routes leading through the public schools into the colleges. Yet the generations of social intimidation that preceded them into today's arena of awareness most certainly can become too much of a burden to bear. The professional coercion of school environments does not appear to be very different from social intimidation—if you are black and aware.

Fortunately, there are echoes from suburban youth that indicate that they, too, are "aware." Although they are not under stress because of deprived physical and social environments, they are under stress *because of the fact that other people are.* The adults who are bewildered by the "senseless" rebellion of suburban youth still hope this is a raccoon coat and goldfish-swallowing phase. They insulate themselves with assurances that "kids will be kids" and sit futilely waiting for it all to pass. It is frightening that many adults cannot see that the young are more aware than the grown-ups can ever be. The students know that institutions such as family, school, church, and supposedly benevolent bureaucracies are those agents that tend to preserve the status quo. The rebellious suburban kids *hear* the system chanting, "Go, go, Status Quo!" Black kids *feel* the pain of status quo. *Everybody is tired of it!*

M. Sylvester King, a many-degreed Harvard man, was principal of an intermediate school in Harlem. King lives in his community and brings a brilliant quality of humanness to his world. He recently startled a group of scientists, educators, teachers, and administrators with the statement, "You'd better thank God for the ghettos. . . . They will give you permission to do the right thing in the suburbs." In my opinion this is one of the most powerful statements I have heard in a dozen or so years of working in education.

What we know from education in city ghettos is that the children have a high capacity for "crap detection." This phrase is borrowed from *Teaching as a Subversive Activity*, by Postman and Weingartner (1969). The authors make a strong case for all kids being able to do this. I feel their point is well taken, but the difference between the ghetto students and suburban kids is the ghetto kids are quicker to *tell you* about it.

In addition to detecting the curricular crap, the ghetto kids are forced to submit (if they are to survive and gain access to the middle class) to the coercion of staying in school. The result is a devastating erosion of their self-images. The destruction of self-image is a characteristic of all minority groups when confronted by social bureaucracy. All young people are essentially members of a minority group in that they are constantly intimidated by the adult social bureaucracy. So in this sense *all* youth represents a minority group.

Society and school expect conformity. The only difference between the "traditional" and "modern" is the nature of the conformity criteria. In traditional curricula, content is stressed; in modern curricula, process is stressed. Though the motives differ, both are completely capable of creating conformity situations. In traditional approaches you conform to the content that is presented; in the modern, to the patterns of behavior inherent in the process approach. Those interested primarily in the content contained in a course of study have lately been cast in the role of the "traditional" villain. The process approach has become the shining method of the innovator. And it would be well to remember that process approaches are constructed by cognitive behaviorists. It is assumed that if an active process approach is employed, students caught up in the euphoria of participation will learn content to much greater depth. This is to say, for example, that you learn much more of the playwright's meaning by acting out the play.

Meanwhile, What of Life?

To twist Shakespeare a bit: I would suggest that "school is but a stage and we are all merely players." We are using this stage for drama lessons while ignoring our capacity to make school more like *life*. Very little goes on in school that is related to life. To avoid wrestling with the disparity between life and school, many educators have chosen to refine the rationalizations that sustain the status quo. What must prevail is a kind of education that transcends the cognitive pitfalls we are now gingerly trying to avoid. The cognitive is dedicated to what one knows—and dangerously little is known about the cognitive. Michael Polanyi (1966) maintains we always know more than we can say. This suggests to me that school experiences structured wholly by overt expressions of the processes of knowing are going to experience a very short life. A strong case against the wholly cognitive school is made by Richard Jones in *Fantasy and Feeling in Education*. Jones' elaborate attack on cognition maintains that it is as important to concern ourselves with how the student *feels* as it is to concern ourselves with what he *knows*.

The structure of most school situations is such that the student is confronted by one decision: Do I play the game or get the hell out? If he leaves, he commits himself to becoming conspicuously defiant. The whole society can then point its collective finger and hiss . . . dropout! If he stays, he acknowledges that he is submitting to coercion. He begins to engage in the processes of self-avoidance and invents reasons for their continuance. It's a job . . . a car . . . a place to hide. In effect he enters the arena of that silent form of mental illness that couches its existence in wrappings of clichés that society generally refers to as recognition of a "sense of responsibility." I have the strange feeling that acceptance of responsibility and acceptance of coercion are synonymous in much of contemporary society.

Extrinsic coercion is remarkably different from intrinsic coercion. Schools can reflect this difference. Enough is known about the kind of school environment that is intrinsically coercive that we have little excuse in avoiding it any longer. Guided in part by the philosophy of the Nuffield Infant Schools in England, hundreds of individuals and groups across the United States have entered this arena with the greatest zeal. Storefront schools, open curricula, and hosts of unlabelable projects have served to precede my remarks here. I am aware that the critical tone of this article seems to ignore the devotion and progress of hundreds of teachers and educators across the country, but it is *because* of these people that such statements must be made.

Five Assumptions for Change

All schools can, and some schools do, serve the intrinsic capacities of students. However, to make such a position viable the following assumptions must be made:

1. *The student (at any level) is a reservoir of relevant experience.* Polanyi's statement that we know more than we can say is the heart of this assumption. Students are at least six years of age when they come to the schools. This is six years of experience in LIFE! The unstructured or self-structured universe of experience they bring to the classroom far outweighs the curriculum for the year. By rewarding the student for drawing upon *his* experience, you provide him with the experience of being an authority. He *is* an authority about what he knows. This is a vital step in establishing a self-image.

2. *The student is capable of making decisions about what happens to him.* In extrinsic coercion all decisions are made for the student. A democratic form of extrinsic coercion is realized when the student is given the "option" of choosing between alternatives that the teacher (or curriculum-maker) provides. The element of choosing between someone else's alternatives is often confused with intrinsic decision-making. For real intrinsic decision-making the student must make choices between alternatives *he* creates. This requires that the student have some control in determining what he does in school.

3. *The student knows the difference between relevant things and crap.* To a black student in Detroit or Watts, the people of his own race who were killed during rioting were relevant. Those rebellious Bostonians killed in the Boston Massacre of 1770 are not. When teachers attempt to lionize the mythology of the one act when the children have

recently experienced the other, they create an environment of crap. The standard mythologies of curricular offerings are easily detectable by the students. The student sees them as stupid and believes that only stupid people could stand before them and try to make them more meaningful than they are. Even more significant than this exhibition of stupidity is the cruelty exhibited in the acts of "evaluation" that punish the child for refusing to accept the curriculum's message. In addition, the intrinsic punishment the child feels when he *pretends* to be coerced by crap is incredibly humiliating.

4. *Nothing is more important for the student than to sense and know himself.* Life is lived by each of us. The worth of the enterprise is a personal thing. We can be tinker, tailor, or candlestick-maker with real pride if we know our capacities are in line with our aspirations. Almost always our aspirations begin higher than our overall capacities. In extrinsically coercive environments the student learns to exert himself in the name of someone else's aspirations. As a result his potential toward goals *he* sets may or may not be realized. Many studies show that students who know themselves do better than students who do not. In a life situation the fondest hope that each of us can realize is to develop a realistic set of aspirations and to progress toward them with the degree of progress directly proportional to our capacity to perform.

5. *Once he trusts the environment to provide a realization of all the previous assumptions, he will learn far more capably than we could possibly predict.* This last assumption, because it embodies all the others and extends them into the arena of learning, is by far the most comprehensive. *Trust* is the key word. If an honest effort born of real involvement in the first four assumptions is attempted, then learning will be achieved. This is not a vacuous hope. The Nuffield Infant Schools approach in England has years of experience to testify to the validity of this idea (Featherstone, 1967). Intellectualization and skill development are inevitable when children feel secure with themselves and their environment. What's more, the entire human condition is served when institutions are at the service of individuals, rather than individuals at the service of institutions.

Such assumptions differ from objectives in that they are statements of faith, not goals that can be evaluated. As soon as these assumptions become goals and progress toward them becomes measurable, they may well go the way of all behavioral objectives: specificity prevails, and they lose the magnetic quality of aspiration and submit to a tone of mechanistic performance. In a sense they become transformed from a human to a technologic condition. The assumptions listed above can be weapons or tools. When used against the child in an extrinsic fashion, they can maim and kill. When they are taken as guides for teachers, they remain what they are: invitations to the intrinsic.

Schools that truly reflect the human condition can honestly sculpture the future. This means that environments of extrinsic coercion in the schools must yield to environments in which students are inspired to learn about and "coerce" *themselves.* This self-"coercion" is in sharp contrast to the external coercion that guides most schooling. To salve our feelings as educators we must take solace in the fact that our infatuation with cognitive research and practices has been an excursion into fertile fields. However, a steady diet of cognition in our schools will result in an unnecessary form of malnutrition. *The affective must be served, and if it is, the cognitive will be inevitable.* We have to understand that we live our lives affectively but explain them cognitively. Living one's life is far more important than explaining it.

REFERENCES

ATKIN, J. M. 1963. Research styles in science education. *Journal of Research in Science Teaching* 5 (4): 338–345.

FEATHERSTONE, J. 1967. What's happening in British classrooms. *New Republic,* 157 (8–9): 17–21.

HAWKINS, D. 1964. *The language of nature.*

———. 1968. Mind and mechanism. *Colorado Quarterly,* 17 (2): 143–161.

JONES, R. M. 1968. *Fantasy and feeling in education.*

POLANYI, M. 1966. *The tacit dimension.*

POSTMAN, N., and C. WEINGARTENER. 1969. *Teaching as a subversive activity.*

leslie rich

teaching for the "real world"

To understand why Kenneth doesn't throw crayons anymore, why Karen has stopped calling her teacher bad names, why Michael finally took off his snowsuit, why Venus thinks the world should know how great she is, and why her father has undertaken a crusade, it is necessary to go back at least as far as 1969.

The Micro-Social Learning Center was opened in Vineland, N.J., in July of that year. Vineland is the largest town in the predominantly Italian farming region of southern New Jersey. It is an old community of quiet streets, vivid rhododendrons, and more than its share of poverty, particularly among the former migrant farm workers—black, Puerto Rican, and Appalachian white—who live in the town's outskirts.

"Micro," as the center is locally known, is a converted supermarket. On the outside it is blank and bricked-over. Inside, it is a bright and teeming place, with three huge classrooms, a nursery for the pupils' younger brothers and sisters, and assorted offices

Leslie Rich, "Teaching for the 'Real World,'" *American Education,* Vol. 7 (August/September, 1971), pp. 3–6. Reprinted by permission.

and storage areas, all brilliantly illuminated and richly carpeted. The classrooms are decorated with the usual merry childish pictures and papers, but there ends the resemblance to ordinary schoolrooms.

Instead of desks there are five oddly shaped "modules" or carrels, each accommodating three pairs of children. The teacher is stationed at a movable standup desk, and elsewhere in the room are easels, books, and an assemblage of interesting, block-like objects forming what is called the "Life Simulator Space."

Next to each classroom, but hidden from it, is an observation area where parents can stop in any time to watch the flow of the classes through one-way mirrors. The children know about these vantage points but are not a bit bothered by them. Only rarely will a visitor take their fancy to the extent that they will walk up to the mirror, peer into its mysteries, and demand: "Is the beautiful lady in there?"

Approximately 150 preschoolers and first-graders come to school here. They were chosen at random from the ex-migrant population, and until a couple of years ago they were among the most downtrodden and disadvantaged children in America. At Micro they are catching up, learning social skills and the language. The old hands among them have by now developed an astonishing, highly verbal kind of self-confidence that borders on arrogance.

When they get to regular public schools, one reflects, their more advantaged classmates had better look out.

Are these typical "open classrooms"? Hardly. The Micro-Social Learning Center— funded in part by the ESEA title I and the New Jersey Migrant Program—is an attempt to simulate life in the "real world" and prepare the child for it. The children follow a carefully planned and regulated course designed to build their self-confidence and self-reliance along with their scholastic skills. They are taught to work with one another but to depend neither on one friendly classmate nor on one particular teacher.

"The children advance," says Myron Woolman, founder of Micro, "because it's the thing to do, not because their teachers coax them, threaten them, or love them."

The goals of the center are impressive. Preschoolers, for instance, are expected to generate a basic speech pool of about 2,000 words and a reading capability of 300 words—and most start from just about zero. Tests (administered by psychologists who are under contract to the State) thus far show that the goals are being met. Scores in the Wechsler-Bellevue Intelligence Test for Children, the Peabody Picture Vocabulary Text, the Goodenough Intelligence Test, and others indicate dramatic gains.

To support the center was a bold decision for Carl L. Marburger, State Commissioner of Education, and his assistant for research, planning, and evaluation, Stanley L. Sallet; for Micro remains a controversial subject in the State and in the profession. Critics at one end of the spectrum say it could turn out robots. Those at the opposite end say there's too much permissiveness. The real hangups, however, are in the little things.

"The little boy is crying his heart out," one visiting educator observed, his eyes boring through the one-way mirror. "Why isn't the teacher paying any attention?"

To understand, it is necessary to go back further than 1969 and consider some precedents. There was, for instance, the Life Simulator Learning System at a Job Corps center in Lincoln, Neb., in the 1960's; catch-up programs for black children whose schools were closed in Prince Edward County, Va., in the mid-60's; and a special reading method developed for mentally handicapped and emotionally disturbed children funded by the National Institute of Mental Health throughout the early 1960's when Woolman was director of the Institute of Educational Research.

To get to the roots of the thing, though, an investigation should reach all the way back to the childhood of Mike Woolman, who developed all these projects and is one of the best-known and most discussed educational psychologists in the country.

"The tininess of my hands," recalls Dr. Woolman, "enabled me to escape the Jewish ghetto of Philadelphia. I couldn't grip a baseball very well, so I fled to the library, where I developed verbal facility—which gave me upward mobility. That's part of what is happening to the kids at Vineland."

Incentive Is a Must

There is, of course, a lot more to it than that. To oversimplify, Mike Woolman believes that almost anybody can be taught almost anything if the learning *system* is planned well enough and then realized in practice. For the disadvantaged, the twin treasures are language and social skills. Upward mobility in our society, he says, is limited to those who have facility with language. But to learn it, the children must have an incentive. They must learn to "live in future time," whereas migrant children particularly have been accustomed to living only in the past and present.

"Language learning," Woolman has written, "will occur only to the degree that it produces meaningful goals with less energy expenditure than nonlanguage behaviors."

"Nonlanguage behaviors"? In this case, that phrase means the big kids grabbing things away from the little kids. Or it means stony withdrawal for the weak.

What the theories come down to at Micro is this: The children work in pairs at their modules, learning to interact. But they change partners every three days or so. They progress through their workbooks from the red module to the green to the yellow to the blue to the white. The system is so structured that an individual learner makes at least 50 responses an hour and sometimes as many as 400 to 500 a day—considerably more than students in an ordinary classroom. The workbooks use picture directions called "ideographs" that tell the children how to learn their work by interacting with one another.

The teachers orchestrate their large classes in a cheerful, friendly way but without showing special affection for any one child. The child who cries is ignored until he stops. Teachers are not supposed to develop brilliant solutions on the spur of the moment. They should be, Mike Woolman says, "much like jet pilots—highly skilled professionals who use the controls with precision but don't have to know how the engine works."

"A zero learning base" is assumed for each new student. The first thing a child learns is what shape in the workbook belongs to him—one partner is the square, the other is the triangle. And the first subject matter he studies is a vertical line, shortly followed by a horizontal line, and perhaps followed thereafter by a circle. After a few pages these various lines begin to form shapes the child either recognizes at once or will come to recognize—the shapes, for example, of letters of the alphabet.

Behind these first simple lessons and the progressively more demanding ones that follow is Dr. Woolman's "lattice" method of organizing information and the "progressive choice" method of organizing the learning materials actually used. One concept is learned. Another is learned. They are combined. A third is added, a fourth, with further combinations at appropriate moments as the preschoolers (in this case) proceed through their workbooks on Common Forms, Body Parts, Food, Household Objects, Nature, Community and Classroom, and Other Lands, cumulating terms at several conceptual levels as they go.

After learning a cluster of concepts in the modules, the youngsters go to the Life Simulator Space, where they would put the concepts into action with blocks and a variety of other objects. But almost everything is too bulky or heavy for one child to lift. Again he must depend on a partner—but a different partner every few days or even hours.

Micro Had Its Doubters

Similarly, teachers change classrooms every two months. No dependence there. They even take turns as center manager to learn the system's administrative aspects.

Such is the system that was launched in 1969 and is progressing today with few changes. But in those early months, there were some who doubted it was going to work. Among them were several of the teachers. Jynell Harris, now assisting Dr. Woolman as a curriculum specialist, joined Micro at the very beginning with the severest misgivings. After her two-week training course she didn't "buy" the system at all and was ready to resign (teachers are all from the Vineland schools and can return to a regular school on their request—or Micro's).

"Then a friend of mine called me one night to ask what was going on over there," she says. "I told her about it, and my friend thought it was terrible. I found myself defending Dr. Woolman and his ideas. So on the day before the end of training, I decided to stay.

"But after my first day in the classroom, I was ready to quit again."

A film made by a staff member shows what happened that day. The little migrant children, carefully dressed by their proud parents, almost tore the place apart. They shrieked in joy and in torment, pulling at the equipment, leaping up on modules, crying in the corner, wrestling with one another. The teachers gestured, invited, herded them toward the modules.

One Puerto Rican father sat stonily in the observation room (parents are invited any time) to see what was happening to his daughter. He left without comment.

Woolman had his own twinges: "When I saw those children, I thought that this time I expected too much of a system. Maybe they were already too psychologically damaged. And the Spanish-speaking children seemed to know no English at all."

The system allows for no coercion. When a child misbehaves in an antisocial way, he is "separated from his peers" for three minutes. An aide then asks him four questions that are printed on a card known as the Learner Guidance Interview Form (LGIF): (1) Do you know why you are here? (2) Do you know what to do in the room with your teacher? (3) Do you want to stay here or go back? (4) Do you know what to do? When all four responses are "yes," the matter is closed. Otherwise, there is a procedure by which the child is progressively interviewed in the same way by the teacher and the center manager. It's all done in a calm, unemotional way—no matter what. LGIF is something those who have seen Micro can never stop talking about.

When Karen called her teacher an s.o.b.—"for openers"—she received no reaction from the teacher, not even a change of expression. She got an LGIF. When Sharon, Karen, and Samantha came into the office and screamed obscenities at Oscar Carter, the unflappable psychology professor who is administrative head of the project, he didn't even look up from his work. They got an LGIF. No one denies that there are continuing behavior problems at Micro, but everyone seems to agree that such problems are no longer very serious.

The other day a new teacher was doing an LGIF with little Walter and mistakenly started with question number two—the business about what to do back in the room with the teacher. "Hold it," Walter commanded. "You forgot to ask if I know why I'm here."

Woolman thinks it was the parents who first convinced the teachers—and even himself—that Micro was working. They began to come to the center with increasing curiosity, peering at the charts (an almost daily report card, even though children can come and go during the year while proceeding at their own pace). And even more telling, the parents reported that wonderful things were going on at home.

One mother, now an active member of the Parents Advisory Group, recalls that at one time her boy would talk to no one in the world but her. Not his grandmother. Not the neighborhood children. He would stand on the porch and silently watch them play. When they laughed, he smiled, faintly. But that was all.

Six months of Micro, and he played normally and happily—and talked fluently.

He is white and Anglo. His Spanish-speaking classmates have made equally impressive progress. For one thing, they have taught the other youngsters to speak their language, which is now the most popular tongue in the hall—but not in the classroom.

Breaking the Mold

Another withdrawn child, little Michael, came in a snowsuit when he first enrolled last winter and refused even to unzip the hood. He just stood there like a wooden Indian for five weeks.

"Then he sat at the red module," says Diana Limpert, the teacher currently serving as center manager, "and his little mouth began to form the words, 'my shape.' The jacket came off, and now he's moving along beautifully through the modules."

Even more dramatic were the changes shown by some of the super-aggressive children. Kenneth charged in the first day like a beautiful black bull, knocking over chairs and children almost without noticing. He spent most of his time after that in the LGIF area, stubbornly not answering. Then one day Jynell Harris noticed that Kenneth wasn't over at LGIF but at the module. He spent three minutes there that day, a little more the next.

"Now he's learning," says Mrs. Harris. "And his behavior is changing. Last week I was handing out crayons and I happened to overlook him. Now, until very recently that would have thrown him into a rage. He probably would have grabbed the whole bucketful of crayons and thrown them at me.

"But this day he was very calm. He just said, 'Teacher, I don't have a crayon.' I almost fainted.

"A day or two later, one of the other youngsters hit him. Instead of striking back and flooring the other child as he would have done previously, Kenneth seemed surprised. 'That kid hit me,' was all he said. He was beginning to be unable to understand aggressive behavior."

Teachers still have difficulty adjusting to the demands of Micro. Mrs. Limper, a Mt. Holyoke graduate whose own children attend private elementary and prep schools, says it took her four months to "come to terms." Now she wishes her expensively educated children had had the benefit of Micro concepts.

The other schools of Vineland, meanwhile, are having adjustments of their own. Now that some Micro "graduates" are joining the regular system the teachers are trooping to the bricked-over supermarket on Main Street to see what's going on. "If you have nerves," a veteran first-grade teacher asked Mrs. Limper recently, "why aren't they shot?"

As a matter of fact, Micro tries to train its children for regular public school. The initial 34 graduates were put in a special room at the end of the summer of 1970 (the school operates year round) and were placed in rows of desks. There were severe restrictions on going to the bathroom and to the pencil sharpener.

There is no scientific data on Micro's grads as yet, but word of mouth has it that they are doing well, though occasionally driving their teachers up the wall. Little Jackie declines to line up with the children going to the lunchroom but hovers in the vicinity. Not content to do just her own assignments, she constantly goes over to help others. Her progress in school is apparently satisfactory. "But you tell me that's not strange!" one of her teachers challenges.

The really amazing thing is that the zombies of 1969 are now patently proud of their school and of themselves. They have even become competitive. "What have I got in my pocket?" a black child repeats, patting the folded-up drawing he did in school that day. And nodding scornfully at some drawings on the wall: "A better tree than any of *those*."

Venus of Micro

Another boy, completely innocent of language until a few months ago, applauds the efforts of the boy whose job it is to get up on the chair and switch off the lights: "Way to go, Christopher."

Little Venus' father, a member of the Parent Group, is constantly being restrained from marching on city hall or the State house in Trenton to demand that Micro be extended for his people all the way through elementary school. And Venus also has a surging self-image.

"Are you taking pictures?" she demanded of the visitor.

"No," said the visitor, pointing to the photographer, *"he's taking pictures."*

Venus wrinkled her brow in annoyance. "I mean, are you going to take the pictures he takes and put them in the newspaper?"

"Do you want your picture in the newspaper?"

"Yes!"

"Why?"

"To show everybody how *great* we are."

Mike Woolman admits that for a time he had his doubts. After the first two months or so, the parents were invited to a mass meeting. More than half seemed to be Puerto Rican, so there was an interpreter. Woolman made a tough speech, saying that this was a hard society and "English as a second language" was intellectual amputation—that Puerto Rican children must learn the English language to move ahead or they would also be trapped.

As the translator took over, Woolman wondered if he had offended the group, who began muttering to one another. Then a weatherbeaten farm worker stood up and spoke in solemn and measured tones. The other parents nodded. They looked grave. Woolman leaned over to the interpreter and asked, "What did he say?"

The translator summarized the man's remarks rather neatly: "He said, 'What have we done here that God should do this good thing for us?' "

edward w. weidner

communiversity

In Green Bay, Wisconsin, home of the legendary Packers, a new kind of university is taking shape, a university conceived as a response to the ecological crisis that threatens man and his world.

This new institution is The University of Wisconsin—Green Bay. After 3 years of planning, we occupied our new main campus and launched our new academic plan in

Reprinted by permission from *National Parks & Conservation Magazine*, May, 1971, which assumes responsibility for its distribution other than through the magazine.

the fall of 1969. Superficially, it may seem that UWGB is like any other university. We train chemists, biologists, physicists and mathematicians. We train business administration specialists, elementary and secondary school teachers, artists, musicians, and actors. A student may select a foreign language, English, philosophy, or history. And courses in all the social sciences are offered as well. There is much that is familiar at UWGB.

But there is a crucial difference at UWGB, a difference well described recently by John Fischer in the February 1971 *Harper's Magazine*. In *Harper's* in 1969 Fischer had proposed what he then considered a wholly imaginary Survival U, "where all work would be focused on a single unifying idea, the study of human ecology and the building of an environment in which our species might be able to survive."

This description, Mr. Fischer later discovered, is an almost perfect summary of the actual academic plan at UWGB, a plan that he characterizes as "the most exciting and promising education experiment that I have found anywhere."

Our focus at UWGB is man and his environment. Whether in teaching, research, or community outreach, our primary objective is to help student, professor, and community member understanding and feel the problems of the environment and do something effective about them. Fundamental to our program at UWGB is the conviction that our mission can be accomplished only in cooperation with the people of our region as they act through their business and industrial enterprises, professional organizations, and governmental and voluntary agencies. To dramatize this relationship, we term ourselves a "communiversity," a socially responsible university relating to a socially responsible community.

What are some of the practical results to date of this new concept of the university and its role?

- The traditional academic department, wholly concerned with a single subject, or discipline, has been discarded. Instead, our faculty members organize themselves around the environmental problem areas in which they are particularly interested, no matter what their disciplinary backgrounds. We call these problem areas "concentrations." Within each concentration, scholars from a variety of fields learn to pool their knowledge for the study and solution of problems of the physical, social, and cultural environments.

- Students discover that their academic work can be relevant to the concerns of the practical world. They learn that most human activity in an industrial society, including their own, results in pollution. They see the community as an extension of the classroom, and cooperation as a more useful tactic than confrontation.

- Faculty-student-community teams are beginning to work together to improve environmental quality. An example is the current multidisciplinary investigation of the problems of an important recreational lake in Marinette County.

- Theory leads to action. Students have eliminated the use of nonreturnable beverage containers in campus clubs and cafeterias. They have organized bottle and paper collections. They have begun cleaning up a creek bed that borders the campus. They have incorporated environmental themes in some of their dramatic and musical productions. They have successfully petitioned the governor to proclaim an Environmental Month.

- The UWGB idea has attracted increasing national attention. Visitors have come from all parts of the United States and from France, Sweden, and Canada. Articles about UWGB have appeared in numerous American and foreign publications.

We cite these accomplishments only as modest examples of the things that become possible within the context of a university that focuses on man and his environment. Although we believe UWGB has made good progress in its beginning phase, we are a long way from achieving our most important goal—the development and widespread acceptance of an environmental ethic.

The ecological crisis, we believe, has not been brought on primarily by lack of scientific and technological knowledge. The crisis is rooted in attitudes that have allowed all of us, in our business, industrial, domestic, and recreational activities, to do things that are producing a cumulative, massive degrading effect on our environment. The great need is for a new set of attitudes that will motivate peoples around the world to apply to the improvement of the environment, the scientific and technological knowledge already available to us. This is what we mean by the development of an environmental ethic.

Conceivably, this new way of viewing our common situation could lead us to solutions of some of our oldest problems, such as war and poverty. The ecological view emphasizes the inescapable relatedness of all of us with each other and of man and his works as a whole with the biophysical environment that produces and sustains life. Thus UWGB is proceeding on the assumption that the old truths formulated by the religious leaders and philosophers of the past apply to the realities of our environmental situation today and may quite literally be the key to our survival.

university without walls
a proposal for an experimental
degree program in undergraduate
education

The time is ripe for the development of fresh designs for college education—more relevant, more flexible in meeting individual needs, more economical, which serve more kinds of students, which utilize a broader range of educative resources, and which foster continuous life-long creative learning.

Union for Experimenting Colleges and Universities, "University without Walls: A Proposal for an Experimental Degree Program in Undergraduate Education," (Yellow Springs, Ohio: Antioch College, September 28, 1970). Reprinted by permission.

Summary

This proposal outlines an alternative plan for undergraduate work which can lead to a college degree. It is called a *University Without Walls* because it abandons the tradition of a sharply circumscribed campus and provides education for students wherever they may be—at work, in their homes, through internships, independent study and field experience, within areas of special social problems, at one or more colleges, and in travel and service abroad. It abandons the tradition of a fixed age group (18–22) and recognizes that persons as young as 16 and as old as 60 may benefit from its program. It abandons the traditional classroom as the principal instrument of instruction, as well as the prescribed curriculum, the grades and credit points which, however they are added or averaged, do not yield a satisfactory measure of education. It enlarges the faculty to include knowledgeable people from outside the academic world and makes use of various new techniques for storage, retrieval and communication of knowledge. It places strong emphasis on student self-direction in learning, while still maintaining close teaching-learning relatonships between students, teachers and others. It aims to produce not "finished" graduates but life-long learners. Moreover, the program is so organized that it promises in time to reduce the costs of higher education,[1] without impairing (and we believe in fact increasing) quality and standards of student undergraduate educational programs.

The project has been developed under the auspices of the Union for Experimenting Colleges and Universities.[2] A total of seventeen institutions will take part in the program to include member institutions of the Union, as well as non-Union colleges and universities. Institutions planning to take part in the program include Shaw University, New College at Sarasota, University of Minnesota, Antioch College, Skidmore College, Loretto Heights College, Goddard College, Friends World College, University of Massachusetts (School of Education), Roger Williams College, Staten Island Community College, Howard University, Bard College, Stephens College, University of South Carolina, Chicago State College and Northeastern Illinois State College.

The UWW programs will seek to meet the needs of a broad range of students. They will provide highly individualized and flexible approaches to learning, making use of a much wider array of resources for teaching and learning than is now recognized, and relying heavily on self-directed independent study. While each institution will plan and

---

[1] For a more detailed analysis of the budgetary implications of the UWW plan and projections of costs and expenditures, see pp. 33–35 and 45–48 of the UWW proposal.

[2] A consortium of 18 institutions that have joined together to foster research and experimentation in higher education. Member institutions at Antioch, Bard, Chicago State, Friends World, Goddard, Hofstra University, Loretto Heights, New College at Sarasota, Northeastern Illinois State College, Roger Williams, Staten Island Community College, Stephens, University of Massachusetts (School of Education), University of Minnesota, University of the Pacific, University of Wisconsin at Green Bay and Westminster College.

design its own UWW unit, each will build its program around the following ideas considered basic to the UWW model:

a) Inclusion of students, faculty and administrators in the design and development of each institution's UWW program.

b) Use within each UWW unit of program components which provide for a broad array or "mix" of resources for teaching and learning, to include regular course work, research assistantships and internships, field experience, independent study, individual and group project activities, seminars-in-the-field, tele-lectures, video-tape playbacks, programmed learning and related media, travel in this country and abroad and other. An *Inventory of Learning Resources* will be compiled and serve as a key guide for students and advisors in the planning of program sequences.

c) Employment of flexible time units so that a student may spend varying periods of time in a particular kind of program experience depending on the special interests and needs he brings to a situation at a particular time. There will be no fixed curriculum and no uniform time schedule (item i, p. 4) for award of the degree. Programs will be individually tailored and worked out between the student and his teacher-advisor. Illustrative models are attached.

d) Inclusion of a broad age range of persons (16 to 60 and older) so as to provide opportunity for persons of all age ranges to secure an undergraduate education and to make for a new mix of persons—young and old—in our programs of higher education.

e) Use of an Adjunct Faculty, composed of government officials, business executives, persons from community agencies, scientists, artists, writers and other persons (many of whom may be alumni of the colleges), who make their living in other ways, but who enjoy teaching and who bring special kinds of expertise and experiences to the UWW program. An extensive *Seminar-in-the-Field* program designed to draw on skills and experiences of this Adjunct Faculty, will be developed by each UWW institution.

f) Employment of procedures designed to maintain continuing dialogue between students and faculty in both one-to-one and small group relationships. Procedures employed to achieve this include: student-advisor meetings at the beginning and throughout the students' program; on- and off-campus seminars; field visits by faculty and use of correspondence, tele-conferences and video playbacks.

g) Design of special seminars and related programs to aid students in the development of skills necessary for learning on one's own. Two such seminars are planned: one will focus on the development of verbal and informational skills (designing and conducting critical inquiries; using library and learning center resources; retrieving and organizing information, etc.) necessary for independent learning; a second will focus on student attitudes and feelings about learning roles and the development of behavior skills that build confidence in one's own capacity for self-directed learning. Similarly, special training and workshop programs will be developed to prepare faculty for the new instructional procedures to be used under the UWW plan.

h) Opportunity to participate in the programs and make use of the resources of other UWW institutions, once these programs have been developed.

i) Concern for cognitive and affective learning, with periodic evaluation by students and their advisors. Each student is expected to produce, before applying for his degree, a *Major Contribution*. This may be a research study, a work of art, a community service, a publishable article or book or some other noteworthy and valuable contribution. Length of time required for award of the degree will vary depending on the experiences a person brings to the UWW program and the time he needs to meet criteria (to be developed by each UWW institution) set for award of the degree. Special attention will be given (UWW central staff and participating institutions) to the development of new evaluation and assessment procedures, so as to provide more adequate criteria for determining individual readiness and time required for award of degree.

j) Participation in a major program of research intended to compare the achievement of graduates of the UWW programs with those graduating from regular programs. Comparison will include measures of both cognitive and affective learning.

To organize, plan and administer the new program it is proposed that a new non-profit university corporation, University Without Walls, Inc., be formed. The UWW Corporation would provide staff support to aid in the development and coordination of the local UWW programs, conduct workshops to bring participant institutions together from time to time for joint planning, program development and evaluation, and would undertake research on the UWW program. The degree will be awarded by the student's sponsoring institution or by the Union for Experimenting Colleges and Universities, in conjunction with the sponsoring college.

Participating institutions will hold membership in the University Without Walls corporation. An advisory board to help in the design and development of the program will be appointed to include faculty members and students from the participating colleges and creative thinkers beyond the campus.

Planning and development for the UWW programs will begin in the Fall (October) of 1970 and continue through August of 1971. While some institutions will admit small pilot groups of students to their UWW programs during the February, 1971, Semester, full-scale operation, which will involve about 50 to 75 students at each UWW institution, is not expected to begin until the Fall of 1971. The funds provided by the U.S. Office of Education will enable teams of students, faculty and administrators to participate in a series of local, regional and national workshops intended to aid institutions in the planning and development of their UWW units. Supplementary funding to provide additional resources needed for the development of the UWW program is currently being sought from several foundation sources.

Rationale and Need

The prevailing paradox in higher education today is a flood-tide of students eagerly seeking admission to college and in too many instances, their subsequent disillusionment, apathy, dissent and protest.

Piecemeal reforms within the traditional structure of the American college have usually proven palliative but not redemptive. Here and there, now and then, for a short time, various colleges have introduced independent study, field experiences, travel abroad, computer-assisted instruction, tele-lectures, interdisciplinary courses and seminars, experiments with the admission of the prevously inadmissible, more intensive orientation and guidance programs, along with a myriad of extracurricular activities. None of these, and no combination of them, has as yet transformed the standard model of the undergraduate college, or eliminated student dissatisfaction.

Meanwhile, pressures are mounting. More students apply for entrance and numerous colleges now despair of any significant improvement in their instruction because they are trying to cope with thousands of students in facilities appropriate to hundreds. The new entrants are more diverse as well as more numerous. They differ from one another, and from preceding college generations, in their values, skills and knowledge. No single prescribed curriculum, no set of optional "majors," is going to meet all these students where they are now, and nourish their continuous growth in curiosity, spontaneity, appreciation, understanding, competence, concern and character.

Financial pressures have grown serious. The future of small private colleges has become precarious. State schools struggle with budget cuts imposed to keep taxes from soaring. If any more economical method of education can be devised which will lower costs while preserving standards of scholarship, it will eagerly be grasped.

Pressures are mounting also from the new needs of a changing society. Recent research continually outruns textbooks in most of the sciences. Technological advance has altered many of the old occupations and created new careers for which few colleges give good preparation. New viewpoints and ideas are arising, not only in science and technology, but also in the social sciences and in all the creative arts. Faculty and students alike have become only too aware that what has been, or what is now being taught, is in too many instances rapidly becoming outdated.

The most immediate indicators of these mounting pressures is the severe crisis in college and university governance which has been building during the past several years. The lines of tactical riot squads and National Guard troops on several campuses, stand as clear warning, even at this writing, that some fault threatens to collapse the very foundations of present programs of higher education. Problems of financing aside, we need to address ourselves to the critical questions of individualization and meaning and impact of higher education.

Rapid advance within a sophisticated civilization produces not only problems beyond the traditional curriculum but also resources which have never been well used in higher education. In most cities there are specialists of high competence in fields which do not appear in the college catalog. New specialties emerge every month. There are banks of systematized knowledge which extend far beyond the college library. There are agencies of communication which link the world more efficiently than some campus switchboards link the department offices. There are not only unresolved conflicts and problems but also continuous experiments in coping with these, which go far beyond the resources of any campus laboratory. There are interesting people working out their own lives in ways which transcend the stereotyped patterns of American child, adolescent and adult roles. In short, there is more going on that has educational significance away from the campus than can possibly be brought onto it.

Attempts at major innovations which have sought to develop radically new forms for undergraduate education, have inevitably encountered resistance from administrators, faculty, students and parents alike. For all of us, having experienced our own education in a particular mode, have become accustomed to think of *the* undergraduate education as having to occur in a certain "place" or buildings known as a college, where students and faculty meet together for a set number of weeks and over a set number of years; after which period one is awarded (or not awarded) the undergraduate degree.

It seems clear that if we really mean to address ourselves to the many problems that now beset our increasingly troubled colleges and universities, that it will no longer be sufficient to fit new pieces into the old framework. Bold new forms are needed, breaking the constraints which have fettered faculties and students and prevented creative adaptation to both individual and social needs in this changing civlization. What this proposal argues for is the development of an alternative model for undergraduate education so as to bring into play a new array of resources for teaching and learning (in, and beyond the classroom), and to allow for a much greater individualization of the student's learning experience than is now the case.

INNOVATIONS

school facility design

theodore osmundson

the school site—our richest untapped environmental education resource

The Need for a New Kind of "Facility"

Environmental education needs study areas beyond the classroom. It ultimately requires going beyond subjective discussion and must deal with the reality of cause and effect on some aspect of the physical world about us. Indeed, the physical world is the focus of environmental education to a far greater degree than any other area of study. Consequently, real-life examples of both natural and man-made environmental situations are highly important to the learning process. How the natural world works and whether or not man works in parallel or in open conflict with nature's processes is the heart of the matter. Land in its many forms; still and flowing water; the movement and quality of air; the continuing dependence of all living things, plants and animals, on the condition of these three major physical, inorganic substances which we lump together in the all encompassing word, "environment," are all tangible and can be seen or felt.

However, the study of any part of this physical world would be academic without the injection of man into the ages-old interaction of land, water, air and the plant and animal life it supports. Man's uses and consequent interference with nature's processes pose the threat to worldwide ecological balance and is the essence of the problem to both the natural world and to man himself. There would be no "problem" otherwise. Because nature and its processes are real, tangible and can be readily observed, as can man's, such observation can be of enormous help in learning. Limitations of time and funds in all school programs make the convenient location of natural areas, mechanical measuring devices, and examples of high and low impact changes in the natural world brought about by man's activities, of primary importance in any attempt to understand the natural world. From that understanding, we must devise new human processes to interrelate and work in parallel rather than in conflict with nature. Such places or devices become what we have traditionally termed educational "facilities" for teaching and learning. They are totally unlike any facilities ever encountered by school curriculum and

Theodore Osmundson, "The School Site—Our Richest Untapped Environmental Education Resource," based on an overview study done for Educational Facilities Laboratories. Reprinted by permission of the author and Educational Facilities Laboratories.

facilities planners before. They do not require buildings, large expenditures of funds, or, necessarily, additional areas of land. They are not static in that they cannot be funded, built and forgotten as a fixed entity. They are living and constantly changing on the one hand and fixed and subject to man's manipulations on the other.

Kinds of Local Facilities Needed

Two types of outdoor facilities are needed. One should have predominently natural elements of land, water, plants, animals and be as nearly in a natural state (that is, unaffected by man) as possible. The other can be largely man-affected, whether for good or evil, and preferably both. The first can be preserved or created on the school ground or a conveniently located site in the region. The second may be the school site as a man-oriented land-use function, the surrounding neighborhood, community, city or countryside. In both cases they should be capable of illustrating certain environmental education principles, and be convenient to use on a daily basis.

The School Site Has Proven Itself

For immediate, daily, and convenient class use, the school site is unquestionably of first importance. It is also the least used. Throughout the country, school districts with commitments and programs for environmental education overlook the environmental problems inherent in their own school sites and the rich potential of developing study areas literally outside the classroom door. On the other hand, funds are spent for co-ordinating, transportation, board, and the multiplicity of secondary costs of moving pupils out of the school district for a day, overnight, or resident experience in a remote nature camp. Because of costs and logistic problems, such experiences can occur usually but once a year at best. Although of unquestioned value, their effect is sharply limited compared to a daily contact with outdoor environmental education facilities within walking distance of the school.

Such remote facilities are usually donated to the school district on a loan or rental basis and because of time and cost limitations are made available to only fifth or sixth grade students. Large school districts, with many such classes, find it difficult to provide more than one outdoor study area experience in the entire elementary school sequence. For example, Los Angeles City Schools, one of the largest districts with almost three hundred elementary schools, can provide a resident experience for sixth grade students but once in seven years, making it impossible for many students to have such an experience at all!

The Miami, Florida area (Dade County), like Los Angeles, is typical of large metropolitan areas throughout the country in focusing day or overnight environmental area experiences toward the sixth grade level only. With approximately 20,000 sixth grade students enrolled, only 200 pupils per week can take advantage of a two-day visit to an environmental education area away from the school site. With approximately 35 weeks in the school year, only 7,000 sixth grade pupils can have such an experience. Although four additional district-wide sites are proposed by Dade County Schools, only the sixth grade would have a two-day program in an environmental study area. In smaller districts, transportation costs and the difficulty of personnel coordination severely limit the use of off-site facilities. The use of such lands is necessary in providing unique day or resident experiences but almost impossible to use adequately as the sole environmental education area. As one teacher in environmental education put it, "The need is not on resident programs. The need is in school site development. We are de-emphasizing the overnight experience. It has been like the 'frosting on the cake'; it has tended to motivate people but certainly is not the kind of thing that changes behavior."

The Center Can Only Supplement the School

Even the finest district-wide or regional centers are, of necessity, devoted to specialized, unique educational experiences which are unavailable to the rank and file individual school. They make available large tracts of land for nature study or possess highly sophisticated and expensive equipment to add a new and often exciting dimension to the total learning process. One of the most outstanding examples of such a center is the Fernbank Science Center owned and operated by the Board of Education of DeKalb County, Georgia. Unquestionably, it is one of the finest facilities of its kind in the United States. Built under the inspired leadership of Mr. Jim Cherry, Superintendent of DeKalb County Schools from County funds, Federal and private grants, and donations from private business and individuals, Fernbank has a capital investment of close to seven and a half million dollars. Its facilities include a handsome new building housing a meterological laboratory equipped to display world weather patterns as read from passing satellites, a modern seismograph, an electron microscope laboratory, a controlled environment room, the nation's third largest planetarium, the world's largest and best outfitted astronomical observatory devoted primarily to public instruction, staff laboratories and offices, darkrooms, a science reference library, exhibition halls and classrooms fitted with the latest in projection and closed circuit television devices. Outdoors, a sixty acre climax forest is maintained and protected as a living laboratory for observing principles basic to the understanding of ecology, taxonomy, conservation and ornithology. In the future, a museum of natural history, an aquarium, greenhouses and a botanical garden are planned. Despite the high sophistication of its equipment, its program is basically like many science centers in districts throughout the country which are moving more and more in the direction of teaching science in its much broader sense, of relating it to man, of reshaping its thrust toward environmental education.

However, although the Center serves most of Georgia and much of the southeast, most classes, even in DeKalb County, experience and use the Fernbank facilities but one day out of a given year. The Center clearly states that its "function is a supplementary one in relation to the curriculums taught within classrooms throughout Georgia." Fernbank, for its stated purposes, is superb. But the void still exists at the school level. The daily curriculum throughout Georgia is devoid of the kinds of facility so urgently needed and which can only be provided on the school ground. But Fernbank, with its center-oriented program now running smoothly and to full schedules, can be enormously influential in leading a new program in the design and development of a system of "satellite" facilities on school grounds in its own district and state. This, it would appear, is its next beckoning major frontier.

Criteria For Effective Environmental Study Areas

On the other hand, the school site is remarkably well suited for use in the creation of environmental education facilities. As pointed out in the booklet "Man and His Environment",[1] an outdoor study area should meet five basic criteria. They are:

1. Have specific educational possibilities.
2. Contain elements that illustrate the effects of human activity.
3. Be easily accessible to students.
4. Have such facilities as parking areas, drinking fountains, and restrooms.
5. Be resistant to repeated use by groups of students.

Obviously, in all but the most extreme cases, the school ground meets all of these criteria or by design can be modified to meet them. It can provide an outdoor environmental education experience and unparalleled convenience at a moment's notice, with a minimum loss of time and continuity in dealing with a given learning problem. In addition, it possesses daily familiarity which enables it to become identified intimately with the life and everyday world of the child.

School Sites Have Proven Their Value

In a recent overview study [2] of the extent to which school sites have been used for environmental education, it was found that, as far as the total number of schools through-

[1] *Man and His Environment* published by the National Education Association, 1970.
[2] "How Are the School Grounds Being Used as a Facility for Environmental Education?", by Theodore Osmundson, FASLA and sponsored by Educational Facilities Laboratories and The American Conservation Association of New York, 1971.

out the country is concerned, relatively little has been done. Among those who have utilized their sites for study, there are several which have made excellent use of the areas immediately outside the classroom doors. Almost all the successful schools have developed their environmental education areas by enthusiastic volunteers with little or no commitment from the school board or administration.

Thomas Kelly School in the San Juan School District near Sacramento, California, is a case in point. When the principal, Mrs. Virginia Adams started an effort to establish a small growing area in 1966, enthusiasm among parents, teachers and children ran so high that they decided to develop 4½ acres of unused school ground. A plan was prepared by Mr. Rudy Yadeo, a parent and landscape architect, and work began. Except for the pond excavation the area has been developed entirely by volunteers. It includes a pond, amphitheater, paths and plantings of California representing the mountains, deserts, and waterbog areas. Simple bridges have been constructed across the pond and the tiny stream on the site. To assist the establishment of planting, $500 was raised from the parents and children to install a water line with hose bibbs throughout the site. Except for providing the land and irrigation water, the school district has not participated financially nor has it committed itself to environmental education by a stated policy. Despite this, about eighteen schools in the North Sacramento area have environmental study areas on their school grounds. Although being on their own has stimulated the imagination and participation of more people in building an area from donated materials and labor, the lack of openly stated support also implies the threat that environmental education will stop with the tenure of the person in charge at the school. The San Juan Unified School District does have a curriculum coordinator, Miss Jeanne Barthelt, whose duties, among many, are to help foster ecological studies. Her dedicated work has done much to build the program throughout the District.

In the Rutland City Schools in Vermont, however, the efforts of the small three man administrative staff led by the Director of Curriculum, Thomas Chesley, saw the potential of turning a swampy portion of a city school site into an environmental study area. They took the leadership, with the support of the school board, in obtaining funds and organizing parent and teacher support. A well-documented proposal for Title III aid funds was prepared and a Federal grant of $50,000 was made. Plans and engineering were provided by the U.S. Soil Conservation Service of which $14,500 was spent for major grading and drainage structures and the balance went for in-service teacher training and the preparation of curriculum and reference materials. All planting and light construction items such as a wooden bridge, observation tower, pier and shelter, were built by parents and student volunteers. The school district supports and coordinates the learning process which uses the area. Other schools in the District look to the North East School as a guide in developing their own school sites and all have the advantage of using district curriculum materials and teacher training coordinated by paid staff.

In Ann Arbor, Michigan, the School Board has adopted a policy of requiring an environmental study area on each of its school sites. They range from one to ten acres of woods at the edge of the school site and are used by the entire school staff in a strongly integrated and pervasive environmental education program throughout all subjects.

At the Highland Oaks School in North Miami, Florida, the school site was preserved in its natural state by the combined efforts of parents and teachers working closely with a sensitive architect. With a rare sensitivity to the landscape, Robert B. Brown, AIA, skillfully designed a school which fits among the canopy of existing native oaks like a series of vacation houses connected by open roofed walkways. Built on an oversized site of 25 acres, most of the area is occupied by the school and natural areas which include a large pond left by home builders in excavating for fill materials. The open fields attract birds, squirrels, rabbits, snakes, and red fox. The children requested and the school board declared the school site a wildlife sanctuary, one of the few in the country. Even the physical education side of the school ground retains numerous trees without interference to the program. Although Highland Oaks School has no environmental education program budgeted by the school district, a happy combination of highly interested parents, an intelligent and enthusiastic principal, Mrs. Virginia A. Boone, plus a fine site with a sympathetic architect has resulted in a learning context that relates all subject matter to man's interaction with the world around. As Mrs. Boone so well stated, "I think the key to environmental education is relating it to the child's own environment, to their being in it and what they are doing to it. You could totally isolate biological science from reality even if you took them to a pond and showed them how things there work. But when they come back and project pond conditions to rivers and large lakes and what is happening to them by the actions of people in dumping industrial wastes, sewage and other pollutants which can kill the entire ecosystem of water, they begin to say, 'Well, if that's the case, why are we doing that?' Then, ultimately a lot of these things can be corrected because they appreciate what the ecosystem means. But too often this connection is never made in the sciences and it becomes a separate entity which has no connection with man. But it's not only related to science, we bring these problems into social studies, mathematics, and everything we teach here."

The Urban School Site

In the usually small urban site, the need for imagination and design becomes even more acute. Although natural areas may be impossible to construct and maintain, the installation of environmental measuring equipment, roof greenhouses, the use of the building as a controlled environment, and the surrounding neighborhood as a man-made environment can be utilized as study examples. Of equal importance, the school ground can be imaginatively modified as a stimulating play place, where art and construction may go hand-in-hand to make an exciting environment for young people where only asphalt and chain-link fences existed before. The Buchanan School in Washington, D.C., whose paved school yard was replaced with a great variety of designed play structure at considerable expense and the Thousand Oaks School site in Berkeley, California, with play equipment built of donated materials and the labor of parents and teachers, are examples of two approaches to changing the school environment itself. It thus becomes an example of the possibilities inherent in man's control of the places he uses; an important lesson in environmental education.

Problems in School Site Use

However, there are obvious conflicts in the use of the school site. Traditionally, the site has been used exclusively for the active outdoor physical education program. But as Mr. Thomas Chesley, Curriculum Director of the Rutland, Vermont City Schools has said, "As a practical matter, the environmental education area should be separated from physical education. But like physical education, it too deserves its own integrity on the school site."

Also, the prevailing attitude toward land in the United States has been one of subjugation rather than adaptation or restoration. The schools have not escaped this. As one teacher in the Tom's River Schools in eastern New Jersey put it upon moving into a new school building, "Just as you saw as you came into the front of the school, the entire woods, that was formerly on the site, was knocked down completely. Somebody put it on a plan and it was done with Board approval. We are terribly aggravated with what they have done but we have to live with it."

An Outline for School Site Planning

At present, most school site facilities consist of wooded areas of one to ten acres left in their natural state on the edge of the school ground or areas which have been planted in a natural state, streams or ponds built, and such devices as bird feeding and weather stations, bridges, walks, benches, amphitheaters, identification signs, and the like installed without a clearly established idea how they are to be used in the curriculum. Only when it is decided what is to be learned can intelligently planned facilities be designed to assist the process. However, what has been done so far points up several fundamental factors which can be applied to the design and installation of facilities on the school site. For example:

1. A coordinator with strong leadership capabilities should be furnished by the school district to work with a highly motivated teacher and parent in each school.
2. The outline of the curriculum for environmental education should be clearly defined.
3. The teachers to be involved should be briefed on the goals and possible approaches in teaching methods.
4. Teachers should be directly involved in arriving at the teaching method to be used, and the needed facilities.

5. A list of physical items should be prepared which will aid each part of the curriculum.

6. All subject areas, such as science, mathematics, the arts, social studies and languages should be analyzed and brought into a pervasive input of environmental education.

7. Curriculum guides and other material should be prepared for each course of study incorporating environmental concerns and problems and related to the outdoor facilities needed.

8. A land-use plan for the entire school site should be prepared by a competent landscape architect in close collaboration with the teachers involved.

9. The design should incorporate all the *educational* elements needed.

10. The design should incorporate all the elements necessary to make the school site a humane environment in itself.

11. The facilities should be designed and detailed by the landscape architect for ease of construction and installation by parents, teachers, and children with flexibility in the design to allow future classes to take on projects after the major parts of the design are completed.

12. Work items too difficult for accomplishment should not be undertaken by volunteers.

13. Items too difficult to be accomplished by volunteers (such as grading and excavation) should be funded and contracted by outside help.

14. Other than initial "seed" money for design and heavy construction, all other funds should be raised by student and parent effort to bring about the strongest community participation in assisting the learning process.

15. Parent and student participation should extend into developing the *entire* school site as a total functioning and beautiful man-made environment.

16. Continuing maintenance of the entire site should be a function of the school district as a community-wide responsibility.

The Importance of Design with Curriculum Planning

The development of school grounds for environmental education is a virtually untouched educational resource. Few schools use their sites for more than physical education and parking. Almost no research has been conducted in the area of site design although billions of dollars have been spent for building construction and the purchase of thousands of acres of school land. A list of the items planned into the Lincoln School at Coldwater, Michigan will indicate the rich variety of facilities possible and the difficulty of designing them into a site which must convey a sense of order and also be used for active physical education and recreation:

rock garden	stream improvement
tree nursery plot	benchmark and compass
bulb beds	sundial

animal food plots	baseline—timeline
cold frame—hot bed	weather station
lawn plots	bird feeders
watershed demonstration	telescope viewing area
rock identification	maps of U.S. and state on parking area
dwarf fruit tree area	bird banding station
footprint walk	insect collecting station
nature trail	nature library
outdoor classroom	space distances
fern garden	planet sizes
garden plots	wildlife pond and nesting island
soil profile demonstration	rustic bridge
swamp garden	shelter belt
boulder area	site orientation center
observation hill	burned land plot
soil variety plots	soil erosion study
topographical lines	living snow and wind control
outdoor cooking	ground cover plants
keyed plantation	air pollution demonstration
playgrounds	water pollution demonstration
weed identification plots	bee hives
windmill	woodlot community
water community	orienteering center
retaining wall	compass course

The complexity of these facilities requires study in working out a curriculum for their use and serious professional design talent working with the curriculum planners in organizing these elements into a cohesive and useable educational facility which will work with the balance of the site. Competent landscape architects, trained and experienced in solving land-use problems in an orderly and beautiful manner are needed to work closely with teachers and curriculum coordinators in designing and programming these facilities. Unfortunately, the traditional limited use of the school site has inhibited the activities of landscape architects in school site design and few have experienced in working closely with school people. Educators and landscape architects must find ways of bridging this void of understanding if better school site design is to be achieved on a large scale. Planning and design are imperative to intensive use of the site for environmental educational purposes. None of these problems are insurmountable but the rewards of discovering and opening a vast new educational resource just outside the classroom door only await our serious thought and planning.

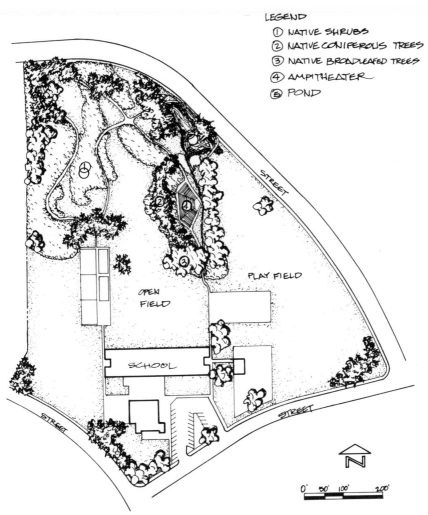

LEGEND
1. NATIVE SHRUBS
2. NATIVE CONIFEROUS TREES
3. NATIVE BROADLEAFED TREES
4. AMPITHEATER
5. POND

STREET

PLAY FIELD

OPEN FIELD

SCHOOL

STREET

STREET

N

0'   50'   100'   200'

THOMAS KELLY ARBORETUM

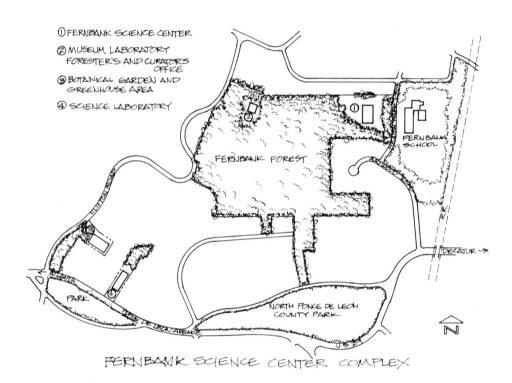

① FERNBANK SCIENCE CENTER

② MUSEUM LABORATORY
FORESTER'S AND CURATOR'S
OFFICE

③ BOTANICAL GARDEN AND
GREENHOUSE AREA

④ SCIENCE LABORATORY

FERNBANK FOREST

FERNBANK SCHOOL

DECATUR →

PARK

NORTH PONCE DE LEON
COUNTY PARK

N

FERNBANK SCIENCE CENTER COMPLEX

guidelines for community schools

Facilities and Equipment

A community's investment in its school plan is often times its largest single investment. Therefore, it is important that school buildings be designed not only for the education of youth, but also to serve the needs of the community school program. Forward-looking communities are now planning elementary and secondary schools to serve community school programs and are locating them with the view that the building and site will provide extended service as a community center.

The following are important factors to consider in the planning and design of community school facilities:

- The facility should be located in an area convenient to the community it serves.
- The multi-use of the buildings and equipment should be an administrative responsibility shared by day and community school administrators.
- Cooperative building and site planning should be initiated with the local government, park board, and other agencies which provide significant community services.
- The classroom furniture and equipment should be adequate for use by children, youth, and adults.
- Adequate storage space should be available for day and community school program needs.
- Space should be available for social activities.
- Lunchroom and kitchen facilities should be available to community groups.
- The parking area should be extended to provide adequate space, and this hard-surface area should be used as a play area during the day.
- Parking areas and grounds should be lighted for safety, security, and convenience.
- Adequate library facilities should be provided to accommodate both youth and adults

"Guidelines for Community Schools," published by State Department of Education, State of Minnesota, St. Paul, 1970. Reprinted by permission.

participating in the community school program—the library can conceivably serve both the school and the general public as a branch public library.

- The building plan should provide for consideration of use by senior citizens and the handicapped.
- Adequate display areas and bulletin boards should be provided for extended use.
- Climate control should be provided for year-round use.
- The business education, industrial education, and home economics laboratories, the gymnasium, the auditorium, the swimming pool, and other areas which have frequent use by community school programs should be readily accessible and, whenever possible, be grouped in wings or areas to provide for building traffic control.
- Multi-use of facilities and grounds should be a basic concept in building a new community school plant or when planning additions.

A total inventory of community facilities and equipment should be made to avoid duplication. In addition to schools, other facilities which lend themselves to community use include:

- City and county park and recreation areas
- City and county buildings
- Churches
- Service clubs
- Business and industrial areas
- Museums
- Art institutes
- Civic theaters
- Neighborhood centers
- Other educational institutions

It is the charge of all agencies in the community to efficiently and effectively incorporate their facilities, equipment, and services into the total community school program for maximum service to the majority of the people in the community. One of the most promising patterns in design and construction of facilities is the park-school complex.

THE SCHOOL AS A COMMUNITY FACILITY

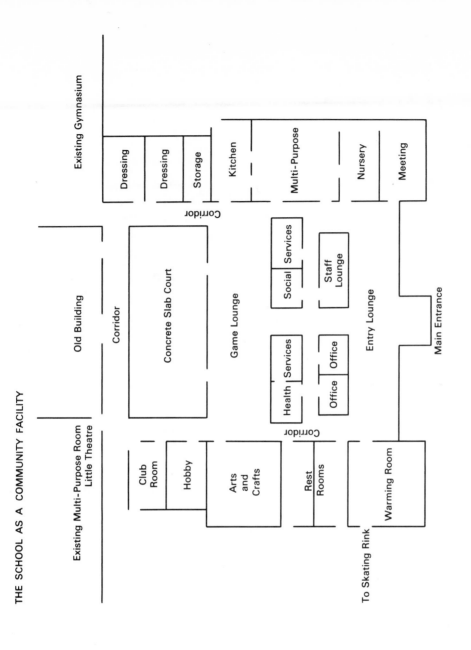

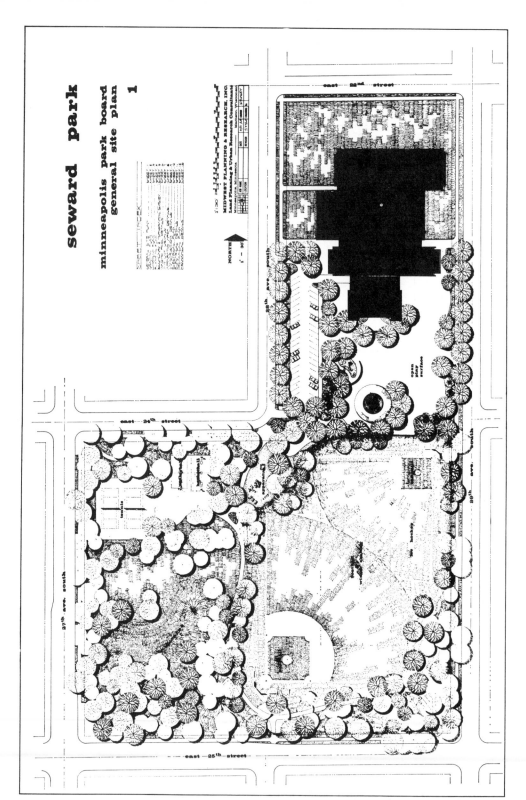

COMMUNITY SCHOOL

Example of Addition to Existing School Structure

Seward Park — School, Minneapolis

william van til

one way of looking at it
the second coming of the
one-room schoolhouse

The anthropologist did not look up from his charts as Herbert eased his frame into a nearby comfortable chair in the lounge of the Explorers' Club. From the paneled walls, masks used in primitive ceremonials stared down unblinkingly. Herbert, an educator ever eager to learn, ventured a conversational gambit, "What are you doing?"

"Extrapolating," responded the anthropologist briefly.

Herbert thought of several facetious comments he might make. But he sensibly refrained. "Extrapolating what?"

"Educational trends," said the anthropologist. "Like everybody else these days, I am speculating on the future. Right now I am extending our current educational trend lines into the decades ahead. They point inexorably to one conclusion."

"Which is—?"

"The return of the one-room schoolhouse."

"Impossible," said Herbert indignantly. "The one-room schoolhouse belongs to earlier centuries. A return to the obsolete one-room schoolhouse is unthinkable. What a peculiar conclusion!"

"That's what I used to think," said the unruffled anthropologist. "But consider my educational trend charts. As an educator, you are no doubt familiar with the present trend to the nongraded school. What do you think of it, Herbert?"

"An excellent innovation which I support wholeheartedly," exclaimed Herbert. "Restrictive grade levels are eliminated. All young children are placed in a primary group. Older children are placed in an intermediate group. Junior high school students are—"

"Extend this trend," suggested the anthropologist. "The logical extension is to eliminate grade lines from the school as a whole. So the one-room schoolhouse, a completely nongraded school, will return."

"One swallow does not make a summer and one trend does not make a peculiar conclusion," said Herbert confusedly.

"Consider also," said the anthropologist remorselessly, "the growing trend in schools toward using older students to help younger students. The one-room schoolhouse is

William Van Til, "One Way of Looking at it," *Phi Delta Kappan* (September, 1971), 16–17.

admirably adapted to this innovation and was long famous for so doing. Or take independent study, now a thriving trend. The one-room schoolhouse offers great opportunities for independent study while individuals are not engaged in group activities, such as recitations. Or consider today's emphasis on each child progressing at his own rate of learning. Clearly the most desirable current educational innovations are best implemented in the one-room schoolhouse."

Herbert said, "But today American education is housed in big buildings—"

"True," interrupted the anthropologist. "But we are talking of *trends* and particularly the trend from present bigness toward future smallness. Surely you have observed that discussion today deals with the desirability of small schools—mini-schools, alternative schools, street academies, the new English primary schools, yet unborn private schools which will grow from the voucher plan, and so forth. Or haven't you been listening to the compassionate critics as they describe their open classrooms, their classes in the corridors, their unadministered schools? Today criticisms of centralization and bureaucracy are heard everywhere. Decentralization and simpler organization are the order of the day. Or haven't you heard the vigorous critics of compulsory education protesting against the giant educational bureaucracies in the cities? Extrapolate, sir—and you have the return of the one-room schoolhouse."

"But the scholars in the social foundations have taught us that it is society which shapes educational developments, not individual critics," said Herbert. "Our society is bureaucratic and the Establishment is—"

"Spare me your tedious recital," said the anthropologist. "Again you are describing the present and ignoring the trends into the future. As the counterculture prevails over the Establishment, the bureaucracy will wither away. Small schoolhouses will prevail. With the greening of America, the one-room schoolhouse will come back into its own. Buses will be used for educational travel, not for carrying students back and forth between home and school. Big schools will become obsolete and may be converted to other uses."

"Such as the making of sandals or the processing of marijuana?" inquired Herbert delicately.

"I will ignore that latter comment, Herbert," said the anthropologist. "Instead, I will generously recognize that you are correct in pointing out that society shapes educational developments. And tomorrow's counterculture—which will be different from today's Establishment—will shape the education of the future."

Herbert abandoned ideology and resorted to an expedient argument. "A one-room schoolhouse in the countryside is all very well. But where would you locate your one-room schoolhouses in the city? This is an urban nation. Surely there aren't enough empty stores in our cities."

The expedient argument did not deter the anthropologist. "On the rooftops," he said.

"The rooftops?" inquired Herbert incredulously.

"Come, Herbert," said the anthropologist. "Have you never flown over an urban area in a helicopter as you traveled from an airport to the center of a city? Have you not noticed the incredible expanse of rooftops below, inhabited only by pigeons and solitary snipers? The rooftops of our cities are our great unused urban resource. They constitute the urban frontier. They top luxury apartments and slum tenements impartially; they cap warehouses, factories, museums, and theaters. They await the second coming of the one-room schoolhouse!"

"And——?" said Herbert inarticulately.

"Can you not see the happy children climbing the stairs or riding the elevators from their homes to the one-room schoolhouses on the rooftops above?" asked the anthropologist rhapsodically. "Can you not hear the pealing of the bells over the city as the one-room schoolteacher pulls the bell rope or clangs a hand bell in the doorway?"

"I assume," said Herbert dryly, "that there would be a privy behind each one-room schoolhouse and that the students will sit around a potbellied iron stove as they study their McGuffey Readers."

The anthropologist was obviously offended. He folded his charts and rose. "You have descended to satire, Herbert," he said. "That is unforgivable in serious discourse. I am sure you recognize that only extremists will insist on privies and potbellied stoves and McGuffey Readers. The characteristic one-room schoolhouse of the future will be a modern and well-equipped school. It will be as new and shiny and efficient as the mobile homes in which Americans increasingly live and the campers in which they increasingly travel and the mobile libraries through which they increasingly supply their schools. Farewell, Herbert." The anthropologist walked away.

Relenting, he turned in the doorway of the Explorers' Club lounge. "I must admit, Herbert, that one thing gives me pause with respect to my prophecy. I suspect that after thousands upon thousands of one-room schoolhouses are established on the urban rooftops, a few radicals will propose something they may call consolidation. They will suggest connecting the one-room schoolhouses on the rooftops through a network of science laboratories and industrial arts shops and such, through auditoriums, gymnasiums, and lunchrooms—and even administrative offices for a new bureaucracy! They will suggest the creation of a complex of interconnected buildings covering the city and crossing its streets. And they may prevail."

"Do not despair," said Herbert. "Even if consolidation were achieved, would not future generations eventually notice the available roof space topping the giant new education complexes?"

The anthropologist's face brightened. "There may be hope for us yet, Herbert," he said.

On the walls, the masks used in primitive ceremonials exchanged winks.

george b. leonard

life-long education: for awareness and delight

Teachers are overworked and underpaid. True. It is an exhausting business, this damming up the flood of human potentialities. What energy it takes to turn a torrent into a trickle, to train that trickle along narrow, well-marked channels! . . . Do not blame teachers if they fail to educate. The task of *preventing* children from changing in any significant way is precisely what most societies require.

George B. Leonard,
Education and Ecstasy

Institutions established to prepare students for goals by specialist courses and credits are being rejected and even defied by their clients. The TV generation wants participation in the educational process. It does not want packages. The students want problems, not answers. They want probes, not exams. They want making, not matching. They want struggle, not goals. They want new images of identity, not careers. They want insights, not classified data.

Marshall McLuhan,
"The Reversal of the Overheated Image"

A boy sits on the floor of the hall next to a classroom door, his back against the wall, his head between his knees. He is a cliché—sweaty, tousled black hair, loose shirttail, a tennis shoe untied. As we pass, one big, luminous eye appears between his knuckles and aims an accusation at me. Why has he been expelled from the company of his peers? I am drawn to the left. "On the right here is our new teachers' lounge." I go right. "I want you to feel free to use this room anytime you want. There's always coffee here, or you can just chew the rag with members of our staff."

We go on, into a classroom at last. It is a fifth grade, presided over by a stout maiden with glasses and reddish hair. Upon our appearance, the electricity within the room changes in a flash; the voltage of tension drops, the amperage of interest rises. Every face turns to us. "Excuse us, Miss Brown. I want our visitor to see one of our new classrooms." At the second seat of the second row, a boy's eyes drop from us to a note-book propped up on his desk. As the principal talks, I drift around to see what the boy is reading. Ah, a copy of *Popular Mechanics* hidden behind the notebook. He glances resentfully at me, then goes on reading, his eyes stubborn and dreamy. An aura of rare intelligence encircles him. I look away. He will need to keep all his stubbornness and all his dreams.

"If you'll notice the placement of the skylight, here, on the side of the room away from the windows, you'll see that the illumination is perfectly balanced at every desk." The principal is happy, and I rejoice with him about the delicious, perfectly balanced flow of outdoor light into a room filled with beautiful children. But something disturbs me, a vinegary tingle at the back of my neck. *There is a witch in this room.* I see her near the back of the fourth row—milk-white skin, black hair falling onto a faded blue blouse, a band of freckles across the bridge of a small, sharp nose. Dark eyes with dilated pupils are fixed on me now, bold and direct, telling me that she knows, without words, everything that needs to be known about me. I return her stare, feeling that this girl, with an education she is not likely to get, might foretell the future, read signs, converse with spirits. In Salem, she eventually would suffer the ordeal of fire and water. In our society, she will be adjusted.

"When it gets dark outside," the principal is saying, "an electric-eye device—here—automatically compensates by turning up the lights." The girl's eyes never leave mine. She is a sorceress, too, for already she has created a whole new world inhabited only by the two of us. It is not a sexual world. What she has in mind—she could never put it into words—bypasses the erotic entirely. But later, when those talents of hers that do not fit the scientific-rationalist frame are finally extinguished, she may turn to sex. And she may become promiscuous, always seeking the shadow of an ecstasy and knowledge that by then she will remember only as a distant vibration, an inexplicable urge toward communion.

"You see, a classroom such as this can never become dark. The illumination will always be even." The principal, I realize, is telling Miss Brown that we are leaving. The girl has no intention of releasing my eyes. The principal is moving toward the door. For a moment, I grow dizzy, then break the connection and follow my host out of the door, quickly reassuming the disguise we all must wear to travel safely in the world that I and the principal and most of us customarily pretend is real.

hugh vallery

a systems approach to educational facilities in metropolitan toronto

KING:

The basic objectives of School Construction Systems Development (SCSD) were to produce schools that were more economical, not cheaper, but at a better price to value ratio, that were higher quality than school buildings that were going up in the state, and that were erected more rapidly. The basic difference between SCSD and the previous systems buildings programs of which we were aware at the time, was that our objective was really to look at the building as a tool rather than an object. To do this we provided a combination, where educators and architects worked together to develop this future role of building in education.

WALTERS:

The total annual value of primary and secondary school construction in the U.K. is around a hundred million pounds, say two thousand four hundred million dollars, very small by North American standards, I'm sure. Of this, around 42 per cent is now being carried out wholly in systems construction, 25 per cent in a hybrid between systems and traditional; and 33 per cent wholly traditional. And the growth in systems use in school building has increased from 23 per cent in 1965 to 42 per cent in 1968. This growth appears to be continuing.

Jonathan King has told you how the original SCSD thinking was to some extent influenced by what we have done. The time has come, I'm sure, for us to be more powerfully influenced by what you are doing here. I think what we have to do ourselves is to

Planning Team: Jonathan King, *Vice President and Treasurer,* Educational Facilities Laboratories, New York, New York, Hugh Vallery, *Academic Director,* The Metropolitan Toronto School Board Study of Educational Facilities, Toronto, Ontario, Canada; Roger Walters, *Director-General of Production,* Ministry of Public Buildings and Works, London, England, R. G. Robbie, *Technical Director,* The Metropolitan Toronto School Board Study of Educational Facilities, Toronto, Ontario, Canada.

Hugh Vallery, "A Systems Approach to Educational Facilities in Metropolitan Toronto," a Report of the Proceedings of the 19th Annual Summer School Planning Institute, co-sponsored by Educational Facilities Laboratories and Stamford University School of Education School Planning Laboratory (New York: Educational Facilities Laboratories, 1969), pp. 17–19.

find out how to move out of our present situation, which is the extensive use of closed systems, the parts of which are not compatible with one another, and into a system which is more truly open and more like the one in fact that you're developing here. I think the main impression I would have as an observer from outer space, so to speak, of what's happening here, is the enormous influence which this work you're doing is going to have on the construction industry as a whole in North America.

I think the effect of the introduction of systems has been to raise the standard of architecture. I'm convinced of this. This may not be in sort of conventional aesthetic terms, whereby you look at a school and you say "my God, isn't that a wonderful invention," but in real terms, good places in which to teach children, and good places to be in and around. There's no doubt that the introduction of systems has made it possible for a large number of architects, many of them very ordinary architects, to produce buildings which have this kind of a quality.

VALLERY:

The directions of education are being profoundly affected by the tremendous population growth and mobility of people, by rapid urbanization, by industrial and technological automation, and by the information technology revolution. Man has entered the age of cybernation where the computer manipulates our machines and our productive output. The day when we needed vast hordes of semi-skilled machine operators is gone. The implications of these changes for education defy the imagination. The goals and methodology of education cannot remain unchanging in a world which is turbulently undergoing transformation at an unprecedented rate.

Our school system, if it is to be effective, must adapt itself to the rapidly changed environment in which it functions. It must recognize that real learning begins with a student's question, rather than with a teacher's answer. Students who receive no hearing for their questions in schools, will soon find schooling highly irrelevant, and sooner or later will tune out, drop out, or rebel against the system covertly or openly.

Starting from the premise that learning is a process that begins with a student's question, rather than with a teacher's answer, the people involved in our project believe our schools require radical change, not only in respect to curriculum and methodology, but also in respect to their building design.

The school designer should assume that education in future schools will rest on the process of learning, rather than exclusively on that of teaching. There will be much less need of having students receiving instruction from a teacher in fixed, enclosed locations capable of seating 30 students. The designer should assume that our highly structured grade organization will become ungraded, and that many flexible forms of organization and scheduling will occur, so that students may proceed at their own interest and achievement rates.

In planning for tomorrow's schools, much more awareness of community needs will be required. The community pays for and owns its schools. The design team should include representatives of the community.

Faced with the reality of open and flexible space, will teachers and students still cling to their practice of teaching and learning in an enclosure? Unless teachers fully participate in planning new learning approaches in flexible space, and are fully committed to the success of new programs, the whole project could be placed in some jeopardy.

Education involves more than the transmission of past culture. It should be much more actively involved in the continuing creation of new culture. It is more than the transmission of factual information, or content. It is more than preparing young people to live with others, or to socialize. It is more than emphasizing process or the structure of subjects, or indoctrinating students in scientific methodology. Above all else, education should be a process of helping young people achieve personal autonomy and of searching for truth. It should involve the nurturing of curious and creative minds. It should assume that education begins with a question by one mind eager to learn. It should assume, as well, that learning takes place when a teacher allows the questioner to arrive at the answer for himself. The emphasis in education should change from what we know to what we can find out.

ROBBIE:

I often feel that there must be deep significance in the fact that North America's most influential social institution—education—in renewing itself is triggering the regeneration of North America's largest industry—building, and building products production.

It was and still is my firm belief that the problem confronting the building industry in North America, at this time, is a desperate need for a total management approach to building, rather than the development of new technology, in other words the systems approach.

May I suggest to you today, that the combined educational interests of the United States, could provide a service of enormous value to the American people by becoming the integrated demand to bring about overall regeneration of the U.S. building industry, and through this regeneration a complex multi-benefit to the social, economic and spiritual aspects of everyday life for all Americans. The prosperity and extended opportunities which the inexpensive automobile has brought to a majority of Americans, is but a shadow of the benefits which a regenerated U.S. building industry could bring to your people.

I have no doubt that education is the institution which will lie at the core of the world of the 21st century, simply because we are now leaving as it were a multi-century muscle era, and entering a mind era. From the education system of today may evolve an institution of tomorrow concerned with integrated social creativity and betterment. The structure of this future system will undoubtedly be fashioned around the needs of the individual rather than the public, and as a consequence will certainly be totally, functionally, decentralized.

The leader and follower form of social organization which we practice, while giving lip-service to individualism, obstructs initiative not only among the followers but also among the leaders. It rewards conformity and purges creativity. It reveres neatness, order and tidiness and seeks to suppress originality, innovativeness and the unexpected.

It is in short the means of social organization appropriate to a species grappling with the problems of raw survival.

The only resource we have to advance our evolution is creativity. Whereas the first era of Man was concerned with conservation, the second in all probability must focus on expansion through the medium of creativity, where creativity is seen as the total use of the total capabilities of every human being.

The education systems of today must be changed to a means for bringing out and applying the creative potential of the populace as a whole, from birth to death. The means must be found to exploit the creativity which lies buried, in all members of the populace. Means must be found of bringing out the vast creativity which lies buried through the lack of contact between the generations.

The ponderous overburden of many concepts whereby we classify human beings as children, boys and girls, students, young people, adults, the aged, good students, bad students, intelligent, stupid students, and trouble makers, must be stripped away to release human creativity.

The school of today must become the "community creative centre" of tomorrow, the core of our urban environments of the future.

In summary, I would appeal to you to ensure that history does not judge us in education as those in the 1960's who could have saved urban North America from banality if we had had the courage to ensure the preservation of sufficient open space, regardless of location, and true public ownership of facilities to ensure unbridled public use in practical perpetuity.

rurik ekstrom

environment

In an invitation to a gathering at Freestone, California in March of 1970, architect Sim van der Ryn, of Berkeley, said that the purpose of the meeting would be "to learn to design new social forms, new building forms, that are in harmony with life . . . to build a floating university around the design of our lives."

This could have been an appropriate invitation to the students who during the Spring of 1970 became interested in designing and building such a campus for Antioch

Rurik Ekstrom, "Environment," a booklet published by the Maryland Art Association, the University of Maryland, Summer, 1971. Reprinted by permission.

College, located in the new town of Columbia, Maryland. It was felt that if the users were directly involved in the making of the campus they would have a greater understanding of the forces that formed it and could perhaps harness some of these forces to serve the needs of the college.

To this end two groups of students formed which resulted in the beginning of two courses in September of 1970. The first group were Antioch students who had become convinced that they could find a way to provide the needed space for their campus. The second group of students were from the University of Maryland School of Architecture. They had become interested in the possibilities for an alternative educational process evolving its own solutions for environmental design. The two groups had met in the Spring of 1970, during a festival, at which they experimented with a series of different experimental structures and began to discuss the problems of the college, both physical and educational.

In the months that followed, the problems were studied primarily from the standpoint of environmental and educational goals. The problems as cited and the resultant goals were as follows:

Problem 1

College and educational buildings have been designed with the best intentions and foresight available—however, changing patterns and philosophies of society and education evolve after the building is built, resulting in the educational program being made to adapt to the space available.

Goal 1—Possibly a campus could be built that could adapt itself easily to educational change. The users, students, faculty and staff, should be able to change the spaces quickly to meet their needs. Seminar rooms, classrooms, and offices could be moved, altered, dismantled, or rebuilt as the need arose with the same effort it takes to arrange chairs or tables in a traditional classroom.

Problem 2

Incredibly high costs—in Maryland educational buildings are costing 17–30 dollars per square foot and more depending upon the sophistication of the program. Antioch was having a tough time meeting rent payments.

Goal 2—A campus must cost much less. Money now being spent on buildings could be used for better education instead of tying it up in deteriorating real estate. A budget was set at six dollars a square foot for the new campus—with hopes of reducing it further if possible.

Problem 3

Educational institutions have been traditionally tied to a single geographic place—largely because the buildings are there. Often the college would be better off educationally if it were able to choose its location in response to its educational goals.

Goal 3—Design a campus that can move easily—either short distances such as within the new town of Columbia or across the country if that need arose. A nomadic campus.

Problem 4

Buildings produced by Western European man have historically been heavy, immobile, monumental and wasteful of resources. This grew from the needs for defense, expediency, and the desire to impress. Today buildings, campuses, and cities are paving the landscape with asphalt—debilitating the land, raping the natural resources for materials to build and requiring huge commitments of energy to keep out snow and rain and to provide a pleasant place to work.

Goal 4—Light weight buildings could satisfy the same need and at the same time rest gently upon the landscape, and just as easily disappear when they are no longer needed—leaving the meadow as it had been found with the smallest possible change having taken place.

Early in the research phase of this project it was discovered that air supported buildings would produce by far the least weight, lowest cost structure available and that the potential spacial quality of the resultant spaces was truly dynamic.

The group received an immense amount of help from the Goodyear Research team under Dr. Robert Pierson. Almost all of the students associated with the project have spent some time living in a half acre experimental building Goodyear built four years ago near Akron. After seeing what was possible and having a vague idea of the complexities of the problem, preliminary designs evolved and a plan of procedure was adopted.

The campus was to be housed in a single one acre inflated air supported building covering a portion of a meadow donated by the Rouse Company, developers of Columbia. All of the internal functions—offices, seminar rooms, laboratories, theaters, classrooms, lounges, etc.—would be light weight, easily assembled and moved, easily disassembled and stored, and each responding to the immediate needs of the people using them. To accomplish these goals the students realized the need for assistance and turned to the Educational Facilities Laboratories of New York.

A grant was given to further study and develop the ideas and to program the way in which the project could become a reality. Dr. Harold Gore, of E.F.L. gave the project the name of "Pneumatic Nomadic Campus." He also was instrumental in securing the services of the Research and Design Institute of Providence, Rhode Island led by Ron Beckman and Howard Yarme. This design group has been developing some of the best research in user design and "off the shelf" implementation of design solutions to educational and health facilities design problems.

By fall of last year, the team included architects, designers, students, faculty, and scientists and work began in earnest.

First, a model of the campus was built to display the idea to the rest of the college community and to provide a working display of the different ways the building could be used. The model was built partially in College Park, partially in Columbia, partially in Providence and was finally assembled in an all-night session in the office of E.F.L. in New York City. Since that time it has been traveling to seminars and conventions around the country in a effort to gather support for the idea.

Parallel to the building of the model was the building of a series of prototype structures to test materials, technology and the skills of the student builders. The first was a fragile fifty foot diameter spherical building held to the ground by a net of parachute cord and inflated by a simple household fan. This structure gave the team the confidence to tackle a more sophisticated project and with the help of Goodyear, two more vinyl prototypes were constructed in Columbia, each thirty six feet in diameter. These buildings were entered through a surplus space flight capsule simulator purchased from NASA. The capsule had two doors in it and served as an air lock through which the visitor would pass on his way into the building. From the capsule he would cross a short bridge, step down a couple of steps and find himself in a beautifully shaped space defined by a clear film envelope—shaped like a symmetrical pumpkin. At night the building glowed and produced extraordinary visual effects and a sense of joy for the beholder.

As an experimental laboratory, the building proved: the need for a great amount of cooling, that it worked as well as a greenhouse (a use the Goodyear Co. is developing extensively), and that the joints, connections, duct systems, acoustics, and lighting needed lots of developmental work.

The next step in the process is to proceed with the building of the campus itself—with some of the questions answered and some awaiting solution to be worked out by the occupants. Hopefully the structure will be constructed during the coming school year and will serve as an example for further experimentation and development. At least, it will provide a low cost alternative to the present way of doing things.

INNOVATIONS

man/environment interactions

gordon a. phillips

awareness inspires creativity

Awareness time for children begins at home in familiar surroundings. Walk with them through the neighborhood. Excite discovery. Ask them: What do you see? What do you hear? What do you smell? How do you feel? This is their environment. Do they like it? How would they change it?

The children will be challenged. They will be chock-full of ideas trying to be revealed. To express these ideas, they must communicate. How?

This is the challenge for teachers, and a natural opportunity to help children express their ideas in a variety of visual ways through the arts and to help them become graphically literate.

Let them draw what they like in their neighborhood. Let them draw what they do not like. Ask them to show you how they would change it to be better. Would they like to build a new kind of place to play, perhaps? A big slide for coasters, a new pond someplace for sailing boats, a bird house, a secret fort? Oh, yes! Exciting!

Now that they have ideas, they can become designers of their own creations.

"Young mind, show us what you see in your dreams. Draw it for us, make a blueprint, build a model."

Language descriptions are entirely inadequate. Measurements must be made and indicated. Scale must be shown. Materials and textures must be considered. Decisions must be made. These children are our decision-makers of tomorrow.

Point out small places that might be developed: The narrow strip between curb and sidewalk, a tiny space between buildings, a small yard, a vacant lot which could become a recreation area, the small area of dirt around a tree growing in the sidewalk. Let them design a kiosk for posters, a shelter for their bus stop, signs for people and automobiles, a stage somewhere for make-believe.

They will have to do some sketching. Now it will be easy to introduce some fundamentals of perspective and to show how forms change in space and distance. And the children can look at forms in different kinds of light, at different times of day. Study with them the effects of brilliant sunshine contrasted with a gloomy day.

Measure things. How high are the trees? How wide is the street, the sidewalk? How many kids abreast can walk on the sidewalk? How much space is needed to park a car? How wide are the doorways? How far can they see down the street?

Gordon A. Phillips, "Awareness Inspires Creativity," Art Education, 23, No. 7 (October, 1970), 55. Reprinted by permission.

And color! Color the neighborhood in different schemes. How are the people affected? Did you ever see houses painted in autumn colors? Nature has beautiful color schemes. Should we dress up the street sign posts with geometric patterns? What if garbage cans were blue and gold? Experiment. Living things are colorful, too, such as birds, flowers, and insects. They are always fun to draw, and to simulate in other ways.

Look at the neighborhood again with the children. Ask them where it is ugly and where it is beautiful. Ask them what they would like to do to make it more beautiful, and to make it safer.

Consider pedestrian traffic. Is it safe to walk to school? How would you make it safer? Let the children express their ideas visually. Are cars the right sizes? Is the transportation system safe and efficient? Perhaps they will enjoy making up a new kind of a car in cardboard. Is bike riding safe? Can they design paths for bicycles only?

Look for utilities, for wires, for poles, for street lights, for fire hydrants, for catch basins and sewers. Lots of room here for re-design, isn't there?

Perhaps some children would like to draw the land as it might have been before man began developing it. Maybe they would like to make pictures of the plant and animal life that has been destroyed or has disappeared. By contrast, some may have great visions of a future environment which has to be shown. Boys and girls, dream your dreams but learn to express them visually.

Invite some local architects, planners, designers, and engineers to come to the school to answer the children's questions, to help them understand some of the problems, to criticize, and to assist in solutions.

Arrange to have the children's creations displayed in public places in the community. Their parents and friends should see that surface beautification is not enough. Man relates to his environment, and we can relate to human problems through perception and expression in art education.

For too long we have been letting our children learn to cope with and live in bad environments with a resulting tragic loss in mental efficiency. Ugliness has a deteriorating effect on the mind. We must now show them how environments can be changed and improved through creative efforts which are mentally stimulating and satisfying.

Awareness + discovery + stimulation + excitement + creativity + expression = satisfaction.

roy l. hyatt/veronica s. lish

environmental sensitivity project

Flow-Chart of Procedures For Participation in Environmental Sensitivity Project

FLOW-CHART OF
PROCEDURES FOR PARTICIPATION IN
ENVIRONMENTAL SENSITIVITY PROJECT

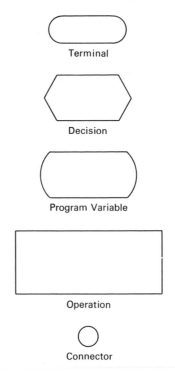

Terminal

Decision

Program Variable

Operation

Connector

This booklet and the application for the Environmental Sensitivity Project were prepared in cooperation with the staff of the Office of Federal Projects, Escambia County School System, C. Boyce Hathorn, Director. Edited by Victoria K. Burney. Reprinted by permission.

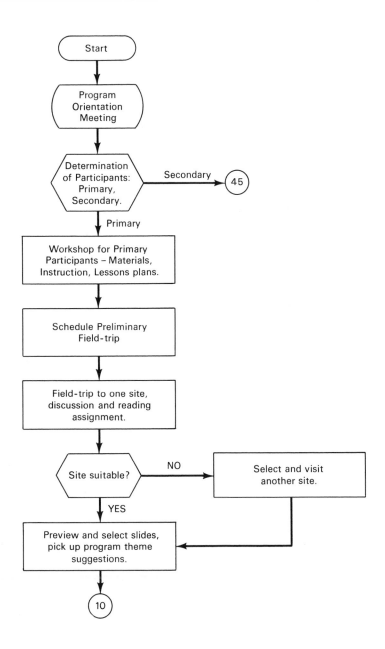

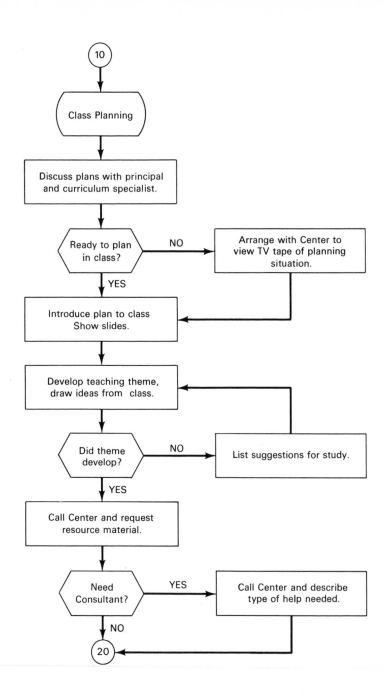

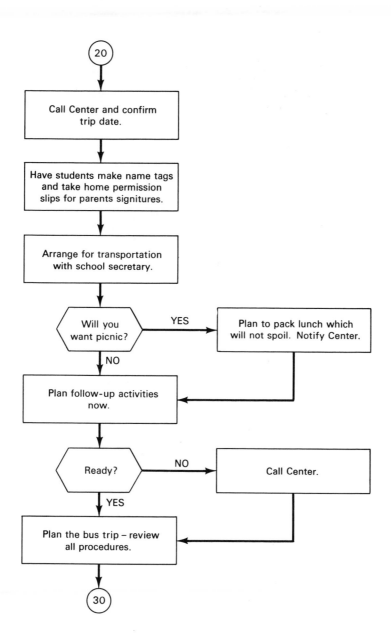

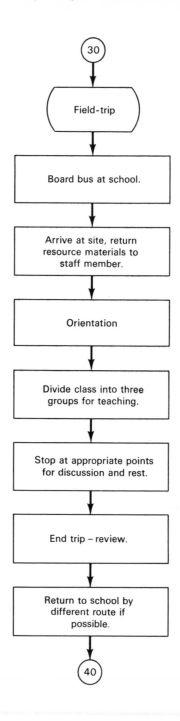

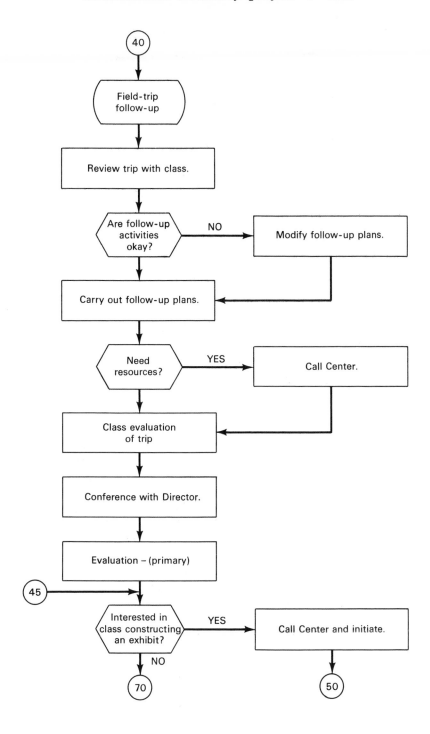

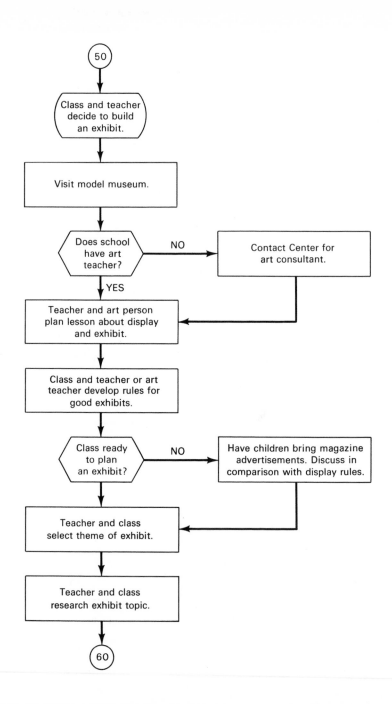

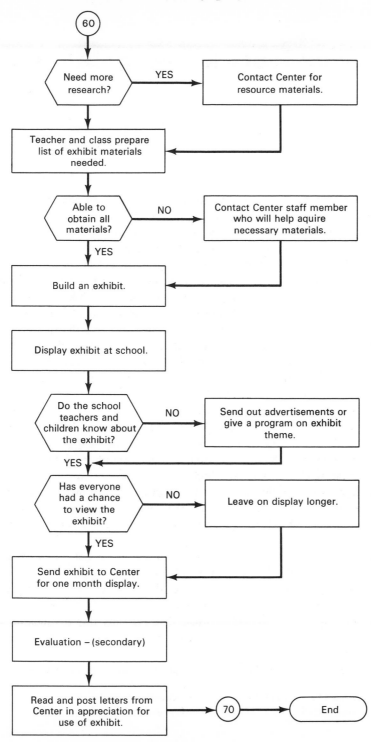

lloyd fraser

outdoor learning on public lands

On a cold wet November day, several groups of high school students huddled intently over various pieces of scientific equipment. They had walked from school to the river which flowed through their community, in order to learn something of the quality of the water. Their noses told them something of the sewage plant upstream. Thermometers showed the effect on water temperature where a municipal incinerator used water to wet down its fly ash and emptied the hot water into a small watercourse feeding into the river. At a storm sewer outfall they saw the oily residue which had run off the streets, shimmering in a foul but beautiful iridescence. More sophisticated tests showed the suspended solids in the water, the biological oxygen demand, and the rate of flow.

The thing which most impressed the casual observer was the enthusiasm and intense interest of these students, undampened by the inclement weather. This study was the real thing. This was their environment, and they were appalled by the mess that had been made of it by us, the older generation. This was a lesson they were not likely to forget. This was a lesson which made a permanent impression on their attitudes toward their environment and their understanding of it. This was *reality*.

A class of Grade 6 students had been out all day doing a geographical study in a wooded valley. In late afternoon they were trudging wearily back to their waiting bus for the return to school. A light rain had come on unexpectedly and had, in a true democratic fashion, soaked the teacher as thoroughly as any of the students. The teacher overheard a student walking along behind him comment in a rather awed tone, that, "he looks just like one of us." He had suddenly come to the realization that the teacher was a human being.

Billy had joined a new Grade 4 class in October. It was not a new experience for him. This was the sixth school he had attended in his four years in school. Three months later, he had fought with all of his classmates, had no friends, and the teacher and Billy loathed each other with equal enthusiasm. Indeed the teacher had just about given up hope of ever being able to deal with him. One February day she took her class out tobogganing, and since there were not enough toboggans to go around, they had to share them with each other.

Before they left the hill, Billy offered some information to the teacher, a thing he

Lloyd Fraser, "Outdoor Learning on Public Lands," *Focus* (Canadian Parks/Recreation Association, Ottawa, Canada) No. 1 (January, 1970). Reprinted by permission.

had never done before. He said, "That's the first time in my life anybody ever shared anything with me." That marked the turning point for Billy. At last he was communicating with the teacher. From that day on he had friends, and was a genuine member of that class.

The water in the lake had not yet warmed up enough to go swimming, but that did not bother the group of boys who were paddling across it on the last leg of a ten-day wilderness canoe trip. They felt a tremendous elation over what they had accomplished on their trip—camping, cooking, navigating, and at the same time mixing in studies in geology, vegetation and animal life. They looked back with pride to their two-day "solo" when they were alone with only their thoughts for company. From now on they would stand a little taller, with a better image of themselves, and a little more aware of their potential, for this is the effect on our youth of genuine adventure.

Who Owns This Place?

These incidents, all educationally valid, have two important things in common. First, they all took place during school hours and under school direction. Second, they all took place on publicly owned land: a municipal park, flood control land, a conservation area, and a provincial park. In three of the cases mentioned, the authorities who have jurisdiction over the land did not even know that the students were there, although they probably would have approved had they known.

As schools gain more and more control over their own curriculum, and as the school doors open more frequently to allow classes outside, the demand for space—particularly natural-state open space—will increase immensely. This demand is certainly going to focus on public park land. The school authorities will say, and rightly so, that the land belongs to their students. They will deny the necessity of buying large blocks of land for their own use when public land lies idle during most of the school year. This attitude could kindle a major power struggle with park authorities, or it could trigger a spirit of co-operation between school authorities and park authorities.

I know several teachers who have adopted the policy of always leaving a place cleaner than it was when their class got there. Each child picks up several items of litter that were left behind by unthinking people. Some park authorities rate litter as their most expensive form of vandalism. These teachers are doing more to create a permanent positive attitude towards this problem than all the signs that have ever been erected in parks.

Many education programs are offered by park authorities at all levels. They are designed to inform the public about the environment of the park and the problems of maintaining that environment or enjoying it fully. Those who should hear the message are many. Those who are preaching the message are few. The high cost of park educational programs prevents their expansion. So the environment continues to deteriorate, and the message which is preached to the public has little effect because so few hear it, and a single one-hour exposure to something as complex as ecology has little lasting effect.

Why do the park authorities not call in the reserve troops? There is an army of teachers in our schools who are willing to help them get their ideas across to the public. The teachers have a captive audience. They can pursue a subject in depth with the students, and they can repeat a message until it gets through. Why do teachers not preach the same message as the park personnel? Remember the boy who discovered that teachers are human. Teachers are no better informed about ecological problems than the general public. This training was missing from their schooling, and not much is done in teachers colleges and colleges of education. Teachers have not had an opportunity to appreciate fully our environmental problems. Park authorities would be well advised to slant their educational programs at teachers by offering sessions for them, and by volunteering to go into teachers colleges. In convincing one teacher, they can reach another thirty-five children for each year that the teacher continues to teach.

It is unfortunate that so many park personnel are well informed in their field, but communicate poorly to children. On the other hand, teachers who know how to communicate are ill-informed. Perhaps now is the time for a shift in emphasis on educational programs.

Whose side are you on? I hope you are working for the benefit of our young people. The schools maintain they are doing this. The park authorities maintain they are doing it. With such unanimity, how can there be a significant difference of opinion?

What Do Schools Need?

As the outdoor movement of schools begins, schools are interested in a "package program." This can be provided by park personnel and conducted on park land. It can vary from one-half hour to a week in length. The class teacher should be involved as much as possible.

As this movement gains momentum, the schools will want, more and more, to "do their own thing." Teachers will learn quickly from participating in the "package program," and they will see that it does not necessarily fit their particular classes at a particular time. They will then develop different programs for their own group, or even different programs for each child in the group, in the interest of making the experience more meaningful.

We know that people react to different things. One child may gain an appreciation of the natural environment by learning to identify all of the wildflowers in an area. Another will be interested in catching fish. A third will be interested through the sounds of nature, and a fourth will gain an appreciation by just soaking up the atmosphere of the place. All people do not react to the scientific approach. An aesthetic approach will appeal to many. It is here that the "package program" falls down. It is here that the teacher can introduce the flexibility needed by knowing the children well. But where can he find the land on which to do it?

Diversity in land types will be essential for a full outdoor school program to develop. A school needs easy access to its school yard, and to nearby parks and ravines. Some far-sighted planners are now locating schools beside ravines or parks. Children should be able to move outside the school as easily as they move to the school library or gymnasium. It will be necessary for children to have day or half-day long trips to regional parks that offer a variety of ecological situations and recreational facilities. These should be no more than 50 miles from the school. It may be possible to develop residential programs on this type of land, using modest buildings, or tents for the period from May to November.

When a residential program is considered, it can be as much as 400 miles away from the school. Distance is not very significant when students are going away for a week. To justify use of facilities that far away, there should be some unique attraction. This could be a different ecological setting, an area of geological, archaeological, or cultural wealth, or a wilderness area.

The facilities required for outdoor programs are not elaborate. In most cases all that is required is land in a relatively undisturbed state. In the areas designated for day use, the most needed facilities include a roof or a heated building for wet or cold weather, a storage area for equipment, a place to build a fire, and a staff member to help teachers run programs and to maintain equipment.

Equipment needs to be of a type which has many uses. Compasses, binoculars, buckets and rubber waders can be used for many different activities. For specific activities, except at a very advanced level, it is useful to have students design and build the equipment they need. Tree calipers are in this category, as are large fishing nets. Each serves one purpose only. If tree calipers are provided, then most of the groups who attend a centre will end up measuring trees. They will tend to go to the same area all the time and the problem of "wear and tear" on the woodlot becomes severe. By contrast, a group of students can go to a woodlot on an art project, spend half a day sitting under the trees, and cause no "wear and tear." It would be interesting to see which group develops a greater understanding of the woodlot and an appreciation of it. It is obvious which group is acquiring a skill which will fit them for recreational activity in their post-school years.

Sleeping Overnight

For residential programs, tents may be adequate for shelter, served by a central dining hall or cooking fireplaces. If a heated building is needed for year-round activities, then it may take many forms. The day is coming when our large secondary schools will each have a school "cottage" that will accommodate a teacher and ten students who will look after their own cooking and housekeeping chores. It will be built by the boys in the shop programs, and the school's own minibus will be used to transport them there. Larger centres designed to sleep 40 students will also develop. They will have facilities where the students can do their own cooking in two kitchens, but no staff will be on hand to run programs, except those who come with their students. Some Girl Guide and Boy Scout camps now rent such facilities to schools. Similar facilities will be needed with a kitchen staff for groups who feel they cannot afford the time to do their own cooking.

There will always be a need for centres that provide beds, meals, and an expert staff to run programs. They will be necessary where the technical details of the area of study are very complex, as in an archaeological centre. They will also be needed for classes whose teachers lack competence to run a program. One of their main purposes will be teacher training.

Large centres will emerge, housing 100 to 200 students, with large staffs to run programs. However, it may not be reasonable to put large groups in a residential centre. A class of up to 40 students is a valid social unit, and largeness destroys the personal characteristics of a good outdoor program. If a student loses his identity and disappears into a large group, he can get little appreciation of his own worth, and his ability to communicate with his teachers in an informal atmosphere is jeopardized. Should it become necessary to put large numbers of students on one piece of land, serious consideration should be given to decentralization to a number of different buildings on the property. It must be remembered that quality, not quantity, is the final standard of judgment for a program.

The Tabernacle in the Wilderness

It appears at this time that certain people, particularly politicians in various municipalities, with the best of intentions, are attempting to establish very elaborate outdoor schools. They want their students to have "the best." They want to be able to point with pride to a palace of learning and say, "Look at what we built." Children neither want nor need that sort of facility. It is far better to build two rustic centres than to build one palace. In most cases an elaborate centre only detracts from the main point of interest —the outdoor natural environment.

Some authorities maintain that a good outdoor program is 20 per cent recreational. This should be remembered when facilities are being planned. It is also worth noting that school physical education programs have begun slowly to swing away from the team sports which students dropped at school-leaving age, and more and more emphasis is being given to the individual activities which can be followed after leaving school. Golf, tennis and skiing are all appearing in the school curriculum. Perhaps it is necessary to consider where to put rifle, archery and trap ranges. Perhaps a few horses will be needed, and maybe a good supply of fishing poles will come in handy.

The most advanced type of residence program requires no buildings at all. It needs only a canoe or a rucksack, plus camping gear. Adventure programs, either hiking or canoeing, must be reserved for those who are ready for them, and need leaders who are very well versed in the techniques used. This is the most difficult type of program, but also the most rewarding. No major capital outlay is necessary. All that is needed is a lot of open country.

Who's Going to do What?

We hear a lot of talk from the agencies which manage public land, and from the agencies which own and operate the schools, about "control." One begins to wonder if either body truly represents the public—the fellow who pays for it all. It sounds too much like a power struggle. The agencies which own the land are worried about abuse of that land by schools, and we must grant that there have been cases where school abuse has justified that attitude. However, the same agency will open its gates to thousands of visitors on hot summer weekends, and, in spite of extensive damage to land and vegetation, point with pride to its rising attendance figures. Perhaps the schools could help protect and maintain the land through a co-operative education program. That weekend crowd could be a much better informed group. Those weekend swimmers do not generally go to the interpretive program anyway, so how else can they be educated except in schools?

Both school and park employees worry about control of programs. The park people want to sell a 'package' to a school board, and the board wants to lay on its own program. It begins to look as though each side considers the other incompetent to do a job of interpretation. Both groups appear to feel that a job needs to be done. It seems to me that the best resources of both sides should be thrown into the job so that the best possible job can be done co-operatively. There must be some grounds for a compromise on these two views.

If the problems of control of land and program can be surmounted, the next question becomes, "Who will pay for the buildings?"

Does this really matter? The money comes out of the public pocket anyway. In some areas it may be easier for the schools to find this money. Elsewhere, park authorities may be in the better position. Perhaps costs could be shared. The important thing is that the buildings should go up where and when they are needed. Over and over, I hear from both sides of the fence, that schools should buy or rent their own facilities. As a taxpayer, this bothers me. Land prices are rising and all that choice public land is sitting idle all week and all winter. Why should I buy more land that will sit idle on weekends and all summer? It does not make sense to me.

The pressure of people in our larger cities is creating a serious demand for open space. We can no longer afford to let land sit idle. Our sixth grade students will not even be able to vote for another ten years. Our aspiration to maintain the quality of our environment depends on an informed electorate, and unfortunately, in some areas, ten years from now is too late. So let us co-operate. Let us get going!

richard saul wurman

two hundred years after

Two hundred years after the founding of America her citizens have more desire to understand the dust of the moon than their own turf.

Two hundred years after, no two major American cities have land-use and planning maps to the same scale or with the same legends. Even the Department of Housing and Urban Development in Washington lacks a uniform mapping system.

Two hundred years after, the desires of the populace for a quality urbanized environment can only be expressed as a list of products instead of as a strategy for performance.

Two hundred years after, public demands come only as reaction to crises, not to reasoned plans for the months and years ahead.

Two hundred years after, we have abrogated the responsibility to make clear our proposals and judgments about our urban world.

In 1776 a group of identifiable men in Philadelphia signed a document that altered the course of history. In 1976 will any act of significance be so clearly identified with the persons or the groups who originate them, and will needs and desires be so clearly stated? In 1976 will planning decisions be based on understanding by our community as a whole or on the decibels and leverage of a few?

1976 could be the year when several of our cities declare fiscal and human bankruptcy, or 1976 could be the year when we declare the interdependency between constructive activities and human understanding.

Public information should be made public. Information about our urban environment should be made understandable.

There is nothing we do with less expertise than tell people what and why we're doing what we're doing.

Architects and designers, educators and managers, contractors and clients—all of us who shape the form of the city—have a responsibility to make the ideas we deal in both observable and comprehensible. We must share a commitment to make the city observable.

Making the city observable can happen through the development of a junior high school curriculum about our man-made environment, or it can be in the form of a clear subway map, as in London, or a ballot that people are able to understand and which enables them to register knowledgeable concern.

Reprinted by permission of the author.

Making the city observable might include creating a city "war room" as part of a pervasive ground floor system of urban observatories. Another piece might be a total urban communications system or a network of utilities whose functions and characteristics are made clear to all the community.

Making the city observable is allowing the entire city to become an environment for learning.

- The New York Times described the moon landing of Apollo 14 with maps and diagrams clearer than any they have ever used to describe the location of a new highway.
- Through their windows on the Avenue of the Americas in New York City, Burlington Industries offers an invitation to the public to see a capsule version of what they do.
- CBS-TV in New York City has a new program called *The Urbanites,* Saturdays at 3:30 pm, which gives information specifically about the city.
- The new Metro System in Mexico City is delightfully comprehensible, even to someone who cannot read.
- ABC took full-page newspaper ads to translate the questions on an election ballot into understandable language—without all the double negatives.
- In tabloid format, the "California Tomorrow" plan addresses a general audience on planning goals for the State.
- The book *Cosmic View, The Universe in Forty Jumps* shows the universe minified and magnified in scale changes. Charles Eames made a remarkable film, *The Powers of Ten,* based on the book. Both book and film manifest the desire to make observable, scale relationships of the elements we perceive and conceive of.
- Jan Blaeu drew maps of all the towns in the Netherlands in the 17th Century clearly and accurately enough to locate each house.
- Giambattista Nolli constructed a plan of Rome in 1748 wherein the public environment was clearly delineated—the white of the streets extended into the ground floor of public buildings.
- Mayor Lindsay proposed a special zoning district for Fifth Avenue, which specified that at least the first two floors of every building be given over to retail space instead of the anonymous and uninteresting invasion of banks and elevator lobbies, open but a few hours a day and dull to the passerby.

But most of us are fooling ourselves and confusing those we serve. We talk in numbers we can't comprehend and about sizes we can't visualize. (To this point, I recommend a recent book entitled *One Million,* which consists simply of 200 pages with 5,000 dots per page.) Proposed changes in our environment are shown as artists' renderings of gift-wrapped packages rather than as indications of measured performances and relationships. Our students concentrate on learning Latin and logarithms instead of on experiencing the environment and coming to terms with their relationship to it.

The jet traveler alights from the plane at the fringe of a city, totally disoriented. A twelve-year-old gets lost downtown. A visitor speaking only a foreign tongue is helpless in almost every subway. The voter is confronted with bond issues for unexplained amounts for unexplained things. School board members spend millions and incur endless debts building new schools to house an educational system they all agree to be largely un-workable, hostile, and irrelevant to the world around them. The front pages of our newspapers report events with such lack of clarity that we find we cannot competently discuss issues with even our closest companions.

In city after city, the local transit authority is losing money. As a result, it cuts back service and raises fares, ensuring both fiscal disaster and loss of ridership. The emperor has no clothes! We polish silver without questioning whether we need silver anymore. We seem afraid or unwilling to say, "I don't understand."

- Why don't we have chartbooks and understandable data books of our cities? Why not a visual summary of the 1970 Census?
- Why don't those industries that are intimately involved with our cities use their advertising to educate us all about the area of their concern? As St. Regis Paper Company; or as a General Motors could about streets, highways, and vehicular storage; or a General Electric could about the quality of urban illumination.
- Why don't we use the tops of our tallest buildings to observe our cities and educate our young? If these rooftops are exciting places for cocktail parties, think of them as special vantage points enabling our kids to understand the growth, form, and networks of our city.
- Why don't in-flight films tell you about where you are going and orient you to your destination? A movie *Michelin Green Guide.*
- Why not paint the streets and make the city a life-sized route map?
- Why can't the newspapers report the potential resources of tomorrow instead of only yesterday's catastrophes?
- Why can't the TV news programs document the daily happenings in the streets, good and bad, focusing attention on the publicly owned sector of our cities?
- Why doesn't each community have a community-made community map? The recently completed community-developed map of the Hill District in Pittsburgh is an example.
- Why can't there be pocket guides to each city? London is blessed with a remarkable hand-sized guide called *Nicholson's.*
- Why isn't the city a schoolhouse?
- Why doesn't each of us care about the parts of the city we jointly own?
- We walk down streets daily and are not able to see them.
- We aren't able to discern the patterns of the movement systems we ride continuously.
- We have an obsessive concern for plots of ownership and the building of private objects.
- We ask for parks, not places of recreation.
- How can we learn to describe spaces and places? How can we insist that the department of highways produce not only studies of the view from the road but the view of the road?
- How do we learn to describe and notate paths, directions, and routes?
- How do we describe and explain the civic dollars we approve to be spent?
- How do we sense ownership of the publicly owned ½ of the city, what I call "City/2?"
- How many of us know that ½ of the total developed land in every American city is publicly owned? We own it and we all should care for it and make constructive changes in it.

- How can we use the city as the educational resource it is?

- How can we recognize and organize a curriculum for students, the basis of which is the why and how the city does what it does?

- How can each of us describe our ideas and allow and encourage the articulate demands of the ideas of others?

Here are some bits and pieces of an answer:

The city is education—and the architecture of education rarely has much to do with the building of schools. The city is a schoolhouse and its ground floor is both bulletin board and library. Everything we do—if described, made clear, and made observable—is education.

Education has been thought of as taking place mainly within the confines of the classroom, and school buildings have been regarded as the citadels of knowledge. The most extensive facility imaginable for learning is our urban environment. It is the classroom without walls . . . offering a boundless curriculum . . . with unlimited expertise. If we can make our urban environment comprehensible, observable, and understandable, we will have created classrooms with endless windows on the world.

Our school buildings then could act as a fine network of administrative nodes and meeting places for identification, faculty and student dialogue, and lockers. A walk through the city's ground floor would then become a continuous learning experience.

Each of us should recognize our role as the developer of an invitation to learning. We should be concerned about real experiences and encourage the development of new learning situations independent of the traditional books and learning products that focus on student experiences in classrooms and school buildings.

We should be interested in the identification and the subsequent communication of the elements that make up the man-made environment.

We should understand the need to develop the skills and abilities to communicate information about the environment both verbally and nonverbally.

We should create the confidence in a student that will enable him to judge and develop criteria for evaluating or creating his own environments. We are all students.

Our children, our friends, and we ourselves should be able to answer the following:

1. What is the man-made environment?

2. Why do we build our environment?

3. What determines the form of our environment?

4. How do we change our man-made environment?

We should understand these concepts:

1. What we want.

2. What resources, human and material, are available.

3. What are the limits—the rules and regulations.

4. And how we can choose the optimum alternative.

We should encourage a sense of ownership of the city and define the extent of the public environment.

We should see the "environment issue" not simply as the causes and effects of air and water pollution, but in broader terms: the understanding of the total physical environment, both public and private.

We should be involved with all that man has made in our consideration of the urban world and with the myriad types of man-initiated pollution that manifest our lack of adequate concern—

- for places to rest and refresh.

- for the need to know where we are or where we are going and for the anxieties of disorientation and disorder.

- for allowing the creation of a human sewer and calling it a subway system.

- for our overwhelming inability to comprehend our interrelationship with the man-made environment and for the perpetuation of this inability in our children.

- for a desire for safety and freedom, masked by the ploy of "law and order."

- for the fouling of our nests with the varied excrements of our civilization.

- for the discordant screams that suffuse our minds with unnecessary noises from unnecessary objects.

- for the interrelationship among the acts and performances that go on in our environment and the physical spaces they occupy.

- for the effect of physical space on our collective mental health.

We own half the land in our cities, yet our concern is only with the look, not even with the performance, of the other half.

We value stylish graphics, not communication.

We are worried and disoriented by our urban problems . . . and yet we will not allow the city itself to become observable.

We don't even allow our children to comprehend the elements that make up, affect, and allow for change in our man-made environment.

I am guilty, and so are most of you. Architects, planners—and their clients—have been participating in a developer's olympics engaging the physical form of our cities, pitting one extruded building against another, gaining support for high-style packages that misrepresent their contents and ignore their neighbors.

A typical trend is the current craze for "city graphics" and street furniture—offering only fashion where the problem is insight. Populating our streets with "pretty" signs may actually increase our massive disorientation—messages for curbing our dog are interesting, but curbing human excrement in the form of the unwanted, useless, and confusing signs, litter, street furniture, wires, fumes, and poisons is of a higher priority. I would far prefer a safe city, a comfortable city, an understandable city to a collection of pretty graphics and stylish products.

Designers have become urban beauticians applying mascara and calling it beautification and promoting urban edsels and calling them street furniture.

Transportation engineers talk of a movement nirvana in terms of actual speed rather than psychological time, comfort, safety, orientation, and information.

City planners have too long thought of the city as a collection of building-of-the-month edifices, the collective ground floors of which are not called on to edify, elucidate, or educate, much less to give comfort and safety.

In our race to invent facades and upgrade technology we have overlooked the need to make clear our performance goals . . . to ascertain publicly their constitution and ensure their development.

It doesn't have to be this way, if we can agree that it doesn't have to: the limited amenities an individual can afford when he lives in isolation are multiplied by thousands when he lives in a community where collective amenities are made economically possible.

Some of these mutual amenities are facilities for—

- free and convenient movement of all kinds.
- the invitation to purchase goods and services.
- protection and shelter.
- orientation, learning, and guidance.

If we do no more than make clear the patterning, disposition, and possible performances of these urban facilities, the city itself will become observable.

It's necessary to consider making the city observable as a single field of concern— all of the disparate projects, ideas, books, guides, maps, advertisements, and curriculums that offer opportunities to provide the public with ways to understand better their urban habitation are means to make information out of data.

Urban information is education; education is communication; and communication— at its best—is both an art and an entertainment.

Many of the ways to make the city observable are visual. I have recently collected a great number of them in an illustrated catalogue entitled *Making the City Observable*. They are represented in ideas not widely discussed and dreams as yet unfulfilled . . . yet many approaches are contained in publications available on local newsstands, in bookstores, and as descriptions of unrelated phenomena. Held within them are the germs of techniques I believe to be applicable to the educational and political problems that engulf the city-dwelling man.

Taken as a whole, the juxtaposition of projects, items, and ideas begin to define a matrix—points in our common field: concern about urban communication.

Public information should be made public.

Will information about our urbanized environment be made more understandable in 1976?

herbert h. swinburne

the environment we see

The environment we see—or rather the environment we perceive, for there is much more to it than we pick up through visual perception

Let's continuously REMIND ourselves of the scope and sweep of creativity as we manipulate the environmental matrix—the urban matrix

Ugly

No place to sit down

Photographs by the author.

Polluted

But some say: give me
rooftops and a gas stove—
you can have your hundred
acres on the prairie

Where man outside a group
is more alone than anyone
else on earth

REMINDER
    We all perceive our environment from the perspective of different sets of values and from
that of the group we are attached to

We all perceive beauty and ugliness from different points of view

What is beauty? How are
we manipulating space,
people, and aspirations to
create a better environment?

Ugliness can be a condition—
a few martinis in this
optimum environment, and a
homely girl is slowly transformed
into a ravishing beauty

REMINDER
    There are many levels of ugliness

blight, squalor, decay—
the social morass of our times

sophisticated bad taste

REMINDER

Be careful of semantics.

Example: alley: a narrow street   alley: an ugly word

How many of these alleys are ugly?

What are the scope and dimensions of beauty in environment?

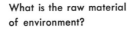

What is the raw material
of environment?

Is it raw stuff such as this

plus imagination and creativity

plus all the arts and all
the disciplines

plus the family, and faith
of any creed?

REMINDER

Man is the focal point of environment.

All of us know that environment goes far beyond the three dimensions of visual perception. We all know that sophisticated perception involves many disciplines, which deal with the most complex part of our environment.

People, and their composite interaction—people, and their goals and aspirations.

Environment, within a total urban composition, is a living, vibrant thing. Human reaction to environment depends on the intellect and the emotions— and his reaction varies.

Perception—what is is? Let's look at three kinds:

Spatial perception begins with light—jiggling, bouncing, vibratory photons of incredible speed

bringing silhouettes at dawn

or sunrise on a mountain lake

bringing glint lights in
late afternoon

or sunset in the clouds

Ambient space has many
qualities—

fog—clinging, spreading

mist—blending, softening

making our cities glow

Atmosphere: sparkling, bright—
scrubbed clean—polished

brilliant, colorful, reflecting

Light and atmosphere: these define and separate space, with moods of infinite variation

Now: to light and mood add
sound and motion

Then: to inanimate sound and
random motion add human sound
and human motion

Psychic influences on perception

claustrophobia

agoraphobia

illusion

REMINDER

Spatial perception has more than three dimensions

Each individual perceives differently and reacts differently to what he sees

What is *psychological perception?*

Man's thoughts probe
complex space

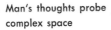

How much do they probe the
simple act of a small child?

Here's a man with a positive
set of values—I know him well;
his name is Tom

He's familiar with the geography
of loneliness

Here's a stranger to me—surely
her set of values is as
positive as Tom's

Does environment mean the
same to everyone? Does it ever
mean the same to children
and adults?

REMINDER
Each man is an individual

His genetic number—family—education—personal values—forever set him apart.

And now—*sociological perception*

Children

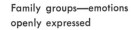

Family groups—emotions
openly expressed

Random groups—involvement
in the scene

Special groups—sharing a new experience

Here are 100,000 people—cheering

Can't you feel the surging millions of a big city at night?

Is environment a daytime thing?

Excitement—turmoil—sound—action—interaction

REMINDER
  We plan for people and their interaction in diverse groups—and with variable concentrations

  But remember, we also design our environment with life, not with statistics

Let's think for a moment about
history and change

Romantic

Old-fashioned?

Curved lines—are these out
of date?

Or do we need straight lines?
Are these up to date?

Art museum—is this out of date?

Is this addition to the same museum up to date?

Monticello—is this *really* out of date?

Motel—up to date of course!

Sculpture—is this out
of date?

Up to date?

REMINDER
    Time changes many things in our environment—sometimes for the better, sometimes not

Let's take a *slow* look at the
automobile

For thousands of years, the
world's cities crystallized
their form around this kind of
transportation

Then—progress!

Sandburg poetry

Who said transportation can't
be beautiful?

A city can be one great
big garage

Transportation—out of date

REMINDER
Perhaps in a few years the automobile will be out of date—and gone forever—like the horse

Now, what is a pedestrian?

Someone who dodges traffic?

Are there two classes of
pedestrian—

those who don't walk

and those who do?

Or is a pedestrian

a little girl on the way to
the zoo?

REMINDER

Perhaps the pedestrian should be given a higher priority when we set the warp and woof of our urban matrix

Let's consider now space and geopolitics

Rivers separate states, generating problems and port authorities

State borders zig and zag at Lake Tahoe, and two jurisdictions split a community of common interests

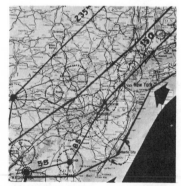

We're running out of urban space in my part of the country— with myriads of overlapping jurisdictions

How can we keep people, space, and resources in equilibrium?

For instance, here's an island
that ran out of space—
inelegantly

In our second largest state—
running out of space in the
middle of square miles of
real estate

In another day (long since gone)
—integrated design—quiet
growth—equilibrium

Is this integrated design in
our day? Do those monuments
against the horizon indicate
our aspirations?

Or do they recall other
monuments against the sky?

Do we want the magnificent
legacy of good planning done
fifty years ago?

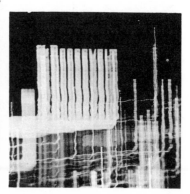

Or do we want the big squeeze   becoming tighter, more crowded

Megalopolis Pacificus

Megalopolis Atlanticus

pushing and extruding our
cities along their natural
barriers

until they are engulfed and
swallowed by their own
dependent perimeters?

REMINDER?

No reminder is needed here. We all know that knowledgeable planning, using all the related disciplines, is the answer. What we must do is continually remind America of this!

Ours is the responsibility to think, plan, and design creatively for all the people— not only in this generation, but the next—

inspired by the wide reaches of nature

the great culture of all our cities

the subtleties of the
countryside

combined with the fabric of
cityscape

searching for beauty

and simplicity

creating a finer environment
for all our children

creating greater cities for
all our people

Let us leave a full, rich
legacy of accomplishment in
the next fifty years

using a total perspective
seen from the vantage point
of all disciplines

INNOVATIONS

accessibility

john foster

hampshire's "campus as an eco-system" way of living/learning

Hampshire College in Amherst, Massachusetts, is a brilliant example of community planning that combines both vision and practicality. It makes some of us here feel good just to know that it exists. Here is an example of the kind of thing Hampshire as a whole is considering:

> Picture if you will an insurance salesman who flies over the Hampshire campus once a month on his way between Boston and Albany. As he looks down on the campus during his May flight he observes vegetation spiralling out from the center of the campus in a pinwheel fashion. Emergent blossoms make each blade of the pinwheel a different color. In his next flight some of the trees now have leaves while other late bloomers are just getting blossoms, so that the scene has changed for him. Not only has it changed in color but he notices that the pinwheel has appeared to rotate. On each subsequent trip he becomes more and more fascinated, for the wheel rotates all through the seasons, reaching a climax when the leaves change in the fall. Then he notices that landowners around the campus are delighted with the idea and the pinwheel grows in size until finally, when he is an old man, this vegetational kaleidoscope encompasses both Boston and Albany. At home and with his business our sales-man participates in the Hampshire scene. He now sees the vegetational pinwheel in another light. It is not just an aesthetic way of manipulating the environment but rather, like a true pinwheel, energy in the form of air, water, and light supplied anywhere on the wheel benefits the whole system.

> There is no reason environmental quality should be limited to the ecologist, the scientist, or the political scientist. Art students should see the possibility of using the landscape as their canvas and knowledge of environment as brush and paint for their creation. In ecology we must return to writing our scientific treatises, as Thomas Huxley did, in verse.

That was written by Ray Coppinger and John Foster, two profs at Hampshire got word of through the *Guide to Organic Shopping and Living*. Here, in total, is a proposal they wrote up for their College Policy Committee.

John Foster, "Hampshire's 'campus as an eco-system' Way of Living/Learning," unpublished paper, 1970. Reprinted by permission of the author.

Hampshire College as a Community Within the Environment—"The Jungle at the Temple Doors"

The major thesis of a program in environmental science is that man, as an organism, must learn to live in harmony with his environment. The purpose of the program is to bring the student to an understanding of the way in which those ecosystems which he is a part of are intended to function, and thereby to learn to make intelligent and creative use of his surroundings in such a way as to produce long-term stability. However, students will want to do more than just study ecosystems; they will want to become actively involved in environmental problems. We propose that this involvement should begin at home on the Hampshire campus. It is here that we can best bring to the student the essential sense of belonging to and being a part of his environment, and begin weaning him away from historical tradition of regarding nature as an adversary.

The basic proposal is that the College embark on a long-term effort to develop itself as a sanctuary, not in the sense of something set apart, but as an area in which ecological, educational and aesthetic features are blended together in such a way as to support and enhance one another. Within the framework of such a general proposal a number of specific projects come to mind. A few of these are outlined below as examples of the sort of thing that could be done.

1. The College is located on land which was for some period of time devoted to agriculture. With the building of the college this land will be converted to other uses, each having an impact of some sort on the ecology of the area. For example, a small pond was drained to prepare for the construction of Merrill House, depriving a population of frogs (Hyla) of their ancestral habitat; trees were cleared, creating a forest border where there was none before; lawns have been created where once there were hayfields or forests. Other areas will, in effect, cease to be used and will, if left alone, revert eventually to forest. Each of these can become a valid and useful subject of study, as examples of the impact of human activity on local ecosystems. This will require as a starting point a thorough ecologic, topographic, hydrologic and geologic survey of the campus. This has been done to some extent in developing present plans for the physical plant of the College, but not with an eye towards creating a stable ecosystem in the biological sense. The necessary field study can be an integral part of seminars in ecology.

2. The campus also presents opportunities for ecological experimentation, thereby creating numerous opportunities for student projects. Some examples are: a). Introducing a new plant species onto an experimental plot to study the ensuing changes in other species. b). Construction of miniature ecosystems, isolated from their surroundings, in order to assess what must be done to maintain them in balance and to study the effects of pesticides and other pollutants under controlled conditions. c). Experimental plantings to create specific new habitats for birds and other small animals. d). Limited agriculture utilizing recycling techniques; e.g., processing garbage from the dining halls for use as fertilizer and feed for wildlife.

3. There are many opportunities for esthetic and landscape design studies. With most of the College's buildings yet to be built, students could take an active part in the concept and

design phases. This would include not only questions of the physical design of the building itself with respect to its intended function, but also such considerations as the location (should this area be used for a building or is it better suited for something else?) Or, the harmonizing of exterior design with the surroundings, and landscaping for ecologic as well as esthetic purposes.

4. A related project calls for some rethinking of traditional campus design concepts. For example, is all that lawn necessary? The University of North Florida, for example, has simply left trees where they were. The result has been lower initial cost, lower maintenance cost, less noise, less wind, and the creation of a campus that doubles as a nature sanctuary.

5. If the College is to take on the function of a sanctuary, it is important that these plans be coordinated with those of the Amherst Conservation Commission and other local groups sharing our concerns. There are also local offices of the U.S. Department of Agriculture, the Fish and Wildlife Service, and others that stand ready to assist with planning and information. Students should know of these groups and learn to work with them in developing their projects.

6. For the social scientist interested in individual and group behavior there would appear to be many opportunities for study and experiment inherent in the concept of developing a balanced community. For example there is the psychology of land use itself. What factors, in addition to economic ones, permit man to plunder his own surroundings? to tolerate pollution? to subject himself to overcrowding? Students could be asked to examine such attitudes in themselves and in their classmates. From such studies could come ideas for experiments students could do with their own groups, such as modifying living arrangements or changing the meal hours to suit some special purpose. In the larger context there will be opportunities for students to gather basic data on attitudes towards environmental quality and pollution in the course of their field studies in the surrounding communities. The object here would be to develop some feeling for the political and sociological realities of implementing pollution abatement programs.

7. An important aspect of the entire program is the extent to which Hampshire College itself contributes to the pollution load on its surroundings. "The College will produce sewage, trash, smoke, garbage, noise, exhaust fumes, and many other pollutants that were not there before. A very important contribution to a program in environmental sciences would be made if the College could adopt whatever steps are available to reduce the pollution which its own existence creates. Some of these steps involve simple changes in human behavior; others will involve wholly new applications of existing techniques or the development of new ones. Particularly important will be an exploration of ways in which the raw materials the college uses can be recycled. For example, can the garbage produced by the dining halls be processed for use as fertilizer on the Hampshire campus, or as feed for some of the wildlife population on it? This may require special facilities and equipment, which will add substantially to the initial cost, especially on the small scale contemplated here. However, all experts agree that recycling of raw materials is going to become essential as the supply of these materials begins to lag behind the demand and the problem of disposing of an ever-increasing flood of waste and trash begins to overwhelm us. Thus the College should assume the obligation of leading the way in developing and implementing recycling techniques wherever feasible.

8. The science building poses some additional problems because of the toxic nature of the waste materials it will produce. This subject has been treated separately in a proposal which

has been prepared for submission to the Dreyfus Foundation. A draft copy of the proposal is attached. (quoted above)

•   •   •

We have made no attempt here to be either comprehensive or detailed. Our intent was only to suggest a few things that might be done in order to stimulate discussion about specific projects that we might cook up for the January term, as a permanent part of the curriculum, for long-term faculty and student research, and for long-term development of the College itself. We have tried to dream up examples that would fall within the scope of all three schools so as to indicate the broad interdisciplinary nature of the overall idea. It is an activity in which we must all be involved if it is going to work, and our personal view is that it could be an exciting focus for Hampshire and its students in the years ahead."

the dance of life

In the early morning hours, it is possible to walk along the beach and, in the inscriptions in the sand, read the night stories of all the little creatures. Here went a snake, a'winding; here a crab, a'crawling, and there a bird a'walking, its tracks ending in eery nothing, as if teleportation were an ordinary part of our lives. Here, in the displaced grains of sand, the patterns and configurations, is a legible record of "mobility."

What we are talking about in "mobility," is observed motion or the record of it. We follow a long, hard trail when we begin to track down what we mean by "motion." It is a trail that leads through the labyrinth of a very few recorded minds. In our limited world of the displaced white European, it appears to begin with Aristotle (in *Physica*) who divided all observed motion into natural and violent. Violent was caused by humans; natural was not.

Something like 1500 years later, we hear Jordanus (in *De ratione ponderis*). "In any motion, whether natural or violent, the velocity obtained is the ratio of the applied force to the resistance which the medium offers."

About 350 years later, Galileo strolled by. He calmly said that "force is something which can change motion; e.g., from rest into motion or from motion into rest." (We kind of doubt he said, "e.g.," but that's the way they put it down, preserved in the amber of encyclopedias.)

The pace picks up, so it is only another hundred years before Newton (in *Philosophiae Naturalis Principia Mathematica*) broke trail by asserting "the three laws of motion."

Ernst Mach wandered along to muse, ". . . It is possible to choose a standard particle, label it as a unit of mass, and determine the mass of every other particle in the universe by allowing it to interact with the standard mass."

So stumbling up the path, his hands full of other people's patent applications, staring into the Prussian glare, comes Einstein, who says, rather diffidently, "Motion is relative to the observer."

Along the way he was helped by other trailblazers in the mathematics of motion: Schroedinger, Heisenberg, Planck. . . .

So that is one trail, not by any stretch of the imagination yet surmounted. In the words of poet Bob Dylan, "Climb that hill, no matter how steep, you still ain't goin' nowhere."

There are other trails. Motion can be defined as the displacement of a figure against a background, or a "surround." Tiger in the bush, scorpion in the sand, adder in the hollow. Move! If you dig rather shallowly, you can pry that one out of contemporary psycho-biology. In the words of the folk song, "the fox went out that night, and he had a long, long way to go, before he reached the town-o." Here we may see a rabbit hopping, because it is hoping; the fox in pursuit, hoping, but not hopping.

It is not a very good trail to follow, because it is circular, and is only observed by a third party, standing outside the two systems, rabbit and fox. The rabbit and the fox, however implicated, are third parties, too. They see each other in relation to a background which, while moving, appears to be static. None of this concerns the rabbit or the fox, their primary question being, "Am I going to have dinner or be one?"

So much for the fox and the rabbit. The small point—the observation of motion—was the function of a third system; in both cases and all around.

We'll try another trail. This is a pretty simple one. Let us say that "x" represents a horizontal in a two-dimensional plane. And that "y" represents a vertical. And that "z" represents depth. Something missing here, so we add "t," for time. Now we can take "xyz," mix liberally with "t," and come up with a model of what is (or has been) going on. We put them on a chart and many businesses and government agencies do this.

And what do we have? What we have is the movement of our eyeballs as we scan a chart from left to right. The "x, y, z, t" bit won't take us very far, either.

Back to the old drawing board. May we make a suggestion? You can't stop us, except to throw this thing into the fireplace or garbage can. But that, too, would be motion, would it not?

So, once more into the breach:

> *MOTION CAN BE DESCRIBED AS OBSERVED OR EXPERIENCED*
> *INTERFERENCE WAVES BETWEEN PLANES OF TIME*
> *AGAINST A HOLOGRAPHIC BACKGROUND.*

If "interference waves," "planes of time," and "holographic" turn you off, then forget it.

These far-out concepts have little to do with mobility as we experience it in our daily lives. We move from room to room, we go to work, or the barber or the hairdresser, the laundromat or the bar; to supermarket or school; to the dentist and the doctor; to a friend's house for dinner or cocktails; to visit relatives, mostly aging aunts and decaying grandfathers.

We are nomads, children of the steppes and plains, of hunters and gatherers long since gone, and we express our mobility in many dimensions.

There is economic mobility; you either get richer, or you go broke, and the middle is all for waiting. There is social mobility; you move up or down and the places that used to say, "Sorry, we're all filled up," now say, "This way, Sir."

It can go the other way, too. A place you were long welcome now says, "beat it, buddy," or "I'm so sorry, we already have guests for that night." So, socially, cut them off at the pass and thus reduce mobility. And then there's political mobility—but we already know too much about that.

In the catch-phrases, "Freedom Now!," "Land of the Free," "Free enterprise," we are essentially ringing the changes on mobility. To be "free" is to be able to move without restraint.

We are restless beasts, and we will move, wheels or not. Short of death sentences, our justice system is based on restriction of mobility; prisons, concentration camps, schools, business offices, bureaucracies. Cut the wire or mount the fence or burrow a tunnel under the wall; the human spirit cannot be confined. We'll move some way.

And we greatly value speed. For some reason, we believe that time is money. The shorter the elapsed time between "A" and "B," the more we "make." And so the horse, the camel, the bicycle, automobile, jet. And this, for humans, is "the dance of life," which threatens to become a tarantella, a mad gyration without substance or meaning, as we find still faster ways to go, and thus annihilate experience. And yet it was experience we sought, was it not? Our little worlds are not necessarily enlarged by the number of miles we have traveled.

Now, let's see if we can get the car out of the garage. . . .

b. ray horn

creating environmental awareness: the development of a mobile environmental education program

Laurance S. Rockefeller recommended that the National Recreation and Park Association consider as a top priority item the "education for use and enjoyment of the environment." [1]

To witness, however, the potential of our Nation's parks that remain unrealized is disheartening. Careful examination reveals that many of our local, state, and national park's biophysical resources are seldom used to full potential. The focus of this article is on how we are *not* using many of our parks. We should view our parks in terms of the total possible effect that their resources *could* have on the American citizenry. We should also consider the subsequent implications for the future.

The aim of this article is to illustrate the process of creating the conditions that encourage an interaction between people and the biophysical resources of local, state, and national parks. Often, activities are carried on within a park's physical boundaries with very little involvement of the participants with the biophysical environment itself. The process of involving people with parks may be called "environmental education," which may be more accurately defined as *the process of recognizing and clarifying the values, attitudes and concepts necessary for the understanding and appreciation of the interrelatedness among man, his culture, and his biophysical environment. Environmental education, moreover, entails practice in decision-making about issues concerning environmental quality.*

The process of creating environmental awareness can be energized by recreation and park professionals through the use of a mobile environmental education facility. The mobile facility may be a portable storage box, a small trailer, a medium sized step-van, or a large moving-van. Whatever the size, the mobile facility can be a catalyst for *involving* people with the park's environment. Before a mobile facility can be a catalyst, however, the recreation and park professional must understand (1) the capabilities and limitations of such a mobile facility, (2) the functions of leadership for an environmental

[1] Opening General Session, The Congress for Recreation and Parks, October, 1966.

B. Ray Horn, "Creating Environmental Awareness: The Development of a Mobile Environmental Education Program," Trends, Vol. 8, No. 2 (April, 1971), pp. 10–14. Published by the National Park and Recreation Association, the National Conference on State Parks and the National Park Service, U.S. Department of the Interior. Reprinted by permission of the publisher and the author.

education program, and (3) the potential of a park as an outdoor laboratory for environmental education and enjoyment.

Capabilities and Limitations of the Mobile Facility

The mobile environmental education facility is not a program. The facility is an intermedium or tool that makes programming for human needs easier. Since the mobile facility is a tool, the facility itself does not do anything. People, through the guidance of trained leadership, perform the doing. Similarly as a screwdriver has been designed to turn screws but can be misused to chisel wood, the mobile facility has been designed for a specific use but can be misused, if misunderstood. Indeed, since a quality program is primarily dependent upon quality leadership, the effectiveness of the mobile environmental education facility is likewise dependent upon good leadership.

Because the facility is mobile, program materials can be easily transported from park to park with little time or effort. Since everyone cannot travel great distances to become involved in a central program or use central facilities, the mobile unit increases participant counts by moving the program to the people. Moreover, the mobility enables the sponsoring agency to maximize use of its equipment, and, therefore, eliminate unnecessary purchasing of expensive equipment for each small park. With a mobile facility a sponsoring agency stretches the tax dollar and increases citizen participation.

A mobile facility has other advantages. For example, requests are often made for park and recreation agencies to involve a great many citizens as rapidly as possible in an active, involving, and advertive recreational activity. Park and recreation specialists are frequently called upon to provide emergency programs and to provide them quickly. The mobile facility is designed to serve a need whether emergency or routine. It can be quickly moved to where interest or circumstances demands, whether to the barren and cement laden parks of many inner-city areas, to Central Park, or to pristine Yosemite Valley. The versatility of the environmental education mobile facility for emergency or routine programming in local, state, or national parks is unlimited.

The mobile facility supplies exploratory equipment to stimulate investigation of a park's biophysical resources. The facility carries an array of environmental study kits (water testing kits, weather kits, etc.); human sensory extensions (temperature guages, hand lenses, etc.); and reinforcing follow-up equipment (field manuals, publications on pollution, etc.). The equipment excites young children as they explore temperature changes, and the equipment quickly attracts youth as they compare, contrast, and map the differences between open-space and closed-space environments. The supplied equipment also encourages adult sensitivity as they focus upon noise pollution by donning blindfolds.

Unfortunately, as indicated by the apparent apathy of many Americans toward environmental problems, large segments of our society have been inadvertently conditioned *not* to carefully observe natural and man-made surroundings. Though each of us nourishes over one-million microscopic nerve endings that specialize in informing the human decision-making apparatus about our environments, many of us seem almost totally unaware of the complexity and interrelatedness of the worlds at our fingertips. We are, as a culture, relatively insensitive to our surroundings, hence, making environmental involvement and intelligent decision-making difficult.

The equipment within the mobile environmental education facility is designed to increase environmental sensitivity, the requisite to eventual understanding. The equipment is designed to extend and vitalize the human sensory antennae to see, touch, hear, taste, and smell the overlooked but critical threads of nature. Focusing on certain vital aspects of our environment, the equipment is carefully selected to function as a tool to environmental concept development upon which sound conservation legislation is based. Senator Henry Jackson has indicated that "Citizens and governmental decision-makers cannot be expected to appreciate the urgency in a need of which they are unaware. They cannot be expected to support expenditures to achieve goals they do not endorse, or understand." [2]

Unique Functions of Leadership for the Program

An environmental education program leader should operate within specific measurable objectives and should work within specific conceptual frameworks which accurately portray an ecological percept of the environment. If the leader does otherwise, then the effect of the program can be void of benefit or even be aversive.

The mobile facility is designed to assist the leader in encouraging certain attitudes toward discovery, inquiry, and the enjoyment of the sensations of our biophysical surroundings. To misuse the facility is human atrophy, the prevention of the satiation of an inherent environmental curiosity. The facility's potential is usually limited only by the restrictions placed by its users. A leader, therefore, must know what the equipment's purposes are and how the equipment can be used before he can maximize outcomes.

The general aims for generating a people/environment interaction are (a) to create within the individual a perceptual awareness of his surroundings and (b) to create an attitude that will evoke additional sensitivity and inquiry beyond the moment.

Accordingly, a participant should learn to recognize his environment as an intertwining complex of an endless web that is not only the ligature to survival of lakes, rivers, and forests but also is the bootstrap of his own survival. A visitor to a park should be encouraged through an active program to seek out the interdependent elements of his environment and fit them together. "Only by realizing and emphasizing the complexity

[2] "Recreation and a Quality Environment," *Journal of Health, Physical Education, and Recreation*, Vol. 40, No. 6 (June 1969), p. 31.

and interrelatedness of the human environment," writes Raymond Dasmann, "can we succeed in the future in keeping it a fit place for people." [3] Also paramount in investigations are the placing of meaning and value on what is observed, the clarifying of feelings toward findings, and the drawing of useful conclusions upon which decisions must be based.

There should emerge a concern for what may happen to the participants as a result of having been in the park. This is often overlooked. After being exposed to the park's biophysical resources, the participant should depart with a better attitude toward that environment than before exposure. If an improved attitude is not developed, then that park may not be around much longer. To yield maximum benefit, exposure to an environmental resource should have carry over value for decision-making beyond the immediate sensation.

Participants should learn to explore as independently as possible, again encouraging carry over. The environmental education program leader should be a guide and partner in discovery and enjoyment; he should be a companion in growth and in understanding. The following are other desirable characteristics of an environmental education program leader:

a) He poses problem questions about environmental issues and concerns in order to orient and motivate the participants to wonder about their environment.

b) He discovers the knowledge levels and interests of the participants and discovers the attitudes that the participants have toward environmental quality and natural-resource use.

c) He is familiar with the use of the sensory equipment and field reference materials within the mobile unit.

d) He provides active guidance and supervision of the participants to encourage investigation of the park's resources.

e) He allows for individual and group discovery through various discussions and activities which recognize individual concerns and stimulate thinking about environmental issues.

f) He communicates a positive attitude toward discovery learning, reflecting enthusiasm, tactfulness, and confidence.

g) He provides multi-sensory experiences which include touch, smell, taste, sight, and hearing.

h) He encourages the participants to become actively involved in problem-solving and decision-making situations.

i) He evaluates experiences to determine whether or not objectives are being met and enjoyment and positive attitudes are being demonstrated by the participants.

j) He uses accurate ecological and resource-use concepts and relates them to the concerns of the participants.

k) He exemplifies responsibility in the use and care of materials, equipment, and environment.

---

[3] *Ibid.* p. 32. Dr. Dasmann is Director of Environmental Studies, The Conservation Foundation, and is author of *Environmental Conservation* (New York: John Wiley & Sons, Inc., 1968).

Park's Potential As An Outdoor Laboratory

Though quality leadership is an aspiration of every agency, someone must first discover the resources available in a park before the leadership can begin interpreting the biophysical environment. The outdoor leader should, therefore, begin by making an inventory of what the park has to offer. He should complete a site-survey which includes all man-made and natural resources. Also, he should determine the population that the park services. In other words, he should know the distance people will travel to use the park and participate in the program. The service area will vary according to numerous factors—such as the esthetic attractiveness of the area, the kind of leadership offered, the ease of access to the area, and the competition with other attractions. Service zones are not static because they vary with conditions: they grow with recreational and educational attraction and they shrink when attraction diminishes.

To determine the existing community interests, the environmental educator should list every organization within the service area and learn its purpose. To present a program without considering community needs would be analogous to fishing without bait on the hook. Furthermore, there may be the best mobile environmental education program in the nation; but if no one knows about it, then it is of little avail to the public. In sum, discover what your agency can do for your participants and then tell them about it. Coordinate your efforts with other agencies and programs concerned with environmental problems. Make a master calendar of all related events throughout the service area. Identify possible resource consultants and request their assistance. Most significantly, provide first-time visitors to the park with a positive and enjoyable experience into the mysteries of the biotic web of life.

Although a mobile environmental education program may be quantitatively small at the beginning when compared to other programs, the influence it could have on environmental attitude development might be qualitatively large. A park is a natural laboratory, functioning as a bridge to more distant fields. The answer to the question of whether or not park and recreation professionals can bother spending the time to involve the American citizenry in sensitivity training to their surrounding environments and related social problems is that they cannot afford to do otherwise. It is now such a priority that many forward thinking states have already made it a matter of public school law. Why must park and recreation professionals procrastinate until it becomes legally mandatory in park and recreation programs? Perhaps it will be too late.

> Those who are not part of the solution, are then part of the problem.

Selected Bibliography

CARPENTER, CHARLES D. "Mobile Science Laboratory." *Science and Children*. Vol. 6, No. 2 (October, 1968), pp. 18–19.

Department of Recreation. "Proposal for a Demonstration of The Effectiveness of Mobile and Portable Recreation Activity Units in Providing Quality Recreation Programs for Inner-City Neighborhoods." Carbondale, Illinois: Department of Recreation, Southern Illinois University, 1969. (Mimeographed.)

DONALDSON, GEORGE W. and HORN, B. RAY. "Mobile Laboratories." DeKalb, Illinois: Department of Outdoor Teacher Education, Northern Illinois University, 1969. (Mimeographed.)

HORN, B. RAY. "Planning Field Libraries." *The Outdoor Teacher*. Vol. V, No. 1 (February, 1969), pp. 8–12. Published by the Department of Conservation and Outdoor Education, Southern Illinois University, Carbondale, Illinois. A discussion of the field library and its function within the environmental education mobile unit.

JOHNSON, JAMES A. "Mobile Science Classroom." *The Science Teacher*. Vol. 30, No. 2 (March, 1963), pp. 21–22.

KNAPP, CLIFFORD E. (ed.). "The Uses of Trailer Equipment." Carbondale, Illinois: Department of Conservation and Outdoor Education, Southern Illinois University, n.d. (Mimeographed.)

National Recreation and Park Association. *Mobile and Portable Recreation Facilities in Parks and Recreation*. Washington, D.C.: The Association, 1967.

Outdoor Education Center. "Equipment for Mobile Education Unit." Carbondale, Illinois: Outdoor Education Center, Southern Illinois University, n.d. (Mimeographed.)

Science and Nature Mobile Unit. Game-Time, Inc., Litchfield, Michigan, 1969. Includes specifications of commercially manufactured unit, sample program plans, a list of equipment, and a basic philosophy.

dick palmer

teachers ride the range

New School District No. 8 is a small district in the range country of western North Dakota —only 348 elementary schoolchildren. It is also a very large district—1,115 square miles, almost the size of the entire state of Rhode Island. Often the combination of a few people scattered across a big space results in an educational desert that slows the nimble-minded children and virtually snuffs out the slow learners. But not so in No. 8.

There the space problem has never yet weakened the residents' purpose to give their children the best possible education within their means. Neither are they neglecting the boy who doesn't tumble to reading and lags behind his classmates. Or the girl who needs that extra push and pat to bring the dawn of long division. They are taking care of their slow learners by moving a remedial classroom right next to the regular classroom.

Before District No. 8 was reorganized in 1950 the children collected in 42 shabby one- and two-room elementary schoolhouses. Today's pupils travel to 16 schools, all renovated and all fulfilling the reorganization promise: more school for the money. Fifteen of the schools even have teacher-ages—basement apartments in the schools or separate, two-room mobile units.

Once the schoolhouses were made comfortably habitable, Leroy Digerness, the district principal, turned to curriculum development and aid to students in low-income areas. He was thinking primarily of the slow learners and what might be done to help.

With a Federal grant under Title I of the Elementary and Secondary Education Act Digerness and his five-man school board purchased, at about $5,000 each, three modified house trailers which are movable from school to school as testing programs show they are needed. Half of each trailer is used as a classroom, half as living quarters for the teacher who travels with it. The living quarters include an average-sized bedroom, a small bathroom, a dining area, and a compact kitchen. Sliding open a folding door, the teacher walks from her quarters to meet and teach her pupils for the day.

The classroom half contains two rows of four or five desks and a teacher's desk. A chalkboard fills the front wall. On both sides there is space between curtained windows for a bulletin board. At the back of the classroom a number of built-in cabinets are used to store supplies. One cabinet has a slide-out bottom for holding a duplicating machine.

In the 1966–67 school year the units were left at schools for six-week periods. This

Dick Palmer, "Teachers Ride the Range," American Education, Vol. 4 (September, 1968) 22–24.
Reprinted by permission.

plan proved faulty; teachers noted that underachievers had just begun to show improvement when the unit was moved elsewhere. This past year two units were left at schools for half the school year; the third unit spent the full school year four miles outside of Williston at "Power Plant" school, which serves an especially large number of disadvantaged youngsters.

Teachers in charge of the units are mostly two-year degree teachers with no special training. But all have several years of experience as rural elementary teachers. This experience with various grade levels helps them to adapt to work as basic skills instructors. They may provide primary reading help for first graders, mathematics help for seventh graders, language or basic English review for fourth graders, or aid in any other subject area for slow youngsters. Few classes are larger than four children, and the teachers usually work with two pupils at a time. Teachers divide the day into 30- or 45-minute periods, which are closely coordinated with the resident teacher in charge of the adjacent school. Because the lessons involve basic skills and nearly a one-to-one instruction ratio, the mobile teachers use no special equipment. "For this type of teaching," Digerness says, "it's just as easy to pull down a map or write on the chalkboard as it is to flip the switch on an overhead projector."

Schools to which the units are assigned are carefully chosen after pupils are tested. Some of the schools in the district will never see the units. "We don't have too many underachievers," Digerness explains, "but evaluations of the units' effectiveness have proven them to be well worth the money where they are being used." Most of the district's teachers agree, but there is not unanimous approval. . . .

carroll g. fader

sea ed

Mountains that climb straight up for 3,700 feet are the backdrop of Ketchikan, a town one block wide and 10 miles long on the southeastern coast of Alaska. The main street is the Tongass Narrows, a narrow channel that is part of the inland passage and the Pacific Ocean. Seaplanes and boats and ships of all descriptions enter and leave the city continually.

Ketchikan's climate is wet, with 13 feet of rainfall per year; its major industries are lumbering, pulp processing, mining, and fishing. The town also produces another product,

Carroll G. Fader, "Sea Ed," Today's Education (December, 1970), 31. Reprinted by permission.

one that is not unique to our area—children! Our school problems are not unique either. We are cramped for space; have a dropout problem or, as I see it, a push-out problem; and need more dollars to provide quality educational opportunities for our young people.

Traditional vocational education courses do not meet the needs of the pupils in the Ketchikan Gateway school system. Auto mechanics? The town has only three garages, with perhaps a dozen mechanics. Agriculture? Hopeless! Office skills and retail sales? There are only limited openings in these areas each year.

For years we had been overlooking a major industry, the maritime and fisheries industry, even though our area needs young people who are well-prepared to fill occupations connected with the sea.

Fortunately, Title III of the Elementary and Secondary Education Act (PL 89-10), which provides grants for innovative education programs, enabled us to remedy this deficiency.

We traveled to New England and to the east coast of Canada to investigate existing vocational programs in maritime industries. We visited two postsecondary programs in the United States and one in Canada that is geared for adults who have had little or no formal schooling but considerable experience on the high seas as fishermen. Since the Canadian program appealed to us, we used it as a guide in developing our own—Sea Ed.

At the start, the classes involved in our program were small, and we had control and experimental groups. The first class had 80 hours of instruction in after-school sessions. Now that the program is in its fourth year, the enrollment is 243 pupils in several classes, with 360 hours of class instruction and 40 to 50 hours of field trips on sea vessels. Initially, the materials used in the program were tried, screened, and tried again, and we continue to use this system today.

Essentially, Sea Ed prepares young men and women to work at sea or in shore-side related industries. But it also includes instruction in other disciplines (science, math, civics) as they relate to the program.

Students enter the Sea Ed program as sophomores with Marine Biology I. In the junior year, they take Sea Ed I, a course which emphasizes navigation skills. Sandwiched in with this are civics, economics, and English as well as communication skills and literature related to the maritime and fisheries industry. During the regular school day, students mend web; repair diesels; learn "rules of the road"; and troll, seine, gillnet, and trawl. When they become seniors, students may elect Marine Biology II, Power Mechanics, Electronics, or Sea Ed II.

Those who elect Sea Ed II learn advanced navigation and help teach the Sea Ed I classes. During the winter months, they sail as cadets with the state ferry system (the Alaska Marine Highway System) for one week. A licensed officer has charge of the students and assigns work responsibilities. In this phase of the program, Sea Ed pays for the students' uniforms and food and the Alaska ferry system provides the living facilities.

Students who take the cadet cruise must express a desire to obtain employment with the ferry system and demonstrate a good attitude in class. Grades do not determine a student's eligibility to take part in this phase of the program.

After a year in Sea Ed I, a student can get a job in the fishing industry. Those who complete Sea Ed II have employment opportunities on the ferries as soon as they graduate. Many of the girls in the program will obtain employment in shore-side supportive industries, and others may marry fishermen and work with their husbands on family boats. This past school year every student who wanted to work in a sea-related industry had a job offer.

We can't claim 100 percent success for the program, but, for the majority of students involved, it is an exciting learning experience. They get "turned on" about school, because their assignments have practical application for their future.

shelter: the cave re-examined

In human communities, networks are the interfaces along which the interaction takes place between organic systems—Nature, Man, Society, Shells, and, of course, other Networks. Rural villages have fairly simple systems of networks, but urban communities interweave many systems of networks at various levels—water supply, sewage and waste disposal, electrical and natural gas systems, movement of people and goods, telephone, radio, television and mass printed media. What is important about the vitality of an urban community is not the number or size of shells it contains, but the degree to which the networks function efficiently. Shown below [p. 302] are analogous network systems in Nature, Man, and an urban community.

Reprinted with permission of Benziger, Bruce and Glencoe, Inc. (Beverly Hills, California), a Division of The Macmillan Company from *Shelter: The Cave Re-Examined* by Don Fabun Copyright © 1970 by Kaiser Aluminum and Chemical Corporation.

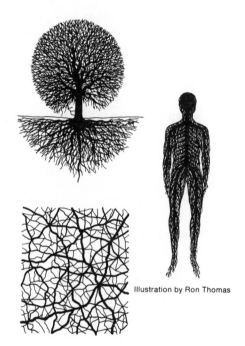

Illustration by Ron Thomas

INNOVATIONS

training

gary nabham

environmental learning!
workship proposal

the ENVIRONMENTAL LEARNING WORKSHIP purposes:

to BRING TOGETHER students, teachers, education and architecture association people (esp. media people), human ecologists, architects in practice, arch. students, educational facilities people, and environmental learning experimenters

so that the

various groups can BE made AWARE of each other's research into the NEEDS and POTENTIAL of KIDS in INTENSIFIED LEARNING ENVIRONMENTS, (i.e. what schools, all schools, should be).

to make it possible for these people to EXPERIENCE TOGETHER a number of PREPARED learning environments, CREATE-IT-YOURSELVES learning environments, and "NATURAL" learning experiences

so that they can EVALUATE PRESENT experiments, research, programs, and materials being used by those interested in environmental learning, and therefore be able to:

AFFIRM! to all interested in LIFE, EDUCATION, and KIDS that the DEVELOPMENT of ENVIRONMENTAL LEARNING is *CRUCIAL* to the
WHOLE EARTH.

SUGGEST! PRACTICAL low-cost MEANS of CREATING ENVIRONMENTS and EXPERIENCES that can HELP KIDS LEARN EASIER and MORE "FULLY."

SUGGEST! how teachers can SENSITIZE themselves and those they're working with to LEARNING through EVERYTHING in an environment.

SUGGEST! FUTURE DIRECTION for RESEARCHERS and BUILDERS

SUGGEST! how ECOLOGY APPLIED to EDUCATION should act as the model for new reforms and experiments, since its principles really govern
HOW LEARNING HAPPENS and
HOW COMMUNITIES SUCCESSFULLY INTERACT.

and

BEGIN WORKING on how all this information and material can be gotten to the PEOPLE
THAT NEED IT!

This material represents rough notes developed by the author and is presented in that form. It is reprinted by permission of the author.

Environmental Learning Workship
Tentative Program

BREAKFAST

program 1—ECO and EDUCATION CRISES, and ENVIRONMENTAL LEARNING—a multimedia happening providing the theoretical base for the workship-place: inside any plain old room, or inside a dome constructed for the workship—near the workship campsite. A written equivalent given at end.

program 2—BASIC INFORMATION on the WORKSHIP and DISCUSSION—a casual mike talk by a staffer on each of the three buses, while driving in to the city, explaining how the workship will float, commune, meet a wide range of experiences, and be expected to synthesize a large amount of data during the next few days. Travelling music, taped, will be played on the bus the rest of the time.

program 3—PRESENT SCHOOLS AS A DISASTEROUSLY LIMITED MEDIA—a casual forum by a few experts, each giving a small, (but qualitatively large), talk on subjects such as: school buildings as institutional traps; schools as indirect ways of learning; the waste of potential learning in schools; and how schools aren't reflecting what is happening in the world, are preparing kids for the world, and what will happen if this keeps up much

LUNCH

longer.—place: in an auditorium of a public building, with all the people in wooden chairs on the stage, with the speakers sitting on the floor in the aisles of the audience seats. A workbook of responses to kids' and experts' opinions of schools and their wasted potential will supplement this forum.

program 4—BUS STOP DISCOVERY TOUR OF SCHOOL BUILDING ALTERNATIVES— Buses will travel through the city, suburbs, and country, stopping when they find what they consider worthwhile alternatives to the institutional school building, and stopping at education alternative places already being used in the area. Discussion and information on the bus will cover;

floating schools (while driving nowhere in particular)

storefront schools (driving in inter-city)

neighborhood schools where learning modules come to you

human resources centers—building used as school, community center, cultural center, etc., (driving near public buildings)

free land schools—camp schools based on learning the ways of nature (while driving thru country and back country)

DINNER

program 5—FEEDBACK TIME—Group dissolves into feedback groups for dinner, group rest and walk time, then sensitivity training for sensory awareness, developing a group basis, and light nonverbal person-to-person contact games. Then discussion and recording of insights and feelings about the day.

nonprogram—FREE MINGLE or ALONE TIME

program 6—ENTERTAINMENT * IMPROVISATIONAL MUSIC *—All of group comes together for do-it-yourself music time—vocal orchestrations—coordinated rounds—instrumentals using what's around you—folk songs *

END OF FIRST DAY

BREAKFAST

program 7—HOW TO TRANSFORM PRESENT EXISTING SCHOOLS INTO SOMETHING LARGER THAN TRAPS—(MORE HUMAN) A collage of speakers, poster manifestos on revolving apparatuses and a balloon (helium or whatever) with pamphlets on it, all giving information on the basics of looking at architecture as a language, multimedia as a language, and how schools have traps because of the unnecessary limits resulting from our traditional uses of these languages. Place—On top of a school building in the area. People will be encouraged to start the transformation by creatively expanding their use of these languages.

program 8—GROWING OLD SCHOOLS INTO NEW SCHOOLS—Discussions by forums on schools as learning places in relation to everywhere being learning places

> Schools as gathering places of particular kinds of people
>
> Schools as resource gathering places
>
> Schools as intensified, directed learning environments
>
> Schools as providers of tools for learning everywhere
>
> Schools as places where kids help build and modify their own environment
>
> Schools as points of departure for field learning, where they can be helped in testing and evaluating their data from field experiences

After a quick discussion of each of these concepts as a group, individuals can go around to special presentation areas on each concept. At each area, a team of three people, either from a school based on the concept, or playing that role, will present the school in any way they feel that is necessary for getting the mood of that school across. Place—At the lodge for the group meeting, then all over the camp.

program 9—HOW TO BUILD A DOME WITH YOUR FRIENDS—An exercise in a community working together. Build a small, temporary dome (considerably different from the one the first program outlined, if the workship needs two domes).

DINNER

program 10—FEEDBACK TIME—nonverbal sensitivity session (body loosening) then group exercises and games. Feedback leader holds up signs relating to the activities of the day and asks people to respond, still nonverbally, to them. Then silent camp walk.

nonprogram—Alone—mingle—staffers meeting-time

program 11—Multimedia ritual drama. Place—new dome. A participational happening in the place the group helped build.

END OF SECOND DAY

BREAKFAST

program 12—HOW CHILDREN LEARN THROUGH THEIR ENVIRONMENT—Specifics on the ecology of the imagination of childhood, synectics and synergy, the fields theory, and how kids perceive the world different than adults do. Talks by experts with role-playing games to get inside of kid's psyches.

program 13—NEEDS OF KIDS—Workshop on the securities kids need, proportioning, and relations with adults. Place for 12 & 13—Nursery school building, or a Kiddie Show TV setting.

LUNCH

program 14—DESIGNERS-NEEDERS FORUM—Teachers and learning experimenters ask facilities people and researchers to help create learning tools and environments that they need, and silence environmental disturbances that they have trouble with. The architects and researchers and facilitators share their information, and ask teachers for insights on applying it. Place—Lodge. Groups face each other.

program 15—WORK-WORKSHIP SIGN-UP TIME. Work-workshops will be small groups that will explore one particular segment of learning environments, one media or method of environmental teaching, accumulate knowledge of it, and synthesize it into some form that can be readily accessible to all teachers and facilitators. Some groups will construct things, some will create activities and programs dealing with environmental learning. The groups will meet after general meetings each morning, in the domes, outside, in the lodge, or at a nearby school. People will switch groups in the afternoon.

WORK-WORKSHIPS

Furniture in schoolrooms
Shapes of workspaces in classrooms, & what they help you do
Colors and graphic patterns in schools, & their implications
Lighting
Textures, & their implications
Acoustics
Smell & taste, & what can be done with them
Flexibilities with floors, ceilings, and walls in classrooms, and halls
Video-taping and closed circuit TV
Tape recorders
Films and slides
Other living things around the school, & in the classroom
Simulation games—field trips combinations
Making associations between the school's activities and ecological
principles

DINNER and FEEDBACK TIME—

A campfire thing, out in some raw land nearby. Relax and chat, near a river, maybe, with only your feedback group in sight. Groups dropped off by bus ½ a mile apart from each other. A storyteller and harmonica player for every fire!

END OF THIRD DAY

BREAKFAST

program 16—EXPERIENCES WITH KIDS MAKING THEIR OWN ENVIRONMENTS— Films and displays of kid-made stuff, (the films can be by kids too), emphasizing that the work-workships should be aimed at informing teachers how to help kids create an environment that they feel partly responsible for. Place—Lodge.

program 17—A quickie suggesting that work-workships should set down specific goals, and suggesting ways they can get this information out to the needers. Place—Lodge.

program 18—WORK-WORKSHIP PURPOSE SESSIONS. Hows, whens, whys, wheres . . .

LUNCH

program 19—WORK-WORKSHIPS

DINNER

Everyone together for some weird primitive feast with guests. Guests are little kids from a local school, and outside earth activist commune, or architects commune, (someone like EARTH LIBERATION FRONT, or FARALLONES INSTITUTE).

program 20—COUPLES OF CREATIVITY—Kids and adults and guests are paired up, then each couple decides what creative thing they'd like to make together. Tape recorders, inexpensive gadgets, paints, paper, cardboard, clay, musicals, costumes, etc., will be available. Then each couple will exchange objects or presentations with another couple.

END OF FOURTH DAY

BREAKFAST

program 21—EARTH FAIR—Outside commune will exchange ideas and constructions with us.

program 22—WORK-WORKSHIPS.

LUNCH

program 23—WORK-WORKSHIPS' WRAP UP

DINNER

program 24—FINAL FEEDBACK TIME—sensitivity group things, and final evaluation.

program 25—SONGFEST AND MASS NATUREWALK AND DESTRUCTION OF DOME

END OF FIFTH DAY
TOGETHER BREAKFAST and CLOSE

WHEN:
early Spring or late Fall, 1971, 3-6 days.

FINANCES:
Hopefully, from foundations and associations who would welcome seeing many re-searchers interact with practitioners for working solutions, rather than funding small research programs that might not do anything. Money could be coordinated by an area committee with advisory help from the foundations and associations, plus special advisory help from someone who has run conventions or conferences before.

Relatively speaking, the workship would not cost that much, because it would stress minimal expense, maximal use activities, and would use only those special resources that could come for free, trusting that if they're worth anything, people at the conference could tune them into people with money after the conference.

Finances would include money for the facilities and services during the workship, special transportation, pre-conference administration costs, and administrators (3-4) part time salary for a period before the workship.

Naturally, part of the finances, if needed, could come from the workship participants, (excluding certain people instrumental to its presentation).

WHO:
Oh, maybe 120 people. Maybe 20 people, student nea, and experts in certain areas would coordinate it. (They could correspond much & get together a couple days before.) Also showing up early could be some building people, architects & students & happening coordinators & facilities people to construct some of the prepared environments & activi-ties. 10-20. Besides that, 10 'media' people for coverage of the thing, other environmental learning freaks and researchers and students, snea people, and people who found out about the thing thru ed. & arch. & media & ecology publications pre-publicity. Maybe up to 140 if we feature that kids & wives & dogs are needed too. Anywhere from 90-140 would be fine.

Specific decisions on who should come, (esp.) with invitations, etc., would be made by the staff with advice from advisory committee of field experts & snea.

WHERE: WITH WHAT:
Oh, how 'bout a kid's camp close to a big city, but yet, out in free land? at a time when kids aren't using it. Minimal buildings. Crude little cabins, a lodge, & maintaining facilities. Really homey, low cost, and simple. Everyone could get that nice awkward feeling watching each other change underwear, & stuff like that. Everything would be kid size, from fountains to chairs. Humbung. It's not hard to find places like this. Also, if

we went to a camp, everyone would hafta wear old clothes. Thoreau said, "Be cautious of anything that makes you wear new clothes." There would have to be some free space near the buildings, for constructions and activities. Also, there would have to be a lot of electric outlets.

Also, we'd need 3 buses, old ones, a pickup truck, and some construction tools, besides multimedia apparatus. Loaned, if possible.

Building materials & environment-creating materials can be loaned hopefully too.

FOOD & LODGING ARRANGEMENTS

We'll somehow break people into tribes of 10-12, which you'll eat breakfast with, sleep with. For lunch, 2 tribes will combine, switching every day. For dinner, you'll eat with your "feedback" group, the group formed for various activities including end-of-day evaluation.

We'll all fix our own food, & the type of food will correspond to the activity of that particular time.

ALTERNATIVE FUTURES

stuart a. sandow

the pedagogy of planning:
defining sufficient
futures

Until the people are solved somehow
For the day and the hour,
Until then, one hears
"Yes, but the people. What about the people?"
Sometimes as though the people
Is a child to be pleased and fed.
Sometimes as though the people
Is a hoodlum you have to be tough with.
But, seldom as though the people is a caldron
And a reservoir of the human reserves
That shape history.   *Carl Sandburg*

Presumably men engage in forecasting for reasons beyond the formulation of forecasts themselves. Usually, forecasting absorbs men because it aids their planning. How can forecasting methods be used to influence the planning process? In short, how can citizens use them as a kind of pedagogical system to affect the ways planners think about the future? How can the future-perspective affect the planning process? These problems are at the heart of this inquiry into the logic of non-data based methods of thought.

A further purpose is to isolate from those methods and catch phrases men use to think about the unknown future the questions they ask themselves, and the nature and uses of their responses when used in planning. This essay is most concerned to develop a way for planners to address the future without forgetting that the future is the future of individuals—of people. It argues the citizen's important role in future planning, and supports sustained divergence of opinion in the planning process, rather than consensus as the desirable outcome of the process.

·   ·   ·

The acceptance of certain arguments is [essential].

Reprinted by permission of Dr. Stuart A. Sandow, fellow, Educational Policy Research Center at Syracuse, N.Y.

What Is the Nature of Information
That Is Useful to Future Planning?

Extrapolations and manipulations of data are useful for predicting and fore-casting. But alone they do not yield decisions in the planning process. Policy and planning imply a concern with goals that is typically omitted from such manipulations of data.[1]

What Is a Goal?

Goal statements reflect beliefs: "it is possible to believe what is false but not possible to know what is false . . . Although belief is a part of any knowledge claim, knowledge is not necessarily a part of belief claims . . . There are vast areas of human concern which are commonly understood not to deal with knowledge at all but with insight, wisdom or simply conviction . . . Beliefs cannot be assessed in ignorance. They cannot be assessed until it is understood how it is that men who have held them have found them reasonable to believe." [2]

On the one hand, we face a lack of data to which we can attach truth or knowledge claims; on the other hand, we confront goals that themselves reflect beliefs—beliefs that need not carry a condition of truth.

What Happens When We Question
the Future?

Questions we ask about the future are of a type whose answer cannot be known to be true at the moment of utterance. Utterances do not fulfill the criteria for answers because they do not satisfy the truth condition imposed on answers. In this pedagogy, I have called all answers to future questions "responses," arguing that a response is an acceptable reply with a logical and believable connection to the question but without necessary truth. This distinction has the pedagogical value of freeing the individual to trust his response almost as a belief, without having to contend that it is true.

---

[1] E. P. Holland and R. W. Gillespie, *Experiments on a Simulated Underdeveloped Economy* (Cambridge, Mass.: M.I.T. Press, 1969).

[2] Thomas F. Green, *The Activities of Teaching* (New York: McGraw-Hill, 1970).

If Questions About the Future Do Not Generate Answers, How Can We Plan At All?

By suspending our disbelief (a cinema concept) and temporarily trusting our conjectured responses enough to treat them as tentative truths, we can proceed to plan.

In effect, we build bridges toward future actions by trusting (as we must) the incomplete knowledge we have in the present. It has often been noted (by policy planners if not by physical planners) that one never has "enough" knowledge on which to base a decision at the moment such decision becomes imperative; if one waits until knowledge is sufficient, the opportunity for effective decision has often slipped away.

What Is the Nature of Expertise About the Future: Does It Exist? If So, Who Has It?

The further into future time we extend our concern and attention, the more unknowns we must face in conjecturing the future possibilities that demand examination. The parameters of the short-term future can be fairly accurately forecast. However, technological innovations not yet conceived will rupture these forecasts. Unlike the short-term future, the long-term future cannot be perceived as a continuous extrapolation of the past in quantifiably larger or smaller terms. Rather, it must be perceived as an array of possible futures. New unknowns in technological innovation have provoked the pursuit of *surprise-free* future projections and the casting of alternative future conjectures—conjectures that are only limited by man's perception of "what could be."

Men try to delimit a plausible future when they pursue goals. All goals are not-yet-occurred states of affairs that are sought by some individual or group. The key argument underlying this essay is that the strategies used in pursuing goals and the groups who chose them need to be examined as rigorously as the goals themselves.

· · ·

Men conceive of the passing of time, both past and future, as aggregate concepts. The past and future are generally disaggregated, for planning, into short-term and long-term periods. The short-term—or more recent—past is examined with the set of techniques appropriate to it—usually by direct examination of the hard evidence which the event has left behind. The long-term—or more distant—pasts are examined with techniques appropriate to them. However, the subjectivity of the historian is imposed on whichever accounts he chooses to believe.

Similarly, the methods for examining the short- and long-term future differ. The short-term future can be rather clearly specified, and its parameters detailed by the extrapolation of the hard data (trends, etc.) available to short-term planners. Through the experts who interpret that data, competent synthesis can delimit options. These 'data based methods' include PERT, PPBS, and the economic and demographic data collected by statisticians over the past several hundred years. In addition, men in the vanguard of their own fields can be interviewed.

The long-term future offers no hard data, and expertise and objectivity toward it are difficult to recognize. The further into the future men project their concern, the greater number of impacts their actions appear to have. The unthinkable events that one cannot conceive through extrapolation of the present become visible and plausible when conjectured into the long-term future.

Processes exist for systematically examining these several alternative long-term futures. These might be called "non-data based methods." (I have coined this term to separate testable knowledge from untestable belief.)

The methods we will consider seem to consist of an array of specific questions which long-term planners confront in their attempt to examine the unknown long-term future. When examined as an array of specific questions, these methods show a natural logic. They seem to focus the long-term planner's attention toward an ever-expanding perception of alternative moments in time.

Responses to questions about the long-term future—like those of the long-term past —are more subjective than those for the short-term. This subjectivity reflects personal perceptions, beliefs and values. Men may attempt to be completely objective, but their objectivity is submerged in their subjective decisions about what they will try to be objective about. The responses long-term planners generate to the questions they ask of the long-term future are value-laden, reflecting their own perspectives.

Long-term planning is concerned with *developing* problems—problems that will not exist for years to come, if at all. These long-term conjectures are not stated in terms of *if-only* goals and are not wishes for a better now.* However, they often reflect aspects of *now* continued into the future unchanged, as if the long-term planner ignored the intervening years and the existing forces which are basic change agents in human behaviors, desires, values, and beliefs.

This essay examines several such methods designed to help long-term planners assess their strategies and goals for the long-term future. They are: Delphi, Future Histories, Scenarios, Value Shift Analysis, and Future History Analysis.

•   •   •

* *If-only* the war were over, I wouldn't mind being drafted *now*.

Delphi: A Tool For Developing Future Environments

The Delphi Technique elicits and refines the opinions of a group of individuals. The individuals remain anonymous to each other, their opinions are continually refined and reiterated, and feedback to participants is controlled. The process is believed to produce either converging group consensus or the polarization of views.

A variant of the panel or committee approach for arriving at consensus or majority opinion, the Delphi Technique eliminates the face-to-face confrontation of a panel or committee. Presumably, it avoids specious persuasion, individual unwillingness to abandon publicly-held positions, and the bandwagon effect of a majority argument. For direct discussion, Delphi substitutes a series of carefully controlled questionnaires that report back edited opinions and new information to participants, while they work in privacy and react to successive inputs. A committee or panel report is replaced by tabulated data from the respondents, from which Delphi coordinators draw their interpretations and analyses in order to arrive at a series of forecasts, opinions, and occasionally scenarios instead of an expository report.[3]

．　　．　　．

With knowledge of a goal, and the groups of society it affects, the Delphi may be used to create a chronologically-linked series of conjectured events which form a "future environment." This is an outcome proposed by Delphi advocates. But in order to specify accurately a future environment, several changes in the present Delphi form are necessary. First, opinions of participants must be focused upon a previously proposed plan or goal whose strategy stretches across the time span reflected by the events in question before the exercise begins. Their anonymous opinions about events can then be set against personal value assessments about the plan, strategy, or goal itself.

Secondly, all persons are experts in their own opinions about the value of any goals. Different people have radically different opinions. Thus, a group cannot be seen as an aggregate from which one can directly extrapolate a consensus about events relevant to those goals. To disaggregate the several subgroups, the inter-quartile ranges of the various expert/interest groups are displayed Delphicly to allow planners to assess those subgroups' perceptions.

Third, the events examined in the Delphi must be displayed along a time line spanning the period between the present and the moment a goal is planned to be attained. We call this time line a "future environment." For this chronology to be sufficiently believable to planners, it must be plausible and internally consistent.

A future environment is an agreed-upon construct of a period of time that has not yet occurred—a period that begins in the present and moves to a date beyond the

[3] N. C. Dalkey, *Delphi* (Santa Monica, Calif.: RAND Corporation Report P-3704, October 1967).

moment of goal achievement. The future environment contains a series of moments in time against which we locate conjectured events. A series of events that is neither implausible nor inconsistent may be considered a set of givens that planners temporarily agree will act as exemplars of the types of events they may confront while pursuing their strategies. Against these events, they assess their strategies and goals.

If each affected subgroup of society is represented by a different interquartile range during successive questionnaires, and if their opinions about the locus of power sufficient to cause the event's occurrence are requested, those events which are perceived by all sub-groups as occurring approximately simultaneously, with the same power base, form key pieces of the chronology. Events that conflict with these are temporarily discarded. Remaining events (those which the Delphi respondents did not agree on) are located on the chronology, according to the planner's assessment of the power base for each event. The probability of an event is increased or decreased depending upon the value ascribed to it by the group who is seen as having the power to make it happen. To this chronology may be added events that fill out the future environment to create plausible links to the present.

.   .   .

When future events are arranged in series, they become an intellectual playground, an environment which planners agree to consider exemplars of a future that will affect their assessment of plans, strategies, and goals. A future environment exists at the whim of planners, reflecting the perceptions and opinions of various groups which may be affected by the planners' actions. A "future environment" has several advantages: it covers the input of relevant populations affected by a plan, is predicated on human desires, and accounts for self-interested perceptions of the future. It plausibly links a future moment—the moment when the goal may occur—to the present. It confronts the goal and its strategy with a series of impinging events that the planners agree are probable and internally consistent with their knowledge.

.   .   .

From these individual histories, alternative futures emerge that specify each individual's perception of the reciprocal impact of events throughout the time span they consider. "Scenarios" of select moments can then be created to specify alternative views of the future.

Expository Methods: Future Histories and Scenarios

The writing of future histories is expository and reflective. The process is similar to the historiography of personally experienced periods. A future history clarifies for the writer his feelings, both reflective and intuitive, about causality. It gives him a chance to order and assess his assumptions about the future.

Because men write histories, different histories will be written about a common theme, set against common contingencies. At any moment, the impact of identical events on each man's goals and plans will be particular, unique, and profoundly important to him in his assessment.

Writing a future history allows individuals who are responsible for planning social change to recognize more clearly their roles as members of a society, not elite beings in some unaffected world. Future histories encourage individual planners to view the long-term future as a series of moments that are linked sufficiently and not necessarily.

Time is dynamic. Moments are linked by a causal chain of events. The relationships we see when we ruminate on past time are of a different quality than those we find when we conjecture forward to a goal. When we trust our evidence of the past in order to extrapolate causation into the future, we assume that the causal links are necessary links—necessary conditions. We *cannot assess causes in terms of alternatives unless we see them as only sufficient conditions when we try to anticipate the future.*

If we examine the future chiefly in order to assess alternative strategies, we must deal with them as sufficient strategies that are amenable to change. Reflections on past causal links as necessary conditions in any future history are a logical fallacy, restricting our freedom to pose alternative sufficient conditions for both the future and the strategies that we pursue toward goals. If we concern ourselves with the interaction of events through time as merely sufficient, each individual may reveal alternatives not posed by others, while assessing his own incremental plans. We impose the past on the future when we extrapolate the past. A necessary past causes a necessary future.

While assessing plans forward through time is cognitive/intuitive, historical assessment is reflective. Each assessment starts from a different knowledge base. In the assessment of a strategy forward through time, we tap memories of our past and all those "future memories" of the strategic interactions we generate during the planning exercise. When one writes a future history from his role in the future as he conjectures it, his assessment of the time spanned draws on his total memories; he draws on his memories of the past which now include his "memories" of the future.

• • •

In the writing of future histories, certain restrictions cover the planner's response:

He must deal with the time span examined in the past tense.

He must posit his plans, and goals pursued, as states of affairs that have occurred.

He must date specific occurrences so that he knows where, in time and space, the event occurred in reference to all other events.

He must posit a "future present role" for himself to explain to himself why he is writing these "memoirs."

Examples:

"I am retiring."

"My successor requests an overview of the institution's work."

"I am transferring and am fascinated by the developments I have seen during the past 20 years."

"I am describing to my children or to someone else why today is necessarily the way it is."

To develop a plausible series of causal events, planners must "suspend their disbelief." They must treat the future they have built as an occurred reality, then reflect back to the present to speculate how it came to be. The strategies, the beneficiaries, the goals, and the decisions that have created it must be explicated to their satisfaction. Their satisfaction is defined as a continuing state of suspended disbelief.

SCENARIOS

In the future's literature a "scenario" is generally treated as synonymous with a "future history." In the logic of the methods developed in this essay, it is appropriate to separate them. This allows them to be used for a crisper analysis of a future conjectured world in order to assess goals. The purpose of constructing "scenarios" is to examine discrete moments in time.

By disaggregating the two ideas, future histories are constructed by several individuals, as histories usually are; scenarios are written from the sum of future histories.

It is useful to treat a scenario as a plausible picture of a single moment drawn from all histories of a period. We do not experience history as a span of time; rather, we are confronted with separate moments, usually experienced as chunks-of-now. We write scenarios to create the perspective from which to examine how men responded to events at certain moments. If we use future histories to specify causal links over a continuum of time, the scenario becomes a tool to examine specific pressure points or strategic points of decision at precise moments in that continuum.

When one writes from his own role, his base of experience is self-centered. The planners who enter the exercise of writing future histories designate differing causal links for events; for other events, they may specify the same causes. These common perceptions may locate those moments which demand more clarification in the choice of alternative goal-bent actions. A commonly perceived interaction may be based on a perception of necessary causality. Such common causal events need examination to determine whether the coincidence demonstrates high plausibility in the conjecture, or whether the causal links have been seen as necessary. Hence common perception of impact, like any consensus of opinion about the future, must be suspect: is the perception based on the group's belief in necessary causality? The various perceptions of individuals as to links over time underlie alternative assessments.

A scenaro, then, is historically free. It records only "what-it-must-have-been-like" for subgroups of the society at some moment, given certain interactions. This "what-it-must-have-been-like" requires a basic pool of several histories, written so that the perceptions of several men can be integrated in a scenario. By thus disaggregating future histories, commonalities and disparities can be identified. The disparities demand that alternative scenarios be devised. One belief about the future holds that it is unknowable, thus the writing of one scenario is inadequate. Several histories allow several alternative scenarios to be built. Advocacy of only one scenario implies a belief that the causal links are necessary, not merely sufficient.

In sum, when we build a future environment from a "Focused Delphi" * and accept its events temporarily as exemplars of the types of events we may face in the actual future, we build a useful playground for planning. If a planning group suspends its disbelief and accepts the environment it builds, it can plot several proposed strategies incrementally, against that array of chronologically-linked events.

Having "lived" through this future in pursuit of their individual goals, the participants develop a past that includes their "memories" of that future. Their "memories" of the interaction of selected events allow them the confidence to reflect on their efforts and then to write their own "future histories." All participants' perceptions span the same period and specify various impacts at various moments not seen by everyone. The existence of many alternative perceptions demands that several scenarios be built of those moments, in order to assess the strategies that will be sufficient to achieve a goal. The sufficient causal links that harm certain segments of society can be assessed in detail to find still other alternatives for the future.

•   •   •

Value Shift Assessment: A Tool to Examine Goal Impact

It has been argued that goals, if achieved, occur at a moment in time. Strategies are pursued towards goals through a continuum of time. The environment spans a period of time; events occur at select moments. We argued that histories of possible interactions between events and strategies may be written about the time continuum, while scenarios may be built of select moments in time. Similarly, values are held at a moment in time, but shift over time.

When individual planners examine goals, they must examine the values on which goal selection was based (values are an ordered set of preferences sustained by a system of belief). Similarly, they must examine the possible plausible values held at the moment of the goal's attainment. Out of these polar examinations, a shift in values over a period should emerge.

The task now is to ask what attaining a goal means in terms of shifting values at the moment it occurs. A most profound reality of the last half of the 20th Century is the *inability of values to keep pace with change*. When individuals adopt goals for the long-term future they pursue a value or try to sustain a value currently held, by trying to

---

* Details of the Focus Delphi described briefly earlier in this essay are available from the author.

promote or reconfirm its future existence. We might think of goals set for the long-term future as attempts to attain or support some value.[4]

It is enough for our purposes to have planners examine their goals in terms of the values implied in the goals' attainment; and to assess their goals against conjectures about a possible shift in values by the time the goal has been attained.

The planners must ask four basic questions in order to examine their goals and the values they imply:

What are some reflectors of the goal's attainment?

What values are implied in the goal's attainment?

What value shifts are implied in pursuing the goal?

What values are probably held now?

The purpose of the exercise is *not* to know what the future might be, but rather to make all planners, each assessing a goal of his choice that he personally chose to work toward, examine the implications of pursuing what has to this point been a cliche goal statement.

.　　.　　.

Future History Analysis and Review:
A Tool to Examine Strategies

Behavior may be thought of as a set of activities. The interactions of men's activities create events. When men's activities and the events they cause are in pursuit of a goal, we might call that set of interactions a strategy. Future History Analysis and Review (FHAR) examines the array of events and activities that may cause the achievement of a goal at a moment in the long-term future.

FHAR is an idea based on concepts originally developed by Warren Ziegler, Acting Director of the Educational Policy Research Center at Syracuse, in 1969. The idea originated in a tool developed for the government called Program Evaluation and Review Technique (PERT). The descriptors are 'events' and 'activities.' Events occur at moments and may be thought static, while activities span time and may be thought dynamic.

FHAR, like PERT, is a tool to help planners focus on the incremental behavior necessary to reach a goal. In each case the planner must specify the intervening events and activities that form causal links to the attainment of the goal. All similarity between the techniques ends there. The author has chosen to polarize the PERT process and technique

[4] K. Baier, "What Is Value? An Analysis of the Concept," in *Values and the Future*, eds.
K. Baier and N. Rescher (New York: The Free Press, 1965).

against the FHAR process in order to more clearly outline the questions FHAR compels the planner to respond to. It is in the differences that the unique value of FHAR may be most evident.

PERT is a useful tool for plotting the necessary events and activities that carry a project from conception to completion. Designed by North American Aviation, under contract to the U.S. Government to build the Polaris missile, PERT organizes the activities of many diverse units of an enterprise to guarantee delivery of sub-parts at critical moments in the development of the final product. Each unit of the whole is thought of as an "event" when it is completed; "activities" represent the effort necessary to create the event. The PERT Chart details the time each activity will take and the moment when finished sub-units must be integrated into a larger unit. It helps the planner keep complex pieces of the strategy integrated.

PERT is very useful regarding projects where goal attainment reflects the end of an investment of energy. Examples of this are: a missile launched, a bomb built, a gas station open for business, or apartments completed. When a goal can be stated in operational terms, the PERT exercise focuses the planner's attention on all intervening events and activities necessary to attain the goal, starting in the present. A pathway to the future is treated as the set of experiences that must occur to have the goal occur.

PERT is an appropriate tool for planning a time and energy strategy toward attainment of a physical goal. PERT does not generate alternatives. Alternative routes to a goal are posited only in terms of shifting time and energy allocations among events in the outlined strategy. No alternative goals are considered.

FHAR also starts with a goal in the future. FHAR first specifies alternative sufficient condition events with no sufficient activities to link them back through time to the present. For each sufficient event posited, starting with the goal, two or more prior alternative sufficient events must be stated. The further into past time one FHARs, the more events are arrayed in any moment in time. Events listed in the present moment must be existing events or ones that are operationally feasible in the present calendar year.

Activities that are sufficient to link the events are then specified incrementally, forward and through time, toward the goal. The tool's purpose is to force the individual planner, as strategist, to confront the myriad starting behaviors that might be sufficient alternatives from which to launch the pursuit of his goal: not to set strategy, but to assess choices among strategies, to confront the magnitude of one's options, and the impact of diverse actions on the planned future.

·   ·   ·

In transferring a tool from physical to social sciences, one problem is that physical entities when constructed and completed no longer demand their former energy investment. Once a car is built, it is built; then it is warehoused, sold, driven. In the social sciences, the focus is on the driver and his ability, attitudes and techniques—rather than on the car itself. The goal is the presence of a continuing behavior we recognize as good driving. To that end, the aggressor must continually invest energy in order for the goal to remain in existence.

This different energy investment is critical to the choice of appropriate tools for examining goals. Physical goals, once reached, exist without the investment of maintenance behavior on the part of the goal advocate—that person who urges support for pursuit of the goal. Social goals demand one type of energy investment to attain the goal, and demand another to maintain it by encouraging an appropriate social behavior. If we cost social projects only to the moment when an exemplar can be identified and call that moment 'goal attainment,' we fail to reach the social goal by not planning investment to maintain the behavior which is genuinely *part* of our goal.

• • •

The FHAR process resembles a brainstorming exercise. In brainstorming, no judgments about ideas generated are made while ideas are being gathered. For any moment, as many sufficient events as possible are detailed, back through the examined period of time. These points in time are then linked by sufficient activities which could cause the event to occur.

By separating the two procedures, the creative exercise of event specification is not constrained by concerns about causality. The specification of events occurs before analysis; the events can be explicated as static entities. Further, the events are the self-imposed parameters of alternative possible occurrences which the planner judges he must account for. By not attending to causality at this first stage, a greater variety of events is elicited.

On the other hand, the activity links, while creative, are thoughtfully introduced and more reasoned. As many causal activity links as events appear, but the dynamic nature of activities differs from the static events they bring about.

As with any series of questions we ask ourselves, the output supplies the base for new questions. The FHAR Chart is no different. Examining the chart, several points can be made to further break the set of necessary causality and to introduce equally important information.

We argued that goals can be thought of as "not-yet-occurred" events. At the moment of the goal's attainment, we can point to it as an event. In addition, all the intervening alternative events we posited between the present and that future moment, if integrated into our chosen strategy, become goals themselves. The activities link our behaviors in our forward pursuit to a goal through time.

All events in the present moment are recognized as occurred goals or the unintended consequences of goal pursuit. Many events listed in the present may harm the society in the present. Men do not pursue bad goals, rather, they are unaware of the goal's impact on the future when they pursue it. We may consider the events in the present calendar year as the goals (or consequences of goals) of men in some past moment. The set of events listed in the present may then be seen as the goals and consequences of the pursuit of some past goal.

Noting this, planners now must operationalize the process they just experienced, only in reverse—this time examining the impact of their (strategy) on the future moment when it will cause a goal to exist. Working forward from a present event, alternative outcomes (events) are posited until the future moment of goal attainment is full of consequences attributable to the pursuit of one goal. An exercise of this type compels the planners to choose their strategy wisely and to consider the detrimental and beneficial impacts of choice.

This effort concerns only one goal and its unique strategy. Within one institution many goals are simultaneously pursued, each with a different moment of attainment. The events that are mile posts in a strategy, and the activities that reflect planned behaviors, are now clearer to each goal advocate. But now a goal is no longer merely a cliche; it reflects the planned values and behaviors of some group. Now, that goal can be set against other goals and assessed to help determine an institution's priorities.

·   ·   ·

The Study of the Sufficient Future:
The Logic of Suspended Disbelief

Throughout this essay the underlying assumption has been that we must see the future as an array of sufficient causal relationships. To study and examine a future, an individual must consider his examination as merely sufficient. To do this, he must suspend his disbelief in order to believe his incremental manipulations of events in time. At the end of a long, internally consistent examination of several sufficient future developments, priorities for a given moment can be specified. When priorities are thus specified and goals pursued, the future necessarily becomes linked to the present. The suspension of disbelief is the sole condition that allows men to examine their sufficient plans before these plans become necessary and are imposed on an unprepared world.

When futurists sell policy-maker's techniques that induce consensus, or conformity to an opinion, each individual's ability to suspend his disbelief is threatened. Those who disagree with the consensus find the foundation of all their responses about the future weak and undermined. Consensus attempts to induce closure. Too early closure prevents suspended disbelief and compels us to operate as if what we do were necessary rather than merely sufficient, inevitable rather than a matter of choice.

Only sustained divergence allows a more thorough examination of plans to exist, yet divergence becomes more difficult to sustain as our play at futures grows formalized. Convergence and consensus methods reach closure but eliminate alternative options; more open methods must be adopted. The real future will be necessary. We do it violence to base our speculations on an insufficient examination of sufficient alternative futures.

francois hetman

modes of understanding
the future

Modes of Understanding the Future

Fr. : modes de perception du futur.

G. : Modelle des Zukunfts-verständnisses.

Understanding of the future may differ from one civilisation to another and from one era to another. Four main « models » may be distinguished:

1. Identification with the present : this method of perception of the future resembles the child's vision of the world where the concept of sequential change is not present; it is the static perception of things which is to be found in primitive societies.

2. Optimism about the future : without actually laying down markers, this attitude consists in having profound confidence in the future, a confidence based on the intrinsic dynamic nature of the society; it was a characteristic of the pioneers in the American West or, on another level, the bourgeoisie at the beginning of capitalist expansion.

3. Integral technocratic planning : an embodiment of the rational order of things; the attitude of those who consider that man and society are malleable at will—this is the Utopian vision of authoritarian planning.

4. Myth of the three ages : the past viewed as the lost golden age, the present as the difficult transition phase and the future as the haven of happiness or the promised land; this myth is constantly reborn and is to be found in widely different forms; determinist philosophies and also the Marxist vision of the redeeming future belong in this category.

(Ref. : WALTER DIRKS, « Die Zukunft als Tabu », in *Deutschland ohne Konzeption*, München, K. Desch., 1964.)

Cf. Future (ontology future—past); Crossroads of futuribles.
Francois Hetman, "The Language of Forecasting," *Futuribles*, Paris: S.E.D.E.I.S., 1969, p. 394.

donald e. hawkins

can we invent the future of leisure?

Your basic tool kit for inventing the future:

Grokker: useful for grokking—a psychological state we enter to totally assimilate something through understanding, identifying, empathizing and feeling. It'll help you cope with future shock.

Prospective Attitude Modifer: essential to create or simulate an intensity of focus on the future. This may seem to be easy, not requiring such a tool. But we need to change the way we think, using foresight rather than hindsight. This requires considerable effort . . . because it goes against our most deeply routed biases, experiences, and habits.

Juxtapositer: helps in examining several objects (graphic or verbal) at the same time, thus helping the creative mind to arrive at new insights, a higher order of thought and abstraction. Often the result is a synthesis that is more than the original, thanks to serendipity and synergism.

Dialogue Focuser: use to bring theory and abstract ideas into a practical and relevant context for you.

Key Words and Their Meanings

SERENDIPITY

Horace Walpole coined the word "serendipity" in 1754, basing it on a Persian fairy tale of the three princes of the Kingdom of Serendip. The legend held that when the princes of Serendip went on a journey something unexpected happened, and they

Prepared for Discover America Travel Organizations, The United States Travel Conference, Atlanta, Georgia, September 30, 1971. Reprinted by permission.

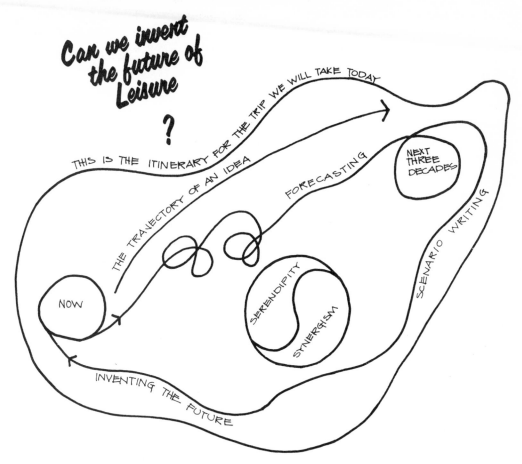

found valuable things not sought for. A serendipity is a bonus that men and nature pay those who can see beyond their noses. And what you find may be far more useful or delightful than what you were looking for.

The discovery of pencillin by Fleming was a serendipity. Some plate cultures of staphylococci had become contaminated and groups of staphylococci around one colony had died. This was not an uncommon experience, but Fleming saw the unusual in the usual and discovered penicillin.

Oliver Evans got the idea of the steam engine by noticing steam blow a cork out of a gun barrel filled with boiling water. Alexander Graham Bell was working to improve the telegraph when he developed the telephone through an accidental occurrence in his laboratory—the sticking of a reed that was being vibrated by an electric current. Goodyear accidentally spilled crude rubber on a hot stove and learned that heating rubber with sulphur would make it firm, would vulcanize it.

Though we cannot work directly for serendipities we can prepare for them and most certainly we can often make them available to others. The word of encouragement, the extra time given to a troubled student, the notes of appreciation are held dear and long remembered. Perhaps, too, the serendipity principle may be taken as a warning to those whose focus on life has been so narrowed that they do not see the flower at the side of the road or the beautiful vista just ahead.

(Ref.: *Edgar Dale.*)

SYNERGISM

In scientific and technological forecasting, synergism stands for cooperative and interactive effects of research activities which tend to result in unexpected solutions and especially in new combinations and new wholes that are greater than the sum of the parts.

Complex synergetic breakthroughs may be composed of a number of layers of interrelated "simple" synergisms, each important in its own right. They may lead to new methods of basic research and consequently to other serendipitous and unpredictable developments.

INVENTING THE FUTURE

Rational thinking, even assisted by any conceivable electronic computers, cannot predict the future. All it can do is to map out the probability space as it appears at the present and which will be different tomorrow when one of the infinity of possible states will have materialized. Technological and social inventions are broadening this probability space all the time; it is now incomparably larger than it was before the industrial revolution, for good or evil.

The future cannot be predicted, but futures can be invented. It was man's ability to invent which has made human society what it is. We cannot stop inventing because we are riding a tiger. But we must start thinking of social inventions to anaesthetise the tiger, so that we can get off its back. Otherwise we are either rushing headlong into catastrophe or we shall have to suppress inventions.

(Ref.: Dennis Gabor, *Inventing the Future*, London, Secker & Warburg, 1963.)

SCENARIO-WRITING

Scenario-writing involves a constructive use of imagination. It aims at describing some aspect of the future: but, instead of building up a picture of unrestrained fiction or even of constructing a utopian invention that the author considers highly desirable, an operations-analytical scenario starts with the present state of the world and shows how, step by step a future state might evolve in a plausible fashion out of the present one. Thus, though the purpose of such a scenario is not to predict the future, it nevertheless sets out to demonstrate the possibility of a certain future of affairs by exhibiting a reasonable chain of events that might lead to it.

(Ref.: Olaf Helmer, *Social Technology*, New York, Basic Books, 1966.)

FORECASTING

When we foresee or forecast the future, we form opinions about the future. When we speak of a "forecast," we simply mean an opinion about the future (but a carefully formed one).

When we speak of "forecasting," we mean the intellectual activity of forming such opinions—serious considered ones, but with an uncertain verification.

(Ref.: B. de Jouvenel, *The Art of Conjecture*, New York, Basic Books, 1967.)

stuart a. sandow

we will be older

The Future Is Where We Get Old

We never think of ourselves being younger tomorrow, only older. Our past is littered with the old ways of doing things and our future is filled with the spectre of our own oldness.

We are taught to look to the past for the successful ways to operate, for the strategies once used that can be used again to reach new goals. Our past is the history of our behavior in pursuing goals. When we look to the past for strategies, we treat a behavior once sufficient as if it were necessary.

So what?

This simple point leads us to several observations: First, when we pursue a new goal, however we behave, the strategy is seen as sufficient if it succeeds. When a similar goal is pursued later, we tend to repeat our once-used sufficient strategies. We develop habits by the repetition of sufficient actions. As habits form, the actions we take become less and less open to change. The behaviors become as if necessary. Secondly, as we age and carry our habits with us into our futures, we are, because of our habits, less open to alternative ways of behaving. We come to have an investment in our habits.

If we are to have futures qualitatively different from our present, we must concern

Stuart A. Sandow, "We Will Be Older," Notes on the Future of Education, *Educational Policy Research Center*, Syracuse University Research Corporation.

ourselves with discarding our once-sufficient, now-necessary habits. If we do not, we may be faced with a *necessary* future—one not unlike the present.

The Future, Then, Is Where Habits Balance Change

Whether it is our golf swing, the knot in our tie, the way we brush our teeth, or the way we make policy, we practice habits. We repeat the simplest activities and they, in turn, comprise the behavioral strategies which determine the more complex issues of our lives.

If our work responsibilities are dynamic, we fill the peripheral activities of our day with habits. Our typewriters in a certain place, letters opened a certain way, our phone calls taken a certain way. If our work responsibilities are static, we fill our peripheral activities with change. We pursue any difference in our stance, modes of travel, attire and appearance—anything to keep monotony to a minimum in those areas in which our responsible actions are not focused. Monotony is a habit gone sour.

Is there a basic difference between monotony and habit? Is there, in fact, anything in our simplest habits that prevents us from dealing with the more important parts of our lives more creatively—more sufficiently?

When a habit becomes boredom or monotony, we strive to change it and in the process make promises to ourselves; we set new goals. We make promises for ourselves and our society about how it will be different in the future. Often, these new goals are pursued with old habits that themselves cause problems.

The Future Is Where We Try to Keep Promises

Goals are promises for our future. Man is an animal who makes promises and sets goals. While our goals are promises for a better tomorrow, our strategies to that goal are often comprised of old habits.

When we behave with old habits to reach new goals we often cause problems that are unintended and disastrous—sometimes so disastrous that the problems overshadow our fulfilled promise, leaving us nothing to praise or commend in our efforts for an ever-better life.

As a nation promising its people equality of education few fault the goal. The promise is taken as sincere; but expectations of many outrun attainment. A strategy of busing students to racially balance schools seems necessary to meet the promise; but it is insufficient as a strategy. It reflects a habit-based perception of equal distribution of resources. Our present is filled with the problems caused not by our promises, but by our strategies—strategies comprised of old habits—strategies that often defeat the hope of the promise by offending in other ways.

The Future Is Where We Will
Live Our Lives

The values of different groups of society shift not because the groups are bad or evil. Values are shifted to meet the demands of the problems we have caused these groups in filling promises. We cause problems by pursuing promises with the blinders of old habits.

For the past decade, individuals in our society have come to demand participation in the processes we set in motion to reach our goals. Leadership recognizes the legitimacy of the claims of these many groups and yet finds it difficult to let them input without threatening the strategy they have chosen to pursue. Should we really be so concerned with "whose strategy" rather than "what goal?"

The Future Is the Only Thing
We Can't Survive

It is commonly believed that youth doesn't think about the future—that they live in the present in some hedonistic "now"—that they refuse to accept the reality of an ever-disappearing present. It could be argued that youth behaves not in ignorance of the future, but in abject fear of what that means for their own life. The future is equated with aging, oldness, and the aggregation of habits.

It is the habits of their elders that cause rejection, not their elders' ideas. It could be argued that youth is not obsessed with the present so much as it is obsessed with future avoidance. If the future develops through the pursuit of old habit-ridden strategies, that future is necessarily a reflector of the past. If it will be the same there is no reason to hope for a better life in the future.

There can be no true alternative futures if the future is seen as necessarily linked to the past. There can only be alternative futures when the future is seen as sufficiently linked to the present.

The Future Is Where We Are Not
Rewarded for Learning

It can be argued that change occurs in our society more often than not by having advocates for certain out-of-date ideas die off. Education is a habit in our society. It is charged with transmitting the past to the students of the present with the hope that that knowledge base will, in some way, prepare them for the future.

We are in an age of serial careerism. We are, each of us, becoming obsolete in our roles and in constant need for retraining and we all know that our lives are terminal, yet our formal educating system is designed only for the young.

If we don't die—and genetic research appears to be leading to this intriguing eventually—how will old ideas and old habits disappear? Will we be capable of changing as rapidly as we do if habits don't disappear by the people who hold them dying?

Can we as a world community, facing our own oldness, describe a realistic and reasonable non-revolutionary process that describes necessary change without the constant fear of revolutionary confrontation over strategy?

Have we lived long enough believing that practice makes perfect?

Are we prepared to believe now that process makes perfect?

Process may be our most important product.

louise odiorne

time gear[©]

Presented at:

Forum #21 White House Conference on Children 1970:

A TIME FRAME IN HUMAN NATURAL MODULES

TIME GEAR[©]

OF UPWARD MOBILITY—TOWARD REALIZATION OF

HUMAN-EARTH POTENTIALS

By

Synchronization of EDUCATION with INDUSTRY

access to earning synchronized with life-time learning options

THE YEAR

Winter break (Christmas)
2 weeks

Fall break
2 weeks

Spring break
1 week

Summer break
3 weeks

Four 11-week quarters
55 teaching days each

All holidays celebrated
during breaks

Copyright © 1969 Louise Odiorne

For Further information write: Hunatech Foundation, Inc.
Box 6, Yellow Springs, Ohio 45387—Louise Odiorne, Director
Phone: 513 767 7852

Louise Odiorne, "Time Gear©." Presented at Forum 21, White House Conference on Children, Washington, D.C., 1970. Reprinted by permission.

Implementing:

1. Most efficient use of existing facilities—year round and clock round, relieving overcrowding and high cost of education.

2. Year round equal quarters for better teacher and student career planning.

3. Time for between-quarter rest, recreation or travel between work-study locations.

4. Family holidays arrangeable any quarter by computerized student registration 2 quarters ahead (teacher contracts 1 quarter ahead) or in any agreeable pattern—with fees for public school registration outside of student's legal residence.

5. Students can follow good teachers and curricular relevance to institutions providing best facilities.

THE DAY

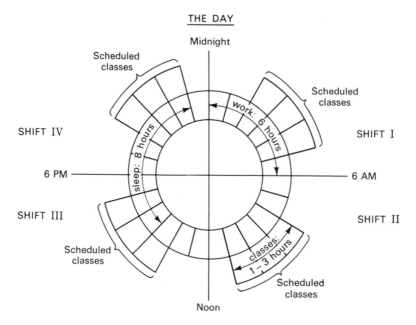

In any community, begin system by scheduling 2 day-time educational sessions. (6 AM – noon & noon – 6 AM). Add evening, then Shift I classes with degree of communities' industrialization.

Implementing:

1. Gradual change to 6 hour work day (4 shifts), 30 hour work week, allowing daily education time to individuals.

2. ⅓ more jobs—for returning GIs and unemployed needing training—without losing jobs existing for skilled workers.

3. Early community participation and responsibility resulting in earlier income production and independence.

4. Younger retirement possibility for parents.

5. Better job opportunities with education and re-training available for all ages.

6. More rapid career advancement by alternating work-study in daily or quarterly patterns.

wayne o. evans

mind-altering drugs and
the future

A researcher in psychopharmacology foresees a growing flood of new drugs that will make man feel happy, cause him to forget his past, arouse his sexual desires, and give him dreams. The dawning of an era of chemically-induced bliss gives new urgency to the ancient conundrum of the philosophers: "Which is better—a happy pig or an unhappy Socrates?" In the coming decades, man may actually have the possibility of attaining sustained happiness —or something like it—through drugs, and so must ask the question, "Is happiness what I most want?"

A study of man shows that throughout recorded history, and in almost every culture, people have taken chemical substances to change their mood, perception and/or thought processes. The earliest recording about such drugs seems to be the hymns of praise sung to "Soma," the magic mushroom of the Aryan invaders of India, found in the Vedas. These indicate its use came from northeastern Europe and had existed since 2000 B.C. Later, about 1500 B.C., the Eber Papyrus documents the use of wine by the Egyptians. The opium poppy, *Papaver somniferum*, appears in records as early as 1000 B.C., and documents from Mesopotamia indicate the use of cannabis (Indian hemp) as a psychotropic drug at least by 500 B.C. The ancient Indian civilizations of Mexico and South America used mind-altering chemicals, e.g., cocaines, tropines, harmines and indoles of various types. Farther west, the natives of the Pacific islands used betel and kava kava, while in Asia, natural products which yield ephedrine and reserpine were common in medical practices. Closer to home, we can consider our own history of opiate usage, laughing gas or ether sniffing parties, cocaine epidemics and a tradition of excessive use of alcohol. Obviously, man always has sought chemical methods to alter his mind and this tendency has not abated and may even have grown in modern times.

Psychotropic Drugs Pour into Market

Today, medicinal and biochemistry, animal and clinical psychopharmacology, neurophysiology and neuroanatomy are advancing at the same rapid rate as the other bio-

Wayne O. Evans, "Mind-Altering Drugs and the Future," The Futurist (published by the World Future Society. P.O. Box 19285, Twentieth Street Station, Washington, D.C. 20036), June, 1971.

logical sciences. Thousands of chemicals are tested each year for potential psychotropic properties. Expeditions have been launched to such dissimilar environments as the upper Congo and the continental shelf in search of new plants or animals which might yield chemicals to alter the mind. New psychotropic drugs have the highest rate of entry onto the market of all types of drugs. Further, our techniques of testing new chemicals for psychotropic properties, in both animals and man, have been refined to the point that one would be hard pressed to name a mood, mode of perception or mental function which now is not testable and roughly quantifiable.

Due to this heightened skill in science and technology, we are achieving a potency and specificity of action in drugs which previously would have been impossible. As an example, K. W. Bentley has synthesized an opiate-like substance which is ten thousand times as potent as morphine. This means that the average effective dose for a human being is 1.5 micrograms to achieve an analgetic equivalence with the usual dose of morphine given for post-operative pain relief. Another example of the capability to produce more potent and specific drugs is the development of certain diazepoxides (Librium®) which can induce sleep at a dose as low as 0.5 mg. We finally may have produced a compound which will live up to the fabled "knock-out" drops of spy fiction.

This greater potency and specificity of drugs comes from a knowledge of the interaction of chemical molecules with receptors on cell membranes, understanding of the affinity and activity of drugs for specific receptor sites, by using molecules with optimal, rigid shapes and appropriate positioning of ionic and polar groups, and by blocking metabolism or facilitating precursor formation. Drug molecules now are better behaved than they were in the past.

A convincing demonstration of this increased specificity of psychotropic drugs is seen in some of the anti-depressant agents, e.g., tricyclic amines. At the proper dose and rate of administration, they do not produce euphoria, but do ameliorate depressive states by reducing the uptake and inhibiting the binding of brain norepinephrine in storage granules of neurons.

Developments in neurophysiology also have contributed to our capacity to design novel and potent psychotropic substances. The chemical and electrical mapping of brain systems for the basic drives, e.g., hunger, thirst, pleasure, fear, sex, excitement, sleep, etc. are well advanced. The faith held by psychopharmacologists that a person's mood and his neurochemical state were equivalent terms from different viewpoints seems to be on the road to justification.

Public Acceptance of Drugs
Is Growing

Science alone is not responsible for the development of new drugs used in a culture. In order for a drug to be developed, people must want it and a social condition favorable to its use must exist. From the evidence of an ever-increasing consumption of psychotropic substances by people today this condition appears to be fulfilled. To gain a perspective in regard to our present social situation, we should remember the resistance to the introduction of anesthetics for childbirth, with its implicit assumptions that pain is "good" and that the "natural" inherently is "virtuous." Anti-psychotic tranquilizers were introduced into our mental hospitals as recently as 1955; in 16 years the previously ever-growing number of hospitalized mental patients has dwindled, to the point where in 1968 occupied mental hospital beds were at the same level as in 1947 in the United States. A more general public acceptance of psychotropic drug use is shown by the number of over-the-counter pharmaceuticals that are purchased. At a local supermarket one can buy drugs reputed to relieve tension, produce sleep, make one become more alert, relieve all sorts of pain, reduce motion sickness, fight fatigue, etc. Most people do not realize that aspirin is the second largest cause of acute drug death in the United States, that caffeine poisonings do occur from the tablets bought in drugstores or supermarkets, that antihistamines in cold tablets can slow reflexes, or that the "safe, non-barbiturate, non-habitforming" sedatives they purchase can induce severe hallucinations at high doses. Finally, we must not forget the most prevalent, socially destructive personally harmful psychotropic drug of them all, alcohol. To call a drug a beverage does not change its chemistry.

Public attention constantly is directed toward psychotropic drug use by mass media advertising, drug education programs, peer group pressures and advice from physicians. Consider how many ads you see on television, newspapers and magazines during a single day for chemicals to make you feel better, become more beautiful, or be the life of the party. Think of the recent flood of opinions you have heard about drugs from both the establishment and from the youth. In almost every town in the United States, drug abuse education programs have sprung up. Energetic, well meaning, but unfortunately, often relatively uninformed people have decided to tell "the truth" about drugs to young people who think they already know everything there is to know about them (4,300 scientific articles were published on psychotropic drugs in 1968 alone). Evidence of this information gap can be seen by considering references to "drugs" without mention of purity, dose, route of administration, schedule of use, situation-person-behavior-drug interactions, etc. The fact is that drugs *qua* drugs are not inherently "evil" nor do they convey "universal truth." Indeed, we have no data to show whether any of the social programs and educational schemes now underway will help to reduce the harmful use of drugs. This lack of evidence has not deterred these activities. Indeed, the programs could be increasing drug use by adding to drug advertisement.

Adults Who Warn Youth Against Drugs Are Using Drugs Themselves

Peer group pressures for drug use are not confined to the young. Recent studies have shown that almost half of middle class adults in the suburbs who occasionally have taken psychotropic substances did not receive them from a physician but from a neighbor or friend who told them that this was "just the pill to make them feel good." Ninety percent of all psychotropic drugs in the United States were not prescribed by a trained psychiatrist, but rather by some other type of physician who may be less aware of drug-behavior interactions. Further, many physcians are not current in their information about these new drugs. The deaths resulting from a use of certain anti-depressants witnesses this fact. Also, few physicians have been trained in the pharmacology of marijuana, heroin, LSD, STP, etc. Non-medicinal drugs aren't taught in medical school. Indeed, parents and physicians who are telling children not to use drugs are themselves using mind-altering chemicals on a massive basis and, frequently, the drugs are not even received legitimately by prescription. When we give up alcohol and tranquilizers, we will reduce the hypocrisy of which the youth accuse us. Perhaps, then, a dialogue can begin.

Even physicians are not totally free from some responsibility for the present extensive use and misuse of psychotropic drugs. Studies have shown that young people who often were ill as children and were taken regularly to a physician and there received pills form the group most likely to enter the drug subculture during late adolescence. Yet some physicians prescribe psychotropic substances merely to satisfy the desire of their patients for some form of chemotherapy, without considering the full psychiatric implications of the complaints or the potential efficacy of the compounds.

In the United States in 1969, 90 million new prescriptions were issued for minor tranquilizers, 17 million new prescriptions for anti-depressive drugs, 12 million people had used marijuana at least once, and one calculates the consumption of diet pills, stimulants, aspirin, sleeping compounds with scopolamine and other psychotropic drugs by the box-car load. We have lived up to the famous comment, "Man is the pill-taking animal."

Potent, Safe Euphorics and Aphrodisiacs Are Foreseen

In the near future—say 20 years hence—we could have available highly potent, minimally hazardous antipsychotics, tranquilizers, analgesics, antidepressives, euphorics, psychedelics, stimulants, sedatives, intoxicants, aphrodisiacs, as well as combinations of these drugs to expediently produce most mood states. There now are over 900 drugs listed as psychotropic by the National Institute of Mental Health and the list is rapidly increasing.

The production of non-sedated states of tranquility has advanced since the discovery of meprobamate (Miltown®) to its present form in the diazepoxide series (Librium®). It seems almost inevitable that this trend will continue. The introduction of pentazocine (Talwin®), a potent analgesic which produces a relatively minimal degree of physical dependence, heralds the probable development of a new class of potent, analgesic drugs which do not have physical dependence as a side effect. This development is continuing so that physical dependence should not be a major medical problem in the near future. Also, research has demonstrated that by combining an opiate with an amphetamine, one produces a greater potency of analgesia without an accompanying depression of vital bodily functions, sedation, or mental incapacitation. These two developments portend that shortly we shall have potent analgesic substances which will interfere minimally with one's daily life. Oral forms of these new analgesics with little dependence or sedation are under development.

The introduction of lithium into manic-depressive therapy is an exciting recent development. Although some types of manic-depression are refractory to any treatment and some depressive states respond best to a short series of electroconvulsive shocks, it appears that a combined therapy of tricyclic amines with a long-term administration of lithium will reduce the impact of this disorder. Further, lithium use has advanced our knowledge of "affect" disorders at a cellular level.

Need for Drugs Less Harmful
Than Alcohol

Compounds to produce euphoria or psychedelic states seldom are discussed in "proper" pharmacological or medical circles. Yet, a member of the National Institute of Mental Health has stated that an urgent need exists to search for compounds which can relieve the tensions of daily life by giving a person the occasional opportunity to become intoxicated without the severe problems associated with the excessive use of alcohol. As population expands and recreational possibilities shrink; as the impersonality of a specialist-run, counter-intuitive society increases and meaningfulness of community life lessens; the tensions easily might cause an episodic desire by some to become intoxicated for a short while to feel wise, strong and loved. If we accept this unpleasant truth, the least we can do is develop compounds less hazardous for use than alcohol (potentially an addicting, physically harmful drug). Additionally, we must provide places and circumstances where these bouts of intoxication could take place, while minimizing the harm a person might do himself or his fellow man. Can we continue to tolerate the fatalities on the highway, overweight, liver damage, psychosis, broken homes, sex crimes, and crowding of public hospitals and jails caused by the unwise use of alcohol? The explorations of the cannabinols, and the extraction of tetrahydrocannabinol as the active principle of Indian hemp, may be a possible first step in a search for new, less hazardous "anti-alienation" drugs and the creation of socially approved, peer-monitored "drag strips" for racing may be our best models for effective social control of intoxicant use.

Recent research on sleep, coupled with data from studies on depressed patients who have received a combination of an amphetamine and a monoamine oxidase inhibiting, antidepressive drug, has demonstrated that man can live quite well on four hours of sleep a night—a fact well known to the Mogul Emperors. This, considered with a development of relatively safe sedatives of the diazepoxide type, should let us arbitrarily decide whether and when to be awake or asleep—as long as we stay within the apparent physiological constraint of at least four hours of sleep per day. Consciousness may become optional and a matter of convenience, personally or for a society run in shifts to prevent overcrowding of limited facilities.

Hedonists' Dream May Be Fulfilled through Sex Drugs

Aphrodisiacs have a fascinating history. Perhaps for no other chemical has man sought so long and avidly. In examining a recent dictionary of purported aphrodisiacs, it was interesting to note that chemicals to aid the flagging potency of the male outnumbered those to aid the female by about 20 to 1. Mass media publicity of L-DOPA and PACA have alerted the public to the fact that the brain centers responsible for the triggering and maintaining of the sexual act already have been discovered. It is possible in animals, by either chemical or electrical means, to initiate the sexual act and have it continue without satiation for prolonged periods. Whether these sexual acts are pleasurable or not to the animal is difficult to know. However, if we combined a euphorogenic agent (to make the sexual act pleasurable), with a cholinergic stimulant (to provide the male an increased capacity for potency without ejaculation), and finally, stimulated the brain centers responsible for the initiation and continuation of the sexual act, we may be approaching the hedonistic philosopher's dream. In some sense, we already have aphrodisiacs (see Aphrodex®, Bennet Pharmaceutical). The only questions remaining are the particular combination of drugs, their ratios and the production of oral forms. If these drugs are developed and widely used, I cannot help but wonder what types of human interactions may result. Where is the warmth, affection and subtlety in a chemically driven liaison?

Peer Group Control Might Limit Drug-Induced Harm

The social consequences of chemically alterable behavior depends on the nature and source of the imposed sanctions. Thus far, through history, we have seen admonitions for individual self-control, prohibitive legal sanctions, peer group control, and, on occasion, imposed use of mind-altering drugs. Individual control is, I believe, a lost battle. The present evidence of the quantity of drugs consumed is proof enough. Prohibitive laws have been attempted since the Empress of China proclaimed the death sentence for opium users and, in Turkey, the use of tobacco was punishable by death in "a means acceptable to God." Our own more recent experience with prohibition of alcohol is additional evidence of the lack of efficacy of this type of sanction. Finally, 12 million people in the United States have used marijuana—though many of the states have harsh laws against its possession. This seems to demonstrate that the threat of harsh punishment does not work well to deter use of psychotropic drugs. Few physiological effects of drugs could be as severe as their legal effects. Peer group control has been used as a sanction for chemical uses—sometimes to limit use to special situations and acceptable doses. Presently, in small groups, some young people learn to 'guide' each other in drug use and can exercise a rather superb degree of control so that group members seldom become too "high" on marijuana. Similarly, in Italy, a tremendous amount of alcoholic beverages are consumed, yet, there are relatively few cases of alcohol dependence or the various other ill effects that sometimes result from continued use of this drug. It appears that introduction of children to the consumption of alcohol in a family situation, during mealtimes, "immunizes" them against later excessive use. In Italy, the family encourages drinking but does not tolerate drunkenness. Perhaps, we should take note of this method in order to reduce drug-induced harm.

Drugs Could Be Used to Slow Social Progress

A frightening possibility exists that psychotropic chemicals could be imposed upon people without their consent or by social pressure. One must wonder if some of child psychopharmacology, as sometimes practiced, is not a form of chemical warfare against our children, and the spread of LSD from one spouse to another demonstrates that pressures for drug use are both close and powerful. Again, the development of incapacitating warfare agents of a psychotropic nature, by the United States and other countries, shows what can be done with these chemicals. At least most of the young have accepted the creed "Thou shalt not alter the consciousness of another without his consent." Are we as honorable? It is not difficult to envision a possible future in which tranquilizers, hallucinogens or euphorogenics, effective in the micro or nanogram range, could be distributed in an aerosol to quiet a "pre-riot" area. What would be the possibility of any social progress in a society in which the authorities might reduce people's level of agitation or disgust by chemical means? We must ask ourselves if agitation, conflict and violence are necessary precursors of social progress, or are these behaviors no longer tolerable in an interdependent, urbanized society?

Drugs Might Produce Dreams or Induce Forgetfulness

The distant future holds many promises—or threats—of memory drugs, amnesia chemicals, dream-producing agents, pills to increase suggestibility, and all manner of other chemicals to make one's phenomenological state a matter of convenience. Although much discussion has revolved around the possible development of drugs to improve memory, people seem to have overlooked the advantages of drugs which will destroy it. Heinz Lehmann has pointed out that the most pathetic aspect of old age is the sense of already having experienced everything. At a recent meeting, he quoted a patient as saying "a pickle doesn't really taste like a pickle anymore." Old age is a state of constant *déjà vu* and *déjà entendu*. To overcome this apathy of experience, we might use drugs to heighten the sensations of the elderly and re-establish their sense of novelty to experiences by producing a temporary condition of amnesia. Why not allow an elderly person to rest and conserve his resources for most of the week, but on weekends or special occasions, allow him the excitement produced by a stimulant and/or psychedelic compound with an amnesic drug as a bonus? Certainly, with this group, we are concerned about dependence, or the other, usual fears associated with drug use by young people. Why should their lives be a constant, grey boredom waiting for death?

We can, if we wish, produce an individualistic "choose your mood" society or a chemically controlled tyranny or an age of ultimate hedonism by chemical manipulation —or any other variant desired. Perhaps the real questions should be: "Can we choose? If so, who should choose? and who will choose?" Technology is doing mankind a great service: It has forced him to define his morals, goals and future. It has exposed him to his ultimate choice; *"What shall I become?"*

ivan illich

the alternative to schooling

For generations we have tried to make the world a better place by providing more and more schooling, but so far the endeavor has failed. What we have learned instead is that forcing all children to climb an open-ended education ladder cannot enhance equality but must favor the individual who starts out earlier, healthier, or better prepared; that enforced instruction deadens for most people the will for independent learning; and that knowledge treated as a commodity, delivered in packages, and accepted as private property once it is acquired, must always be scarce.

In response, critics of the educational system are now proposing strong and unorthodox remedies that range from the voucher plan, which would enable each person to

Ivan Illich, "The Alternative to Schooling," Saturday Review, June 19, 1971. Copyright 1971 Saturday Review, Inc. Reprinted by permission.

buy the education of his choice on an open market, to shifting the responsibility for education from the school to the media and to apprenticeship on the job. Some individuals foresee that the school will have to be disestablished just as the church was disestablished all over the world during the last two centuries. Other reformers propose to replace the universal school with various new systems that would, they claim, better prepare everybody for life in modern society. These proposals for new educational institutions fall into three broad categories: the reformation of the classroom within the school system; the dispersal of free schools throughout society; and the transformation of all society into one huge classroom. But these three approaches—the reformed classroom, the free school, and the worldwide classroom—represent three stages in a proposed escalation of education in which each step threatens more subtle and more pervasive social control than the one it replaces.

I believe that the disestablishment of the school has become inevitable and that this end of an illusion should fill us with hope. But I also believe that the end of the "age of schooling" could usher in the epoch of the global schoolhouse that would be distinguishable only in name from a global madhouse or global prison in which education, correction, and adjustment become synonymous. I therefore believe that the breakdown of the school forces us to look beyond its imminent demise and to face fundamental alternatives in education. Either we can work for fearsome and potent new educational devices that teach about a world which progressively becomes more opaque and forbidding for man, or we can set the conditions for a new era in which technology would be used to make society more simple and transparent, so that all men can once again know the facts and use the tools that shape their lives. In short, we can disestablish schools or we can deschool culture.

In order to see clearly the alternatives we face, we must first distinguish education from schooling, which means separating the humanistic intent of the teacher from the impact of the invariant structure of the school. This hidden structure constitutes a course of instruction that stays forever beyond the control of the teacher or of his school board. It conveys indelibly the message that only through schooling can an individual prepare himself for adulthood in society, that what is not taught in school is of little value, and that what is learned outside of school is not worth knowing. I call it the hidden curriculum of schooling, because it constitutes the unalterable framework of the system, within which all changes in the curriculum are made.

The hidden curriculum is always the same regardless of school or place. It requires all children of a certain age to assemble in groups of about thirty, under the authority of a certified teacher, for some 500 to 1,000 or more hours each year. It doesn't matter whether the curriculum is designed to teach the principles of fascism, liberalism, Catholicism, or socialism; or whether the purpose of the school is to produce Soviet or United States citizens, mechanics, or doctors. It makes no difference whether the teacher is authoritarian or permissive, whether he imposes his own creed or teaches students to think for themselves. What is important is that students learn that education is valuable when it is acquired in the school through a graded process of consumption; that the degree of success the individual will enjoy in society depends on the amount of learning he consumes; and that learning *about* the world is more valuable than learning *from* the world.

It must be clearly understood that the hidden curriculum translates learning from an activity into a commodity—for which the school monopolizes the market. In all countries knowledge is regarded as the first necessity for survival, but also as a form of currency more liquid than rubles or dollars. We have become accustomed, through Karl Marx's writings, to speak about the alienation of the worker from his work in a class society. We must now recognize the estrangement of man from his learning when it becomes the product of a service profession and he becomes the consumer.

The more learning an individual consumes, the more "knowledge stock" he acquires. The hidden curriculum therefore defines a new class structure for society within which the large consumers of knowledge—those who have acquired large quantities of knowledge stock—enjoy special privileges, high income, and access to the more powerful tools of production. This kind of knowledge-capitalism has been accepted in all industrialized societies and establishes a rationale for the distribution of jobs and income. (This point is especially important in the light of the lack of correspondence between schooling and occupational competence established in studies such as Ivar Berg's *Education and Jobs: The Great Training Robbery.*)

The endeavor to put all men through successive stages of enlightenment is rooted deeply in alchemy, the Great Art of the waning Middle Ages. John Amos Comenius, a Moravian bishop, self-styled Pansophist, and pedagogue, is rightly considered one of the founders of the modern schools. He was among the first to propose seven or twelve grades of compulsory learning. In his *Magna Didactica,* he described schools as devices to "teach everybody everything" and outlined a blueprint for the assembly-line production of knowledge, which according to his method would make education cheaper and better and make growth into full humanity possible for all. But Comenius was not only an early efficiency expert, he was an alchemist who adopted the technical language of his craft to describe the art of rearing children. The alchemist sought to refine base elements by leading their distilled spirits through twelve stages of successive enlightenment, so that for their own and all the world's benefit they might be transmuted into gold. Of course, alchemists failed no matter how often they tried, but each time their "science" yielded new reasons for their failure, and they tried again.

Pedagogy opened a new chapter in the history of Ars Magna. Education became the search for an alchemic process that would bring forth a new type of man, who would fit into an environment created by scientific magic. But, no matter how much each generation spent on its schools, it always turned out that the majority of people were unfit for enlightenment by this process and had to be discarded as unprepared for life in a man-made world.

Educational reformers who accept the idea that schools have failed fall into three groups. The most respectable are certainly the great masters of alchemy who promise better schools. The most seductive are popular magicians, who promise to make every kitchen into an alchemic lab. The most sinister are the new Masons of the Universe, who want to transform the entire world into one huge temple of learning. Notable among today's masters of alchemy are certain research directors employed or sponsored by the large foundations who believe that schools, if they could somehow be improved, could also become economically more feasible than those that are now in trouble, and simultaneously could sell a larger package of services. Those who are concerned primarily with the curriculum claim that it is outdated or irrelevant. So the curriculum is filled with new packaged courses on African Culture, North American Imperialism, Women's Lib, Pollution, or the Consumer Society. Passive learning is wrong—it is indeed —so we graciously allow students to decide what and how they want to be taught. Schools are prison houses. Therefore, principals are authorized to approve teach-outs, moving the school desks to a roped-off Harlem street. Sensitivity training becomes fashionable. So, we import group therapy into the classroom. School, which was supposed to teach everybody everything, now becomes all things to all children.

Other critics emphasize that schools make inefficient use of modern science. Some would administer drugs to make it easier for the instructor to change the child's behavior. Others would transform school into a stadium for educational gaming. Still others would electrify the classroom. If they are simplistic disciples of McLuhan, they replace blackboards and textbooks with multimedia happenings; if they follow Skinner, they claim to be able to modify behavior more efficiently than old-fashioned classroom practitioners can.

Most of these changes have, of course, some good effects. The experimental schools have fewer truants. Parents do have a greater feeling of participation in a decentralized district. Pupils, assigned by their teacher to an apprenticeship, do often turn out more competent than those who stay in the classroom. Some children do improve their knowledge of Spanish in the language lab because they prefer playing with the knobs of a tape recorder to conversations with their Puerto Rican peers. Yet all these improvements operate within predictably narrow limits, since they leave the hidden curriculum of school intact.

Some reformers would like to shake loose from the hidden curriculum, but they rarely succeed. Free schools that lead to further free schools produce a mirage of freedom, even though the chain of attendance is frequently interrupted by long stretches of loafing. Attendance through seduction inculcates the need for educational treatment more persuasively than the reluctant attendance enforced by a truant officer. Permissive teachers in a padded classroom can easily render their pupils impotent to survive once they leave.

Learning in these schools often remains nothing more than the acquisition of socially valued skills defined, in this instance, by the consensus of a commune rather than by the decree of a school board. New presbyter is but old priest writ large.

Free schools, to be truly free, must meet two conditions: First, they must be run in a way to prevent the reintroduction of the hidden curriculum of graded attendance and certified students studying at the feet of certified teachers. And, more importantly, they must provide a framework in which all participants—staff and pupils—can free themselves from the hidden foundations of a schooled society. The first condition is frequently incorporated in the stated aims of a free school. The second condition is only rarely recognized, and is difficult to state as the goal of a free school.

It is useful to distinguish between the hidden curriculum, which I have described, and the occult foundations of schooling. The hidden curriculum is a ritual that can be considered the official initiation into modern society, institutionally established through the school. It is the purpose of this ritual to hide from its participants the contradictions between the myth of an egalitarian society and the class-conscious reality it certifies. Once they are recognized as such, rituals lose their power, and this is what is now beginning to happen to schooling. But there are certain fundamental assumptions about growing up—the occult foundations—which now find their expression in the ceremonial of schooling, and which could easily be reinforced by what free schools do.

Among these assumptions is what Peter Schrag calls the "immigration syndrome," which impels us to treat all people as if they were newcomers who must go through a naturalization process. Only certified consumers of knowledge are admitted to citizenship. Men are not born equal, but are made equal through gestation by Alma Mater.

The rhetoric of all schools states that they form a man for the future, but they do not release him for his task before he has developed a high level of tolerance to the ways of his elders: education *for* life rather than *in* everyday life. Few free schools can avoid doing precisely this. Nevertheless they are among the most important centers from which a new life-style radiates, not because of the effect their graduates will have but, rather, because elders who choose to bring up their children without the benefit of properly ordained teachers frequently belong to a radical minority and because their preoccupation with the rearing of their children sustains them in their new style.

The most dangerous category of educational reformer is one who argues that knowledge can be produced and sold much more effectively on an open market than on one controlled by school. These people argue that most skills can be easily acquired from skill-models if the learner is truly interested in their acquisition; that individual entitlements can provide a more equal purchasing power for education. They demand a careful separation of the process by which knowledge is acquired from the process by which it is measured and certified. These seem to me obvious statements. But it would be a fallacy to believe that the establishment of a free market for knowledge would constitute a radical alternative in education.

The establishment of a free market would indeed abolish what I have previously called the hidden curriculum of present schooling—its age-specific attendance at a graded curriculum. Equally, a free market would at first give the appearance of counteracting what I have called the occult foundations of a schooled society: the "immigration syndrom," the institutional monopoly of teaching, and the ritual of linear initiation. But at the same time a free market in education would provide the alchemist with innumerable hidden hands to fit each man into the multiple, tight little niches a more complex technocracy can provide.

Many decades of reliance on schooling has turned knowledge into a commodity, a marketable staple of a special kind. Knowledge is now regarded simultaneously as a first necessity and also as society's most precious currency. (The transformation of knowledge into a commodity is reflected in a corresponding transformation of language. Words that formerly functioned as verbs are becoming nouns that designate possessions.) Until recently, dwelling and learning and even healing designated activities. They are now usually conceived as commodities or services to be delivered. We talk about the manufacture of housing or the delivery of medical care. Men are no longer regarded fit to house or heal themselves. In such a society people come to believe that professional services are more valuable than personal care. Instead of learning how to nurse grandmother, the teen-ager learns to picket the hospital that does not admit her.) This attitude could easily survive the disestablishment of school, just as affiliation with a church remained a condition for office long after the adoption of the First Amendment. It is even more evident that test batteries measuring complex knowledge-packages could easily survive the disestablishment of school—and with this would go the compulsion to obligate everybody to acquire a minimum package in the knowledge stock. The scientific measurement of each man's worth and the alchemic dream of each man's "educability to his full humanity" would finally coincide. Under the appearance of a "free" market, the global village would turn into an environmental womb where pedagogic therapists control the complex navel by which each man is nourished.

At present, schools limit the teacher's competence to the classroom. They prevent him from claiming man's whole life as his domain. The demise of school will remove this restriction and give a semblance of legitimacy to the life-long pedagogical invasion of everybody's privacy. It will open the way for a scramble for "knowledge" on a free market, which would lead us toward the paradox of a vulgar, albeit seemingly egalitarian, meritocracy. Unless the concept of knowledge is transformed, the disestablishment of school will lead to a wedding between a growing meritocratic system that separates learning from certification and a society committed to provide therapy for each man until he is ripe for the gilded age.

For those who subscribe to the technocratic ethos, whatever is technically possible must be made available at least to a few whether they want it or not. Neither the privation nor the frustration of the majority counts. If cobalt treatment is possible, then the city of Tegucigalpa needs one apparatus in each of its two major hospitals, at a cost that would free an important part of the population of Honduras from parasites. If supersonic speeds are possible, then it must speed the travel of some. If the flight to Mars can be conceived, then a rationale must be found to make it appear a necessity. In the technocratic ethos poverty is modernized: Not only are old alternatives closed off by new monopolies, but the lack of necessities is also compounded by a growing spread between those services that are technologically feasible and those that are in fact available to the majority.

A teacher turns "educator" when he adopts this technocratic ethos. He then acts as if education were a technological enterprise designed to make man fit into whatever environment the "progress" of science creates. He seems blind to the evidence that constant obsolescence of all commodities comes at a high price: the mounting cost of training people to know about them. He seems to forget that the rising cost of tools is purchased at a high price in education: They decrease the labor intensity of the economy, make learning on the job impossible or, at best, a privilege for a few. All over the world the cost of educating men for society rises faster than the productivity of the entire economy, and fewer people have a sense of intelligent participation in the commonweal.

A revolution against those forms of privilege and power, which are based on claims to professional knowledge, must start with a transformation of consciousness about the nature of learning. This means, above all, a shift of responsibility for teaching and learning. Knowledge can be defined as a commodity only as long as it is viewed as the result of institutional enterprise or as the fulfillment of institutional objectives. Only when a man recovers the sense of personal responsibility for what he learns and teaches can this spell be broken and the alienation of learning from living be overcome.

The recovery of the power to learn or to teach means that the teacher who takes the risk of interfering in somebody else's private affairs also assumes responsibility for the results. Similarly, the student who exposes himself to the influence of a teacher must take responsibility for his own education. For such purposes educational institutions—if they are at all needed—ideally take the form of facility centers where one can get a roof of the right size over his head, access to a piano or a kiln, and to records, books, or slides. Schools, TV stations, theaters, and the like are designed primarily for use by professionals. Deschooling society means above all the denial of professional status for the second-oldest profession, namely teaching. The certification of teachers now constitutes an undue restriction of the right to free speech: the corporate structure and professional pretensions of journalism an undue restriction on the right to free press. Compulsory attendance rules interfere with free assembly. The deschooling of society is nothing less than a cultural mutation by which a people recovers the effective use of its Constitutional freedoms: learning and teaching by men who know that they are born free rather than treated to freedom. Most people learn most of the time when they do whatever they enjoy; most people are curious and want to give meaning to whatever they come in contact with; and most people are capable of personal intimate intercourse with others unless they are stupefied by inhuman work or turned off by schooling.

The fact that people in rich countries do not learn much on their own constitutes no proof to the contrary. Rather it is a consequence of life in an environment from which, paradoxically, they cannot learn much, precisely because it is so highly programed. They are constantly frustrated by the structure of contemporary society in which the facts on which decisions can be made have become elusive. They live in an environment in which tools that can be used for creative purposes have become luxuries, an environment in which channels of communication serve a few to talk to many.

A modern myth would make us believe that the sense of impotence with which most men live today is a consequence of technology that cannot but create huge systems. But it is not technology that makes systems huge, tools immensely powerful, channels of communication one-directional. Quite the contrary: Properly controlled, technology could provide each man with the ability to understand his environment better, to shape it powerfully with his own hands, and to permit him full intercommunication to a degree never before possible. Such an alternative use of technology constitutes the central alternative in education.

If a person is to grow up he needs, first of all, access to things, to places and to processes, to events and to records. He needs to see, to touch, to tinker with, to grasp whatever there is in a meaningful setting. This access is now largely denied. When knowledge became a commodity, it acquired the protections of private property, and thus a principle designed to guard personal intimacy became a rationale for declaring facts off limits for people without the proper credentials. In schools teachers keep knowledge to themselves unless it fits into the day's program. The media inform, but exclude those things they regard as unfit to print. Information is locked into special languages, and specialized teachers live off its retranslation. Patents are protected by corporations, secrets are guarded by bureaucracies, and the power to keep others out of private preserves—be they cockpits, law offices, junkyards, or clinics—is jealously guarded by professions, institutions, and nations. Neither the political nor the professional structure of our societies, East and West, could withstand the elimination of the power to keep entire classes of people from facts that could serve them. The access to facts that I advocate goes far beyond truth in labeling. Access must be built into reality, while all we ask from advertising is a guarantee that it does not mislead. Access to reality constitutes a fundamental alternative in education to a system that only purports to teach *about* it.

Abolishing the right to corporate secrecy—even when professional opinion holds that this secrecy serves the common good—is, as shall presently appear, a much more radical political goal than the traditional demand for public ownership or control of the tools of production. The socialization of tools without the effective socialization of know-how in their use tends to put the knowledge-capitalist into the position formerly held by the financier. The technocrat's only claim to power is the stock he holds in some class of scarce and secret knowledge, and the best means to protect its value is a large and capital-intensive organization that renders access to know-how formidable and forbidding.

It does not take much time for the interested learner to acquire almost any skill that he wants to use. We tend to forget this in a society where professional teachers monopolize entrance into all fields, and thereby stamp teaching by uncertified individuals as quackery. There are few mechanical skills used in industry or research that are as demanding, complex, and dangerous as driving cars, a skill that most people quickly acquire from a peer. Not all people are suited for advanced logic, yet those who are make rapid progress if they are challenged to play mathematical games at an early age. One out of twenty kids in Cuernavaca can beat me at Wiff 'n' Proof after a couple of weeks' training. In four months all but a small percentage of motivated adults at our CIDOC center learn Spanish well enough to conduct academic business in the new language.

A first step toward opening up access to skills would be to provide various incentives for skilled individuals to share their knowledge. Inevitably, this would run counter to the interest of guilds and professions and unions. Yet, multiple apprenticeship is attractive: It provides everybody with an opportunity to learn something about almost anything. There is no reason why a person should not combine the ability to drive a car, repair telephones and toilets, act as a midwife, and function as an architectural draftsman. Special-interest groups and their disciplined consumers would, of course, claim that the public needs the protection of a professional guarantee. But this argument is now steadily being challenged by consumer protection associations. We have to take much more seriously the objection that economists raise to the radical socialization of skills: that "progress" will be impeded if knowledge—patents, skills, and all the rest—is democratized. Their argument can be faced only if we demonstrate to them the growth rate of futile diseconomies generated by any existing educational system.

Access to people willing to share their skills is no guarantee of learning. Such access is restricted not only by the monopoly of educational programs over learning and of unions over licensing but also by a technology of scarcity. The skills that count today are know-how in the use of highly specialized tools that were designed to be scarce. These tools produce goods or render services that everybody wants but only a few can enjoy, and which only a limited number of people know how to use. Only a few privileged individuals out of the total number of people who have a given disease ever benefit from the results of sophisticated medical technology, and even fewer doctors develop the skill to use it.

The same results of medical research have, however, also been employed to create a basic medical tool kit that permits Army and Navy medics, with only a few months of training, to obtain results, under battlefield conditions, that would have been beyond the expectations of full-fledged doctors during World War II. On an even simpler level any peasant girl could learn how to diagnose and treat most infections if medical scientists prepared dosages and instructions specifically for a given geographic area.

All these examples illustrate the fact that educational considerations alone suffice to demand a radical reduction of the professional structure that now impedes the mutual relationship between the scientist and the majority of people who want access to science. If this demand were heeded, all men could learn to use yesterday's tools, rendered more effective and durable by modern science, to create tomorrow's world.

Unfortunately, precisely the contrary trend prevails at present. I know a coastal area in South America where most people support themselves by fishing from small boats. The outboard motor is certainly the tool that has changed most dramatically the lives of these coastal fishermen. But in the area I have surveyed, half of all outboard motors that were purchased between 1945 and 1950 are still kept running by constant tinkering, while half the motors purchased in 1965 no longer run because they were not built to be repaired. Technological progress provides the majority of people with gadgets they cannot afford and deprives them of the simpler tools they need.

Metals, plastics, and ferro cement used in building have greatly improved since the 1940s and ought to provide more people the opportunity to create their own homes. But while in the United States, in 1948, more than 30 per cent of all one-family homes were owner-built, by the end of the 1960s the percentage of those who acted as their own contractors had dropped to less than 20 per cent.

The lowering of the skill level through so-called economic development becomes even more visible in Latin America. Here most people still build their own homes from floor to roof. Often they use mud, in the form of adobe, and thatchwork of unsurpassed utility in the moist, hot, and windy climate. In other places they make their dwellings out of cardboard, oil-drums, and other industrial refuse. Instead of providing people with simple tools and highly standardized, durable, and easily repaired components, all governments have gone in for the mass production of low-cost buildings. It is clear that not one single country can afford to provide satisfactory modern dwelling units for the majority of its people. Yet, everywhere this policy makes it progressively more difficult for the majority to acquire the knowledge and skills they need to build better houses for themselves.

Educational considerations permit us to formulate a second fundamental characteristic that any post-industrial society must possess: a basic tool kit that by its very nature counteracts technocratic control. For educational reasons we must work toward a society in which scientific knowledge is incorporated in tools and components that can be used meaningfully in units small enough to be within the reach of all. Only such tools can socialize access to skills. Only such tools favor temporary associations among those who want to use them for a specific occasion. Only such tools allow specific goals to emerge in the process of their use, as any tinkerer knows. Only the combination of guaranteed access to facts and of limited power in most tools renders it possible to envisage a subsistence economy capable of incorporating the fruits of modern science.

The development of such a scientific subsistence economy is unquestionably to the advantage of the overwhelming majority of all people in poor countries. It is also the only alternative to progressive pollution, exploitation, and opaqueness in rich countries. But, as we have seen, the dethroning of the GNP cannot be achieved without simultaneously subverting GNE (Gross National Education—usually conceived as manpower capitalization). An egalitarian economy cannot exist in a society in which the right to produce is conferred by schools.

The feasibility of a modern subsistence economy does not depend on new scientific inventions. It depends primarily on the ability of a society to agree on fundamental, self-chosen anti-bureaucratic and anti-technocratic restraints.

These restraints can take many forms, but they will not work unless they touch the basic dimensions of life. (The decision of Congress against development of the super-sonic transport plane is one of the most encouraging steps in the right direction.) The substance of these voluntary social restraints would be very simple matters that can be fully understood and judged by any prudent man. The issues at stake in the SST controversy provide a good example. All such restraints would be chosen to promote stable and equal enjoyment of scientific know-how. The French say that it takes a thousand years to educate a peasant to deal with a cow. It would not take two generations to help all people in Latin America or Africa to use and repair outboard motors, simple cars, pumps, medicine kits, and ferro cement machines if their design does not change every few years. And since a joyful life is one of constant meaningful intercourse with others in a meaningful environment, equal enjoyment does translate into equal education.

At present a consensus on austerity is difficult to imagine. The reason usually given for the impotence of the majority is stated in terms of political or economic class. What is not usually understood is that the new class structure of a schooled society is even more powerfully controlled by vested interests. No doubt an imperialist and capitalist organization of society provides the social structure within which a minority can have disproportionate influence over the effective opinion of the majority. But in a techno-cratic society the power of a minority of knowledge capitalists can prevent the formation of true public opinion through control of scientific know-how and the media of communication. Constitutional guarantees of free speech, free press, and free assembly were meant to ensure government by the people. Modern electronics, photo-offset presses, time-sharing computers, and telephones have in principle provided the hardware that could give an entirely new meaning to these freedoms. Unfortunately, these things are used in modern media to increase the power of knowledge-bankers to funnel their program-packages through international chains to more people, instead of being used to increase true networks that provide equal opportunity for encounter among the members of the majority.

Deschooling the culture and social structure requires the use of technology to make participatory politics possible. Only on the basis of a majority coalition can limits to secrecy and growing power be determined without dictatorship. We need a new environment in which growing up can be classless, or we will get a brave new world in which Big Brother educates us all.

erika pfeufer

an adult education experience 2000 a.d.

Introduction: In the following telephone conversation "DI" refers to the **Department of Information,** while "MB" refers to a Mrs. Brown.

DI: "Department of Information, may I help you?"

MB: "Well, my name is Mrs. Brown. My family and I left the USA in 1975 to become missionaries on the island of Tobe in the Pacific. Our friends have told us from time to time that things have changed a great deal here—but nothing like this! We have been assigned this house in District 164NW/19. It looks just like a computer center —and I don't know how to go about living in it. My husband and our 3 children are due to arrive tomorrow. So, could you please help me to get acquainted with just a few of the "gadgets" until my husband gets here. Then I presume all of us better go to a school and learn more about it."

DI: "Madame, can you see me now?"

MB: "No . . ."

DI: "Well, you better push the button next to your phone—the one saying "picture."

MB: "Oh, I can see you now! Are you a doctor?"

DI: "No, I am the head of the Computer Department. But let me and my associates here spin the computer back to the year 1975—oh, I see . . ."

Erika Pfeufer, "An Adult Education Experience 2000 A.D.," June 6, 1966. Reprinted by permission of the author.

MB: "I am sorry to be of so much bother. Are all 10 people working just for me?"

DI: "Of course Mrs. Brown. You have a problem and all of us are glad to help you. First, you'd better put away your pencil. You will not need to make notes. We will program your personal computer with all the information you will need. Please give me the number on your phone?"

MB: "It is a long one: BCJH 56734f/2."

DI: "This is your permanent phone number. The last number 2 stands for the second eldest member of your family. Number 1 will be your husband's number and so on. You can use this number wherever you are in the world. There is no other number like yours. When your telephone rings it will always first repeat this number. You can't forget it since it is listed on all your equipment at home—on the computer or credit card, medical report, expenses or income tax, your garment size—even on food. You mentioned something about a school or class—what type of class were you referring to? We have 150 computers here. They have been programmed to contain all existing knowledge, all publications and of course all this is available to you if you so desire."

MB: "Well, I wanted a class sort of . . . sort of a class how to get along with the computers, the neighbors, my friends and . . . and to catch up with all those new things that are here now. I would call the class 'Getting along with people.'"

DI: "These four men are looking up 'Getting along'—in the meantime shall we proceed to the Healthroom? It is the room to your left. Please lie down on the couch and make sure that the blue arm can swing freely over your body. Now place two orange and one blue disk on your skin. This will give us your chemical data. Thank you! Now for the physical data: place two green and one blue disk on your skin. That's all. Thank you. We now have your chemical as well as your physical data. You see, getting along with people as you put it, is really a chemical, as well as a physical reaction toward other people. Now to your reading. It is F49/6¼6a. You use this number whenever you talk to a person—even on the phone or at a party. You also dial their personal number on your computer, find out their chemical and physical data, feed both numbers into your computer and you always get along with people. Do you understand this?"

MB: "Well, no . . . you mean a chemical and physical wavelength is all—that makes a person compatible? How about morals??? Are those 'chemical' too??? . . ."

DI: "One moment please. I must inform myself on the term "MORALS." Oh, here it is. Well, let me explain: When you left the USA you probably realized that there were riots and wars and dissent going on here. Well, that was a time when we allowed the luxury of morals. In other words we left it up to a person whether he cared to kill another person—according to his morals or his irrational thinking—and later society tried this person for a 'crime' he committed. Well, things got very much out of hand and morals were found to have variances, according to different individuals. Now even a first-time-user of the computer realizes the teaching of the absolute strength of the law, that there is no individual choice as it was with 'morals.' There is no point in trying a person *after* he has committed a crime. We do not allow crimes to happen—therefore we have morals with laws. We are now dealing with exact sciences. The computer, if programmed correctly, will not make any mistakes. So, why should we leave it up to people to make mistakes? The social sciences or humanities as you knew them were not precise or correct. Researchers and the trial and error method used to find new ways—quite often the wrong ways. Therefore we had to establish a new, safe and law-abiding society."

MB: "But how about religion? How about God?"

DI: "Again, allow me to spin the computer to read to you the 1970 version of Webster's College Dictionary: *RELIGION:* The service and worship of God or Supernatural. Committed or devoted to religious faith or observance, or it can mean a personal set or instructionalized system of religious attitudes. God: The supreme or ultimate reality as the Being perfect in wisdom and goodness whom men worship as creator and ruler of the universe . . ." Well, there too, we have changed very much. We now try to get close to what you call religion by getting as godlike (to use 1970 terms) as possible ourselves. We do not use religion as a crutch, a leaning post or even as a force to be blamed when things go wrong, or people are unkind. It is now called 'Creativity.' Every man has the ability to create anything his mind can conceive and with the help of his computer he can then achieve his creation. We strive to create daily. We don't ask anymore: What do I create? or How do I create? We are proud to improve ourselves with the help of our own creativity, to get as close to a godlike being as possible ourselves. It makes us a kind of God or Lord within ourselves, better everyday. We have no strange god whom we worship. Man used to drift; he didn't know his purpose. Now he knows."

MB: "But how did you figure all this tremendous knowledge the computer has?"

DI: "Well, we reversed the malfunctioning of any machine, and found out that any mistake is caused by 2 parts not carrying out what they are designed to do. It works the same way with people. Can I ask you to look at the yellow box on top of the computer. It reads 'test pills.' Would you please take one and then turn the knob 'Test' to the left. We will now test your KQ—that is your knowledge quotient. You have a very heavy reading on household, and practical experiences, as well as something called farm and outdoor experience. You greatly lack computer languages, data retrieval, efficiency reporting and oh!!—oh the RED LIGHT! Gentlemen, did you see the RED LIGHT! Mrs. Brown, please excuse our astonishment, but the red light shows negative attitudes, thoughts or deeds. In some isolated cases that might even be due to evil or wrong thoughts. You see, we have outlawed all negative thoughts and deeds to free society."

MB: "Just how does one live in your society? Is there a daily plan or schedule?"

DI: "Of course, excuse me for not mentioning this earlier to you and having therefore caused you some anxious moments, but you see, we never worry, since our lives have been greatly programmed by computers. Let me explain your daily schedule. The computer rings a bell every morning to wake up the family. This has been programed by the nerve center of each individual and according to how much sleep was required—a result based on yesterday's health test. Your morning household chores are done simply by telling the computer—by that I mean pressing the button "Household Chores." You might also want to dial—according to yesterday's health test—the nutritional needs for the day. The computer will then not only give you the name of the food your family should consume today—but also the amounts, the substitutions and the time desired. Everything will be ready to serve, either cooked, heated or chilled, at the time you designated. Reordering is being done automatically by the pantry. Your children will have individual programs. According to the test results a complete allotment for studies and play has been arranged. They also have their own computer centers, in different colors. Let me remind you that there is no laundry or drycleaning problem, since anyone entering the home goes through a cleaning chamber all items deposited in closets will be automatically cleaned during the night. If you should want to replenish any family clothing, just dial the number for 'catalog.' There will be pictures moving on your screen in correct sizes, pleasant colors, since you will be using your telephone-permanent number. The cost of each article is clearly stated—the amount also includes delivery charges. Your husband, having formerly been a missionary, has probably a great deal of studying to do, this too will be programmed. When you are serving lunch it would be good to verify again the menu and preparation, just in case someone should change his mind on a choice of food or preparation—the item of course will be replaced only with an equally nutritious selection. After lunch the family meets in the health room for the daily medical check-up to spot a possible illness or re-arrange the diets. Every afternoon there is a nationwide family information pro-gram—some games, and most important: The CREATIVITY Contests! The daily program has some of our elected officials introducing new goals to be voted on by the entire population. That's what keeps this country free! Since there is a guar-anteed national income, further remuneration can only be earned by a citizen through his own creative contributions to the national program, or by 'hitch-hiking' on someone else's idea. After the evening meal there is, of course, television enter-tainment. You might prefer your own family party or take one of the tube-rail transportations to the downtown entertainment center. If for any of your parties one or more of your friends might be unable to attend in person, he can always participate on a fullsize wall TV unit from anywhere in inner or outer space. Any correspondence you desire is, of course, done by telephone vision as are the daily news broadcasts from inner and outer space. At the end of the day with pro-grammed 'sleep,' the world awaits another computer day.

You see, there is very little difference in outside appearance between today and the 1970's. The only real difference is that we have now arrived at a scientifi-cally computerized life, the precise and correct ideas of the humanities. Humane, isn't it??"

MB: "Heaven help us!"

teg's 1994

During her year of travel as an Orwell Fellow, Teg learns that her contemporaries' concept of the "communication society" is increasingly flawed by interaction failures between diverging communities. A full expression of each community's sub-culture, or myth, has been achieved only at the cost of increasing mutual incomprehension, and even a re-emergence of an aggressive community ethnocentricism.

In the last decade of the twentieth century there is a growing awareness that maximizing social interaction is as much an avoidance of the individual's responsibility for full self-development as were earlier a reliance on the control-systems of the "economic mechanism" and later the "technological imperative." As the book ends we see Teg and her contemporaries beginning the struggle for full human awareness through reappraisal of communication techniques and a new understanding of the role of the individual as a member, not only of a face-to-face community, but also of the larger human society—terran society.

I must share what I've just learned with somebody and it had better be somebody of my own age. During yesterday's facilitation session with C I learned about the "education system" of the sixties. If I tell anyone who was "at school" then how entropic it was, they may feel attacked.

After the session with C, one of the apprentices here and I were having a relaxed evening. We'd set the computer on random search among sixties-films on the first three life-periods. We discovered a behavior-pattern which amazed us: during the sixties protest about educational conditions was expressed in a way which could not possibly have been expected to bring about change.

I'm sure I've been told about this reality in a dozen different ways but somehow I never really got inside the system before listening to C. During the sixties it appears that *only one form of "education"* was valued—"authoritarian teaching" and "rote assimilation of materials": inside schools for those up to eighteen and inside colleges for those up to 22 and in many cases beyond.

Schools and colleges contained large numbers of "students" who were taught in classes of up to 40 in schools and 1000 and beyond in colleges. This size of class was considered practical because people were expected to rote-memorize what previous scholars

Robert Theobald and J. M. Scott, Teg's 1994: An Anticipation of the Near Future (Chicago: The Swallow Press, 1972). © *1972. Reprinted by permission.*

had learned and then reinform the teacher about existing theories. Apparently no one expected that students would retain the knowledge beyond the "exam" period designed to test people for recent-information-recall.

I can't make sense of this pattern. If the object had been to train people in a specific skill, classes of this size would have been a possible technique, given the fact that auto-training with computers and robots did not exist at that time. But then those involved would have continued practising the same skill until it became automatic and their constant need for the skill would have ensured that it was retained. Tests to discover information-recall would have been unnecessary. On the other hand, if the object was education, repeatedly forcing existing concepts on the student would prevent him from internally rearranging the information into new patterns and perceiving new insights which is the function of any effective educational process.

In the sixties the confusion about appropriate techniques of learning was not apparently due to any lack of concern. In addition, the films we saw made it clear that many of those involved in education as teachers and learners saw how dysfunctional the entire educational system was. But those who protested didn't seem to have any idea of the way in which change is achieved. They held "rallies" and "sit-ins" protesting the actual detailed functioning of the educational system without recognizing that changes in part of a system are not possible without changing the total system and that it is not possible to change total systems unless those involved comprehend a changed perception of the nature of the universe.

The increasing disruption and violence which accompanied student "rallies" and "sit-ins" during the late sixties set in motion two forces which led to the collapse of many government and private universities. First, private donors and government agencies cut back on the funds they applied. Second, an increasing number of young people no longer saw college as essential to their life-development and sought alternative patterns of learning.

By the mid-seventies, colleges and universities were attempting to develop programs which would attract both new donors and students. It was unfortunate that many of the colleges which had the clearest comprehension of the new approach to learning, and which were therefore able to attract students, did not have the merchandising skills to attract funds. By the end of the seventies, a large proportion of colleges and universities had disbanded.

In a few cases the buildings of a college or university were purchased by groups of individuals who created new forms of communities in which learning was an integral part of the community style: the sharp age-breaks between those learning and those working began to disappear. These new institutions, often organized consentives, and those colleges which did survive moved in one of two directions; they became either local or transnational nodes in the de-Chardinian noosphere. As such they acted as transmission points for information.

The local nodes began to develop ways in which they could serve their immediate community. These local organizations used, among other innovations, patterns of learning interaction developed by the Street Universities and also brought in by individuals from India and other nations with traditions of personal facilitation. They were able to demonstrate how real education could take place within the community rather than cut off from it in schools and colleges.

In the second case, when institutions and colleges moved toward being transnational nodes in the noosphere, they concentrated increasingly in a single p/p area (problem/possibility area). It was made clear to those who wished to join these emerging institutions that their purpose was to elucidate a specific p/p area and that nobody should seek admission if they were not interested in this area of knowledge. As this process of moving toward being a transnational node continued, it was understood that information structured around p/p areas required new forms of presentation. It became necessary to replace those methods which had been used for deduction and transfer of data within "disciplines," such as rote learning texts and personal interpretation of facts written by an "authority" for his followers. The continuing transformation of transnational nodes later converged with the efforts of those who were interacting following the Scientists Synergy to create the invisible college and the p/p Institutes.

edward stainbrook

environmental education and psychological behavior

An ecological model of man-in-nature and of man-as-nature is now being organized intellectually by integrating a broad range of scientific and humanistic knowledge into the structural and dynamic concepts of applied ecosystems. The urgent concerns of applied ecology may militate against any cautionary preoccupation about whether the existing information is organizing the theoretical models or whether the conceptual models are organizing the useful knowledge. In contemporary education, however, and particularly in environmental education, it may be imperative to consider how much the existing curricular structure and process should determine the organization of the knowledge to be learned and taught and how much the relevant extant knowledge should organize or reorganize the curriculum.

At the moment the critical focus for the selection and integration of information

Reprinted by permission from Robert S. Cook and George T. O'Hern, eds., Processes for a Quality Environment, a report of the National Conference on Environmental Education, the University of Wisconsin-Green Bay.

and of directing values about man and his environment is on the prospective teachers of human ecology, whatever their disciplines and wherever in the total educational system they may teach. Properly informed themselves and committed to superordinating humanistic values which both "save" the present and suggest the most resourceful and fulfilling future for man, ecologically oriented teachers and educators can then shape the educational experiences specifically, flexibly, responsively, and innovatingly, no matter where they are in the teaching-learning process.

One of the lamentable happenings of the times seems to be the increasing maladaptation of social institutions, and particularly of educational institutions, to the changing definitions and evaluations by contemporary man of his present and emerging human situation. Indeed, perhaps the basic crisis for modern technetronic man is a crisis of conceptualization and its attendant necessity for the conceiving of new cultural and social directives.

Moreover, in a society of slowly but steadily increasing affluence characterized at the same time by an augmenting number of people who experience a more extensive formal or informal educational contact with currently emerging knowledge and thought, the redefinitions of values and ideas about the nature of man become not only a task of social institutional change but also an urgent soul-saving and soul-creating individualized existential goal.

Contemporary thought, both scientific and humanistic, has now brought us to an inescapable encounter with our own existence. We are self-studying, self-aware, self-directing men. We are that part of nature which has developed the capacity to conceptualize itself and which now within certain degrees of freedom has achieved the ability to direct itself. And this acceptance of the responsibility for our own destiny, so insidiously and imperceptibly thrust upon us by our evolution, is a second loss of innocence more fraught with apocalyptic significance than our first Edenic desertion by Providence. The active self-directing responsibility for ourselves that we once accepted can never be given back. From now on to ourselves we must be enough.

Hence, education for ecological awareness and adaptation must provide a comprehensive conception of the nature of man, that is to say of man as and in nature. It must insist upon an active, responsibility-accepting society. And it must provide those experiences in perceiving, conceptualizing, informing, integrating, valuing, creating, and acting that lead to gratifying, competent, and effective individuation both in adapting the self to the environment and in shaping the physical and psychosocial environment to the self.

Since the essential concepts guiding content selection for environmental education must certainly include comprehensiveness and cross-disciplinary integration, some superordinating conception of man, which all the intellectual disciplines will accept but with which none may enthusiastically agree, must be proposed as a sort of manifesto for curriculum construction.

Men live both as bodies and in and with an environment. Or, excusing the reality-distorting and reifying outcomes of language usage, the simpler, more succinct statement is that men live both in their bodies and in an environment. Or, more complicatedly, we live as a population of socialized bodies transactionally adapting among ourselves within our social organization and enduring through time as an organized population by transacting our adaptational existence with the natural environment, much of it man-altered, and with the man-created and man-maintained artifactual and psychosocial surround.

Key Concepts

Adaptive, maladaptive, and non-adaptive behavior are key concepts in ecological thinking. Indeed, the genetically determined programming of the biological structures and processes of modern man are conceived as the resultants of past adaptational success. The hidden determinants of much of the behavior of contemporary man are not only the individual experiential unconscious of Freud, but are something, in a way, closer to Jung's collective unconscious. As bodies, we are what we are, largely because of our ecological history. The genes are constantly organizing and reorganizing the morphology and physiology of the body whose adaptive transactions with its investing environment may then either be enhanced or impaired.

The recognition that some of the basic behavior of man is evolved behavior which at some time in the past was adaptational leads at once to the importance of contemporary behaviorial biology and especially its subdivisions of molecular biology, genetics, neurophysiology, and ethology as sources of knowledge for environmental education.

Similarly, the study of animal behavior is also confirmed as relevant to an understanding of the adaptational capabilities and vulnerabilities of man. The observation of animal behavior is, among other things, a way of studying our own behavioral and ecological past.

In the pursuit of resourceful and effective ecologic planning and administration, we must center both on actively adapting the environment to man and on adapting man to the environment. The knowledge being developed by behavioral biology can be used, like most behavioral science knowledge, to achieve both these goals.

Consider, for example, some of our evolved behavior such as the quick arousal into rage, or the rapid frantic amplification of attentive appraisal into acute anxiety, or the constraint imposed upon ordinary thinking by the binary organization of the up-down, right-left, yes-no brain, or the compelling control over behavior exerted by the pleasure-reward organization of the nervous system. Some of this genetically maintained, evolved behavior, once adaptive, may now be maladaptive for much of the contemporary human situation. Hence, it is already beyond the scientific fiction stage of application to be teaching seriously the extant and developing knowledge about genetic "surgery," electrical stimulation, and computer programming of the brain; pharmacologic motivation and capacity control; biofeedback creation of perceptual awareness and the consequent possible self-control of biological processes; and the burgeoning psychotechnology of behavioral control as directives and methods for enhancing (or diminishing) the capacity of man to adapt himself effectively to his present and emerging circumstances.

Thus, an underlying emphasis for environmental education from behavioral biology is the insistence that human bodies are neither standard nor empty organisms. On the contrary, they are filled, each one uniquely, with life and with all of man's past and present living. And they are open systems constantly transacting with and cross-organizing into the environment around.

This latter conception leads to a consideration of another focus for an organization of the funded knowledge of the behavioral sciences. The environment—physical, social, and cultural—may provide gratification, confidence, security, effectiveness, competence, and health for the inhabiting individuals, or it can be a source of deprivation, threat, conflict, and of biophysical or of biosocial stress.

A comprehensive public health model of man-environment transactions would be concerned with both biophysical and biosocial threat and stress. As is understandable, the current medical interest is much more on biophysical pollution and reactive organic disease than on the biosocial interactions.

Nevertheless, in an open systems model each body organ is in a transacting relationship within the organization of the body, as well as directly and indirectly with the physical and psychosocial world around. The lungs are actually invaginated external surfaces in direct contact with the atmosphere; but they are also under the control of a large number of learned interpersonal and other symbolic stimuli centered largely, though of course not exclusively, around the expressive and communicative functions of startling, crying, laughing, and talking. Similarly, the biosociology of other organs has both general and specific characteristics, depending in significant part upon the particular psychosocial transactions in which each organ participates differentially. Many of the problems in psychosomatic disease theory are related to biosocial organ specificity.

Hence, the ecological import of environmental life stresses must be related not only to the general psychophysiology of the body but also to the specific biosociology of each organ system.

In terms, however, of general biosocial conceptions, it is apparent that certain incrementing environmental stimuli, such as noise and the increasing number of persons and events, particularly in urban environments, demanding attention, appraisal and response, are stress hazards evoking ecologic concern. It has recently been suggested that simply the number of significant changes occurring in one's life, whether valued as desirable or undesirable, may be positively correlated with psychosomatic complaints, if not also with demonstrable symptoms.

Psychophysiologic correlations seek to identify the convergence of psychosocial and constitutional influence on biological structure and process. Although part of the information directing biologic action comes from the genetic control room in the nucleus of each cell, much of the information which induces, intensifies, suppresses, or maintains cell and organ physiology is brought to the cell from stored, learned experience, from the surrounding here-and-now and even from the individual's scan and appraisal of his future.

The psychophysiologic communication channels can be specified. Verbal or nonverbal symbolic information transacted in a sociocultural context is within the person transduced as electroneurophysiologic information. Some of this basically electrical, or "dry," neurophysiology is then transformed, in the hypothalamus particularly, into "wet" neurophysiology or hormonal information. This hormonal communication system, in which quite literally the medium is the message, was evolved, as was the nervous system, to integrate the various organ systems and functions of the internal environment and to mediate between them and the frequently suddenly-arising and quickly-shifting demands and changes of the external environment.

The hormonal messengers bear what was originally highly specified symbolic psychosocial information now reduced to the parameters of biochemistry and physiology. In association with the electrophysiologic information of the nervous system, the hormonal information affects either enzyme production, enzyme activity, cell permeability, or in some other way impresses its influence upon the inherent and existing system properties and action of the cell.

It is in this way that an abstract conception such as a value about social or economic status may induce anxiety and perhaps depression in a patient and concomitantly alter his physiology. Or a bit of external interpersonal information such as an unloving or rejecting look on the face of another may influence and regulate biologic processes.

The many recent demonstrations, both in unicellular organisms and in complex animals and man, of recurrent, genetically programmed, biological rhythms with 24-hour, 7-day, lunar, seasonal, and annual cycles point to an evolved locking-in to our biological processes of a correlation between once parallel and coexisting sequences of bodily and environmental events. But modern environments are now regulated by climatic and illumination control, and work organizations and other social institutions structure wakeful activity around the clock. A distressingly high and insistent daily input of inadequately integrated information demands delayed and belated attempts at mastery, perhaps most particularly in sleep. There is also the much discussed psychophysiology of the rapid transportation of persons through space and time. All these transformations in and of the environment may now conflict with the innate programmed tempo of the body and with the inherent biological scheduling and readiness for anticipated happenings in the cyclical natural spans of time.

Fatigue, inefficiency, and other perhaps more subtle temporary or enduring impairments of adaptation and optimal biological responsiveness may be the price exacted for a mismatch between the preferred inherited ongoingness of the body and the out-of-phase demands of the surround.

Emotional Behavior Needs Study

One additional conception arising from contemporary behavioral biology and neuropsychology concerning the meaning of emotional behavior may be helpful in confirming the importance for environmental education of anchoring itself securely in the behavioral sciences. Emotional states are frequently used as evidence of psychological health or impairment. The formulation of directives about the human goals and outcomes of environmental planning and management relies significantly upon an assessment of the emotional behavior of persons.

From the aspect of stress reactions, with or without the implications of psychosomatic illness, and also considered as motivational sources for both adaptive and maladaptive action, emotional states are largely the results or the effects of man-environment transactions. They are associated with event-perception and event-resolution in the ongoingness of behavior. They can be measured in terms of frequency, intensity, and duration. They can be analyzed and subjectively experienced as the changing and shifting resultants of stimulus-appraisal, self-appraisal, available response-appraisal, and outcome-appraisal.

Emotional states can be "hung-up" and remain unresolved through time. They can occur too frequently or too intensely. The associated adaptive impairment may occur because the person can do nothing effective either in cognitive informational problem-seeing or in cognitive executive problem-solving.

Environments may strain persons, therefore, by presenting alerting change too frequently. The characteristics of the surround may create ambiguity and other uncertainties of information-presentation. Both historically and currently the environmental structuring of personal experience may induce self-appraisals of low worth, inadequacy, insecurity, ineffectiveness, impotency, and inconfidence about the future. An environment, general or local, may offer inadequate physical, economic, social, and cultural resources to make possible the learning and maintenance of gratifying and effective responses for adaptive action.

A relatively newly designated area of behavioral science concern is called environmental psychology and is described by some of its protagonists as the interrelations of man and his physical setting. This is somewhat related to the study of behavior in natural settings labelled by Roger Barker as ecological psychology. Properly speaking, these disciplines represent social and cultural environmental science. Allied with the broad range of the sciences of social man, from social psychology to economics, political science, and the law (and to history as retrospective social science), these constitute the general sociology of the biosociology superordinating and integrating behavioral science knowledge.

For guidance in environmental education an intellectual ecosystem of behavioral disciplines can very roughly be described. An individual man can be both studied as an object and yet experience himself as a subject. Man is both the knower and the known. This is why the crucial self-reported knowledge from man the subject must always inform the observed knowledge of man the object.

An apt metaphor for ecologic transactions is a circuit. The circuit can be entered at different places. In suggesting a cognitive model for biosociology, we can begin with culture which directs the structure, process, and functions of social organizations, which shapes and determines the individual behavior and the self-conceptions of the persons who enact social roles in organizations, which, in turn, brings biological structure and process under social and physical environmental control. Or for some other purposes, we can begin with the inherited directing genome in each body cell, which structures the evolved morphology and physiology of the body and the associated patternings of organization and function, which then experience individuation, differentiation, and reorganization in social organizations, which maintain and create culture.

Most of us would agree, presumably, that basic value changes are necessary in order to properly plan and manage our most insistent ecologic problems. Social organizational change can then follow and the long ecologic march through the social institutions can begin.

But it is essential also that we maintain an awareness of our superordinating biosocial model. It is still not generally appreciated, for example, that urban ecology is too serious a matter to be left to the architects. The human needs for a fulfilling social and cultural environment cannot be satisfied by merely renewing the physical artifactual environment. A city is a network of human services and resources as well as architectural design and structure.

Finally, it is obvious that the multidisciplinary character of education for environmental and ecological awareness necessitates an integration of a faculty before any integration inside the skull of the student can be achieved. As already suggested, some superordinating cognitive model must be accepted which will allow the biologist spontaneously and gladly to refer to the sociologist, and which will enable the anthropologist to suggest happily for the biologist's elaboration that a cultural value is capable of modifying "the guts of the living," to use a phrase of Wystan Auden's.

Whether this integration of faculty is achieved by interdisciplinary programs, by abandonment of departmental segregation, or by institutes is a matter of organizational decision and innovation. Integration by mere contiguity, either of departments or of professors, will not achieve the desired goal. Nothing short of a task force of interdisciplinarians working together informing and educating themselves and creating a directing model of an integrated curriculum will do.

Indeed, if we are in an intellectual revolution of a new awareness of ourselves in nature and of ourselves as nature, then our planning and our imagination for environmental awareness as an outcome of education must be revolutionary too.

A SELECTED BIBLIOGRAPHY

BARKER, ROGER G. *Ecological Psychology*. Stanford, Calif.: Stanford University Press, 1969.

PROSHANSKY, HAROLD M., WILLIAM ITTELSON, and LEANNE G. RIVLIN. *Environmental Psychology*. New York: Holt, Rinehart and Winston, Inc., 1970.

STAINBROOK, EDWARD. "Human Behavior and the Natural Environment," *Man and Nature in the City*. Washington, D.C.: U.S. Department of Interior, 1969.

alfred a. arth/
ronald n. short

city planning in the
elementary school

Approximately 140 million Americans live in urban areas. Some 251 million urban dwellers will be counted by the year 2000. The American city has literally happened—with limited forethought to the creation of a liveable and enjoyable urban environment.

Conditions of physical hazards, overcrowdedness, discomfort, ugliness, and frustration plague today's urban dwellers. They have resulted from a lack of knowledge and apathetic attitudes of the majority of population. Such unknowledgeable and apathetic populace are strong, contributing factors to the default of intelligent city planning.

Only a few years ago, for example, the governing body of a small city in northeastern New Jersey—an overdeveloped community where open space is almost non-existent—presented its people with a choice in regard to the last three adjoining vacant lots in the city. One alternative was to allow the city to develop these lots into a city park; the other was to sell these lots to a private builder to create additional tax base and housing.

The city elected to sell the lots to private interests. The development of multiple housing units on the lots overtaxed the existing, undersized water main to the detriment of fighting local fires. In addition, soil conditions not conducive to urban development resulted in serious wall cracks only a month after the first occupants were housed.

The social studies have always taught degrees of knowledge and skills. But, it appears that the "old" social studies may have lacked the ability to influence developing values, attitudes, and responsibility necessary to community betterment.

The lack of citizen involvement in city planning and administration is an example of a missing link in environmental responsibility. If the people of the city previously mentioned had been exposed to the relationships between land use and such factors as land capabilities, density, utility capabilities, open space, traffic, aesthetics, etc. beginning in elementary grades; there might have been adequate parks and open space in that city today.

The elementary student of today will sit in the city governments of the year 2000 or sooner. He will voice opinions and legislate policies on city planning in relation to the accumulated theories and knowledge with which the school, primarily, has exposed him.

The distance that a child covers between home and school is laboratory ground. It

Alfred A. Arth and Ronald N. Short, "City Planning in the Elementary School," NJEA Review (December, 1969), 42–43. Reprinted by permission.

is the laboratory for providing awareness of the many aspects of intelligent city planning. And, the school can assist in sharpening such awareness.

With this in mind, "A Student's City Planning Survey" is offered for classroom use. It is suggested that familiarity be made of the questions before and evaluation of the answers be made after the survey in the form of a discussion with teacher-student participation.

The survey has been divided into two parts for the benefit primarily of younger students, who may find it easier to do half of the survey at a time. In addition, preparing maps and taking field trips to particular portions of the survey area, as well as a visit from the city planning director, would be especially valuable.

If the basic principles and standards of intelligent city planning are taught to today's children, it will be an enlightened public that will:

- Object to a proposed elementary school location adjacent to a major and potentially dangerous street;
- Not sacrifice important parks and open space to private development pressures;
- Demand and benefit from the amenities and services that urban life can provide, instead of becoming hardened to their environment; and
- React in similar situations with an awareness of other aspects that are important to the creation of a liveable and enjoyable urban environment.

The following survey includes comments to assist in an evaluation discussion:

A Student's City Planning Survey

PART I

1. Underline each city service you observed—police, garbage pick-up, road construction, street cleaning, firemen, or other _____. Underline each condition you observed —speeding cars, overloaded garbage containers, holes in streets, leaves and litter in streets, or other _____.

(Relating the extent of local government employees in action providing the various necessary maintenance and protection services to the corresponding conditions points out the level of community service.)

2. Underline the amount of vehicles traveling beside you—cars (many, few, or none); trucks (many, few, or none); and buses (many, few, or none).

(The presence of many cars, trucks, and buses along the route to school indicates the danger of school children being routed along major arterial streets and relates to the site selection policy of the school board.)

3. Underline on what you walked to school—sidewalk (all of the way, part of the way, or none of the way), street (all of the way, part of the way, or none of the way), other _____ (all of the way or part of the way). Other could refer to lawn, path, ditch, etc.

(Children walking any portion of their way to school in the street or other non-pedestrian way intimates the absence of a requirement by the local governing body for sidewalks or other safe pedestrian ways in all subdivisions.)

4. How many blocks did you walk to school? _____

(This reveals whether or not the school is situated in a location offering a convenient and reasonable walking distance to the children it serves.)

5. Give the name of any street you crossed that had a heavy flow of traffic. _____

(If the elementary school child has to cross a major arterial street, it intimates the school is located nearby that arterial. Such a location violates a planning standard that the elementary school should be located in the center of the neighborhood. Major streets should be located on the periphery of the neighborhood, whereby no elementary school child should be required to cross a major street for access to an elementary school.)

PART II

6. Give the name of any park you passed and underline what each contained—
     a. _____
     playground equipment
     picnic tables
     baseball diamonds
     tennis courts
     other _____
     b. _____
     playground equipment
     picnic tables
     baseball diamonds
     tennis courts
     other _____

(The number of parks passed suggests the adequacy of convenient parks in the neighborhood. The degree to which the parks are developed indicates the present useful-ness to the family.)

7. Underline the open areas and landscaping you passed—vacant lots, ponds, streams, trees, gardens, woods, or other _____.

(The absence of open areas and landscaping, such as: vacant lots, drainage channels, small plazas, etc., intimates the area is heavily developed without important gaps in urban development to provide a sense of spaciousness and rural atmosphere in the city. The city's acquisition of streams and other open-space worth preserving is important before it is built upon and lost to the public.)

8. Underline the businesses you passed—gas station; large grocery store; small grocery store; restaurant; ice cream, hamburger, taco, chicken, root beer drive-ins or drive-ups; drug store; beauty parlor; barber shop; cleaners, clothing store; laundromat; or other _____.

   Underline the locations of these businesses you passed—in a particular shopping center, just along the street, or in a home.

(If many stores, gas stations, etc. are passed by the child, it is likely that incompatible commercial uses have been allowed to penetrate the residential environment—creating noise, smoke, odor, glare, etc. detrimental to enjoyable living. Commercial establishments should be clustered into attractive shopping centers. Also, the presence of businesses located in homes seriously threatens the stability of the residential neighborhood.)

9. Underline the amount of business signs you passed—many, few, or none.

   Underline the size of business signs you passed—mostly large or mostly small.

   Underline how the signs appeared to you—mostly neat, mostly messy, or mostly _____ _____ (other description).

(The presence of many commercial signs that appear messy to students intimates the absence of a sign-control ordinance by the local government.)

10. Did you pass any new construction, _____ If so, what is being constructed? _____ and where is it located? _____

(New construction testifies to the economic and physical growth of the city. Also, the latter two questions at this point in the survey will hopefully lead the child a step further in recognizing and gaining understanding of compatible land use and acceptable standards for urban development.)

11. Underline the amount of homes or businesses that looked "worn-out"—many, few, or none.

(The passing of many "worn-out" homes or businesses indicates a blighted area of the city. There can be discussion as to why the area became blighted. Blight has been traced to incompatible land use, excess traffic, poor community services, limited and outdated community facilities (schools, parks, etc.) and residents economically unable to improve the area by themselves. Also, there can be discussion as to methods of stopping the decay and making the neighborhood a better one.)

. . .

Educational systems should provide our youngsters with information and exposed involvements that will lead to the acquisition of basic skills of city planning.

These basic skills will inevitably provide attitudes and understandings that will enable future citizens to influence and control the elements of city structure that surround them. This process will, in turn, afford the public more healthy and richly stimulating cities.

index

THE ENVIRONMENTAL CLASSROOM

Donald E. Hawkins and Dennis A. Vinton

Emphasizing that man's environment is a "far more exciting place in which to learn than any one school" and a "far more exciting teacher than any one person," this important new book proposes that through the discovery, exploration, and use of the total resources of the environment a learner can develop awareness, understanding, and above all, motivation to act to improve man's environment. Suggesting specific educational reforms, the authors argue that education can truly "recreate and revitalize people, places, and things" and reverse the present trend of isolating and insulating man from his environment.

THE ENVIRONMENTAL CLASSROOM develops a dynamic structure for learning by examining the traditional ideas and methods of education, reviewing the issues of the current environmental crisis and the educational crisis, and giving step-by-step descriptions of more innovative approaches that can be applied in the area of education. The authors provide systematic models for achieving an environmental classroom through practical means, give numerous examples of programs that have already been successfully introduced, and offer reading selections meant to stimulate creative thought about reconnecting human beings with their environment.

Valuable reading material for everyone involved in the educational field, THE ENVIRONMENTAL CLASSROOM offers a unique approach for transferring the traditional concepts of education to a process of lifelong learning in the environmental classroom.

PRENTICE-HALL, Inc., Englewood Cliffs, New Jersey